The American
CATHOLIC ALMANAC

The American

CATHOLIC ALMANAC

A

Daily Reader of

Patriots, Saints, Rogues,

and Ordinary People

Who Changed

the United States

BRIAN BURCH AND
EMILY STIMPSON

IMAGE

New York

Copyright © 2014 by CatholicVote.org Education Fund

All rights reserved.
Published in the United States by Image, an imprint of the Crown Publishing Group,
a division of Random House LLC, a Penguin Random House Company, New York.
www.crownpublishing.com

IMAGE is a registered trademark and the "I" colophon is a trademark
of Random House LLC.

Library of Congress Cataloging-in-Publication data is available upon request.

ISBN 978-0-553-41872-9
eBook ISBN 978-0-553-41873-6

Printed in the United States of America

Cover design by Jessie Sayward Bright

10 9 8 7 6 5 4 3 2 1

First Edition

Books take you places you never expect to go. That's true for their readers, and it's doubly true for their writers. When you sit down to write a book, you think you know where you're headed. But along the way, something happens—obstacles arise, different paths open up, or new ideas present themselves. By the time you reach the end, you find precious little has gone as planned. And yet, you're incredibly grateful for that.

This book was no exception.

When we first set out to write *The American Catholic Almanac,* we wanted to accomplish two things. First, we wanted to tell the stories of the men and women who built the Catholic Church in America. Second, we wanted to demonstrate just how much America has benefited from what those men and women did.

Our reasons for that were simple.

Many American Catholics have studied the history of the Faith in Europe and know about the lives of the saints who built the Church there. We know about the Crusades, the Inquisition, the martyrs of the English Reformation, and Saints Francis and Clare.

But for all that American Catholics know about Church history elsewhere, much of our own history remains a mystery. We don't know about the suffering and sacrifice that went in to building Catholic parishes in Maine and Catholic schools in Oregon. Only a few among us have heard of the Venerable Father Samuel Mazzuchelli, the great apostle of the Upper Midwest, or the Most Reverend Joseph Machebeuf, the first bishop of Denver. In most corners of America, the work of "The Angel of the Delta"—the laywoman Margaret Haughery—or "The Angel of Andersonville"—the priest Peter Whelan— has simply been forgotten.

Because we don't know those stories, because we don't know what those early American Catholics sacrificed, we also don't know how much we've gained. And that puts us at a serious disadvantage, especially when it comes to the ongoing debate over the place of religion in public life.

THE AMERICAN CATHOLIC WITNESS

In the years that immediately preceded the American Revolution and for more than a century afterwards, America's dominant Protestant majority questioned the compatibility of Catholicism and democracy. They couldn't see how Catholics, with their "medieval superstitions" and papal loyalties, could be good citizens. Accordingly, many attempted—through both law and mob violence—to silence Catholic voices.

Ultimately, they failed. But today, anti-Catholicism has returned with a vengeance. Growing numbers of Americans again contend that Catholic voices don't belong in the public square, and growing numbers of Catholic dioceses again find themselves fighting legislation that limits Catholics' ability to practice their faith. Behind both those problems lurks a creeping militant secularism, which views religious faith in general (and the Catholic Faith in particular) as harmful to a free society.

The witness of the past, however, tells a different story than the polemics of the present.

That witness shows us Catholics, such as Saint Marianne Cope and Mother Frances Warde, building hospitals and schools for America's immigrants. It also shows us the Venerable Father Nelson Baker and Dorothy Day establishing institutions to serve the poor; Cesar Chavez and Lucy Burns fighting for the rights of the marginalized; Commodore John Barry and Rear Admiral Jeremiah Denton serving bravely in battle; and countless other Catholics living ordinary lives with extraordinary virtue.

The Catholic Faith wasn't incidental to what these men and women accomplished; it was central. It motivated and inspired them. It guided them. It shaped their thinking and formed their characters. You can't tell their stories without also telling the story of their faith. And you can't hear those stories without coming to a deeper understanding of what America owes to the Catholic Church.

LESSONS FOR THE NEW EVANGELIZATION

So, in the beginning, that's what we wanted to do—tell stories and demonstrate how the Catholic Faith helped shape America. We believe we've done that. But along the way, we found more than just greatness in the past. We also found guidance for the present.

In America and elsewhere in the West, the Christian faith is dying. According to a 2012 report by the Pew Research Center, "none" is the United States' fastest-growing religious affiliation, with one in five Americans now identifying as an atheist or agnostic. The Catholic Church has responded to that crisis of faith by calling for a "New Evangelization"—a renewed proclamation of the Gospel. Many within the Church, however, don't quite understand what the New Evangelization entails. All too often, Catholics find themselves at a loss about how best to lead others to Christ.

But the men and women in this book can show us the way.

In the lives of early American missionaries such as Bishop John Dubois, Bishop Simon Bruté, and Father John Bapst, we see conviction, not compromise. And in the lives of religious women such as Fanny Allen, Saint Frances Cabrini, and Saint Rose Philippine Duchesne, we see selflessness, not self-absorption. In the lives of both priests and religious, we see poverty, simplicity, and humble acts of service. We see men and women nursing victims of yellow fever and cholera, building parishes and schools, tending to the poor, and proclaiming the Gospel in the most dangerous and remote corners of America.

What we see are men and women who thought little about their own comfort and much about Christ.

Similarly, among the laity, we see Catholics such as Blessed Carlos Rodriguez, Venerable Pierre Toussaint, and Catherine Doherty, who lived what they believed. They incarnated the Church's teachings in the businesses they built, the laws they wrote, and the charities they founded. They prayed. They loved. They served.

And it worked, all of it—the humility, the service, the sacrifice. It won people to the Faith. It changed minds, and it transformed hearts. It built the Church in America from the ground up, giving rise to greater Catholic devotion and a flourishing Catholic intellectual life.

What worked once can work again—but only if Catholics know the stories of the people who made it work, only if we know our story as American Catholics.

In the end, the best gift we received from writing this book was getting to know the men and women in these pages. They charmed us, amused us, inspired us, and encouraged us. They brought us to a deeper faith in Christ and a deeper love for the Church. Most of all, they helped us see what a great treasure we've received from those who went before us.

Without realizing it, we took much of that treasure for granted. We didn't fully know what we had. We didn't realize what a great blessing it is to call ourselves not Irish Catholics or French Catholics or German Catholics, but American Catholics. Now we do.

Perhaps, because so few of America's first Catholics have the title "Saint" before their name, we often forget that clouds of witnesses have lived on our shores. But they did. Through the centuries, countless holy men and women have called America home. There were far more of them than we could find room for in the 365 days covered in this almanac, and they did far greater things than we could do justice to in the limited space each entry afforded. Nevertheless, this is at least a start.

And we do need to start somewhere. For the more we get to know our spiritual forebears—the more we grow in friendship with them—the more we can continue the great work that they began. We can not only preserve our heritage as American Catholics but also cultivate it, enrich it, and pass on to future generations more, not less, than what we received.

—Brian Burch and Emily Stimpson
Pentecost 2014

January

Early on the morning of **January 1, 1892,** as the J. E. Moore Barge approached its destination, eleven-year-old Anthony Moore and his seven-year-old brother Phillip knew nothing about what their new life in America would hold. The brothers did know, though, that it was their sister Annie's fifteenth birthday and, with a little teamwork, they could help her become the first immigrant to set foot on the newly opened Ellis Island.

Twelve days earlier, the three young Catholics had boarded the steamship *Nevada* in Queenstown (County Cork, Ireland). Along with 145 other steerage passengers, the Moores spent Christmas in the ship's crowded belly. Finally, late on December 31, they arrived in New York Harbor.

The next morning, the *Nevada's* steerage passengers disembarked and boarded a barge bound for Ellis Island. There, immigrants would undergo a medical and legal inspection before being cleared for entry into the country.

It was on the barge that the Moore brothers concocted their plan. Enlisting the help of a chivalrous Irishman (who bellowed, "Ladies first!"), they blocked the path of a large German and pushed their sister onto the gangplank. The girl half ran and half tripped across the dock, receiving a $10 gold piece from the Immigration Bureau upon her arrival.

After the fanfare subsided, the siblings were reunited with their parents, who lived in a Manhattan tenement. Annie eventually married a German bakery clerk and bore him 11 children. She died in 1924 at the age of 47.

Today, a bronze statue of the little Catholic girl from County Cork—young, slim, and suitcase in hand—still stands on Ellis Island, an enduring symbol of the 12 million souls who passed through that particular portal between 1892 and 1954, as well as the countless others who arrived elsewhere after journeying across land and sea to make a new home for themselves in the United States of America.

January 2: A GENERAL MALIGNED

General James Longstreet was not popular with the Episcopalians in New Orleans. On Sundays, when the former Confederate commander entered his pew, his fellow worshippers routinely rose and walked out. To them, honoring God mattered less than dishonoring Longstreet.

It wasn't just the Episcopalians, however, who had it in for Longstreet. By 1877, most everyone in the former Confederate States of America loathed General Robert E. Lee's one-time second-in-command. Many blamed the South Carolina native for the Confederacy's devastating loss at Gettysburg and blamed him even more for his support of President Ulysses S. Grant's Republican Administration. The value of the services rendered by Longstreet—Lee's "Old War Horse"—at the Battles of Fredericksburg, Second Bull Run, Antietam, and Chickamauga, as well as in the Wilderness Campaign, was lost on his contemporaries. Or, at least, most of his contemporaries.

Hearing of the Episcopalians' scorn for Longstreet, Father Abram Ryan, a former Confederate chaplain, paid the general a visit.

Catholics, Father Ryan informed him, didn't care who worshipped in their midst, and if Longstreet ever decided to convert, they would welcome him with open arms. Longstreet took Ryan up on his offer. He entered the Catholic Church in 1877 and remained a devout communicant to the end of his life.

Over the course of the next 27 years, Longstreet would go on to serve his country as ambassador to the Ottoman Empire, a U.S. marshal, and U.S. railroad commissioner. History would clear Longstreet's reputation; he had adamantly opposed Lee's battle plan at Gettysburg, ordering the infamous Pickett's Charge only under protest. Longstreet had also been close friends with Grant since their days at West Point.

But Longstreet never lived long enough to see his good name restored in the South. He died of pneumonia on **January 2, 1904,** at the age of 82.

Two million. That's how many Irishmen migrated to America in the wake of the Great Potato Famine of 1845. The majority passed through New York City, where many stayed.

With no money and little education, the immigrants crowded into tenements overrun by disease, crime, and poverty. In New York, anti-Irish and anti-Catholic sentiments rose.

The city's Irish, however, had a champion in Archbishop John Hughes.

Described by a contemporary as "more of a Roman gladiator than a follower of the meek founder of Christianity," Hughes himself immigrated to the United States from Ireland in 1817. A few years later, as a gardener at Mount St. Mary's Seminary, he so impressed the visiting Elizabeth Ann Seton that she convinced the seminary to admit him.

After his ordination in 1826, Hughes went to Philadelphia, which, at the time, was a hotbed of anti-Catholic nativism. Outspoken, forceful, and determined to prevent Catholics in America from becoming second-class citizens, Hughes routinely sparred with Nativist preachers, whom he called the "the clerical scum of the country."

Accordingly, by 1842, when Hughes became New York's fourth bishop, he was well seasoned for his role as champion of the Irish.

Hughes initiated the campaign for his flock by waging a legal battle against the Protestant monopoly of New York's educational system and founding more than 100 schools. He then invited the Society of St. Vincent de Paul and the Sisters of Mercy into his diocese, trusting them more than the state to care for the city's poor. He likewise promoted temperance pledges and devotion to the Sacred Heart, believing discipline and piety could overcome poverty and violence.

History proved him right. Within a generation, the moral squalor of the Irish slums was eradicated, and instead of composing the majority of the city's underclass, the Irish of New York composed a majority of the city's schoolteachers, policemen, and civic leaders.

Hughes died on **January 3, 1864,** 14 years after becoming New York's first archbishop.

January 4: THE INDEPENDENT CATHOLIC CHURCH
OF AMERICA

If not for an Irish Franciscan's loyalty to Rome, the Independent Catholic Church of America could have been established in 1819.

The trouble began years earlier, when, with the appointment of America's first bishop, John Carroll, Irish-American Catholics began demanding the right to hire and fire their own priests. As trustees of the churches they financed and built, they believed the right to choose the priests belonged to them. Following the death of Carroll's successor, Archbishop Leonard Neale, and the appointment of the Frenchman Ambrose Maréchal, as Archbishop of Baltimore, tensions rose even higher.

First, the Catholics of Newport, Virginia, sent a letter to Rome demanding the right to appoint their own clergymen. Then, on **January 4, 1819,** Catholics in Charleston, South Carolina, had Father Thomas Carbery of New York forward a letter for them to Father Hayes in Dublin.

The letter requested that the Franciscan priest travel "in the most secret manner" to the Netherlands, where a schismatic Jansenist bishop resided. It then instructed him to "have yourself consecrated Bishop of South Carolina."

The letter concluded with the promise that, "On your arrival in America your expenses shall be made good to you, but you must agree to consecrate other bishops in this country, otherwise your salary may be doubtful."

Alarmed, Hayes immediately had the letter translated into Italian, then sent it on to the Holy Father in Rome. Recognizing that schism loomed, the Vatican responded by creating new dioceses in Virginia and South Carolina, and sending two Irishmen to lead them: Patrick Kelly to Richmond and John England to Charleston.

Schism was averted, but the battle against what would come to be known as "trusteeism" was far from over.

January 5: AMERICA'S MOST USEFUL CITIZEN

By October of 1917, six months after America entered into the fray of World War I, Catholics constituted less than 17 percent of the country's population. Despite that, they accounted for 35 percent of new army recruits.

Credit for those numbers belonged largely to one man: Baltimore's Archbishop James Cardinal Gibbons.

The Baltimore-born, Irish-American prelate had served as a Union chaplain at Fort McHenry, Baltimore, during the American Civil War, and was almost as strong a believer in the United States and the virtue of patriotism as he was in the tenets of the Catholic Church.

That support was evident in April 1917, on the eve of Congress' declaration of war against Germany, when Gibbons issued the following statement to the press:

> *In the present emergency it behooves every American citizen to do his duty, and to uphold the hands of the President and the Legislative department in the solemn obligations that confront us. The primary duty of a citizen is loyalty to country. This loyalty is manifested more by acts than by words; by solemn service rather than by empty declaration. It is exhibited by an absolute and unreserved obedience to his country's call.*

For his support of America's military in World War I—including initiating the founding of the National Catholic War Council (the forerunner to the United States Conference of Catholic Bishops), which coordinated spiritual, medical, and material support for U.S. troops—Gibbons earned nearly universal praise from top government officials.

No praise, however, touched that of former President Theodore Roosevelt, who, even before America entered the war, wrote to Gibbons on **January 5, 1917,** saying, "Taking your life as a whole, I think you now occupy the position of being the most respected and venerated and useful citizen in our country."

How do you reconcile the religion of the Old World with the political doctrine of the New World?

That question dogged Catholics in both America and Rome throughout the nineteenth century. Although Americans loved their faith and respected their bishops, the laity in the United States also observed their Protestant neighbors exercising great sway in the governance of their churches. For Protestant Americans, democracy was a way of life in matters of faith as well as politics. Catholics observed the fruits of that, and many thought them good.

To an even greater degree, both the Catholic laity and Catholic hierarchy in America instinctually championed prototypical American values—the separation of Church and State, freedom of speech, independence, and self-reliance. Many also wanted to see Catholics integrated into the mainstream of American life, and worked to find common ground with their Protestant neighbors.

In Europe, those American attitudes were met with a mixture of admiration and suspicion. In some places, particularly late-nineteenth-century France, they were imitated. In others, notably the Vatican, they seemed cause for concern. The *curia* appreciated the energy of the American Church, but they also remembered the threat of schism brought on by trusteeism earlier in the century. Some feared that the attitude of American exceptionalism—championed by Catholics and non-Catholics alike on questions of politics—might bleed over into questions of faith and morals.

To check that possibility, Pope Leo XIII issued the encyclical letter *Longinqua Oceani* ("The Wide Expanse of the Ocean") on **January 6, 1895.**

Although the letter primarily praised the work and faith of U.S. Catholics, it nevertheless reminded them that the Church did not view the separation of Church and State as ideal, and that the Church in America "would bring forth more abundant fruits if, in addition to liberty, she enjoyed the favor of the laws and the patronage of the public authority."

On **January 7, 1789,** the United States' first presidential election took place. In each of the 13 colonies, presidential electors were chosen. A month later, General George Washington became the nation's first president.

Upon hearing the news of Washington's election, a number of prominent Catholics, including Father John Carroll, S.J. (soon to be bishop of Baltimore) and his cousin Charles Carroll (recently elected to the U.S. Senate from Maryland), sent their new president a letter of congratulations.

Washington, known for his friendships with Catholics and admiration for their Church, promptly replied, writing:

> *I feel that my conduct, in war and in peace, has met with more general approbation than could reasonably have been expected and I find myself disposed to consider that fortunate circumstance, in a great degree, resulting from the able support and extraordinary candour of my fellow-citizens of all denominations.*
>
> *As mankind becomes more liberal they will be more apt to allow that all those who conduct themselves as worthy members of the community are equally entitled to the protection of civil government. I hope ever to see America among the foremost nations in examples of justice and liberality. And I presume that your fellow-citizens will not forget the patriotic part which you took in the accomplishment of their Revolution, and the establishment of their government; or the important assistance which they received from a nation in which the Roman Catholic faith is professed. . . .*
>
> *[M]ay the members of your society in America, animated alone by the pure spirit of Christianity, and still conducting themselves as the faithful subjects of our free government, enjoy every temporal and spiritual felicity.*
>
> *G. Washington*

January 8: AMERICA'S FIRST BISHOP

The funeral procession of Archbishop John Carroll in December 1815, was, as one Baltimore paper reported, a site to behold.

"We have never witnessed a funeral procession where so many of eminent respectability and standing among us followed the train of mourners," it noted. "Distinctions of rank, of wealth, of religious opinion were laid aside in the great testimony of respect to the memory of the man."

The man in question was born 80 years earlier, on **January 8, 1735,** to an Irish immigrant and an American heiress of English descent. Educated largely at a school for English Catholics in Europe, Carroll entered the Jesuits at 18, became a priest 14 years later, and remained in Europe, traveling and teaching, until he was almost 40.

The suppression of the Jesuits in 1773 finally brought Carroll back to his native Maryland, where he was soon drawn into the struggles of the fledgling movement for American independence, as well as the struggles of the fledgling Catholic Church in America.

In the years that followed, as a friend of both George Washington and Ben Franklin, Carroll worked to guarantee religious liberty for Catholics and helped secure the Constitution's prohibition of religious tests for public office. Likewise, as the first American bishop and archbishop, he helped lay the foundation for the future of the Church in America. Credit for the first American cathedral (the Cathedral of the Assumption of the Blessed Virgin Mary in Baltimore), the first American seminary (St. Mary's in Baltimore), and the first American Catholic college (Georgetown University in Washington, D.C.) all goes to Carroll.

Known for his intellect, energy, piety, and preaching (some Protestants even attended his Masses just to hear his homilies), Carroll helped quell early waves of anti-Catholicism in the newly founded United States, while still strengthening the faith of his flock.

The spectacle of his funeral procession was thus a fitting tribute to a man whose contributions to both country and Church endure to this day.

William "Buffalo Bill" Cody was many things: a trapper, a bullwhacker, a Pony Express rider, a wagon master, a stagecoach driver, a hotel manager, and a Civil War soldier.

He was also a Catholic, for all of one day.

Born in LeClaire, Iowa in 1846, Cody spent most of his childhood in Kansas, where his father's outspoken opposition to slavery earned the family few friends.

In the years immediately following the American Civil War, Cody gained a reputation as an "Indian fighter." He also gained a reputation as one of the finest shots in the West, a reputation bolstered by his claim to have killed 4,280 American bison over an 18-month period, while fulfilling a contract to supply meat to railroad workers.

In 1872, that reputation earned him an invitation to appear in the Chicago stage show *The Scouts of the Prairie.* The show toured for 10 years before it evolved into "Buffalo Bill's Wild West," a traveling extravaganza featuring the likes of Annie Oakley, Calamity Jane, Lillian Smith, and Sitting Bull.

Between 1883, when the show made its debut, and 1907, more than two million people across Europe and America, including Queen Victoria, watched Cody and company show off their sharp-shooting skills and reenact skirmishes between American settlers and the country's original inhabitants.

Although Cody profited off depictions of Native Americans as savages, in private he lamented that "every Indian outbreak that I have ever known has resulted from broken promises and broken treaties by the government."

In 1917, while visiting his sister in Denver, Cody fell deathly ill from kidney disease. On **January 9, 1917,** the day before he died, he summoned a Catholic priest, Father Christopher Walsh, to his bedside. He told Walsh that he had never belonged to a religion, but believed in God and wished to die a Catholic. Walsh examined him, then administered the sacraments, and received him into the Church.

Cody died the following day.

January 10: THE IRISH SPEAKER

On **January 10, 1963,** as John William McCormack was sworn in as the first Catholic Speaker of the House, everyone watching knew the Democratic congressman from Massachusetts had big shoes to fill.

McCormack's predecessor, the legendary Sam Rayburn, had ruled the House for the better part of the last two decades and ruled it like few others. Throughout those decades, McCormack served alongside Rayburn as House Majority Leader and (during the rare years when Democrats lost the House) as Minority Whip. Following Rayburn's death, he was the natural successor, but skeptics feared the Irish politician was too interested in being likeable to be effective.

But McCormack was stronger than he looked.

Nearly 60 years before, McCormack dropped out of eighth grade to help support his mother and siblings. His first job as a newsboy eventually led to a job as an errand runner for a law firm. Intrigued by his employers' work, McCormack began studying law at night. Although he never attended high school or college, he passed the bar at the age of 21.

McCormack's years of practicing law were few. After fighting in World War I, he served in the Massachusetts House, then the State Senate, before his election to Congress in 1928. He served there for 43 years, including nine as Speaker. Although dissent from younger Democrats drove him into retirement in 1971, McCormack's tenure was a historic one, which saw the passage of landmark legislation on civil rights, education, and welfare.

McCormack's greatest love, however, wasn't politics. It was his wife, Harriet. Legend has it that the couple never spent a night apart, and even when Congress kept McCormack late, they still dined together in the Capitol. During the last year of her life, a year spent in the hospital, McCormack took up residence in the hospital room next door.

He died nine years after Harriet, in 1980, at the age of 88.

If you want to become a saint, it helps to know one. Case in point: Blessed Francis Xavier Seelos.

Born and baptized in Bavaria on **January 11, 1819,** Seelos came to America as a seminarian in 1843 to minister to German-speaking Catholics. After completing his theological studies in Baltimore and becoming a priest for the Congregation of the Most Holy Redeemer (the Redemptorists), Father Seelos was assigned to serve under the future Saint John Neumann in Pittsburgh, Pennsylvania. As a parish priest at St. Philomena's, Seelos spent hours in the confessional, drawing penitents from across the region because of his believed ability to read souls.

Together, Neumann and Seelos also preached missions throughout the city. Of their relationship, Seelos once said: "He has introduced me to the active life . . . and guided me as a spiritual director and confessor."

After leaving Pittsburgh, Seelos went on to serve in parishes in Maryland, Michigan, and Louisiana. During the American Civil War, he also served as an itinerant preacher, taking the Gospel and sacraments to Catholics in Connecticut, Illinois, Michigan, Missouri, New Jersey, New York, Ohio, Pennsylvania, Rhode Island, and Wisconsin. Although Pope Pius IX offered him the see of Pittsburgh in 1860, Seelos declined, preferring the life of parish priest to that of bishop.

And it was as a parish priest that Seelos died. In New Orleans in 1867, while ministering to his parishioners who suffered from yellow fever, Seelos contracted the illness, passing away at the age of 48.

Seelos, like Saint John Neumann, is considered a model for all parish priests. In 2000, he was declared "Blessed" by Pope John Paul II.

On **January 12, 1892,** Cardinal Mieczyslaw Ledóchowski, Prefect for the Congregation for the Propagation of the Faith in Rome, sent a greatly anticipated letter to a German-American priest in Ohio.

The letter informed Father Joseph Jessing that Rome was conferring upon his seminary the title of "pontifical college," making the Pontifical College Josephinum the only pontifical seminary outside of Italy at the time.

Jessing requested the title for his seminary early in 1892. He wanted to ensure that even after his death, his school would endure. That request was necessary because, unlike most other seminaries in the United States, the Josephinum was not under the auspices of a diocese. Rather, Jessing had founded it on his own in 1888, to provide impoverished young men with a path to the priesthood.

In the beginning, most of those young men came to the seminary straight from St. Joseph's Orphanage, the boys' home Jessing had opened almost two decades earlier. Located first in Pomeroy, Ohio, and later in Columbus, the orphanage supplied the parentless boys in Jessing's parish with food, shelter, and an education. When some of the older boys began expressing an interest in the priesthood, Jessing responded by founding the Josephinum, which provided six years of minor seminary education and six years of major seminary education to German Catholics from the Columbus area. The focus later shifted to educating seminarians from dioceses that lacked their own major seminary and the minor seminary then closed.

Long before then, however, on September 1, 1888, 23 young men began their studies for the priesthood under Jessing. Six of those men were ordained to the priesthood in 1899.

More than 1,500 Josephinum seminarians have been ordained in the years since.

Bishop Edward Fenwick, O.P., inherited a love of his country from his father, the Revolutionary War hero Colonel Ignatius Fenwick. From his mother, Sarah Taney, he inherited a love of his Catholic faith. And from both, Bishop Fenwick inherited a vast fortune that he used to build the first Dominican Priory in the United States and the first Catholic educational institution west of the Allegheny Mountains.

Born in Maryland and educated in Belgium, the young Father Fenwick spent several years teaching at a Dominican college near Antwerp before the advent of the French Revolution led to the college's closing and Fenwick's imprisonment. When he was released, he traveled to England, where he continued teaching for the Dominicans.

Fenwick's dream, however, was to return home and help evangelize the United States. In 1804, his Superiors finally granted him permission, and with three companions, Fenwick journeyed across the Atlantic to Maryland. There, he met with Bishop John Carroll, who asked the Dominicans to evangelize the American frontier, including the territories acquired through the Louisiana Purchase of 1803.

In 1806, with Fenwick as their Superior, the foursome arrived in Washington County, Kentucky, where Fenwick used his inheritance to purchase a 500-acre farm and begin construction of St. Rose Priory. In 1809, construction of the church was complete. Three years later, the doors to St. Thomas Aquinas College opened. And in 1816, its first four graduates were ordained to the Dominican priesthood.

In St. Rose Catholic Church, on **January 13, 1822,** Fenwick became Bishop Fenwick, the first bishop of the newly created Diocese of Cincinnati, a diocese that then encompassed all of Ohio, Michigan, and the Northwest Territories. He went on to build 22 churches, as well as the diocese's first cathedral, establish St. Francis Xavier Seminary, and found *The Catholic Telegraph,* the oldest continually published Catholic newspaper in the United States.

A cholera epidemic took the 64-year-old bishop's life 10 years later, in 1832.

In 1882, the St. Augustine Society of Chicago hosted a bazaar to raise funds for a new church building. Nothing unusual about that, right?

Wrong.

The St. Augustine Society of Chicago was no ordinary society. It was, as explained by its founder, Father Joseph Rowles, "a Negro apostolate" that sought to encourage black Catholics in the city and evangelize other black Chicagoans.

Likewise, the church they sought to build was no ordinary church. It would be the first parish in both the city and the nation constructed exclusively for the black Catholic community.

At the time, although black Catholics could worship at any parish in Chicago, many preferred to attend Mass with other black Catholics in the basement of St. Mary's Church on 9th and Wabash.

Over time, a desire in the community for their own parish and pastor grew. Hence the fund-raising bazaar.

Thanks to that bazaar (and generous gifts from the Chicago Catholic community), that desire was realized on **January 14, 1894,** when the newly constructed St. Monica's Catholic Church, on 35th and Dearborn, was dedicated.

The congregation's pastor was Father Augustus Tolton, the first Catholic priest in the United States to self-identify as black. (Others, of mixed heritage, chose to identify as white.)

Eight years later, Mother Katharine Drexel and five of her Sisters of the Blessed Sacrament arrived at the parish to help found St. Monica's Catholic School. Within a year, 200 students were enrolled.

By 1922, that number had risen to nearly 500, while Easter Mass attendance at St. Monica's topped out at 1,200. No longer able to accommodate its growing population, St. Monica's merged with nearby St. Elizabeth's, which soon became known as the Mother Church for the city's black Catholics.

Today, St. Elizabeth's remains a vital center for black Catholics in Chicago, as both a parish and a school.

In November 1842, the 28-year-old French priest Father Edward Sorin, C.S.C., and seven companions from the newly established order of the Congregation of the Holy Cross, arrived in northern Indiana. The bishop of Vincennes had entrusted to them over 500 acres in his diocese, on which they intended to build a college dedicated to the Blessed Virgin Mary.

Fourteen months later, on **January 15, 1844,** the Indiana Legislature officially granted Sorin his college charter, and the University of Notre Dame du Lac ("Our Lady of the Lake") was born.

In the early years, only a few dozen students took advantage of the school's classical college curriculum. More came as novices to receive their theological education or for primary schooling and vocational training. By 1879, however, when a fire destroyed the campus' main academic building, the school had grown to the point that Sorin could remark, "I came here as a young man and dreamed of building a great university in honor of Our Lady. But I built it too small, and she had to burn it to the ground to make the point. So, tomorrow, as soon as the bricks cool, we will rebuild it, bigger and better than ever."

In the years that followed, Notre Dame came to be known as *the* Catholic university in America, with more than 120,000 alumni as of 2013. A co-educational institution since 1972, the university is made up of five colleges and one professional school. Its alumni have included nearly 30 college presidents, two Nobel Laureates, 19 members of the U.S. Congress, nine state governors, six U.S. ambassadors, three astronauts, two national security advisors, one attorney general, one secretary of state, and one solicitor general.

War, as the saying goes, makes for strange bedfellows. The American Revolution was no exception.

In Virginia, for more than a century prior to the Revolution, the Church of England had been the official state religion, with a tax imposed upon those who refused to attend Anglican services. Religious dissenters, however, were numerous: by 1776, they made up at least one-fifth of the state's population.

Accordingly, as war against Britain became imminent, the Anglicans in Virginia's House of Delegates found themselves in desperate need of dissenters' friendship. To obtain it, they made generous concessions on the religious liberty question, including eliminating the dissenters' tax.

As the war progressed, however, the dissenters' votes became less important. And in 1779, when Thomas Jefferson authored a "Bill for Establishing Religious Freedom," Virginia's House of Delegates tabled it without a vote.

Not until seven years later, when Virginia's legislators tried to establish yet another religious tax, could advocates for religious liberty muster enough votes to pass Jefferson's bill.

On **January 16, 1786,** the "Virginia Statute for Establishing Religious Freedom" passed the House. It states:

> *No man shall be compelled to frequent or support any religious worship, place, or ministry whatsoever, nor shall be enforced, restrained, molested, or burthened in his body or goods, nor shall otherwise suffer, on account of his religious opinions or belief, but that all men shall be free to profess, and by argument to maintain, their opinions in matters of Religion, and that the same shall in no wise diminish, enlarge or affect their civil capacities.*

As the most sweeping religious liberty law of its time, the Virginia Statute became a model for the First Amendment to the Bill of Rights and an important legal touchstone in religious liberty law for centuries to come.

It's the simplest and humblest of gravestones: just a marker in the ground, with an epitaph—"My Jesus Mercy"—and a name—Alphonse Capone.

It's an unlikely epitaph for America's most notorious gangster. And yet, there never was anything "likely" about Al Capone. From first to last, he was an enigma.

Born in Brooklyn on **January 17, 1899,** Capone was a bright student who didn't take well to the rules of his Catholic school. He dropped out at the age of 14 and quickly moved up through the ranks of Brooklyn's most notorious gangs—the Junior Forty Thieves, the Bowery Boys, the Brooklyn Rippers, and finally the Five Points Gang.

In 1923, his work with the Five Points Gang took him to Chicago. Within two years, he was king of the Chicago underworld, the city's most notorious bootlegger, gunrunner, speakeasy operator, and crime boss. His disregard for the law and ruthless treatment of his enemies (including gunning down seven rival gang members in the 1929 St. Valentine's Day Massacre) knew no limits.

But neither did his generosity.

Although Capone rarely darkened a church's door, a large donation to a local Catholic parish followed every big score. He founded the city's first soup kitchens when the Depression hit, distributed coal and clothes to Chicago's poor every winter, and routinely paid for the hospital bills of indigent strangers.

All that came to an end, however, with his arrest and imprisonment for tax evasion in 1931. Soon after, the syphilis he'd contracted as a teenager flared up. Throughout his time in prison, his health deteriorated, finally earning him parole in 1939. By 1946, his physician declared that he had the mental capacity of a 12-year-old.

Al Capone died of cardiac arrest a year later, with his only hope—Christ's mercy—carved into his gravestone.

On the night of January 17, 1943, Rita Rizzo was in pain. Nine days earlier, she had begun a novena, asking God for healing from what her doctors called "incurable abnormalities" in her stomach and intestines. But by January 17, the ninth and last day of the novena, the pain that had afflicted her for nearly two years had only grown worse. That night she went to bed, praying that sleep would bring relief.

It did.

When she awoke the next morning, on **January 18, 1943,** the pain was gone. It never returned.

In the days that followed, Rizzo became convinced that God was calling her to religious life. Her mother, Mae, disagreed. Abandoned by her husband soon after Rita's birth, Mae had long battled depression and poverty. All she had was her daughter and feared losing her.

But Rizzo knew God healed her for a purpose.

Leaving only an explanatory note behind, Rizzo left their home in Canton, Ohio, for a convent in Cleveland on the night of August 14, 1944. The next day she became a postulant at the Adoration Monastery of the Poor Clares of Perpetual Adoration. The following November, she received the novice habit and a new name: Sister Mary Angelica.

Seventeen years later, after another mysterious healing, Sister Angelica became Mother Angelica, the foundress of a new Claretian Monastery in Irondale, Alabama. The first postulant to enter was her mother, Mae.

In the years that followed, Mother Angelica became a familiar face on television, first on local channels, then on Pat Robertson's Christian Broadcasting Network, and finally on the Eternal Word Television Network (EWTN), which she founded in 1981.

Today, EWTN is the largest religious media network in the world, reaching more than 148 million homes in 144 countries and territories. Although two strokes in 2001 ended her television career, Mother Angelica remains a prayerful presence in her Claretian monastery—the Shrine of the Most Blessed Sacrament—in Hanceville, Alabama.

January 19: THE SNOWSHOE PRIEST

"The Snowshoe Priest." That's how the Ojibway (Chippewa) Indians referred to Father Frederic Baraga, the young missionary newly arrived in their territory.

In 1830, seven years after his ordination, Baraga journeyed to America from his home in present-day Slovenia. Bishop Edward Fenwick of Cincinnati needed priests for his mission territories and issued a call in Europe for help. Baraga, already a polyglot who spoke a half-dozen languages, answered that call. He spent a year with Fenwick in Cincinnati, learning the Ottawa tongue, then traveled north to an Ottawa mission in Michigan. While serving the Ottawa people, Baraga also completed work on the first book written in the Ottawa language, *Otawa Anamie-Misinaigan*—a Catholic catechism and prayer book.

Baraga left the Ottawa in 1835 to take up a new assignment ministering to the Ojibway (Chippewa) Indians in northern Wisconsin and Michigan. There, during the long, harsh winters, Baraga earned his nickname, traversing thousands of miles via snowshoe to minister to the people in the region. Before long, he had mastered the Ojibway language as well, publishing an Ojibway dictionary and grammar book in 1850. He also worked tirelessly to protect the region's Native American population from government relocation efforts.

In 1853, Father Baraga returned to Cincinnati to be consecrated Bishop Baraga, the first bishop of the Diocese of Sault Sainte Marie, Michigan (now the Diocese of Marquette). As bishop, he faced the enormous task of ministering to the Ojibway, as well as French-Canadian settlers and a growing flood of Irish and German immigrants. A perpetual priest shortage made his work all the more difficult.

The letters Baraga sent to the Congregation for the Propagation of the Faith, however, were read throughout Europe and helped attract priests such as Saint John Neumann to America.

Baraga died on **January 19, 1868,** at the age of 70. He was declared "Venerable" by Pope Benedict XVI in May 2012.

The whole of the nation's capitol was covered in snow when, on the afternoon of **January 20, 1961,** John F. Kennedy stood on the East Front of the U.S. Capitol Building and was sworn in as the 35th president of the United States.

The 43-year-old Massachusetts native was the youngest man and only Catholic yet to be elected to the nation's highest office. He was also a war hero, civil rights proponent, staunch anti-communist, proponent of supply-side economics, and champion of the poor, as well as (unfortunately) a philandering cad. He served three terms in the U.S. House of Representatives and one in the U.S. Senate before overcoming significant anti-Catholic prejudice to win the White House.

He overcame that prejudice, in part, by promising, "I am not the Catholic candidate for President. I am the Democratic Party candidate for President, who also happens to be Catholic. I do not speak for the Church on public matters—and the Church does not speak for me."

In his inaugural address, Kennedy noted that "the same revolutionary beliefs for which our forebears fought are still at issue around the globe—the belief that the rights of man come not from the generosity of the State, but from the hand of God."

He continued:

> *Since this country was founded, each generation of Americans has been summoned to give testimony to its national loyalty . . . Now the trumpet summons us again—not as a call to bear arms, though arms we need; not as a call to battle, though embattled we are— but a call to bear the burden of a long twilight struggle, year in and year out, 'rejoicing in hope, patient in tribulation'—a struggle against the common enemies of man: tyranny, poverty, disease, and war itself.*

Kennedy led that struggle for less than three years. An assassin's bullet ended his presidency and his life on November 22, 1963.

January 21: THE HANDS OF A WOMAN

In 1648, the existence of the Catholic colony in Maryland depended on one woman: Margaret Brent.

A decade earlier, Brent and three of her siblings (all Catholics) fled Great Britain for America, looking to escape the religious troubles of Post-Reformation England. In 1645, however, the troubles from which they'd fled came to them.

That year, Richard Ingle, an industrious Puritan sea captain, set sail along the Maryland coast in the ship *Reformation,* attacking Catholic settlements, imprisoning two priests, and ultimately exiling Maryland's governor, Leonard Calvert, to Virginia.

There, Calvert hired mercenary soldiers who returned with him to Maryland, defeated Ingle's men, and executed Ingle. All should have been well, but Calvert fell ill and died before he could pay the mercenaries. That task he entrusted to the unmarried but wealthy landowner Margaret Brent, telling her to "Take all. Sell all."

Unfortunately, as his executrix soon discovered, Calvert's property wasn't sufficient for payment. With the mercenaries threatening to wipe out the colony they'd just saved, the Maryland Provincial Court took action. Rather than tax themselves to pay the mercenaries, they named Brent the attorney for Calvert's brother, Cecil, the absent Lord Baltimore, granting her the authority to sell his property as well.

Brent, who appeared before the council on **January 21, 1648,** protested and demanded a vote in the proceedings. She knew their decision would not please Baltimore.

Although her request was denied, she dutifully carried out the court's order. Her prediction of Baltimore's displeasure, however, proved correct.

In a letter defending their decision, the court wrote him, saying: "We do verily believe, that your estate was better for the colony's safety at that time in her hands than in any man's else. For the soldiers would never have treated any other with civility and respect."

Brent, the first woman to appear before a court of Common Law in the American colonies, died in 1671.

If at first you don't succeed, try and try again.

When it came to stifling the creeping heresy of Americanism in the nineteenth century, that was the Church's motto.

In 1895, concerned with certain secularizing and modernizing tendencies within the Church in America and Europe, Pope Leo XIII penned the encyclical letter *Longinqua Oceani* ("The Wide Expanse of the Ocean"). In the main, it was a gentle letter, offering more praise than chastisement, and simply reminding Catholics in America that the government of their nation would bear more fruit if it were more illuminated by the Church's teachings.

Around the same time, however, a biography of the Reverend Isaac Thomas Hecker, founder of the Paulist Fathers, became popular in France. The translation of the book was somewhat problematic, and a group of French priests began pointing to Hecker as their inspiration for liberalizing and modernizing the Church in ways arguably less than Catholic.

By 1899, the Vatican feared that in both France and America too much emphasis was being placed on individual initiative in the spiritual life and not enough on the guidance of the Church. They also feared that the principles of democracy were being applied to the Faith, with some Catholics (ordained and lay) believing they could pick and choose which doctrines of the Faith they believed.

Hoping to put an end to those trends, which together came to be known as "Americanism," Pope Leo XIII sent a much more strongly worded letter to Baltimore's Cardinal James Gibbons on **January 22, 1899:** *Testem Benevolentiae Nostrae* ("Witness to Our Benevolence").

In it, the pope emphasized the singularly important role of the Church's magisterium and clergy in the formation of conscience, argued against Catholic assimilation in a Protestant nation, and questioned the wisdom of unlimited freedom of speech and press.

The American bishops protested, denying Americanism's existence in their midst. Time, however, told a different story, and Americanism (or, as a strain of it later came to be called, "cafeteria Catholicism") would rear its head again in the decades to come.

January 23: THE BLUE AND THE GRAY

The boys of the Georgetown College Boat Club had a problem.

The 1876 rowing season was upon them, and, unlike their rivals—Harvard and Penn State—Georgetown had no distinctive colors to help their fans on shore identify them. To solve the problem, they formed a committee and weighed their options.

Their decision? Blue and gray. The blue would represent the students from the Northern states, the gray would represent the students from the Southern states, and together the two colors would represent the unity of the students on campus, a unity that just 10 years before seemed unthinkable.

Georgetown, the oldest Catholic and Jesuit institution in the United States, had nearly closed its doors in the immediate wake of the Civil War. Nearly 1,200 students and alumni had fought in the conflagration, and in 1861 the U.S. Army took over the university's campus to house Union soldiers. By 1869, its graduates numbered exactly seven.

The Jesuits who ran the school, however, were determined to see it survive. The land for the college had been purchased on **January 23, 1789,** by America's first bishop, the Jesuit John Carroll, and since then, Catholic men from across the country had worked hard to attend the school.

In 1873, Father Patrick Francis Healy assumed the presidency of the college. Some thought he would close its doors. Healy, however, became like a second founder, erecting new buildings, reforming the curriculum, and improving alumni relations. Within a decade, the school was on sure footing once more.

Today, Georgetown University educates more than 7,000 undergraduate and 9,000 post-graduate students. Considered one of the most prestigious schools in the country, with more than 23 Rhodes Scholars, a U.S. president, and dozens of civic and cultural leaders on its alumni rosters, its blue and gray colors still represent the university and its 23 intercollegiate athletics teams.

January 24: GOLD FOR GOD

On **January 24, 1848,** a foreman building a lumber mill for Sacramento farmer John Sutter noticed a few shiny metal objects in the water wheel. He took the metal to Sutter. Tests confirmed their suspicions: Gold.

In the years that followed, nearly 300,000 men and women made their way to Northern California, hoping to find their fortune in the territory's streams and riverbeds. Most were disappointed. But not all. One of those lucky few was Patrick Manogue.

In 1854, the 22-year-old Irish immigrant arrived in San Francisco. Six foot three and powerfully built, Manogue had no trouble finding work on one of the gold-mining crews. His team had even less trouble finding gold.

Manogue used his initial profits to pay for his siblings' passage from Ireland. He used the rest to pursue his vocation to the priesthood, promising the bishop of San Francisco that if he was accepted as a seminarian for the diocese, he would pay his own way through seminary in Europe.

The bishop agreed, and Manogue soon sailed for France, where he studied at the Seminary of Saint-Sulpice in Paris. Ordained in 1861, he returned to the States, serving as a missionary in Nevada, before becoming co-adjutor bishop of the Diocese of Grass Valley in 1881 and then the first bishop of Sacramento in 1886.

Upon his arrival in Sacramento, Bishop Manogue began raising funds for a cathedral. For help, he turned to his friends from his gold-mining days, most notably John Mackey, who, at the time, was the richest man in the world. Construction on the cathedral began in 1887 and was financed almost entirely by those who made their fortune in the Great California Gold Rush. Once complete, the Cathedral of the Blessed Sacrament was the largest church west of the Mississippi.

Manogue died in 1895, in the cathedral he built.

"If you really were a Catholic priest, could you please prove it by reciting the 'Our Father' in Latin?"

That request, posed by the young Father John Noll to anti-Catholic preachers who claimed to be former priests, never failed to bring the preachers up short. They came to Northern Indiana expecting to find easy prey for their virulent anti-Catholicism. Instead, they found their lies quickly unmasked and their arguments against the Church dismantled by a man no older than 25. By the end of the night, anti-Catholic audiences would ask Noll questions about joining the Catholic Church.

Noll, who was born on **January 25, 1875,** and ordained a priest when he was only 23, tried to never let an argument against the Catholic Faith go unanswered. When anti-Catholic preachers came his way in 1898, he rode on horseback to their revivals. And when Communist agitators began targeting the Church in a series of print publications, he responded to those attacks by founding *Our Sunday Visitor* (*OSV*) in 1912.

In less than a decade, the circulation for the national Catholic newsweekly topped half a million, while the Communist paper that sparked its founding, *The Menace,* had folded. Eventually, *Our Sunday Visitor* would reach more than one million Catholics every week.

Ordained bishop of the Diocese of Fort Wayne in 1925 (and named archbishop in 1953), Archbishop Noll went on to help found the Catholic Press Association and the Legion of Decency (which combatted explicit sexuality in the media), as well as expand *Our Sunday Visitor*'s reach, publishing magazines and books, along with parish-giving envelopes, a concept he introduced to Catholics in 1916. All profits generated by the publishing empire went back into the Our Sunday Visitor Institute, which funded missionary and apostolate work in the Church at home and abroad.

Noll died in 1956 at the age of 81.

January 26: THE GERMAN PROFESSOR

Shortly after midnight, on March 12, 1938, three Gestapo agents pounded on the door to Dietrich von Hildebrand's home. When no answer came, they broke the door in, only to find the Viennese apartment empty. Hildebrand and his wife, Margaret, had left just five hours before and were already on the other side of Austria's border with Czechoslovakia.

Later that morning, Austrians awoke to find their country occupied by the German army. Austria's political leaders had been arrested in the middle of the night. After the heads of government, von Hildebrand had been next on their list.

What made the philosopher such a threat to the Nazi Party?

Von Hildebrand, who was born to German parents living outside of Florence, Italy, converted as an adult to Catholicism. In 1933, he fled to Austria from Germany knowing that his outspoken opposition to the Nazi Party would threaten his life. Once in Austria, he took up a position teaching philosophy at the University of Vienna and founded a popular Catholic newsweekly, *Der Christliche Ständestatt,* for which he penned more than 70 articles against National Socialism. Those articles were what brought the Gestapo agents to his door.

From Austria, von Hildebrand went on to France, and then to America in 1940, where for the next two decades, he taught at Fordham University. In 1959, two years after the passing of his first wife, Hildebrand married his colleague, Alice Jourdain. He retired from teaching a year later and devoted the rest of his life to writing.

When he died on **January 26, 1977,** von Hildebrand left behind one of the most impressive philosophical legacies of the twentieth century. His large body of work profoundly influenced the Church's understanding of the human person, sexual love, and holy matrimony, so much so that decades before his death, Pope Pius XII described von Hildebrand as "the Twentieth Century Doctor of the Church."

January 27: MISSION CONTROL

On **January 27, 1967,** a fire broke out in the Apollo 1 command module. Its launch into outer space was a month away, but the crew was onboard, going through an important launchpad test. All three astronauts died.

Gene Kranz, NASA's 33-year-old Flight Director at the time, watched the tragedy unfold from the control room. Hoping to avert further such tragedies, Kranz crafted a statement of professional ethics for his team: "Foundations of Mission Control." Kranz has credited the ideas that underlie that document to his Catholic faith and the education in virtue he received from Catholic schools. Historians have likewise credited Kranz and the professional ethic he cultivated at NASA for saving the Apollo 13 crew in 1970, when an explosion crippled the ship in space. The statement read:

Foundations of Mission Control

To instill within ourselves these qualities essential for professional excellence:

- Discipline: Being able to follow as well as lead, knowing that we must master ourselves before we can master our task.
- Competence: There being no substitute for total preparation and complete dedication, for space will not tolerate the careless or indifferent.
- Confidence: Believing in ourselves as well as others, knowing that we must master fear and hesitation before we can succeed.
- Responsibility: Realizing that it cannot be shifted to others, for it belongs to each of us; we must answer for what we do, or fail to do.
- Toughness: Taking a stand when we must; to try again, and again, even if it means following a more difficult path.
- Teamwork: Respecting and utilizing the ability of others, realizing that we work toward a common goal, for success depends on the efforts of all.

To always be aware that suddenly and unexpectedly we may find ourselves in a role where our performance has ultimate consequences.

To recognize that the greatest error is not to have tried and failed, but that in trying, we did not give it our best effort.

In 1973, when *Roe v. Wade* legalized abortion in the United States, Catholic politicians were nearly unanimous in their condemnation of the decision. Republican, Democrat: It didn't matter. On the question of abortion, Catholic legislators stood with the Church.

Throughout the 1970s, however, that unity began to crumble. One by one, formerly pro-life Democrats, including Ted Kennedy, Joe Biden, John Kerry, and Mario Cuomo, reversed their position on abortion and embraced their party's pro-abortion platform. Helping them make that switch and giving them theological cover was Father Robert Drinan, a lawyer, a Jesuit priest, and a U.S. Congressman from the Commonwealth of Massachusetts.

Ordained a priest in 1953, Drinan served as Dean of the Boston College Law School from 1956 until 1970. That year, he ran for a seat in the U.S. House of Representatives. He won. Two years later, he won again, taking his seat in the same month that the decision in *Roe v. Wade* came down.

From the beginning, Drinan supported the Supreme Court decision, arguing that while he found abortion personally reprehensible, he believed it legally necessary. Other Catholic politicians soon followed, taking Drinan's argument as their own.

For years, Drinan's religious superiors tried to persuade him to step down, concerned over the scandal and confusion generated by his pro-abortion views. Only in 1980, however, when Pope John Paul II authoritatively forbade priests from holding political office, did Drinan retire from political life. As a writer and professor at Georgetown University Law Center, however, he continued to expound his theories on law and abortion.

Although he led countless humanitarian missions to Latin and Central America during his 27 years at Georgetown, Drinan's enduring legacy remains his tragic contributions to the abortion debate.

Drianan died on **January 28, 2007.**

January 29: THE POET OF THE ANGELUS

Fame found Edgar Allan Poe late. On **January 29, 1845,** four years before his death and 14 long years after he began attempting to earn his living as a writer, "The Raven" was published in *The New York Evening Mirror.* It was an overnight sensation, and Poe, suddenly, a household name.

Its success, however, did little for Poe in his lifetime. He made almost no money from the poem, and he took little consolation in the applause. His beloved wife, Virginia, was dying of tuberculosis, his debts were mounting, and his reputation as a hard drinker made it difficult for him to find steady work as an editor and critic.

Not long after the publication of "The Raven," Poe and Virginia moved to a small cottage in Brooklyn. Following her death in 1847, Poe befriended his neighbors, the Jesuits of St. John's College (the future Fordham University). There, the father of the modern detective story spent long nights in conversation with the (mostly) French Fathers, and, when he couldn't bear the thought of returning home to an empty house, he would remain with the priests at the college.

After the 40-year-old poet died in 1849 under mysterious circumstances, those Jesuits continued to pray for Poe's soul. That soul never embraced the Catholic Faith, but, as his poem, "Hymn of the Angelus," attests, it was touched by the Faith's beauty nevertheless.

At morn, at noon, at twilight dim,
Maria, thou hast heard my hymn!
In joy and woe, in good and ill,
Mother of God, be with me still!
When the hours flew brightly by,
And not a cloud obscured the sky,
My soul, lest it should truant be,
Thy grace did guide to thine and thee;
Now, when the storms of fate o'ercast
Darkly my present and my past,
Let my future radiant shine
With sweet hopes of thee and thine.

January 30: A GIFT BEYOND PRICE

On the American frontier, there were no extras. Most families had barely enough food and money for themselves, let alone extra food and money to support priests, religious, the building of new churches, and the education of seminarians. But they needed priests and churches just the same.

So, the American bishops turned to Europe. Few did so more successfully than Cincinnati's Bishop Edward Fenwick.

In 1827, Bishop Fenwick sent his vicar-general, Father Frederick Rese, on his behalf to Austria-Hungary, where the priest was granted an audience with Emperor Francis I. Rese regaled Francis with stories of Catholics beset by Protestant missionaries and priests who traveled hundreds of miles on horseback to administer the sacraments.

Rese's tales so impressed the emperor that he entrusted his brother— Archduke Rudolph, the Cardinal Archbishop of Olmütz—with the task of overseeing a missionary society to benefit the Catholics of the United States.

On **January 30, 1829,** Pope Leo XII, by papal bull, gave his sanction to the new society, which bore his name: The Leopoldine Society.

In the decades that followed, the Society provided more than half a million dollars in aid to the Diocese of Cincinnati, as well as the dioceses of Baltimore, Bardstown, Boston, Charleston, Chicago, Detroit, Dubuque, Galveston, Hartford, Little Rock, Marquette, Milwaukee, Mobile, Nashville, Natchez, New Orleans, New York, Philadelphia, Pittsburgh, Richmond, St. Louis, St. Paul, and Vincennes. At the time, that was a staggering amount of money, which enabled the bishops to educate their priests, build and furnish churches and cathedrals, support elderly priests, and provide material aid to their parishioners.

The money also paid for missionary priests to leave Europe and journey to America. To The Leopoldine Society goes the credit for some of America's greatest priests, including Venerable Frederic Baraga and Saint John Neumann, which, in and of itself, was a gift beyond price.

Their rivalries were the stuff of legend: the Hatfields and the McCoys, the House of Lancaster and the House of York, Juneautown and Kilbourntown.

Maybe "legend" is a stretch for the latter, but in 1840s Wisconsin, the animosity between Juneautown and Kilbourntown was no laughing matter.

Fueled in large part by the rivalry between the town's respective founders—the Catholic Solomon Juneau and the Protestant Byron Kilbourn—citizens of the two towns spent the better part of five years warring over the bridges that spanned the Milwaukee River. Juneautown lay to the east of the river, Kilbourntown to the west. In order for trade to flourish, it was important that those bridges be well placed.

Kilbourn, however, didn't want to see any flourishing trade in the more Catholic Juneautown. His hope was to make the town dependent on his own, so that he could exercise control over both towns.

Accordingly, when the Wisconsin Territorial Legislature ordered a new bridge built over the Milwaukee River, Kilbourn opposed the plan. When his opposition failed, he and the citizens of Kilbourntown destroyed the newly built bridge. In retaliation, men from Juneautown destroyed two smaller bridges along the river, cutting off Kilbourntown from trade in the east and south.

There were riots and fires, and more than a few injuries, although thankfully no one was killed. The dispute finally ended on **January 31, 1845,** when a treaty united the two towns, as well as Walkertown to the south, into the modern-day city of Milwaukee.

Milwaukee elected Juneau as the town's first mayor. He served one term. Then, in 1848, when Kilbourn was elected to the same office, Juneau moved north, leaving behind the town he had founded, as well as St. Peter's Parish and St. John's Cathedral, which were built upon land he had donated to the Church. He died in 1856.

Kilbourn served two terms as mayor, and eventually retired to Florida, where he died in 1870.

February

February 1: THE APOSTLE TO THE SIOUX

When Father Martin Marty set sail for America in 1860, he expected his stay to be short—just one year or slightly more.

Earlier that year, his order—the Benedictines of Einsiedeln Abbey in Switzerland—discovered that their daughter-house in St. Meinrad, Indiana, was riddled with corruption and laden with debt. To correct the problem, their superior turned to the 26-year-old Marty, booking him passage across the Atlantic and giving him one year to turn the situation around.

Which he did. Upon Marty's arrival, morale among the monks improved immediately, and before the year was out, the Abbey was financially solvent. Impressed, the Benedictines decided Marty should stay in St. Meinrad. He remained there for 16 years, becoming abbot of the house in 1870.

In 1876, however, a dispute with his fellow Benedictines led Marty to resign his post and accept another with the Bureau of Catholic Indian Missions.

Arriving in the Dakotas just one month after the Battle of Little Big Horn, Marty's success with the Sioux was almost as immediate as his success with the monks. His personal asceticism impressed them, and when he journeyed to Canada in 1877, hoping to convince Sitting Bull to return to the United States, he quickly won the great chief's trust. Although it took four more years before Sitting Bull surrendered, Marty purportedly baptized him, along with 2,000 other Sioux, in 1883.

On **February 1, 1880,** Father Marty was consecrated Bishop Marty of the newly created Vicariate Apostolic of Dakota, which nine years later became the Diocese of Sioux Falls.

Even as a bishop, however, Marty never lost his missionary zeal and devoted the bulk of his episcopacy to evangelizing the Sioux, founding schools and parishes for them, and petitioning the U.S. government on their behalf. He also wrote a dictionary of their language and translated numerous Church writings into Sioux.

In 1895, Marty left the Dakotas to serve as bishop of St. Cloud, Minnesota. He died there one year later, his stay in America lasting 35 years longer than expected.

Bishop Benedict Joseph Fenwick, S.J., was determined to open a Catholic college in Boston. But not just any college. He wanted a Jesuit college.

In 1827, shortly after his ordination to the episcopacy, the former Georgetown University president launched his first attempt at founding his college. He furnished a classroom in the cathedral's basement and personally began instructing the city's most promising Catholic youth. He called the school "Boston College."

Unfortunately, it took him 15 years to convince other Jesuits to join him, and by then Protestant city officials had put their foot down. They wanted no Catholic college in Boston.

Unwilling to admit defeat, Fenwick began looking elsewhere for property on which he could build a proper school. He eventually found that property in the small town of Worcester, Massachusetts. He purchased it on **February 2, 1843**.

The following November, six boys ages 9 to 19 began their studies at Fenwick's school, which he named "College of the Holy Cross."

Six years later, the young James Augustine Healy—later America's first bishop of African descent—was valedictorian of the college's inaugural class.

Despite its successes, however, anti-Catholicism continued to dog the school, with Commonwealth officials repeatedly denying the college a charter. Until 1865, when the governor finally relented, diplomas had to be granted through Georgetown University.

In the years that followed, the school flourished, eventually becoming one of the most academically respected liberal arts colleges in the nation. In the years leading up to and following the Second Vatican Council, it also earned a reputation as a center for the emerging Catholic social justice movement and, in 1974, *TIME* magazine dubbed it "the cradle of the Catholic left."

In recent years, the college has stood at the center of an ongoing debate about the nature of Catholic higher education and has come under fire for welcoming pro-choice politicians and groups to campus, at times putting it at odds with its local ordinary. Despite the controversy, the school continues to flourish, educating nearly 3,000 undergraduates each year.

The directive from the Captain of the USAT *Dorchester* was clear: "Sleep in your clothes and wear your life jackets at all times."

Unfortunately, his men, hot and tired in cramped quarters below, didn't listen. And when a torpedo from a German U-Boat struck the ship shortly after midnight on **February 3, 1943,** panic ensued.

At that moment, four chaplains emerged from the chaos: the Methodist preacher George Fox, the Jewish rabbi Alexander Goode, the Presbyterian minister Clarke Poling, and the Catholic priest John Washington.

The son of Irish immigrants, Father Washington enlisted in the days immediately following the attack on Pearl Harbor. Throughout most of 1942, the 33-year-old New Jersey native remained stateside, stationed first in Indiana and Maryland, then in Massachusetts, where he began Chaplain School at Harvard University. Among his classmates were Fox, Goode, and Poling.

The four became friends and together boarded the *Dorchester* in late January 1943. They had been at sea for less than 10 days when the torpedo struck. In the aftermath of the attack, the four chaplains calmed the men, organized an evacuation, and distributed life jackets. When the life jackets ran out, they gave up their own.

Life jackets, however, weren't the only thing in short supply: the *Dorchester* had only enough lifeboat space to accommodate one quarter of its men. The officers offered spots to Washington and his fellow chaplains, but they refused to go.

As the survivors rowed away from the ship, they could see the four chaplains—linked arm in arm, praying for the souls and safety of their men.

Before the sun rose, the *Dorchester* was gone. So were her four chaplains and nearly 700 others. Only 230 men survived.

Posthumously, Washington and his fellow chaplains received the Distinguished Service Cross and the Purple Heart. In 1988, Congress declared February 3 "Four Chaplains Day," and the Episcopalians honor all four men on that day with a liturgical feast.

Maryland was lost. Following a Protestant revolution in 1689, control of the colony's government passed out of Catholic hands. That loss of political power brought with it the loss of religious liberty, with public Masses banned and dissenters' taxes imposed.

As the years passed and the anti-Catholic laws in the formerly Catholic colony grew more stringent, many Maryland Catholics began looking for a new home. Some found that home along the Little Conewago Creek (from the Lenape word meaning "at the rapids") in the present-day Diocese of Harrisburg, Pennsylvania. There, in 1730, Charles Calvert, the fifth Lord Baltimore, deeded 10,000 acres to Catholic settlers.

At first, the settlers celebrated Mass in their homes, with Father Joseph Greaton, S.J., as their priest. By 1741, however, a small chapel was built. Although it was christened "Our Lady of the Assumption Catholic Church," almost no one called it that. To the locals and the travelers who passed through the growing Catholic settlement, it was known simply as "Conewago Chapel."

Twenty-seven years later, the community expanded the chapel, and it became the motherhouse for all Jesuit priests serving west of Philadelphia. By 1784, however, even that expansion couldn't accommodate the 1,000 plus Catholics who worshipped there. The old church was taken down and a new one built in its place. Construction wrapped up sometime around **February 9, 1787,** though no one knows exactly when. A fire and the departure of the Jesuits left the parish with no records from its first century.

Once complete, the newly named Sacred Heart Parish was the largest Catholic church in the young nation.

A basilica since 1962, the church still commonly goes by the name Conewago Chapel. It is the oldest stone Catholic church in the United States and holds a well-deserved place on the National Register of Historic Places.

In 2007, Francis Beckwith caused a stir when he resigned from his post as president of the Evangelical Theological Society to return to the Catholic Church. Beckwith's announcement, however, paled in comparison to the controversy caused by the conversion of Congregationalist minister John Thayer in 1783.

Boston born and Yale educated, Thayer hailed from one of New England's wealthiest families. During the American Revolution, he distinguished himself as a chaplain. Then, after the war, Thayer used the family money to fund an extended European tour.

As he journeyed through France and Italy, the Catholic piety he encountered surprised him. It also aroused his curiosity. Upon arriving in Rome (and with no intention of converting), Thayer set out to learn more about what Catholics believed.

Months of discussions and debates with Jesuit priests followed. Eventually, the sheer reason of Catholicism overwhelmed him, and Thayer began wrestling with the implications of conversion. Even so, it took the death of the beggar Saint Joseph Benedict Labre and the firsthand accounts of the miracles that followed his death to convince Thayer to enter the Catholic Church in 1783.

Four years later, while studying for the Catholic priesthood in France, Thayer published his conversion story. An overnight sensation, it was printed in England, Ireland, Spain, and France, as well as America, where Catholic priests praised him and Protestant preachers from Boston to the Carolinas denounced him.

Thayer took it all in stride, and was ordained in 1789. He then returned to the United States, where he was stationed for short periods of time in Boston, Virginia, and Kentucky. He never managed to hold a pastoral assignment for long though. Catholic priest or not, his preaching style remained decidedly Congregationalist—forceful and uncompromising—and Catholics in America didn't take to it.

Upon Bishop John Carroll's advice, Thayer finally moved to Limerick, Ireland, where his preaching found a more appreciative audience. He lived out the rest of his days there as a beloved parish priest, dying on **February 5, 1815.**

February 6: PROVIDENCE, THE POPE AND THE PRESIDENT

He should have been Catholic. And he almost was.

America's fortieth president, Ronald Wilson Reagan, was born on **February 6, 1911**. His father, Jack, was Catholic, as was his older brother, Neil. A little over a year before Reagan's birth, however, his mother joined the Disciples of Christ, and, when her second son was born, insisted he be baptized in her community. So he was.

For the next 19 years, the future president worshipped without question in his mother's church. Then, not long after his nineteenth birthday, he announced to his family that he wanted to become Catholic. The pronouncement, however, proved more an act of teenage rebellion than genuine conversion, and Reagan's enthusiasm for joining his father's Church soon passed.

After graduating from college in 1932, Reagan worked briefly in radio, then embarked on a successful career as a film star. More successful still was his political career, which included one term as governor of California and two terms as president of the United States.

Through it all, Reagan retained his affection for his father's Church. That affection grew in June 1981, when the visiting Mother Teresa told the president of her community's prayers for him following the assassination attempt on his life three months earlier. She then added, "You have suffered the passion of the cross and have received grace. There is a purpose to this . . . this has happened to you at this time because your country and the world need you." Reagan was noticeably moved. His wife Nancy cried.

The following year Reagan met Pope John Paul II for the first time. Three more meetings, an extensive correspondence, and a great partnership followed. One of the first fruits of that partnership was the restoration of U.S. diplomatic ties to the Holy See in 1983. The greatest fruit, however, was helping bring a peaceful resolution to the Cold War by the decade's end.

Ronald Reagan passed away in 2004. The pope whose friendship he treasured died one year later.

The American Civil War didn't just divide a country; it also divided a Church.

Some U.S. Catholic bishops stood proudly with the Union. For example, Archbishop John Baptist Purcell of Cincinnati hung the U.S. flag over his cathedral throughout the war.

Others, such as Bishop Martin John Spalding of Louisville, found themselves sympathizing with the South.

As the Kentucky native saw it, slavery was "a great moral evil." But abolishing slavery via civil war, he feared, would only lead to more evil.

"But how can we free ourselves of [slavery] without ruining our country and causing injury to the poor slaves themselves?" he asked. "Those who are in such a way liberated ordinarily become miserable vagabonds, drunkards and thieves."

If Spalding's position before the war was typical of many American bishops, so was his response once war began. Setting aside his reservations, he committed diocesan resources to the care of families and Union soldiers, even closing St. Joseph's College in 1861 and converting it into a hospital for wounded men.

After the Civil War, as archbishop of Baltimore, Spalding showed equal concern for the devastated South and the former slaves who found themselves with neither home nor work.

Asking, "Can we be held blameless before God if our brethren, whom we are solemnly commanded to love even as ourselves, should perish through our coldness and neglect?" Spalding inspired the Catholics of Baltimore to send thousands of dollars in relief money to the South. He did the same for former slaves, raising funds to feed and clothe those in need and recruiting missionaries from England to minister to the vastly expanded population of freemen in his archdiocese.

As he explained to New York's Archbishop John McCloskey, "Four million of these unfortunates are thrown on our charity, and they silently but eloquently appeal to us for help."

Shortly after returning from the First Vatican Council in Rome, the sixty-one-year-old archbishop contracted bronchitis. Spalding passed away on **February 7, 1872.**

February 8: PASCAL'S WAGER

In 1930, the 26-year-old John von Neumann met and fell in love with Mariette Kôvesi. Von Neumann was an agnostic Jew, born, raised, and educated in Hungary. Mariette was a German Catholic. If von Neumann wanted to marry her, he needed to convert. He was baptized shortly before their wedding day.

Von Neumann's conversion, however, was in name only. He rarely went to Mass after their marriage (and never after their 1938 divorce). Publicly and professionally, he continued to profess agnosticism.

Von Neumann moved to the United States in the fall of 1930 to teach at Princeton University. Three years later, he received one of the first two faculty positions at Princeton's Institute of Advanced Study. The other went to Albert Einstein. There, von Neumann made landmark contributions to quantum mechanics, game theory, computer science, and mathematics. He eventually joined the Manhattan Project—helping develop, test, and launch the world's first nuclear bombs. Later, he led the U.S. Atomic Energy Commission and helped devise the Cold War "peace-keeping" strategy of Mutually Assured Destruction. For his work, von Neumann received numerous awards and honors, including the U.S. Navy's Distinguished Civilian Service Award and the Medal of Freedom.

In 1955, however, when cancer appeared in his bones, von Neumann began rethinking both his agnosticism and his life. One year later, shortly before he died, the loud, boisterous, brilliant polymath who had annoyed Einstein by playing deafening marching band music at the office, summoned a priest to his bedside.

Reiterating Pascal's Wager, von Neumann explained to the priest that, in the time that remained to him, he'd rather run the risk of believing in God than run the risk of not believing in God. Von Neumann then confessed his sins and received Last Rites.

Although many of his colleagues doubted the sincerity of his conversion, von Neumann remained in good standing with the Church until his death on **February 8, 1957**.

February 9: THE ANGEL OF THE DELTA

Margaret Haughery was alone in New Orleans. She'd moved to the city from Baltimore with her husband in late 1835, but two years later both he and their infant daughter had died. An orphan herself, the 23-year-old Haughery had no family to whom she could turn. She was uneducated, illiterate, and penniless.

Thanks, however, to her years as a domestic servant in Baltimore, Haughery did know how to iron. That helped her find work at a local laundry where, as she ironed, she would watch the children who lived in a nearby orphanage play. Within months, she became friends with the children and the women who cared for them—the Sisters of Charity. She visited the Sisters regularly, and began giving them part of her wages.

From what Haughery kept for herself, she saved up enough money to buy two dairy cows for the orphans. Whatever milk they couldn't drink, Haughery sold to local hotels and restaurants. Her little business grew rapidly, and within two years, she owned more than 40 cows, whose milk paid for the construction of two new orphanages.

A few more years passed, and Haughery took over a local bakery. As she did with the milk, she carried the bread around town on a small cart and sold it to hotels and restaurants, giving the surplus to the poor. Almost all her profits went back to the orphans. She kept little for herself, never owning more than two dresses at a time.

When she died on **February 9, 1882,** the woman who had given more than $600,000 to the poor of New Orleans and built more than half a dozen orphanages received a state funeral. City newspapers were edged in black as a sign of mourning for the woman dubbed "The Angel of the Delta," and on her coffin rested a singular crucifix—a gift, sent with thanks from Pope Pius IX.

Shortly after World War II, the New Jersey State Legislature voted to reimburse parents for the cost of busing their children to school. It didn't matter if parents sent their children to a public school or private school; either way, New Jersey would pay for it.

One Arch R. Everson of Ewing Township, however, took issue with the legislature's action. He didn't like the state using his tax dollars to transport students to Catholic schools, so he sued the state, arguing that the law violated the First Amendment of the U.S. Constitution.

After losing in the New Jersey court, *Everson v. Board of Education* went to the U.S. Supreme Court. The Court's decision, handed down on **February 10, 1947,** was something of a mixed bag.

On the one hand, a majority of the justices agreed that transporting children to and from Catholic schools did not constitute the establishment of a state religion. That was a bridge too far for them.

At the same time, however, the justices implicitly acknowledged that the Fourteenth Amendment's Due Process Clause required the Constitution's prohibition against state-sponsored religion to apply to individual states. Before that, the First Amendment had only been interpreted as applying to the Federal Government, and some states had indeed adopted policies preferring one religion over another.

Additionally, both the majority and minority opinions in *Everson* affirmed an understanding of the separation of Church and State that was harder and firmer than that of past decisions.

Explained Justice Hugo Black, writing for the majority, "The First Amendment has erected a wall between Church and State. That wall must be kept high and impregnable. We could not approve the slightest breach."

Ultimately, the *Everson* decision set the stage for future judicial decisions banning prayer, religion classes, and even mentions of God from America's classrooms and civic life.

But, at least for a time, Catholic school students in New Jersey did get free bus rides.

You never want to let the good ones go. Such was the case with Bishop Benedict Joseph Flaget.

In 1832, after 26 years of shepherding the Diocese of Bardstown, Flaget submitted his resignation to the Holy See. It was accepted, but the outcry against Flaget's retirement, from clergy and laity alike, grew so intense that the Vatican reappointed him in 1833.

The Holy See's reluctance to let Flaget go was understandable.

Born and educated in France, Father Flaget fled to the United States in the midst of the French Revolution. He arrived in America in 1792, and within months had nursed the dying in Pittsburgh, taken over a mission in Indiana, and evangelized Native Americans in the Miami Valley. In 1795, he was called back to Baltimore where he spent three years teaching at Georgetown University. He then traveled to Havana to establish a college. While in Cuba, Flaget befriended the exiled future King of France, Louis Philippe. When he returned to America, Flaget convinced 23 Cubans to come with him to Georgetown to study for the priesthood.

In 1808, Flaget again left Georgetown when the Holy See named him bishop of the newly created Diocese of Bardstown. The size of the diocese was immense, encompassing 10 future states and 44 future dioceses and archdioceses. He had seven priests assisting him.

As bishop, Flaget was beloved by Catholics and non-Catholics alike thanks to his personal care for the poor and the sick. He also proved to be a gifted administrator, helping with the repeated subdivisions of his diocese, founding four colleges and 11 girls' academies, establishing eight religious orders, building a hospital at his own expense, and constructing two cathedrals and dozens of parishes.

In 1841, the Diocese of Bardstown was transferred to Louisville. And it was as bishop of Louisville that Flaget died on **February 11, 1850,** this time giving his flock no choice but to let him go.

How do you celebrate the Mass when Catholics cannot publicly worship and the Catholic Church cannot own land?

In colonial Maryland, some Catholics decided to look for a home elsewhere, while others found more creative solutions.

On **February 12, 1728,** James Carroll (a relative of the future Archbishop John Carroll) deeded two thousand acres near Maryland's Patuxent River to the Jesuit Fathers. Although the priests could not legally own land as Jesuits, they could as private citizens. They also could offer the Mass on their private property, and invite Catholics to attend.

So, that's what the Jesuits did: they built a manor house and chapel that they called White Marsh Plantation.

Completed in 1741, White Marsh quickly became the center of Catholic life in Colonial America. In addition to the Masses said on their plantation, the White Marsh Jesuits traveled throughout the mid-Atlantic region—to Annapolis, Baltimore, current-day Washington, D.C., and beyond—celebrating Mass and administering the sacraments in private homes and chapels.

Later, in the wake of the American Revolution, the Jesuit Fathers hosted three general chapters at White Marsh, during which they organized the Church in the newly independent nation. They also made the decision to put forth Father John Carroll's name as their recommendation for Prefect Apostolic of the Missionary Church in the United States. That recommendation eventually led to the Vatican appointing Carroll as the country's first bishop.

In 1853, the original chapel at White Marsh—Sacred Heart Church—was destroyed by fire, then rebuilt in 1856. A larger, modern parish was constructed nearby in 1969, but the older chapel still stands, with the Catholics of Bowie, Maryland, continuing to worship there today.

February 13: AN EPISCOPAL APOLOGIST

The Most Reverend John Baptist Purcell, second bishop of the Diocese of Cincinnati, was a man of many talents. Walking away from a debate was not one of them.

In 1837, during a meeting of the Ohio College of Teachers, the discussion turned to the teachings of Catholicism. Typical of the time, the discussion was fraught with misconceptions. Bishop Purcell, present at the meeting, spoke up, trying to make the Church's positions clear.

Time, however, cut the discussion short, so one of the Protestant pastors in attendance offered Purcell the use of his church for a lecture on the topic. Purcell agreed and delivered what history tells us was a "masterly discourse." It was so masterly, in fact, that the revivalist preacher Alexander Campbell challenged the bishop to a public debate.

The bishop, once again, found himself incapable of refusing, and on **February 13, 1837,** squared off against Campbell in a Baptist church to debate the following propositions:

1. *The Catholic Church is . . . an apostasy from the Church of Christ.*
2. *The notion of Apostolic succession is without foundation in the Bible and reason.*
3. *She is not uniform in faith, but fallible and changeable as other sects in religion and philosophy.*
4. *She is the Babylon of St. John.*
5. *Purgatory, indulgences, confession, and transubstantiation are immoral in their tendencies, injurious to the well-being of society, political and religious.*
6. *The world is not indebted to the Church for the Bible.*
7. *If the Church is infallible and unchangeable, she is opposed to the spirit of the institutions of the United States, which means progress.*

Cincinnati's Protestant papers called the debate a draw, which in the *lingua franca* of the day, meant Purcell drubbed Campbell soundly. Accordingly, in the years that followed, Purcell became known as one of the Church's greatest apologists and was repeatedly called upon to expound upon Catholicism, in person and in print, all around the nation.

Not surprisingly, he rarely declined.

Some men find their faith in times of war. Other men lose it. William Tecumseh Sherman numbered among the latter.

Baptized a Catholic at the age of nine (by his foster mother and future mother-in-law Maria Ewing), the future Civil War general was never a deeply devout man. But as a cadet at West Point, a soldier in California, and a banker in San Francisco and New York, he faithfully attended Sunday Mass. He also supported his wife Ellen's decision to relocate the family to South Bend, Indiana, so their eight children could attend the University of Notre Dame and St. Mary's College.

Sometime after his return to military service at the outset of the American Civil War, however, his attitude towards the Church and God changed. By the time he conquered Atlanta, marched south to Savannah and back north through the Carolinas, leaving total devastation in his wake, any faith Sherman had was gone. Not only did he refuse to attend Mass with his family from that point on, but when his son Thomas entered the Jesuits, he described it as one of the greatest sorrows of his life.

Once peace came and Ulysses S. Grant became president, Sherman's Civil War fame and close friendship with Grant helped him to succeed his friend as commanding general of the U.S. Army. In that position, he was responsible for the Indian Wars that both facilitated the progress of the railroads and decimated Native American settlements in the West.

Sherman retired from the army in 1884, refusing all requests that he run for public office. He died nine years later, on **February 14, 1891**. A state funeral was held for him on February 19, but another funeral for Sherman, a Catholic one, took place the following week in St. Louis. The celebrant was his son, Father Thomas Ewing Sherman, S.J.

René Auguste Chouteau was not yet 16 when he received an order, via letter, from his stepfather, Pierre de Laclede: "You will come here as soon as navigation opens, and will cause this place to be cleared, in order to form our settlement according to the plan I will give you."

"This place" was on the west bank of the Mississippi River, in present-day Missouri. A wealthy trader, Laclede wanted more for his goods than a mere warehouse. He wanted to create a new a community of French settlers.

Accordingly, on **February 14, 1764,** Chouteau and 30 other men crossed the mighty Mississippi. Following his stepfather's instructions, he called this new city St. Louis.

As the men cleared the land, Chouteau marked off a large portion of it, reserving it for a future church. In those first days, Mass was celebrated there in a small tent. Within six years, a log cabin stood in its place. The cabin then served as the town's chapel for six more years, until Chouteau finally expanded it into a proper parish church.

In that church, Chouteau, who now ran his late stepfather's trading business, was married. His seven children were baptized there. And in 1829, he was buried in its cemetery.

Two years after Chouteau's death, the Diocese of St. Louis began constructing an even bigger church, still in the same spot where the tent had been plotted. When the Cathedral of St. Louis, King of France was completed in 1834, it was the first Catholic cathedral west of the Mississippi.

Although the Archdiocese later built a larger cathedral elsewhere, John XXIII recognized the importance of that first cathedral in 1961 when he designated it a basilica. The City of St. Louis similarly recognized the church's importance by preserving it from destruction in 1939, when it razed 40 blocks of buildings to make room for the Jefferson National Expansion Memorial.

The basilica still stands there today.

February 16: A LIFE TRANSFORMED

February 16, 1969, was one of many days Dr. Bernard Nathanson would live to regret.

A few days earlier, the obstetrician had traveled to Chicago, where he joined feminist Betty Friedan and journalist Lawrence Lader at the First National Conference on Abortion Laws.

That weekend, Nathanson spoke about the medical consequences of illegal abortions, exaggerating (as he later confessed) the number of maternal deaths resulting from "back alley" procedures. Then, at the close of the conference, on February 16, he helped found an organization that would put the conference's agenda into action: the National Association to Repeal Abortion Laws (NARAL).

Within a year, NARAL had its first major victory in New York State, enabling Nathanson to establish the Center for Reproductive and Sexual Health (CRASH) in New York City. There, he oversaw more than 60,000 abortions and performed 5,000 himself.

Two years later, Nathanson's group repeated more of the false statistics he'd presented at the Chicago conference, this time in testimony before the U.S. Supreme Court. The justices bought the lies and, with their 1973 *Roe v. Wade* decision, legalized abortion nationwide.

In the wake of that victory, NARAL changed its name to the National Abortion Rights Action League. Around the same time, Nathanson began distancing himself from the organization he helped found. Rapidly advancing ultrasound technology had convinced him that abortion destroyed a human life, not a clump of cells. By decade's end, one of the pro-choice movement's greatest champions had become outspokenly pro-life.

For the next 30 years, Nathanson devoted himself to undoing the damage he had caused. He also found forgiveness and healing in the Catholic Church, where he was baptized and confirmed in 1996. Of his baptism, he said, "I was in a real whirlpool of emotion, and then there was this healing, cooling water on me, and soft voices, and an inexpressible sense of peace. I had found a safe place."

Nathanson died on February 21, 2011. His Mass of Christian Burial took place in New York City's St. Patrick's Cathedral.

February 17: A TOAST FOR SENATOR BLAINE

Tonight, raise a glass to Wisconsin Senator John J. Blaine, author of the Blaine Act, which passed the U.S. Senate on **February 17, 1933,** and, in doing so, initiated the end of prohibition in the United States.

Prohibition had begun 13 years earlier, when the Eighteenth Amendment to the U.S. Constitution took affect. As legislated by the Volstead Act, the amendment banned the sale, production, transportation, and importation of any and all alcoholic beverages.

Many Catholics, along with Lutherans and Episcopalians, did their best to fight the amendment's passage, but in the end they were no match for the Methodists, Baptists, Quakers, Presbyterians, and other Protestant congregations who made up the Dry Crusade. For nearly a century, the momentum for state-mandated temperance had been growing, with anti-Catholic and anti-immigrant sentiments compounding the problem. (Some supporters believed that if the unwashed immigrant masses could be kept from strong drink, they just might manage to civilize themselves.)

Alas, experience proved otherwise. Instead of ridding the U.S. population of its taste for wine and whisky, prohibition had the opposite effect, with almost everyone from President Woodrow Wilson on down violating the new law. Bootlegging rose, and organized crime flourished.

Some, however, found more legal means to purchase drink. For example, the Volstead Act permitted the sale of alcohol for medicinal purposes. Not coincidentally, doctors made $28 million in 1928 writing prescriptions for whisky.

Likewise, wine was permitted for religious use and permits were granted to parishes, allowing them to purchase wine for the Mass. Again, not by accident, the amount of wine for which such permits were granted jumped by more than 800,000 gallons between 1922 and 1924.

In 1933, three days after the Blaine Act passed the U.S. Senate, it passed the U.S. House of Representatives as well. Thirty-six states then ratified it in quick succession. When Utah, Pennsylvania, and Ohio voted Yes on December 5, prohibition was no more.

And then, many glasses were raised.

February 18: COME HOLY SPIRIT

In 1967, Catholics around the world found themselves in a state of profound confusion. Changes in Catholic liturgy and life abounded. Priests and religious were shedding their habits and titles. Some even shed their vocations. Doctrine itself seemed up for grabs. Many, both inside and outside the Church, believed Catholicism was in a state of collapse.

Yet, in the midst of the confusion, graces still abounded, including the graces that manifested in a particular way just outside of Pittsburgh, Pennsylvania, on Saturday, **February 18, 1967**.

That weekend, a group of Duquesne University students and faculty went on retreat. In the days leading up to the retreat, the students read the Acts of the Apostles and a book, *The Cross and the Switchblade,* which recounted the experiences of two Protestant Pentecostals ministering in New York. Then, when they arrived at The Ark and The Dove Retreat House, they began their retreat with the ancient hymn *"Veni Creator Spiritus"* ("Come Creator Spirit").

The Holy Spirit answered that call. On Saturday night, in the retreat house chapel, numerous students experienced an overwhelming outpouring of grace and multiple manifestations of the gifts of the Holy Spirit.

From there, the graces and manifestations spread. The Catholic Charismatic Renewal had begun.

Emphasizing a personal relationship with Christ, the power of the Holy Spirit, and the charismatic gifts (such as healing, words of prophecy, and praying in tongues), as well as fidelity to the Magisterium, the Charismatic Movement became a primary instrument of renewal for the Church throughout the latter half of the twentieth century. Reaching more than 230 countries and touching tens of millions of lives, it received the enthusiastic support of Pope Paul VI, Pope John Paul II, and Pope Benedict XVI.

As Pope John Paul II explained on Pentecost 1998, "It is from this providential rediscovery of the Church's charismatic dimension that . . . a remarkable pattern of growth has been established for ecclesial movements and new communities."

He seemed invincible. And for a while he was.

Born in Buffalo, New York, in 1916, John Basilone was the sixth of 10 children brought into the world by Salvatore Basilone, an Italian immigrant, and his first-generation Italian-American wife, Dora. A typical Catholic boy of his age, the future Marine was educated by nuns, good at boxing, and not interested in school.

In October 1942, however, Gunnery Sergeant Basilone proved anything but typical when, with two machine guns and a .45 caliber pistol, he fended off 3,000 Japanese soldiers on Guadalcanal. At the outset of the attack, Basilone had 15 men with him. When the Japanese finally surrendered, only two remained. Almost miraculously, Basilone kept the machines guns firing for three days and three nights, stopping only once to fight his way through hostile territory and secure more ammunition.

Overnight, the newly minted Medal of Honor winner became a household name. The U.S. government took advantage of that, pulling Basilone out of combat and ordering him to sell war bonds. In just over a year, the Marine raised more than $1.4 million for the war effort. He hated the attention though and repeatedly asked to return to combat. He finally did in late 1943.

On **February 19, 1945,** Basilone was among the first to land on Red Beach II during the invasion of Iwo Jima. Almost singlehandedly, he fought his way past enemy fire to the blockhouses that sheltered Japanese troops. Within minutes, Basilone destroyed the blockhouses with grenades and small arms. He then navigated three American tanks through a minefield, all the while exposing himself to enemy fire.

A short while later, however, something (no one knows what), struck Basilone while he stood briefing his men. He died in an instant.

After Iwo Jima, the U.S. government posthumously awarded Basilone the Navy Cross, making him the only enlisted Marine in World War II to win both the Navy Cross and the Medal of Honor.

The Freemasons, the Illuminati, the Carbonari—those are just a few of the secret societies the Church has long forbidden Catholics to join. All are either anti-Catholic, require of their members the kind of absolute obedience that Catholics owe only to God, insist on their members keeping secrets from their Confessors, or some combination of all three.

But what about the Noble Order of the Knights of Labor?

In 1884, the archbishop of Quebec, who mistrusted the North American trade association, asked the Vatican to add the group to its list of banned secret societies. The Vatican quickly granted the request. Up to that point, most of its experience with labor organizations had been negative, with anti-clerical European associations.

Immediately, American bishops protested. With over 700,000 members, most of whom were Catholic, the Knights were then the country's largest labor union. Moreover, the group's primary focus was securing an eight-hour workday and abolishing child labor—two causes near and dear to the U.S. bishops' hearts.

Recognizing that any condemnation of the Knights risked alienating the masses of working-class Catholics, James Cardinal Gibbons, Baltimore's Archbishop and three other prominent American churchmen (Bishop John Ireland of St. Paul, Minnesota; Father Denis O'Connell, rector of the North American College in Rome; and Bishop John Keane, rector of the newly created Catholic University of America in Washington, D.C.) drew up a petition asking Rome to reconsider its decision.

At the same time, the bishops convinced the Knights to remove "Noble Order" from their name and end certain membership rituals—two organizational details that they knew would be sticking points with Rome.

On **February 20, 1887,** following a series of delicate negotiations, Bishop Ireland presented the document (known as the "Gibbons' Memorial") to the Prefect of the Congregation for the Propagation of the Faith in Rome. He received it favorably. Permission for Catholics in America to belong to the Knights of Labor was granted and, more important, a change in how Rome viewed labor unions had begun.

For almost 500 years, the world sent priests to America. In the early part of the twentieth century, however, America began sending priests to the world. One of the first of those priests was Bishop Francis Xavier Ford, M.M.

Brooklyn born and raised, Ford was the first man to enroll in the Maryknoll seminary, founded in 1912 to support the work of the also newly founded Catholic Foreign Mission Society of America. Five years later, Ford became the first Maryknoll seminarian to graduate and was ordained to the priesthood on December 5, 1917.

Early the following year, Father Ford headed to China, arriving in October 1918 with three other Maryknoll missionaries, including Maryknoll co-founder Father Thomas Frederick Price. Ford then proceeded to the southern province of Canton (now Guangdong), where he established two Catholic missions, one in the north and one in the south.

Consecrated a bishop in 1935, Ford's evangelization efforts included building schools and churches, establishing the first convent of Maryknoll sisters in the region, and cultivating priestly vocations among the native Chinese. Within 20 years, the number of Chinese Catholics in the region had grown from less than 9,000 to more than 20,000.

Throughout World War II, Ford provided shelter and food to countless refugees, as well as to Allied and Chinese troops combating the occupying Japanese.

All that was forgotten, however, when the Communists came to power. In 1950, Mao's men put Ford and his secretary, Sister Joan Marie Ryan, M.M., under house arrest. The following spring, soldiers took Ford from his home and marched him through the villages where he'd served, organizing mobs to torture and beat him along the way. They finally led Ford back to a prison in Guangdong, where he died on **February 21, 1952**.

Amerigo (or Americus) Vespucci is a historical enigma.

He may have sailed to the New World four times. Or he may have sailed only twice. He may have written a series of famous letters about those journeys. Or someone else might have penned them, using Vespucci's original letters as their inspiration. And he may have sought to displace Christopher Columbus' legacy. Or he may have found fame purely by accident.

The confusion surrounding Vespucci arises from those famous letters, which recall four journeys by Vespucci to the New World. Due to some glaring inaccuracies (such as the failure to mention the Rio de la Plata), his authorship of the letters, as well as the exact nature of his expeditions, has long been in doubt.

What is certain is that Vespucci was born in Florence on March 9, 1454, educated by a Dominican uncle, and employed as a clerk for the House of Medici. Shortly before the turn of the century, he lost his taste for trade and turned to exploring. History grows fuzzy at this point; it is unknown if he set sail in 1497 or 1499. If 1497, he was indeed the first European to happen upon South America. If 1499, then that honor goes to Columbus.

Vespucci did, however, discover the mouth of the Amazon River in 1499, and it's possible he sailed as far south as Patagonia in 1501. Later, in 1505, he became a citizen of Spain, and three years after that assumed the office of Master Navigator of Spain, a position he held until his death on **February 22, 1512**.

As for his continental namesakes, credit for that goes to Martin Waldseemüller, a German cartographer, who in 1507, decided to name the southernmost part of the New World in honor of the man who allegedly discovered it. Thirty-one years later, another mapmaker working from Waldseemüller's maps, labeled both the northern and southern landmasses in the Western Hemisphere "America," thereby securing Vespucci's legacy (deserved or not) for the ages.

February 23: "THE PATRIOT PRIEST"

When Father Pierre Gibault arrived in the small French settlement of Kaskaskia, on September 8, 1768, he had his work cut out for him.

The newly ordained priest had been sent from Quebec to minister to Catholics living in the Illinois Territory. Those Catholics had been without a priest for five years, ever since the English assumed control of the area and evicted the Jesuit missionaries. To Gibault, his bishop entrusted the care of all the Catholics in present-day Illinois, as well as parts of Indiana, Missouri, and Michigan. No other priests accompanied him.

For the better part of the next decade, Gibault traveled on horseback with his Mass kit, shotgun, and two pistols, administering the sacraments wherever he went. No amount of ministering in British territory, however, could make him forget his French roots. Accordingly, when the American Revolution broke out and American military officer George Rogers Clark arrived in Kaskaskia, intent on capturing the Illinois Territory for the Americans, he found a friend in Gibault.

The priest not only convinced the people of Kaskaskia, Vincennes, and other settlements to switch their allegiance to the Americans—enabling Clark to take key British forts without firing a shot—but he also traded Spanish silver for the Continental Army's worthless paper currency, in effect financing a substantial portion of Clark's Illinois Campaign.

When the British eventually retook Vincennes (and with it, the Spanish trader and friend to the Americans, Francis Vigo), Gibault and his entire congregation marched to Fort Sackville, informing British Commander Henry Hamilton that his troops would not receive supplies until they released Vigo. Later, Gibault blessed Clark's troops before they launched their attack to recapture Vincennes. The campaign began on **February 23, 1779,** and by February 25, the American flag hung over the fort once again.

After the war, Gibault, who was never honored by the U.S. government for his contributions, moved across the Mississippi to the Spanish town of New Madrid, where he ministered until his death in 1802.

February 24: FATHER McSWEENEY'S SCHEME

Why must parents who send their children to Catholic schools pay taxes to support public schools?

That is a question people ask today, and it's also a question Father Patrick McSweeney asked in 1873. Father McSweeney, however, didn't just ponder the problem; he came up with a solution.

That year, as pastor of St. Peter's parish in Poughkeepsie, New York, Father McSweeney made an offer to the city's school board. He would rent them two newly refurbished parochial school buildings for a mere $1 a year. The parish would also supply the teachers: Sisters of Charity. In return, the school board would maintain the buildings and operate the schools during hours amenable to the parish, with the parish retaining the use of the building during non-school hours.

For the school board—who, since 1840, had rented all the buildings in which public education took place—the offer was too good to refuse. It gave them the use of two excellent buildings, virtually for free, and enabled them to enroll more students in ostensibly public education.

In turn, Catholic parents could send their children to a school where they would be taught by nuns but at no cost to them. Moreover, because Sweeney arranged for the school day to run from 9 a.m. until noon and 1:30 p.m. until 4 p.m., the sisters could provide prayer and religious formation to the Catholics before and after school, as well as during the extended lunch hour.

Despite criticisms from Catholics outside Poughkeepsie, the plan was a rousing success with the locals, both Catholics and non-Catholics. It also so impressed St. Paul's Archbishop John Ireland that he tried it in his own diocese as well.

Unfortunately, in 1898, after 25 years of happy cooperation between Church and State, the New York Superintendent of Schools found fault with the arrangement and brought McSweeney's scheme to an end.

The clever priest died nine years later, on **February 24, 1907.**

February 25: THE FIRST CATHOLIC CONFERENCE

Most of the American bishops saw it as a dirty, underhanded move.

In 1922, when Boston's Archbishop William Cardinal O'Connell and Philadelphia's Archbishop Dennis Cardinal Dougherty traveled to Rome for the papal conclave that would elect Pope Pius XI, they missed the vote by mere hours. But the pair still had time to discuss with the European cardinals what they perceived as the growing problem of America's National Catholic Welfare Council (NCWC).

Founded in 1917, as the National Catholic War Council, the NCWC first existed to coordinate the Catholic response to World War I. After the war, America's bishops recognized the usefulness of an administrative body that could address the U.S. government on programs and policies affecting Catholics. So, in September 1919, 95 prelates from 87 dioceses gathered in Washington, D.C. There, they changed the "War" in NCWC to "Welfare," set up a permanent administrative staff, and appointed committees on education, legislation, social welfare, lay organizations, and publicity.

For the next several years, the bishops met annually. Not everyone was happy though with the groups' decision-making process, most notably Cardinals O'Connell and Dougherty, who went behind their fellow bishops' backs and convinced the Consistorial Congregation in Rome to suppress the NCWC on **February 25, 1922**.

Upon learning of the two cardinals' politicking, the other American bishops, outraged, convinced Rome to delay publishing the decree until they could make their case. Led by Cleveland's Bishop Joseph Schrembs, the bishops petitioned Rome to reverse the decree of suppression. Rome agreed, with the condition that the bishops remove "Council" from the organization's name and make it clear that its decisions were non-binding.

The bishops complied, changing the name to the National Catholic Welfare Conference. The Conference continued to operate under that name until 1966, when it split into two organizations, the National Conference of Catholic Bishops and the United States Catholic Conference, only to reunite again in 2001 as the United States Conference of Catholic Bishops.

February 26, 1734, was a day long awaited by Catholics in the American colonies.

More than 30 years prior, in the wake of the Protestant Revolution of 1689, public Masses had been banned in Maryland. Private celebrations of the Mass remained licit, but even that permission had been granted by the colonial government reluctantly.

Prohibited from practicing their faith and exercising the rights of citizens in Maryland, many Catholics and Jesuit priests eventually moved to Pennsylvania, with several families settling in Philadelphia. There, Joseph Penn's famous charter granted religious liberty to all, including Catholics. In 1729, Father Joseph Greaton, S.J., was sent by his order to serve as a permanent pastor in the city, and four years later he began constructing a chapel in which Catholics could worship.

The chapel, Old Saint Joseph's, was completed early the following year and on February 26, 1734, for the first time in decades, a Catholic priest publicly celebrated the Mass in the American colonies.

Not surprisingly, not everyone thought Penn's promise of religious liberty should apply to Catholics, and later that summer a case was brought before the Provincial Council protesting that "a House lately built in Walnut Street, was sett apart for the Exercise of the Roman Catholick Religion and it is commonly called the Romish Chappell, where Mass [is] openly celebrated by a Popish priest, contrary to the Laws of England."

After deliberating the matter, the Provincial Council determined that Penn's charter superseded England's laws, and allowed the public Masses to continue.

That meant, for the next four decades, until the American Revolution, Old Saint Joseph's was the only place in the English-speaking world where priests could offer the Mass both publicly and legally.

February 27: GEORGETOWN'S "SECOND FOUNDER"

On **February 27, 1830,** Michael Healy and his common-law wife, Mary Eliza, welcomed their third son, Patrick, into the world.

A devout Catholic, the Irish-born Michael would have liked to wed Mary Eliza in his Church, but she was of both African and European descent, and in 1820's Georgia, interracial marriages were a long way from becoming legal.

The couple would go on to have 10 children. Since their mother was technically their father's slave, legally their children were too. Manumission, which could be obtained only through an act of the Georgia legislature, was difficult. And so not wanting to see his children grow up as slaves, Healy sent both his sons and daughters to the North for school and forbade them from ever returning home.

Accordingly, when Patrick Healy was old enough, he joined his brothers, first at a Quaker school in New York, then later at the College of the Holy Cross in Worcester, Massachusetts. After graduating in 1850, he entered the Jesuits and continued his formation in the United States for another eight years. Although Healy and all his light-skinned siblings self-identified as white, the approaching American Civil War and heightened racial tensions convinced the Jesuits to send Healy overseas for the remainder of his formation.

A gifted student, Healy earned his doctorate at the University of Leuven in Belgium, the first American of mixed-African descent to do so, and was ordained to the priesthood in 1864.

Two years later, he returned to the United States and began teaching at Georgetown University. He remained there for the next 16 years, becoming president in 1873 and so transforming the struggling college that today, Healy is often referred to as the school's "second founder." Since 1881, the school's most iconic building, Healy Hall, has borne his name.

In 1882, Healy stepped down from his position. He spent the next 28 years traveling, writing, and assisting his brother, Bishop James Healy, the first American prelate of African descent. He returned to Georgetown University during the last years of his life, dying in the infirmary there on January 10, 1910.

February 28: BROKEN TIES

In Washington, D.C., some things never change. Rumors populate the nation's capital today, and they populated the nation's capital 150 years ago, when, on **February 28, 1867,** the U.S. Congress voted to cut off diplomatic relations with the Holy See.

Ever since the presidency of George Washington, the United States and the Vatican had enjoyed cordial formal relations. Americans weren't always happy about the diplomatic ties that bound the two nations—the Catholic Church being less than popular with America's mostly Protestant population—but the ties were tolerated nonetheless.

In 1867, however, anti-Catholic sentiments reached new heights as waves of Catholic immigrants poured into America from Europe. That year, rumors spread around the capital, including conspiracy theories alleging that the Church had plotted to assassinate President Abraham Lincoln and that the pope had forbidden the celebration of Protestant services at the home of the American Minister in Rome. President Andrew Johnson's support of diplomatic relations with the Vatican didn't help either, given his low approval rating at the time.

Legislation was soon introduced that blocked any future funding of U.S. diplomatic missions to the Holy See. It passed by a wide margin, effectively severing all diplomatic ties between the two nations.

For more than 100 years after that vote, those ties remained severed. Beginning in 1933, presidents occasionally appointed special envoys to handle diplomatic negotiations with the recently formed Vatican City State, but they made no attempt to formalize relations until 1951, when President Harry Truman nominated General Mark W. Clark to serve as the country's official emissary to the Holy See. Clark withdrew his nomination after Protestant groups vociferously protested.

Finally, in 1983, Senator Richard Lugar of Indiana successfully introduced and passed legislation repealing the 1867 prohibition. The reinstatement of diplomatic relations between the United States and the Vatican was officially announced on January 10, 1984, and two months later the U.S. Senate approved President Ronald Reagan's nomination of William A. Wilson as the first U.S. ambassador to the Holy See.

March

March 1: A PLEDGE OF FIDELITY

If you want to teach Catholic theology in a Catholic school, you actually have to teach Catholic theology, not your personal opinion.

This was the gist of the Vatican's message to bishops, seminary rectors, and Catholic theology professors in a note published by the Congregation for the Doctrine of the Faith (CDF) in 1989.

Dating back to the infamous Land O' Lakes Conference in 1967, dissent had reigned in more than a few of America's Catholic colleges and universities. Theologians justified that dissent with appeals to academic freedom, claiming that it fell within their purview to disagree with the Church on matters of faith and morals.

To correct that problem and help clarify what was expected of those charged with teaching the Faith, the CDF revised both the Profession of Faith and Oath of Fidelity to stress the importance of fidelity to the Church in all her doctrines and disciplines. The note that included those revisions went into effect on **March 1, 1989**.

Unfortunately, March 1 came and went with few theologians in the United States taking heed of the changes. Many simply dismissed the document, arguing that such pledges were a private matter, and refused to acknowledge whether or not they had made any such profession. Persisting in dissent, their schools supported them.

Exceptions did, however, exist: Within weeks of the revisions going into effect, Franciscan University of Steubenville became the first U.S. Catholic school to require its theology professors, friars, and chapel ministry staff to publicly pledge their fidelity to the Church. A handful of other colleges soon followed suit, including Thomas Aquinas College and Christendom College.

In the decades since, that handful has grown, but not by much. Today, only 32 of the country's 244 Catholic colleges and universities have publicly confirmed that those who teach the Faith at their schools have sworn to teach it faithfully. The status of the other 212 schools remains unknown.

When Guy Carleton Bayley (half brother to the future saint and Catholic convert Elizabeth Ann Seton) married Grace Roosevelt (the descendent of English royalty), two of New York City's oldest and wealthiest Protestant families united. And when their first son was born in 1814, both families had great plans for the boy, envisioning a career for him in the military or medicine. But the boy—James Roosevelt Bayley—had plans of his own.

In 1836, Bayley entered a Protestant seminary in Connecticut. Three years later he became an Episcopal priest. His ministry often took him among the Irish poor, and through that work, his fascination with the Catholic Faith grew. Prolonged conversations with New York's future cardinal, Father John McCloskey, and his own Catholic cousins—the children of Mother Seton—soon turned that fascination into conviction. Within two years of his Episcopal ordination, Bayley entered the Catholic Church. Two years later, on **March 2, 1844,** he became a Catholic priest.

Upon his ordination, Bayley's grandfather wrote him out of his will, using his grandson's multi-million dollar inheritance to build a hospital instead. But Father Bayley didn't mind. He was where he wanted to be— first teaching at St. John's College, then pastoring a parish on Staten Island, and later working as private secretary to Bishop John Hughes of New York.

In 1853, Father Bayley reluctantly became Bishop Bayley, the first bishop of the Diocese of Newark, New Jersey. He remained in Newark for nearly 20 years, transforming the diocese through an expansive building and vocations campaign that doubled the number of its priests and parishes.

In 1872, Bishop Bayley left Newark to become archbishop of Baltimore—again, reluctantly. His tenure there, however, was short-lived. Kidney disease forced him into retirement in the spring of 1877, allowing him for a short time to return to the humble priest's life that he loved. As he explained, "I am Archbishop; I have been Bishop; but I like Father Bayley best of all."

Bayley died on October 3, 1877.

In 1761, Thomas Fitzsimons, a 24-year-old Irish immigrant, and his brother-in-law, George Meade, formed a small West Indies trading company based in Philadelphia. The fledgling company was just beginning to thrive when the British passed the Stamp Act of 1765. The legislation—which helped fund British troops stationed in the American colonies—hit merchants like Fitzsimons particularly hard. Accordingly, Fitzsimons soon joined those rallying against the Crown.

In 1774, Fitzsimons led Philadelphia merchants in protests against the Coercive Acts, and in 1776, when the Revolution began, he immediately enlisted in the Pennsylvania militia. Through the course of the war, Fitzsimons led troops in the Battle of Trenton, defended the New Jersey coastline as part of the home guard, and oversaw the newly formed Pennsylvania Navy. He also dug deep into his own pockets, supplying Pennsylvanian and French forces with ships, money, and supplies.

That patriotism earned him a spot as one of the delegates to the Congress of Confederation in 1782. He returned the following year, and later served two years in the Pennsylvania State Legislature.

In 1787, Fitzsimons entered Independence Hall as one of Pennsylvania's delegates to the Constitutional Convention. Although he opposed the provisions for slavery incorporated into the final draft, Fitzsimons nevertheless signed the Constitution on September 17, 1787, one of only two Catholics to do so.

In 1788, Pennsylvania elected Fitzsimons to the U.S. House of Representatives. He served two consecutive terms, stepping down from office on **March 3, 1793**.

Upon leaving politics, Fitzsimons devoted himself to education and commerce. An early supporter of Bishop John Carroll's endeavor to found Georgetown University, he also served as a trustee for the University of Pennsylvania, president of Philadelphia's Chamber of Commerce, director of the Delaware Insurance Company, and director of the Bank of North America.

The merchant patriot died in Philadelphia on August 26, 1811.

"What is an American?"

In 1782, with the colonists' victory over the British nearly certain, all of Europe was asking that question. To it, J. Hector St. John de Crèvecoeur had an answer: The American was a new man, transformed by the frontier and remade by his adopted homeland.

In his book, *Letters from an American Farmer,* Crèvecoeur explained that transformation by coining the notion of America as a "melting pot."

"Here individuals of all nations are melted into a new race of men," he wrote, "whose labours and posterity will one day cause great changes in the world . . ."

Although in the writing of the book, Crèvecoeur assumed the persona of a simple immigrant farmer, he was actually a Jesuit-educated French gentleman, who fled to Canada after escaping an overbearing father. An occasional apostate from Catholicism, Crèvecoeur married a Protestant American and built a sizeable home in New York State. There, in the decade leading up to the American Revolution, Crèvecoeur reflected upon the strengths and weaknesses of his adopted homeland in the epistolary style of fiction so popular at the time.

When the Revolution came, Crèvecoeur's Tory sympathies forced him to flee his farm (unpublished manuscript in hand), first to British-occupied New York City, then to Great Britain, where he sold *Letters from an American Farmer* to a British publishing house. Two years later, after he reconciled with his father in France, a revised manuscript (with all the pro-British parts taken out) was published there. An American edition finally went to print on **March 4, 1793**.

Although the book caused an initial sensation on both sides of the Atlantic, Crèvecoeur and his *Letters* were all but forgotten by the time of his death in 1813. In the early twentieth century, however, literary scholars rediscovered Crèvecoeur's "melting pot" metaphor. In the wake of World War I, the letter that contained that passage became standard in American literary anthologies, helping shape how generations of school children answered the perennial question, "What is an American?"

In 1834, Mother St. John Fontbonne, C.S.J., superior of the Sisters of St. Joseph in Lyons, France, received an unusual visitor: the French Countess Felicite Duras.

Not long before, Countess Duras had received a request for help from Bishop Joseph Rosati, the first bishop of the Diocese of St. Louis in Missouri. The bishop needed aid for his poor but growing diocese. More specifically, he needed religious sisters who could teach the diocese's children.

Promising to cover the costs of the sisters' work, the Countess asked Mother St. John to help the bishop. Mother St. John agreed, and in mid-January 1836, six sisters from the Lyons' convent set sail for the Port of New Orleans. The oldest was 30 and the youngest was 21 years old.

After a harrowing 49-day crossing, the sisters landed in New Orleans on **March 5, 1836**. Bishop Rosati was there to meet them.

The group rested for two weeks in New Orleans, then boarded a steamer ship bound for St. Louis.

Upon their arrival, the French sisters lived with the Sisters of Charity. Soon, however, they settled into their new home in Carondelet, doing the work (and then some) that they'd crossed an ocean to accomplish.

In St. Louis, the sisters founded schools for both white and black students and administered a school for the hearing impaired. They also opened a college for women and ministered to the poor and the sick in their community. Their example of service rapidly inspired vocations, and in less than 25 years, the community was sending out sisters to serve all across the country.

Today, more than 175 years later, the Sisters of St. Joseph continue their work in the Archdiocese of St. Louis and nearly 20 other cities around the United States.

Shortly after midnight, on **March 6, 1854,** the watchdog at the Washington Monument construction site stopped barking. Soon afterwards, the guard patrolling the grounds had a gun to his head. Nine armed men made short work of binding and gagging the guard and then tossed him into the watchman's shack. When his replacement found him four hours later, the Pope's Stone was gone.

A gift from Pope Pius IX, the Pope's Stone was just one of 200 donated stones slated for placement inside the Washington Monument. This stone in particular was a 2,100-year-old slab of marble, measuring 36" x 18" x 10", taken from the ruins of the Temple of Concord.

As far as gifts go, it was a fantastically generous one. But not everyone saw it that way. Some saw it as just another example of the Church of Rome trying to leave its mark on a Protestant nation. Government officials offered a $500 reward for information leading to the capture of the thieves, but no arrests were made.

Twenty years after the robbery, one of those thieves, a Washington, D.C., saloonkeeper, confessed his crime to a *Washington Post* reporter. According to his account, he and eight fellow members of the anti-Catholic Know-Nothing party chipped off pieces of the stone with sledgehammers, smuggled what remained onto a boat, then dumped it into the Potomac River.

"That's the true story," he said, adding, "If the dredges at work in the Potomac strike the right spot, they will fish up something that will create a sensation."

Sure enough, a decade later, bridge workers found a large piece of marble right where the saloonkeeper said they would. Although the water had worn down the Gothic engraving on the stone, traces of the pope's message—"From Rome, To America"—remained.

Unfortunately, no sooner did authorities put aside the stone for safekeeping, then it was stolen once more. Not until a century later, in 1982, was a new Pope's Stone commissioned and installed in the Washington Monument by the National Park Service.

March 7: BLOODY SUNDAY

They've been called the unsung heroes of the Civil Rights Movement. But the Edmundite priests of St. Elizabeth's Catholic Church in Selma, Alabama, didn't set out to be heroes. They set out to be faithful.

In the three decades leading up to the 1965 Selma civil rights marches, the Edmundites devoted their lives to advancing the spiritual and physical well-being of African-Americans in Alabama. They provided them with food, clothing, medical care, and most important, the sacraments, operating the only integrated Catholic parish in the state.

For their work, they were targeted by the Ku Klux Klan and received a steady stream of death threats.

Yet, as racial tensions grew, the Edmundites risked even more, offering food and shelter to visiting civil rights activists. One priest even placed a full-page ad in the local paper that explained why all Christians should support the struggle for voting rights.

On the morning of **March 7, 1965,** as 500 peaceful protestors prepared to march from Selma to Montgomery, the priests began to pray. Their bishop had forbidden his clergy to march, but the Edmundites encouraged their parishioners to participate nevertheless, and now feared for their safety.

Once sirens began wailing, signaling the outbreak of violence, the priests made their way to the hospital they administered, Good Samaritan. It was the only one in the city that admitted black patients. There, they spent what would become known as "Bloody Sunday" caring for the peaceful protestors who'd been beaten by law enforcement officers when they attempted to cross the Edmund Pettis Bridge.

In the weeks that followed, the Edmundites opened their rectory and unused rooms in Good Samaritan to the priests and religious who came to Selma from across the nation to participate in subsequent marches.

The Edmundites continued to house civil rights activists and workers for the next several years, until the battle for voting rights was won. Then, they carried on with the work they'd begun in 1937, ministering to the African-Americans of the Deep South.

March 8: THE LAST-MINUTE CATHOLIC

It's been said that to succeed in politics, one must make an art of indecision. In this regard, Thomas Ewing, Sr., was the consummate politician.

Born in Virginia in 1789, Ewing moved to Ohio as a young man. There, he established a successful practice as a country lawyer. That success led him to the U.S. Senate in 1830, then to an appointment as U.S. secretary of the treasury under Presidents William Henry Harrison and John Tyler. Later, on **March 8, 1849,** he again secured a place in the presidential cabinet, becoming the first secretary of the interior under Presidents Zachary Taylor and Millard Fillmore.

Unfortunately, the most notable feature of Ewing's tenure at Interior was the culture of corruption he created. His nickname as Secretary was "Butcher Ewing," a wry tribute to his summary dismissal of good civil servants who were not his political cronies and were unwilling to pay him for their positions.

Despite his questionable professional ethics, Ewing was devoted to his Catholic wife, Maria, and their children, including his foster son and future son-in-law, William Tecumseh Sherman. At Maria's request, Ewing raised the children Catholic, faithfully attended Mass with her, and even became close friends with Cincinnati's colorful archbishop, the Most Reverend John Baptist Purcell.

Despite his affinity for all things Catholic, Ewing nevertheless held off on making any formal commitment to the Church until he was 80 years old. He might have delayed even longer, had he not collapsed in 1869, in the midst of arguing a case before the U.S. Supreme Court. Believing he had only moments to live, Ewing called for a priest and was baptized on the spot in the courtroom.

Ewing soon recovered. However, he took no further steps towards full reception into the Catholic Church. Not until September 1871, when it became clear to him that the time for indecision was finally at an end, did Ewing summon Bishop Purcell to his house to hear his Confession and administer the sacraments.

Ewing died one month later.

On **March 9, 1988,** President Ronald Reagan spoke before a crowd at the University of Notre Dame. He'd come to unveil a U.S. postal stamp commemorating the man the College Football Hall of Fame called, "American football's most renowned coach": Knute Rockne.

Born in Norway and raised in Chicago, Rockne found deserved fame in his 13 years as head football coach at Notre Dame. During that time, he led the "Fighting Irish" to 105 victories, five ties, three national championships, and five undefeated seasons.

More impressive than his coaching record was his character. Revered by his players, their opponents, his fellow coaches, and countless fans, Rockne was known for his kind heart, generous spirit, and unfailing work ethic. He also was known as a man of deep faith, a faith he found through the help of his players.

As Rockne recalled in his autobiography, one fall morning before an away game, he couldn't sleep, so he left his hotel room and went to the lobby. As he sat there, he saw several players come down the hotel stairs just before dawn and leave. On a whim, he followed them . . . straight to the nearest Catholic church.

"They didn't realize it," he wrote, "but these youngsters were making a powerful impression on me. When I saw them walking up to the Communion rail to receive and realized the hours of sleep they had sacrificed, I understood what a powerful ally their religion was to them in their work on the football field."

In 1923, Rockne, who had been raised Lutheran, entered the Catholic Church. He died eight years later, at the age of 43, in a plane crash. When they found his body, Rockne had a rosary in his hands and a prayer book by his side.

Speaking on that March night in 1988, Reagan concluded his remarks by noting that through his lived example of faith, "Knute Rockne did more spiritual good than a thousand preachers. His career was a sermon in right living."

Arranging a miracle can be tricky. Just ask Father Anthony Kohlmann, S.J.

In 1823, the Georgetown University president and professor heard that one of the city's most devout Catholics, Mrs. Ann Mattingly, suffered from an aggressive form of breast cancer. In addition to a large and painful lump, she was disoriented, vomiting blood, and rarely able to leave her bed.

Around the same time, Kohlmann learned of Prince Alexander von Hohenlohe, a German priest with a gift for healing. Unfortunately, the German priest was actually in Germany, and Mrs. Mattingly couldn't possibly make the trip.

Determined to help the woman, Kohlmann came up with a plan. He wrote to Hohenlohe proposing that Mrs. Mattingly begin a novena for healing. On the ninth day, at the hour of completion, one priest would offer Mass near her bedside, while Kohlmann offered one in the Georgetown chapel and Hohenlohe offered one in Germany.

Hohenlohe agreed to the plan. Kohlmann continued the correspondence, and named the date to celebrate Mass. Then Hohenlohe wrote back yet again to confirm the plan. So, it went, back and forth, as the two priests, without the help of phones, e-mail, or even reliable postal service, attempted to coordinate a miracle.

Through it all, Mrs. Mattingly's condition worsened, and the impatience of her family grew. Invariably, Kohlmann replied to their concerns by saying that the miracle would seem all the greater for occurring at the last minute.

Finally, the plan was set and, on the appointed day, **March 10, 1824,** was carried out. The novena was prayed, all three Masses said, and within minutes of receiving the Eucharist, Mrs. Mattingly rose from her bed, both her pain and the lump gone.

Catholics celebrated the miracle. Protestants dismissed it. The Church hierarchy ignored it. But Mrs. Mattingly and Father Kohlmann didn't care. Their prayers were answered.

Ann Mattingly lived another 31 years, all of them healthy ones.

"The most important vehicle for exploring the tangled web of religion and society in the English-speaking world."

Writing in the pages of *Newsweek,* papal biographer and political commentator George Weigel used these words to describe the ecumenical journal *First Things.* It's high praise, but nevertheless praise with which many would agree.

Launched on **March 11, 1990,** *First Things* was the brainchild of then-Lutheran priest, soon-to-be-Catholic convert, Father Richard John Neuhaus.

For more than 30 years, Neuhaus had stood at the intersection of religion and public life in America, first as an early civil rights activist and co-founder of Clergy and Laymen Concerned About Vietnam, then, in the wake of *Roe v. Wade,* as a staunch opponent of abortion. Over time, Neuhaus grew more conservative, eventually becoming one of the great intellectual lights of the neo-conservative movement.

Noting that "Where orthodoxy is optional, orthodoxy will sooner or later be proscribed," Neuhaus sought to facilitate dialogue between different faith traditions and build constructive coalitions where he could. To that end, he founded the Institute on Religion and Public Life in 1990 and began publishing *First Things* soon after, with the stated mission of creating a "religiously informed public philosophy for the ordering of society." Among the journal's contributors in its first year were U.S. Ambassador to the Holy See Mary Ann Glendon, historian Robert Louis Wilkin, and ethicist Gilbert Meilaender.

Although the journal features commentary from members of the Protestant, Orthodox, and Jewish faiths, Catholics have long predominated both in its pages and in the top editorial positions. Neuhaus himself entered the Catholic Church just six months after launching the journal and was ordained a Catholic priest the following year.

Father Neuhaus died of cancer in 2009, but the journal he created continues to both reflect and shape the discussions of intellectually minded, committed Christians in America.

Near the end of his life, Jack Kerouac said, "I don't want to be known as a beat poet anymore; I want to be known as a Catholic."

Since his death in 1969, however, the author of *On the Road* has been memorialized as many things—the father of the "Beat Generation," the grandfather of hipsterdom, a drunk, a libertine, and even a Buddhist—but rarely as a Catholic.

Born on **March 12, 1922,** Kerouac was the son of two French-Canadian Catholics living in Lowell, Massachusetts. Although his father eventually fell away from the Church, his mother's devotion remained strong. From her, Kerouac learned to see the world as a place of grace, touched everywhere by God.

He continued to see it that way his whole life, although he stopped going to Mass when he was 14, and not long afterwards embarked on a journey across America that was marked primarily by moral dissolution. But according to Kerouac, even in the dissolution, he looked for grace.

As he said of the book that memorialized that trip, "[*On the Road*] was really a story about two Catholic buddies roaming the country in search of God."

With a personal diary tattooed on nearly every page by a sketch of a crucifix or a scribbled prayer for mercy, Kerouac was, in some sense, Christ-haunted. He knew that, and he was surprised when others didn't know it as well. When one reporter had the temerity to ask him why he never wrote about Jesus, he replied, "I've never written about Jesus? You are an insane phony. All I ever write about is Jesus."

A lifetime of heavy drinking led to Kerouac's early death in 1969, at the age of 47. He did, however, receive a Mass of Christian burial in his boyhood parish, remembered as a Catholic, at least in death, by the Church of his youth.

When the West was still wild, Native Americans coined names for the priests who ministered in their midst. For Father William Ketcham, they coined the name *Wambli Wakiata,* or "the Watching Eagle."

Born in Iowa and raised in Texas, Ketcham was intrigued by Catholicism as a teenager. Before his eighteenth birthday, he told his Puritan parents he wished to convert. Rather than oppose the decision, his parents encouraged him. Years later, they would surprise everyone by converting as well.

Before then, however, the family moved to Oklahoma, where Ketcham first encountered the Catholic missions to the Native Americans. His desire to work with the missions in turn led him to the priesthood. Ketcham was ordained on **March 13, 1892**—the first vocation for the Indian Territory of Oklahoma.

Over the next eight years, with the help of Mother Katharine Drexel, Father Ketcham built six churches and several schools for the Native Americans in his region. Opposed by Protestant missionaries at every turn (they accused him of "sheep-stealing"), Ketcham withstood legal challenges as well as threats to his life in order to carry out his work.

In 1900, Ketcham was put in charge of the Bureau of Catholic Indian Missions. Despite the waning interest in their work, Ketcham nevertheless pieced together enough funding to keep the schools open.

Ketcham died suddenly, in 1921. At his funeral, the presiding priest recalled his Indian name, *Wambli Wakiata,* saying:

> *For 10 years in Indian Territory, he watched at the doors of the Indian homes. He noted as a father their comings in and goings out. For twenty years more, as a faithful guardian, he watched in Congress where laws were made, and in courts lest they might be unmade; and before the altar of God he daily watched and prayed . . . Father Ketcham was, indeed,* Wambli Wakiata, *the Watching Eagle, the truest and best and most powerful friend of the Indians of his generation.*

In 1663, a young Italian boy, Eusebio Kino, fell deathly ill, and doctors held out little hope for recovery. Privately, Kino offered God a deal. If God let him live, he would become a Catholic priest.

God took him up on the offer, and as soon as Kino recovered, he entered the Jesuit novitiate. Sixteen years later, as a recently ordained priest, he set off for the Jesuit missions in Mexico.

Upon arrival, Father Kino's first major assignment was to peacefully colonize the Baja peninsula, establishing a mission with a church, a farm, and housing for native converts. A drought and a corrupt government official worked against him, however, leading to the mission's dissolution in less than two years.

Kino returned to Mexico City. Two years later, on **March 14, 1687,** he began a second missionary journey. Traveling north to Pimería Alta, he established a new mission at Nuestra Señora de los Dolores. It would be the first of more than two dozen missions he would found in present day Northern Mexico and Arizona.

Over the next 24 years, Kino baptized 4,500 Native Americans and helped convert nearly 30,000 in total, riding more than 50,000 miles on horseback in the process. In addition to instructing converts in the Faith, he also instructed them in European methods of farming and livestock management. By the time of his death, his missions owned more than 70,000 head of cattle.

An outspoken opponent of slavery in the New World, Kino earned the ire of Mexico's silver miners when he obtained a guarantee from the King of Spain protecting all converts to the Faith from enslavement (in the mines or elsewhere) for 20 years. He tried for more, but two decades was the best he could do.

Twenty-four years and one day after his mission in the Pimería Alta began, Kino died from fever in one of his Sonora missions. He was 65.

It was a decision so horrible in its scope, so inflammatory in its language, and so far-reaching in its consequences, that more than 150 years later, it still overshadows the legacy of an otherwise respected jurist.

The desicsion was 1857's *Dred Scott v. Sanford*. And the jurist was Roger B. Taney, the first Catholic to sit on the U.S. Supreme Court. The decision came near the end of his 28-year tenure as Chief Justice, and from the beginning, there was little doubt about how the Maryland native and ardent champion of state's rights would decide the case. What was surprising was the sweeping nature of the decision—the majority ruled that the spread of slavery couldn't be stopped in newly acquired territories—as well his intemperate language, including the assertion that black people weren't fit to associate with white people.

As a younger man, Taney might have written a different decision. Although slaves worked his family's plantation and Taney himself once owned several, he eventually freed them all. As an up-and-coming lawyer, he likewise defended a Methodist minister accused of inciting slave rebellions and described slavery as "a blot on our national character."

Somewhere, however, in the midst of his journey from country lawyer to U.S. secretary of war, then U.S. attorney general, U.S. secretary of the treasury, bank president, and finally, on **March 15, 1836,** to Chief Justice of the Supreme Court, Taney's support for slavery as a legal right grew stronger, ultimately resulting in the decision that helped rend a nation in two.

There was more to his legacy than just the *Dred Scott* decision though. In fact, for his strong defense of *habeas corpus* rights during Abraham Lincoln's administration, as well as for the bulk of his judicial career, Taney has earned the respect of many modern legal scholars.

History, however, judges him by the *Dred Scott* decision alone. Perhaps not wrongly. Although one hopes, after Taney died in poverty at the age of 87, he met a far more merciful judge than history.

It is, arguably, the largest Catholic diocese in the world. It spans not one state, but 50, not one country, but more than 100. It is the Archdiocese for the Military Services, USA (AMS), and it was created on **March 16, 1985.**

In the centuries prior to that, the Catholic Church had found different ways to care for America's soldiers.

From the American Revolution into the early twentieth century, individual priests had offered their services to the armed forces, traveling with men into battle wherever battle took them. Then, in 1917, the Catholic Church formalized the arrangement, first creating the Military Ordinariate of the United States of America, and later the Military Vicariate. At the helm of both the Ordinariate and the Vicariate were auxiliary bishops from New York, who divided their time between their diocese and their work with chaplains. New York was chosen because so many U.S. soldiers passed through the city before departing for Europe.

In the early 1980s, noting the strain such double duty put on his auxiliaries, Archbishop Terence Cardinal Cooke of New York began advocating for a different arrangement. Pope John Paul II soon came up with one, creating the AMS in 1985 and naming Archbishop Joseph T. Ryan (previously of the Archdiocese of Anchorage) as its head.

Today, the Archdiocese is served by nearly 300 active-duty priests, with more than 200 additional priests serving in Veterans Affairs (VA) hospitals, all "on loan" from their dioceses or religious orders. Those priests oversee the liturgy, sacramental life, and faith formation of America's armed forces, support personnel, and their families in more than 220 installations in 29 countries. They also provide pastoral care to patients in 153 VA Medical Centers and federal employees serving outside the United States in more than 100 other countries.

All told, 1.8 million men, women, and children around the world depend upon the work of the AMS and the generosity of Americans across the country who fund its ministry.

President Ulysses S. Grant was tired of scandal, particularly in the Bureau of Indian Affairs. Hoping to put an end to corruption and graft in the Bureau (or at least avoid further blame for the problems), he initiated a "peace policy" in 1869, effectively handing over control of the 72 agencies responsible for overseeing Native American tribes to various religious congregations.

Based upon the number of missions they already ran, the Catholic Church expected to oversee 38 of the 72 total agencies. Instead, the government only granted them authority over seven. Even worse, the policy forbade Catholic Native Americans on the now-Protestant-run reservations from leaving to attend Mass or receive the sacraments.

After the U.S. bishops' initial protests against the arrangement went unheard, the Church formed the Catholic Bureau of Indian Missions (later the Bureau of Catholic Indian Missions) to give them a stronger presence in Washington, D.C. They then asked General Charles Ewing to head the organization.

The son of Thomas Ewing, Sr.—the former U.S. senator and cabinet secretary—and brother-in-law of General William Tecumseh Sherman, Charles Ewing was a devout Catholic who had distinguished himself on the battlefield during the Civil War, and then later as a Washington lawyer.

Eager to serve the Church, Ewing took up his appointment as the first commissioner of the Catholic Bureau of Indian Missions on **March 17, 1873**.

Over the next 10 years, although the Church never recovered her lost missions, the Bureau under Ewing helped found dozens of new ones. They also successfully lobbied the federal government to protect existing Catholic missionary interests, raised money for the missions, and strove to protect Native American lands from further encroachment by the U.S. government.

Charles Ewing died in 1883, but the work of the Bureau went on. Today, under the auspices of the Black and Indian Mission Office, it goes on still—funding Catholic schools, encouraging vocations, and defending the rights of Native American Catholics, just as it has since its beginning.

For members of the American Protective Association (APA), no rumor about Catholics was too wild to believe.

Catholics started the American Civil War? Of course they did. Catholic priests burned the American flag during Mass? Not surprising. Catholics exercised secret control over the White House via blackmail and more nefarious means of manipulation? No news there.

Founded in Clinton, Iowa, in **March 1887,** the APA was the late-nineteenth-century successor to the Know-Nothings, Nativists, and other American anti-Catholic groups. Like their predecessors, the APA believed Catholics threatened the prosperity and culture of their Protestant nation. Also like their predecessors, they were determined to do something about it.

Over the next 10 years, the APA aggressively recruited members, claiming, by the mid-1890s, 2.5 million men among their ranks. They also published over 70 different newsweeklies, and sent men and women posing as ex-priests and nuns to Protestant revivals to spread rumors about the Catholic Church.

Expert fund-raisers, who used the money they raised to put candidates that sympathized with their views into political office, the APA had its greatest success in the midterm and off-year elections of 1894 and 1895. In just two short years, their activity helped elect at least one governor (New Jersey) and as many as 100 congressmen (including 20 APA members).

What they wanted those newly elected officials to do was fairly straightforward: impose stricter regulations on immigration, prevent non-native-born citizens from voting, impose literacy tests at the polls, strengthen public schools, weaken Catholic schools, tax church property, and inspect all religiously run hospitals, schools, and reformatory institutions, as well as monasteries, convents, and seminaries.

In essence, they wanted to reduce the number of Catholic immigrants coming to the United States and make life difficult for Catholics already here. Unfortunately for them, more pressing national concerns arose before the 1896 election, and the APA's influence soon diminished. Its demise was also helped along by *Our Sunday Visitor*'s founder Archbishop John Noll, who worked to undermine the reputation of the group and their publications. After 1923, the APA was never heard from again.

It was a legacy built on quarters—quarters and Our Lady of Victory.

In 1882, Father Nelson Baker, who had been ordained several years earlier on **March 19, 1876,** found himself in charge of two orphanages in the Diocese of Buffalo. With a combined debt of $60,000, the homes seemed fated to close. Baker, who had run a successful grain and seed store prior to entering the seminary, had already drained his personal savings to pay off creditors. But it wasn't enough.

Desperate, he turned to Our Lady of Victory. After praying to her, he began writing letters to postmasters around the country, asking for names and addresses of Catholic ladies disposed to charitable giving. Once he received those names, he sent the ladies letters of their own, asking them to send one quarter a year to the orphans. In return, he promised to pray for them at Mass.

The money came pouring in, sometimes in quarters, sometimes in much larger amounts. In the decades that followed, those donations not only paid off the orphanages' debts, but also helped expand the buildings, construct a new chapel, and finance Baker's seemingly endless charitable endeavors.

In addition to the orphanages, those endeavors included a maternity home, where women could leave unwanted newborns; a maternity hospital, which provided free medical care to unwed mothers; a general hospital that served the poor; a kitchen that fed the hungry; and eventually Our Lady of Victory National Shrine and Basilica in Lackawanna, New York.

In Baker's 60-plus years as a priest, it was said that he never turned away a soul in need. He gave shelter to widows, orphans, and out-of-work men. He started a workers' home for boys who left the orphanage to work in Buffalo's factories, and he converted and baptized countless African-Americans who came north looking for work.

Father Baker, now Servant of God Baker, died in 1936, but his legacy lives on in the network of charitable and educational institutions he left behind, known today as Baker Victory Services.

In 1817, when the Italian-born Father Joseph Rosati arrived in St. Louis, he found a ramshackle church, a windowless log cabin for a rectory, and 2,500 people disinterested in religion of any sort.

On the best of days, that would fail to cheer a missionary's heart. But this wasn't just any day. Rosati had come to St. Louis to prepare the church for the arrival of the Most Reverend Louis William DuBourg, the newly ordained bishop of Louisiana and the Two Floridas, who was coming to set up his episcopal see in St. Louis.

The 28-year-old Vincentian priest had no time to waste. He rolled up his shirtsleeves and got to work.

He didn't stop for 26 years.

After DuBourg's arrival, Rosati took over a parish and opened a seminary, teaching all the classes himself. Two years later, he became the Superior for the Vincentians in America. Three years after that, he became DuBourg's coadjutor bishop. And four years after that, once St. Louis became its own diocese, he became the first bishop of St. Louis. Rome issued the appointment on **March 20, 1827**.

With an episcopal see that spanned almost the entirety of the Louisiana Purchase, Rosati knew he needed help. He began recruiting, and within a decade the Sisters of St. Joseph were running schools and teaching the deaf, while the Sisters of Charity administered a hospital.

As the diocese flourished, debt mounted. Hoping to find benefactors who could put his flock on firmer financial footing, Bishop Rosati set sail for Europe in 1840. His efforts were successful, but his return to St. Louis was delayed when Pope Gregory XVI asked him to undertake a mission to Haiti. Upon his return to Rome, illness struck.

Rosati never recovered, passing away in Rome in 1843. His remains were later returned to St. Louis and interred in the cathedral he had built.

Contrary to popular opinion, not all Irish politicians in the nineteenth century were a product of Tammany Hall. Case in point: William R. Grace.

Born in Ireland in 1832, Grace traveled from the Emerald Isle to Peru when he was 18 to help his father launch an agricultural community for victims of the Irish Potato Famine. The community failed and his father soon left, but Grace stayed on, finding work with a shipping firm. He became a partner in 1854, and gradually expanded the business until it became one of the most successful shipping companies in the world. By 1860, W. R. Grace and Company had offices in New York, San Francisco, and every major city along South America's west coast.

In 1866, Grace decided he'd had enough of Peru and moved to New York with his wife, Lillius—the daughter of a prominent ship builder from Maine—and their six-year-old daughter (two other children had died as babies). Over the next 16 years, the couple would have eight more children. Only five of the 11 would survive to adulthood.

In early 1880, Grace paid for more than a quarter of the aid Americans sent to a starving Ireland via the famine relief ship *Constellation*. Thanks to his generosity, Grace's popularity with the New York electorate skyrocketed and he was urged to run for office. He complied, and later that year, became the first Catholic mayor of New York City.

Over the course of two terms (1880 to 1882 and 1884 to 1886), Grace fought the Irish political machine of Tammany Hall, going after corruption and organized vice while also lowering tax rates. During his second term in office, he welcomed the Statue of Liberty to New York.

A regular at daily Mass for most of his life (morning Mass at St. Agnes was his first stop every day as mayor), Grace devoted his later years to the work of the Grace Institute, the charitable organization he founded in 1897 to provide education and job training for female immigrants.

William Grace died on **March 21, 1904.**

As far as sound investments go, Uncle Sam isn't always the best bet. Just ask Francis Vigo.

Born in Italy in 1747, Vigo came to the New World as a soldier in the Spanish Army. When his enlistment expired, he remained in Louisiana and launched a fur trading business in the Mississippi River Valley.

Over time, the business grew prosperous, so prosperous that by the time the American Revolution began, Vigo had become wealthy enough to bankroll much of George Rogers Clark's military campaign in the Illinois territory. The transactions were simple. Clark had the Continental Army's worthless paper dollars. Vigo had gold. Vigo handed over his gold to Clark in exchange for those worthless dollars . . . with the understanding that the exchange was a loan, not a gift. Once independence was secured, Vigo would get his money back, plus interest.

In addition to ranking as the single-largest financier of the Revolution in the Northwestern territories, Vigo did the occasional bit of spying for Clark. One such tour of duty landed Vigo in the cellblock of Fort Sackville as a prisoner of the British Army. He remained there until the local Catholic priest and fellow Revolutionary financier, Father Pierre Gibault, intervened.

When the war ended, and Britain's American colonies became a country unto themselves, Vigo politely attempted to collect the money owed to him. But no money came.

Vigo soon asked again. And again. And again.

In the end, he kept asking for more than 40 years, right up until his death on **March 22, 1836**.

Not until 1875 though, did the U.S. federal government agree to pay Vigo's estate the $8,016 he had lent Clark, as well as $41,282.60 in interest. But, because Vigo had no living blood relatives, there was no one to whom the government could actually pay out the claim. So, they purchased a small bell for a town that had been promised one by Vigo in his will. The remaining money stayed in the U.S. Treasury.

March 23: THE LEPER PRIEST

As a seminarian with the Congregation of the Sacred Hearts of Jesus and Mary, Damien de Veuster prayed every day before an image of St. Francis Xavier, the patron saint of missionaries. His prayer never varied. The Belgian-born farm boy wanted to become a missionary too and take the Gospel to the Hawaiian people.

His prayer was answered in 1863 when his brother, also a member of the Congregation, fell ill shortly before sailing for Hawaii. Although not yet ordained, Damien received permission to take his brother's place. He and a group of fellow missionaries left France before the New Year, arriving in Hawaii in March 1864.

Shortly after landing, Damien was ordained a priest. He then served the native Hawaiians for nine years, until 1873, when at his request, he left to care for the lepers in the recently established colony on Molokai.

Once Father Damien arrived in Molokai, he began constructing a graveyard to bury the dead. Honoring the dead, he believed, was the first step towards helping people honor their lives. Next, he expanded the small chapel and built the lepers homes, schools, orphanages, and hospitals, all the while evangelizing and catechizing his flock. When he arrived, 200 of the island's 600 lepers were Catholic. Within six months, he had 400 catechumens.

As Father Damien worked beside the lepers, he realized that if he was truly going to touch their souls, he needed to touch their bodies as well—to bathe their wounds and hold their hands as they lay dying. So, he did, eventually contracting the disease himself by December 1884.

Father Damien continued his work without pause for four more years. But by **March 23, 1889,** he was too ill to go on. On that day, he was confined to his bed. He died soon after, on April 15, 1889.

One hundred and twenty years later, on October 11, 2009, Pope Benedict XVI declared Damien the Leper, Saint Damien of Molokai.

The first people to notice that Joseph Barbera (born **March 24, 1911**) had a knack for drawing were the Catholic sisters who taught him in his New York City grade school. When they needed artwork for the classroom or illustrated teaching aids, the sisters turned to him. Unfortunately for them, they turned to Barbera so often that his mother eventually asked them to stop, explaining that his other studies were suffering.

Barbera, however, never did stop.

After graduating from high school, he worked at a bank by day while focusing on his artistic pursuits at night. In 1932, his persistence was rewarded with a job as a cartoonist at Van Beuren Studios. Five years later, he made the move to Hollywood for a job with Metro-Goldwyn-Mayer (MGM). There, he found himself sharing office space with another illustrator, William Hanna, and a partnership that would last more than 60 years began.

Over the next six decades, first at MGM and later through their own studio, Hanna-Barbera, the pair produced some of the most successful cartoon series of the twentieth century: *Tom and Jerry, The Flintstones, The Huckleberry Hound Show, Scooby Doo, The Jetsons, Yogi Bear,* and many more.

Surprisingly, despite winning seven Academy Awards and eight Emmys for his work, Barbera claimed that the work of which he was most proud was his series of animated Bible stories.

"It took me 17 years to get it done," he said in a 1993 interview with the Catholic News Service, explaining that the studios were convinced cartoons about salvation history would "cause too many problems."

Nevertheless, every year without fail, Barbera pled his case. Finally, in 1985, with the help of Taft Broadcasting, Barbera's *The Greatest Adventure: Stories of the Bible* was made for direct-to-home-video release. Within seven years, it had brought in more than $20 million.

Barbera died in 2006. He was 95.

English Catholics needed safe harbor. That much George Calvert knew all too well. The fines imposed by the British government on dissenters were crippling Catholics in seventeenth-century England, and saying goodbye to their homeland seemed the best hope for many. What Calvert—the first Baron of Baltimore and a convert to Catholicism—didn't know was where English Catholics could find that safe harbor.

In 1627, he thought perhaps they could find it in Newfoundland and financed a colony there, but the French and the harsh climate ended that attempt almost as soon as it began. Next, in 1629, Calvert looked to Virginia. This time, too many powerful people in the region were adamantly anti-Catholic. Finally, in 1632, he settled on Maryland, obtaining a promise from his good friend King James I, for a land charter.

Two months before the land charter was granted, however, George Calvert died. His son Cecil carried through with the project, though, and on November 22, 1633, *The Ark,* a 400-ton merchant ship, departed for America. On board were two Jesuit priests, a lay brother, 16 Catholic families, about the same number of Protestant families, and Cecil's brother, Leonard. Their intention was to found a colony in the New World, where all Christian religions, Protestant and Catholic alike, were equally respected.

The Ark met up with a second ship, *The Dove,* in Barbados, and together the ships made landfall on an island in the Chesapeake Bay on **March 25, 1634,** the Feast of the Annunciation. The passengers disembarked, and the first Mass in the British colonies was offered that day on the beach of the newly christened St. Clement's Island.

After Mass concluded, the Catholics took a cross—carved out of one of the island's trees—and completed their celebration with a procession across the beach. Then, as the Jesuit priest who celebrated the Mass, Father Andrew White, described in a letter, "We erected a trophy to Christ the Savior, humbly reciting, on our bended knees, the Litany of the Sacred Cross, with great emotion."

Daniel Patrick Moynihan has been called "The Great Catholic 'What If' of American public life"—a brilliant thinker who brought the Church's insight to Washington, D.C., politics, but who remained mostly silent when it came to protecting the right to life.

Born in Oklahoma, Moynihan grew up in a poor New York City neighborhood. With the help of a Naval officer's training program scholarship, he earned his B.A. at Tufts University, then served in World War II before going back to Tufts for his M.A. and Ph.D. in sociology. He finished his education as a Fulbright Scholar at the London School of Economics.

After that, Moynihan entered public service, first working in New York State politics, then in four successive presidential administrations (Kennedy, Johnson, Nixon, Ford), and finally as New York's four-term Democratic senator.

In the beginning, Moynihan's politics had a decidedly Catholic bent. During the Kennedy administration, he angered liberals by arguing that the U.S. national welfare policy destroyed African-American families by "defining deviancy down," enshrining through law behaviors once considered immoral. Later, as U.S. Ambassador to the United Nations and India, he opposed communism more stridently than the Republican administrations he served.

Once Moynihan moved into the Senate, however, his reputation as a champion of Catholic social teaching waned. Although he continued to stress the importance of culture to a healthy democracy and wielded his razor-sharp wit on behalf of the poor, on the foundational issue of the sanctity of unborn human life he parted ways from his Church.

Moynihan was no abortion champion. He once told a group of feminists, "You women are ruining the Democratic Party with your insistence on abortion." Nevertheless, with the exception of a vote against partial-birth abortion in 1996, he refused to defy the pro-abortion lobby, leaving many wondering how abortion politics might have changed had the prolific author lent his wit to the cause of life.

"The Great Catholic 'What If'" retired from the U.S. Senate in 2001, and died two years later, on **March 26, 2003.**

Henriette DeLille was destined for a life as a white man's mistress—a highly privileged mistress, but a mistress no less.

Born in 1813 New Orleans, DeLille was the daughter of a wealthy Frenchman and his common-law wife—a Creole freedwoman who was one-quarter African. Her grandmother had lived the same sort of life, as had her mother before her. DeLille was expected to follow suit.

Accordingly, in her father's home, she lived a life of luxury and received a gentlewoman's education, studying French, music, literature, and dancing—all to prepare her to become a white man's mistress or common-law wife.

But DeLille had different ideas. Her love for the Catholic Church was strong, and she knew the *plaçage* system of common-law marriage, in which her parents participated, was wrong. Wanting no part of the future planned for her, she began teaching in a Catholic school at the age of 14. The older she grew, the more she devoted herself to works of charity among poor blacks. Her ultimate desire was for religious life, but the opposition of her family combined with refusals from the Carmelites and Ursulines made that difficult.

Finally, in 1836, after her mother's assets passed to her, the 23-year-old DeLille took matters into her own hands, forming a small community of freed black women like herself. They called themselves the Sisters of the Presentation. In 1837, the group received ecclesiastical recognition, and in 1842, they changed their name to the Sisters of the Holy Family.

For nearly 30 years, as Superior of her community, DeLille worked among the black and Creole population of New Orleans. They cared for the elderly and infirm, operated parochial schools for the city's free blacks, and helped bring countless freed slaves into the Church.

DeLille died in 1862, but her order lives on. On **March 27, 2010,** she was declared "Venerable" by Pope Benedict XVI.

In 1835, John Neumann wanted to become a priest. The twenty-four-year-old seminarian had recently completed his studies in theology and had a reputation as a good and pious man. But, as his bishop explained to him, Bavaria was full up with priests that year and didn't need any more.

So, Neumann booked passage to America, where priests were in short supply. He arrived in 1836, and Bishop John Dubois of New York ordained him soon after.

For the next four years, Father Neumann ministered to German immigrants in the Niagara Falls area. Then, in 1840, with the permission of his bishop, he joined the Redemptorist Fathers in Pittsburgh. He made his final vows with the community in 1842, and five years later became the order's Superior in the United States. The following year, he became an American citizen.

Neumann continued his work as a priest in Pittsburgh and the Ohio Valley until 1852, when Rome named him bishop of Philadelphia. Neumann was less than pleased with the appointment and begged the Vatican to pass him over. The Vatican did not comply, and on his 41st birthday, **March 28, 1852,** Neumann was consecrated as Philadelphia's fourth bishop.

Unpopular with the city's wealthy Irish Catholics and plagued by the anti-Catholic Know-Nothing party, Neumann nevertheless went about his job undaunted. In his eight years in Philadelphia, he set up the first diocesan-administered system of parochial schools in the United States, founded one religious order of women (the Sisters of St. Francis), brought in another order from Germany (the School Sisters of Notre Dame), and pioneered the practice of the 40 Hours' Devotion in the States.

In 1860, the 48-year-old Neumann suffered a stroke while running errands and died in the streets of Philadelphia. In 1977, 117 years after his death, he was canonized by Pope Paul VI.

On the night of October 2, 1881, a group of men gathered at St. Mary's Church in New Haven, Connecticut. They'd been summoned to the parish by their assistant pastor, Father Michael J. McGivney, to discuss the formation of a new fraternal organization for Catholic men.

After observing the struggles of his immigrant parishioners, McGivney wanted to create a mutual benefit society, where members' dues helped fund insurance benefits for Catholic widows and orphans. He also wanted to encourage civic and religious pride among Catholic men, providing a fraternal service association for them similar to that provided by other organizations, but from which Catholics were often banned.

On that October night and the many nights that followed, McGivney and his men hashed out various schemes for organizing the association. By the following spring they'd settled on a plan, and on **March 29, 1882,** the Knights of Columbus was officially incorporated in the State of Connecticut.

In the beginning, their efforts were met by rabid anti-Catholic prejudice. Groups such as the Ku Klux Klan spread rumors that Fourth Degree knights had sworn to "exterminate Freemasons and Protestants, as well as flay, burn alive, boil, kill, and otherwise torture anyone, including women and children, when called upon to do so by church authorities."

Nevertheless, the group flourished. In fewer than 10 years, there were more than 40,000 knights throughout New England. By 1909, there were 230,000 knights across the country. Today, the number of knights around the world has reached nearly two million.

The organization's modest insurance program has likewise grown and now holds $90 billion worth of existing policies. In the last decade alone, the Knights have given more than $1.44 billion to charity, with members performing over 664-million hours of volunteer service.

For both its charitable work and its strong defense of Catholic teaching in the public square, Pope John Paul II once described the Knights as, "the strong right arm of the Church."

Can a Catholic university fire a tenured professor of theology who flagrantly dissents from Church teaching?

That was the question in 1989, when Father Charles Curran filed suit against The Catholic University of America (CUA), in Washington, D.C., for what he believed was wrongful dismissal.

Born on **March 30, 1934,** Curran grew up in Rochester, New York, was ordained a priest for the diocese in 1958, and then traveled to Rome, where he earned a licentiate and doctorate in sacred theology. Upon returning to America, Curran taught briefly at his diocesan seminary before joining the theological faculty at Catholic University in 1965.

Just two years later, however, with Curran's support for artificial contraception common knowledge, Catholic University made the decision to let his tenure-line position lapse. Outraged, faculty and students went on strike, demanding the university reverse course. Which it did.

In 1968, the professor joined 600 other theologians who penned a letter dissenting from *Humanae Vitae,* Pope Paul VI's encyclical on artificial contraception. After that, he parted ways with the Church on other key teachings, both in the classroom and in his writing, claiming that homosexual acts, masturbation, premarital sex, and divorce could all be moral goods. Along the way, Curran served as president of the Catholic Theological Society of America and earned its highest honor, The John Courtney Murray Award.

By 1986, the Catholic Church had heard enough. That year, the Congregation for the Doctrine of the Faith forbade Curran from teaching Catholic theology at Catholic institutions. Catholic University complied with the decision and fired Curran. Curran, in turn, filed suit.

In the end, the courts sided with the university. If a person is going to teach Catholic theology at a Catholic institution, the court said, it's not unreasonable to expect that they actually teach what their employer believes and professes.

Accepting defeat, Curran went on to enjoy a successful publishing career and become a lauded professor of "human values" at Southern Methodist University in Dallas. He has yet to recant from his dissent.

As a child in Northern Italy, Frances Cabrini looked forward to the stories her father told each night about the missionaries and martyrs of the Church. Her favorite stories were about the missionaries who went to China. Despite her chronically bad health, Cabrini dreamed that one day, she too would serve the Church there.

But, it wasn't to be. First, her hopes were dashed by the religious orders that turned her away because of her poor health. Later, after she formed her own religious order, the Missionary Sisters of the Sacred Heart of Jesus, those hopes were dashed by the pope himself.

The thirty-seven-year-old Cabrini had served as Mother Superior of her order for seven years when she went to Rome in 1887, seeking permission to take her sisters to China. Pope Leo XIII, however, had different ideas.

"Not to the East," the pope told her, "but to the West."

Mother Cabrini did as instructed, and soon left with six of her sisters for New York City, where Archbishop Michael Corrigan needed help caring for Italian immigrants. She arrived in New York on **March 31, 1889**.

Within two years, Mother Cabrini and her sisters had opened two orphanages for Italian children in New York. Soon, they added a third orphanage; this one was in New Orleans. Next, back in New York, they opened a hospital for the Italian poor, then more hospitals and orphanages in Chicago and Seattle.

In the years that followed, Mother Cabrini was seemingly everywhere, opening 67 orphanages, hospitals, and schools in New York, Pennsylvania, Illinois, Louisiana, Colorado, California, and Washington, as well as Italy, France, England, Spain, Brazil, Argentina, and Nicaragua.

Given that, it's little wonder that after her death in 1917, it took less than 30 years for the Church to declare Mother Cabrini a saint. That happened on July 7, 1946, making her the first American to enter the Church's canon.

April

April 1: THE POP ARTIST

Andy Warhol's body of work is a study in contrast, juxtaposing commercialism, celebrity, and fine art. His life was something of the same.

Born Andrew Warhola, Jr., in Pittsburgh, Pennsylvania, in 1928 to Byzantine Ruthenian Catholic immigrants, the future pop artist spent much of his childhood bedridden. Throughout his long illnesses, his mother kept him entertained with art projects, the radio, and celebrity news. Later, as an adult, Warhol made a career out of those childhood entertainments, first as a graphic artist for magazines and advertising firms, then as the most celebrated pop artist of the twentieth century.

Using a host of different mediums—including film, music, sculpture, photography, performance art, and painting—Warhol repeatedly violated the art world's established boundaries. For him, no subject was too ordinary (Campbell's soup cans) or too mundane (dollar bills). Likewise, no matter how perverse, no subject was too taboo.

During his lifetime, Warhol's public image mirrored his art. Openly gay, he lived at the center of a countercultural community that pushed society's boundaries as thoroughly as Warhol pushed art's boundaries. Yet, while unquestionably homosexual, by his own account Warhol was continent, refraining from sexual relations with others. He also was a closeted Catholic.

After Warhol's death, the world discovered that the legendary pop artist had never left the Faith, as most assumed he had. He visited his New York parish daily (sometimes for Mass, sometimes just to pray), and regularly volunteered at a soup kitchen. In his apartment, he kept a small altar, dedicated to the Virgin Mary, and by his bed he kept a prayer book and rosary. He also proudly paid for his nephew's seminary studies and spent the last year of his life painting more than 100 variations of DaVinci's *The Last Supper.*

On February 22, 1987, following a routine surgery, Warhol unexpectedly passed away. He received a Catholic funeral at Holy Ghost Byzantine Catholic Church in Pittsburgh. A memorial service took place a month later, on **April 1, 1987,** in New York's St. Patrick's Cathedral.

April 2: THE FEAST OF FLOWERS

On the evening of April 1, 1513, the governor of Puerto Rico, Juan Ponce de León, and his company of Spanish explorers sailed into the (soon-to-be-named) Bay of the Holy Cross.

He and his crew, however, were looking for something else. A month earlier, Ponce de León sailed from Puerto Rico hoping to explore the unknown lands to the north. As legend has it, he wanted to find Bimini, a mysterious island where the waters grant eternal youth. By the evening of April 1, the crew made landfall and believed they might have found that island. They had no way of knowing that the landmass before them wasn't an island at all, but rather the southeastern tip of the future United States.

The next morning, **April 2, 1513,** Ponce de León and his men disembarked from their ship. Once on shore, a procession formed. The company's chaplain, carrying a golden cross high in the air, led the way. His fellow priests followed close behind. In their arms, they carried an altar.

With kettledrums beating and bugles blowing, the priests prepared for Mass. And there, on the shore of the Bay of the Holy Cross, they offered the first Eucharistic sacrifice celebrated in the future continental United States.

After Mass, Ponce de León formally claimed the new land for Spain's Ferdinand V. He also named the land "Florida" (*La Florida*), supposedly because he'd discovered the place, blooming with flowers, during Eastertide (in Spanish, *Pascua Florida* or flowery festival).

Ponce de León left Florida several weeks later, after exploring its coastline. The following year, back in Spain, the king made him Florida's governor. Not until 1521, however, did Ponce de León return to the peninsula, this time with 200 soldiers, farmers, and priests, plus orders to colonize the new land.

Unfortunately, death, not eternal youth, awaited Ponce de León among the flowers. An Indian arrow struck the explorer soon after he landed in Florida. He died days later in Cuba.

Everyone knew Michael Kelly was a born troublemaker. The only question was what sort of trouble he would grow up to make—the good kind or the bad.

After catching the teenage Kelly drinking beer in the high school parking lot, one of Kelly's teachers, a Jesuit priest, told him, "You can either be a fantastic con-artist or shape up and do something serious." Kelly weighed his options and chose the better part. He straightened up, studied hard, and went to the University of New Hampshire, where, following in his father's footsteps, he studied journalism. Kelly's troublemaking spirit lent itself well to reporting, and after graduating from college in 1979, he found work with ABC News, the *Cincinnati Post,* and the *Baltimore Sun.*

Then, the First Gulf War broke out.

In 1991, Kelly headed to Kuwait as a correspondent for *The New Republic.* Rather than wait with the approved pool of reporters for official government updates, Kelly hitched a ride on an Egyptian tank and went to the front lines to investigate, sealing his reputation as one of the best war correspondents of his generation.

After the war, Kelly turned to editing, first heading up the *New Republic,* then the *National Journal,* and finally *The Atlantic.* In the pages of those magazines, Kelly stood out as a populist Catholic pro-lifer, routinely taking positions that squared with his faith, but put him at odds with his peers.

Kelly headed back to the Middle East when the Second Gulf War began, this time as an embedded reporter with the Third Infantry Division in Iraq. On the night of **April 3, 2003,** as his division attempted to secure Baghdad International Airport, the Humvee in which Kelly rode came under enemy fire. An evasive maneuver went wrong, and both Kelly and his driver died.

A troublemaker of the best sort to the very end, Michael Kelly was the first American journalist killed in Operation Iraqi Freedom.

April 4: NEW YORK'S NATIVE CARDINAL

On the evening of **April 4, 1968,** the Most Reverend Terence Cooke was supposed to attend an exclusive reception in a tony Manhattan neighborhood. He went to the streets of Harlem instead.

Earlier that day, Cooke had become New York's seventh archbishop. The reception was set to celebrate the appointment of a poor Irish kid from the Bronx to one of America's premier sees. But shortly before the reception began, an assassin gunned down Martin Luther King, Jr.

With riots breaking out across the country, the archbishop couldn't sip champagne. New York was his city. He'd spent most of his priesthood there—from his first parish work after his ordination in 1945, to his most recent post as the city's auxiliary bishop. He understood the struggles of his city, and wanted its citizens to know they weren't without a voice.

So, Archbishop Cooke thanked the organizers of the reception, then left. Once in Harlem, he addressed the crowds, calming tensions and helping the city avert the destruction endured in Chicago, Washington, D.C., and elsewhere.

In the years that followed, Cooke (who became a cardinal in 1969) continued to defend the destitute, the marginalized, and the weak, founding Birthright, a home for expectant mothers in crisis; heading the bishop's pro-life committee after *Roe v. Wade;* starting Courage International, an apostolate to help Catholics who struggled with same-sex attraction fully live their faith; opening homes for the elderly, infirm, and indigent; and launching an inner-city scholarship fund.

In October 1983, days before he died from leukemia, Cardinal Cooke's last public act was to publish a letter affirming the dignity of those he served. He wrote:

> *The gift of life is no less beautiful when it is accompanied by illness or weakness, hunger or poverty, mental or physical handicaps, loneliness or old age. Indeed, at these times, human life gains extra splendor as it requires our special care, concern and reverence. It is in and through the weakest of human vessels that the Lord continues to reveal the power of His love.*

April 5: A QUESTION OF HABITS

In the first years of the twentieth century, Catholic missions to the Native Americans were booming. By 1912, the Catholic Church operated 137 Native American missions, 55 boarding schools, and eight day schools, all thanks to the generosity of some 10 million Catholics.

Many Protestant Americans, however, were less than thrilled by that success and some began looking for ways to cool the Catholics' missionary fervor.

In January 1912, a group of Protestant missionaries nearly succeeded. They convinced Commissioner Robert Valentine, their ally in the Bureau of Indian Affairs, to ban religious garb and symbols from reservation classrooms. Because Protestant missionaries weren't given to wearing habits or placing crucifixes and statues of the Virgin Mary in their schools, the ban was a clear swipe at Catholics.

Catholics recognized the snub and sent Father William Ketcham to talk some sense into the federal government. Ketcham didn't quite manage that, but he did persuade President William Howard Taft to block the enforcement of the order until federal hearings could examine the matter more closely.

In **April 1912,** both Protestants and Catholics made their case before a special commission, convened to examine the question. The final decision, rendered by Interior Secretary Walter Fisher, was a draw. The ban on religious garb and symbols stood, but the government also carved out an exemption for current habit-wearing employees.

In other words, teachers who wore habits could continue wearing them. But only if they served in reservation schools prior to the ban. All future religious teachers would be required to dress as laypeople.

Despite the new restrictions, Catholic missions on the Native American reservations continued to thrive . . . much to the chagrin of their Protestant peers.

April 6: AN AMERICAN CATECHISM

Catholics in early nineteenth-century America needed to know their faith better. The country's bishops knew that. They also knew that couldn't happen without an English-language catechism—an easy-to-use teaching tool that would ensure the Faith was taught in all its fullness across the fledgling nation.

What the bishops didn't know was just how difficult producing such a catechism would be.

Their quest for a catechism began in 1829, at the First Provincial Council of Baltimore, There, they decreed:

> *A catechism shall be written which is better adapted to the circumstances of this Province; it shall give the Christian Doctrine as explained in Cardinal Bellarmine's Catechism (1597), and when approved by the Holy See, it shall be published for the common use of Catholics.*

Unfortunately, after the Council, the bishops were too busy seeing to the more immediate needs of their fledgling dioceses to write a catechism, so no one moved ahead with the idea.

In 1852, when their successors reconvened at the First Plenary Council of Baltimore, a catechism once more topped the agenda. But again, nothing came of it. Nor did anything come of the bishops' call for a catechism after the Second Plenary Council of Baltimore in 1866. Other pressing concerns—from the anti-Catholic Know-Nothings to the American Civil War's aftermath and Reconstruction—took precedence.

Finally, after the Third Plenary Council of Baltimore in 1884, the bishops formed a committee, and six prelates undertook the arduous task. A year later, the first edition of the four-volume, English-language catechism went to press. It received an imprimatur, guaranteeing its theological orthodoxy, on **April 6, 1885**.

In the years that followed, "The Baltimore Catechism," as it became known, was used throughout the United States and Canada to form the faithful, both young and old. Its popularity endured for almost a century, and even with the publication of the universal *Catechism of the Catholic Church* in 1992, The Baltimore Catechism remains in print, offering solid religious instruction for children and adults alike.

When asked about his religion, John Wayne usually gave one of two responses. Either he claimed to be a "presbygoddamnterian" or a "cardiac Catholic."

In the end, only one answer proved true.

Born Marion Robert Morrison, John Wayne was the son of lackadaisical Presbyterians who never baptized their son. Wayne followed in his parents' footsteps, keeping faith on the sidelines until 1933, when the budding movie actor married a devout Catholic. Although he never became one for churchgoing, Wayne helped raise his children Catholic and sent all of them to Catholic schools, later crediting those schools for how well his children turned out. ("Not a Jane Fonda in the bunch," he once said.)

Unfortunately, as Wayne's fame grew, so did the number of temptations that came his way. An extramarital affair ended his first marriage, as well as his second and third. Wayne often spoke with regret about his broken marriages and moral failings, but he never seemed inclined to do anything about them. To him, a deathbed conversion seemed his best bet.

On **April 7, 1969,** Wayne won his first and only Oscar for his role as Rooster Cogburn in *True Grit.* Rumor has it, Wayne had been passed over before because of his outspoken conservatism—he was a die-hard anti-communist and a free market champion—but no one knows for certain.

Regardless, no other Oscars followed, and 10 years later, Wayne lay dying in a Los Angeles hospital. At last, the time for joking about cardiac Catholicism had ended. His son Patrick, at his father's request, summoned a priest to his bedside, and two days before his death, "the Duke" was baptized and received into the Catholic Church.

Posthumously awarded the Presidential Medal of Freedom and the Congressional Medal of Honor, Wayne left behind a legacy of 175 films, seven children, and many more grandchildren, including one who became a Catholic priest.

In 1803, Bishop John Carroll had a problem—a big problem.

Fourteen years earlier, when Carroll became bishop of Baltimore, his diocese spanned all of the former American colonies, and most of the Eastern half of the present-day United States (Florida and the Gulf Coast excepted). Anywhere from 35,000 to 50,000 Catholics lived within that territory.

It was, from the start, an unwieldy diocese to shepherd, larger in size than his European counterparts could even begin to imagine. Then came 1803, and his diocese's size went from unwieldy to overwhelming.

That year, Napoleon Bonaparte sold the entirety of France's land holdings west of the Mississippi River to the United States. For a mere $15 million, America acquired more than 828,000 square miles of land. Overnight, the country doubled in size.

Moreover, because the acquired territory had belonged alternately to the French and Spanish, it was chock-full of Catholics, who, at the time of the purchase, were without a bishop of their own. Their previous bishop had been recently transferred, and with the Vatican otherwise occupied with Napoleon Bonaparte, his replacement had yet to be named. Accordingly, when the United States purchased the land, Rome decided Bishop Carroll could see to the Diocese of Louisiana and the Two Floridas himself. Carroll appointed an administrator to help him, but he remained the only bishop in the United States.

The promise of relief finally came on **April 8, 1808,** when (at Carroll's request) four new American dioceses were created—Bardstown, Boston, Philadelphia and New York. Two years later, in 1810, four new shepherds were also named: for Bardstown, Bishop Joseph Flaget; for Boston, Bishop Jean-Louis Lefebvre de Cheverus; for Philadelphia, Bishop Michael Francis Egan; and for New York, Bishop Richard Luke Concanen.

Even then, all did not flow smoothly for Carroll. Egan died within four years from stress, and Concanen passed away before he reached his see, leaving Carroll again responsible for both dioceses. At the very least, however, Carroll was no longer alone. And for that, he was grateful.

April 9: THE FRENCH EXPLORER

René-Robert Cavelier's fortune was lost. Gone with it were his prospects for success, at least in his native France.

Six years earlier, in 1660, the young Sieur de La Salle renounced his fortune when he joined the Jesuits. By 1666, though, La Salle knew religious life wasn't for him. Nearly destitute and with few other options, he decided to travel to New France, where his older brother served as a Sulpician priest.

Later that year, La Salle arrived in New France with the little money he had left. There, he purchased land on the island of Montreal and quickly established a successful fur trading business. Three years later, hoping to make that business even more successful, La Salle organized the first of many expeditions to explore the riverways of his new home. Native Americans had told La Salle of a great river, which led to an even greater sea, and La Salle hoped that river might offer a route to the Orient.

Although he never found the Orient, La Salle's explorations weren't in vain. His journey around the Great Lakes helped establish forts throughout the region and secured the future of the French fur trade. He also was the first European to see the Ohio River, traveling along it as far as Louisville, Kentucky, and to canoe the length of the Mississippi River.

Upon arriving at the mouth of the Mississippi, on **April 9, 1682,** La Salle claimed the entirety of the Mississippi River basin for France. He also named it *La Louisiane,* after King Louis XIV.

Two years later, La Salle attempted to return there to found a colony. With four ships and 300 colonists, he sailed from France in 1684. They overshot their mark, however, ending up in modern-day Texas, and lost three ships along the way. La Salle attempted to find the Mississippi on foot, but to no avail. Finally, his remaining colonists mutinied, killing La Salle in 1687. He was 43.

What makes *A Man for All Seasons* one of the greatest movies of all time?

For starters, there's the story upon which it was based: Saint Thomas More's refusal to betray his conscience and Church at the whim of king and country.

There also is the cast: Paul Scofield, Orson Welles, John Hurt, Wendy Hiller . . . a director couldn't ask for more.

Best of all, there's Robert Bolt's witty, erudite, and quintessentially Catholic screenplay, a screenplay that made *A Man for All Seasons* perhaps the most quotable Catholic movie of all time.

Case in point? The following exchange between the Duke of Norfolk and More:

> **Norfolk:** *Oh confound all this. I'm not a scholar, I don't know whether the marriage was lawful or not but dammit, Thomas, look at these names! Why can't you do as I did and come with us, for fellowship!*
> **More:** *And when we die, and you are sent to heaven for doing your conscience, and I am sent to hell for not doing mine, will you come with me, for fellowship?*

Then there are these classic lines from More:

> *When a man takes an oath, Meg, he's holding his own self in his own hands. Like water. And, if he opens his fingers then, he needn't hope to find himself again.*

> *I think that when statesmen forsake their own private conscience for the sake of their public duties, they lead their country by a short route to chaos.*

> *I die the king's good servant, but God's first.*

For all those reasons and more, *A Man for All Seasons* proved a film for all seasons, receiving six Academy Awards on **April 10, 1967:** Best Picture, Best Director, Best Adapted Screenplay, Best Actor (Scofield), Best Cinematography, and Best Costume Design.

In 1819, Catholics in Charleston, South Carolina, threatened schism. Rome responded by creating a new diocese—the Diocese of Charleston— and ordaining an Irish priest—Father John England—to keep them in line.

Born and educated in County Cork, Ireland, England was only 34 when the Church plucked him out of an Irish parish, made him bishop, and sent him off to South Carolina. Awaiting him in his new diocese— which consisted of North Carolina, South Carolina, and Georgia—was a scattered flock of a few thousand Catholics, precious few parishes, even fewer priests, and a sizable number of parish trustees who believed they, not their priests, should run the Church.

Rather than do battle with the trustee system, England neutralized it, drawing up a constitution for the parishes in his diocese that gave lay-people a voice in how their parishes were governed. At the same time, the constitution ensured proper recognition of episcopal and priestly authority.

As the threat of schism passed, England set about bringing order to his diocese, traveling to wherever Catholics lived, organizing parishes, building churches, and recruiting priests. In Charleston, he founded a seminary and college of classical learning, as well as an academy for young women and a religious order to help catechize both free black women and slaves. England also attempted to open a school for free blacks, but it closed in the wake of violent opposition from the local community.

More than anything else, England wanted his flock to know and understand their faith. To that end, he wrote an English-language cat-echism, as well as an English-language missal. He also launched the first diocesan newspaper in America—the *United States Catholic Miscellany*— and started a diocesan-wide book club in which all parishes were asked to participate.

Respected by Catholics and Protestants alike for his preaching, char-ity, and practice of personal poverty—reportedly the soles of his shoes were perpetually marked by holes—England died of fever on **April 11, 1842.**

April 12: THE LITTLE NAPOLEON

When Confederate Brigadier General Pierre Gustave Beauregard arrived in Charleston, South Carolina, in March 1861, he faced more problems than he'd bargained for.

Although South Carolina and six other states—including Beauregard's native Louisiana—had already seceded from the Union, armed conflict had not yet commenced. And Beauregard, despite his nickname ("Little Napoleon") didn't want to fire the first shots in the American Civil War. Unfortunately the regiment of Union troops stationed at Fort Sumter, positioned in the middle of Charleston's harbor, refused to leave of its own accord.

Furthermore, the commanding Union officer inside Fort Sumter was Beauregard's friend and teacher, General Robert Anderson. Before fighting in the Mexican-American War, Beauregard had studied under Anderson at West Point, and then later worked as his assistant. Beauregard valued their friendship and did not want to aim fire at Anderson.

Hoping Anderson would leave South Carolina peacefully, Beauregard repeatedly sent aides to the fort, requesting as much. He also sent cases of whisky and cigars, hoping the gifts would buy him some goodwill. Anderson only sent the gifts back.

Beauregard saw the writing on the wall, and began preparing the batteries surrounding Fort Sumter for attack. Then, in April 1861, when word came that President Abraham Lincoln had sent a small fleet to replenish the Fort's limited supplies, Beauregard acted on Confederate President Jefferson Davis' orders.

On April 11, he gave Anderson one final chance to surrender. Anderson refused. The next day, on **April 12, 1861,** under the Catholic general's command, the Confederate Army launched its assault. The Union Army responded in kind. Thirty-four hours later, Anderson admitted defeat.

The end of the fight at Fort Sumter, however, only meant the beginning of something worse. In its wake, Lincoln called for 75,000 volunteers to help end the rebellion. In response to that call, four more Southern states, including Virginia, joined the Confederacy. The Civil War, which saw more than 50 Catholics serve as generals or admirals in the Union and Confederate armies, was underway.

On **April 13, 1743,** in Shadwell, Virginia, Thomas Jefferson was born. In the years that followed, Jefferson would become a farmer, lawyer, architect, inventor, clockmaker, philosopher, patriot, author of the Declaration of Independence, first U.S. secretary of state, third U.S. president, founder of the University of Virginia, and more.

The "more" includes his authorship of the Virginia Statute for Religious Freedom.

Drafted in 1777 by Jefferson, the statute disestablished the Church of England as Virginia's state religion and forbade the state from setting up another church in its place. It also guaranteed freedom of religion to people of all faiths. Once adopted, the statute became a model for subsequent statutes across the country, as well as the First Amendment to the Constitution.

Although Jefferson later coined the phrase, "wall of separation" to describe the relationship he envisioned between Church and State, a letter he sent to the Ursuline Sisters of New Orleans following the Louisiana Purchase made it clear that, as he saw it, the wall was there to protect the Church as much as the State. As he explained to the Ursulines:

> *I have received, holy sisters, the letter you have written me wherein you express anxiety for the property vested in your institution by the former governments of Louisiana.*
>
> *The principles of the constitution and government of the United States are a sure guarantee to you that it will be preserved to you, sacred and inviolate, and that your institution will be permitted to govern itself according to its own voluntary rules, without interference from the civil authority.*
>
> *Whatever the diversity of shade may appear in the religious opinions of our fellow citizens, the charitable objects of your institution cannot be indifferent to any; and its furtherance of the wholesome purposes of society, by training up its younger members in the way they should go, cannot fail to ensure it the patronage of the government it is under.*
>
> *Be assured it will meet all the protection which my office can give it.*

April 14: THE UNSHAKABLE PRIESTS OF THE UNSINKABLE SHIP

On the night of **April 14, 1912,** the unsinkable *Titanic* struck ice. In the terrifying hours that followed, more than 1,500 men, women, and children died a cold and horrible death in the North Atlantic Ocean. But they didn't die alone. In their last moments, as the unsinkable *Titanic* sank, three priests stood by the doomed passengers' sides, hearing their confessions, praying the Rosary, and, at the very last, granting general absolution.

One of those priests was Father Thomas Byles, an Englishman who, almost 20 years before, had converted to Catholicism while studying at Oxford. Since 1905, he'd served as a parish priest in Essex and was on his way to New York to celebrate the wedding Mass of his younger brother.

Another was Father Juozas Montvila. Only 27 at the time, Father Montvila was fleeing the Tsarist regime in his native Lithuania, which had forbidden Ukrainian Catholic priests from ministering to their flocks. As an Eastern Rite priest in union with Rome, Montvila had three options: convert to Russian Orthodoxy, endure persecution, or flee. He chose to flee, planning upon his arrival in America to serve the country's growing Ukrainian Catholic population.

The third priest on board the *Titanic* was the 41-year-old German scholar Father Joseph Benedikt Peruschitz, who was traveling to St. John's Abbey in Collegeville, Minnesota, to take up a teaching position on the school's faculty.

Father Byles was a first-class passenger on the *Titanic*. His fellow priests traveled in second class. All, however, received offers to enter the lifeboats and row away to safety after the ship struck an iceberg. None accepted those offers. Each knew his vocation called him to remain with the dying, even at the cost of his own life.

When the *Titanic* slipped below the water line at 2:20 a.m. on April 15, all three priests disappeared with her. Their bodies were never recovered.

April 15: A PAPAL VISIT

It was an extraordinary move, something that would have shocked and scandalized earlier generations of Americans. Yet, to those awaiting Pope Benedict XVI's arrival at Andrews Air Force Base on **April 15, 2008,** President George W. Bush's presence on the tarmac seemed entirely appropriate.

True, it broke with precedent. As a rule, U.S. presidents don't leave the White House to greet arriving foreign dignitaries; they wait at the White House for dignitaries to come to them. But for Bush, precedent mattered less than showing his respect for the pontiff. He showed that respect by his presence on the tarmac. He also showed it through his remarks the following day, saying:

> *Holy Father, you will find in America people whose hearts are open to your message of hope. And America and the world need this message. In a world where some invoke the name of God to justify acts of terror and murder and hate, we need your message that "God is love." And embracing this love is the surest way to save men from "falling prey to the teaching of fanaticism and terrorism."*
>
> *In a world where some treat life as something to be debased and discarded, we need your message that all human life is sacred, and that "each of us is willed, each of us is loved, and each of us is necessary."*
>
> *In a world where some no longer believe that we can distinguish between simple right and wrong, we need your message to reject this "dictatorship of relativism," and embrace a culture of justice and truth.*
>
> *In a world where some see freedom as simply the right to do as they wish, we need your message that true liberty requires us to live our freedom not just for ourselves, but "in a spirit of mutual support."*
>
> *Holy Father, thank you for making this journey to America. Our nation welcomes you. We appreciate the example you set for the world, and we ask that you always keep us in your prayers.*

April 16: BESTING BABE

The Catholic farm boy from Fargo, North Dakota, had always been a promising athlete. In high school—Shanley Catholic—he stood out in baseball, football, basketball, and track. Later, when he moved on to the minor leagues, he excelled there as well.

Nevertheless, when Roger Maris made his major league debut with the Cleveland Indians on **April 16, 1957,** nobody expected the kid from Fargo to do the unthinkable: break Babe Ruth's home-run record.

Yet within four years, that's exactly what he did.

Maris was 26 years old and a New York Yankee when the 1961 season began. Kansas City had traded him to the Yankees after 1959, and although Maris won the American League's Most Valuable Player Award for the 1960 season, New York fans hadn't taken to him. Quiet and shy, Maris was a faithful family man, more interested in spending time with his wife and (eventually) six kids, than schmoozing with the press.

Then, when it became clear that Maris and his teammate Mickey Mantle were in a race to break the Babe's record of 60 home runs in a single season (albeit, a slightly longer season than Ruth's), things got ugly.

Every time Maris took to the field in 1961, boos, not cheers greeted him. Threats and hate mail poured into the Yankee's office, and the press routinely savaged him. People didn't want to see Ruth's record broken by an outsider. Maris, however, handled it with grace, keeping his cool and finally hitting his 61st home run in the last game of the regular season.

Maris went on to play five more seasons with the Yankees, before finishing up his career in 1968 as a St. Louis Cardinal. Seventeen years later, Hodgkin's lymphoma took the 51-year-old father's life. In his funeral Mass at the Fargo cathedral, concelebrated by the bishop and four priests, nearly 1,000 people turned out to honor Maris, not simply for the way he played baseball, but more fundamentally, for the way he lived life.

April 17: LA CHAPELLE DE L'ASSOMPTION DE LA SAINTE VIERGE A LA BELLE RIVIÈRE

In Pittsburgh, Pennsylvania, three rivers meet. Right in the middle of the city, the Allegheny and the Monongahela come together to form the Ohio.

Today, the city's Point State Park, filled with runners, bikers, and tourists, overlooks the confluence. But in the days when the French and British fought over the fur trade and the American interior, that meeting point offered more than river views: It offered control of the interior's waterways. Accordingly, long before Pittsburgh was a settlement, a chapel stood where a fountain now stands.

The chapel was part of Fort Duquesne.

In February 1754, the British began building a small fort on the site of the future park. Upon discovering what the British were up to, French forces decided to take it for themselves. They launched their attack on April 16, and by the next day, the fort was theirs.

Hours later, on **April 17, 1754,** Father Denys Baron, a Recollect friar and chaplain to the French army, arrived and celebrated Mass for the soldiers.

Soon, the French soldiers completed building a second and much larger fort at the confluence—naming it Fort Duquesne, after New France's governor, the Marquis Michel-Ange Duquesne. They also built a chapel inside the fort, which Baron christened "The Assumption of the Blessed Virgin of the Beautiful River."

The chapel served the soldiers, Native Americans, and far-flung Catholic settlers for four years. Parish records, carefully preserved by Baron, tell of a few marriages, many baptisms (including one Iroquois chief who asked for baptism at the age of 95), and many more funerals.

In 1758, rather than see the fort fall into British hands, the French burned it to the ground. Today, the only remaining traces of the fort and its chapel are a row of stones in Point State Park, marking where the fort once stood, and a small plaque in the nearby St. Mary of Mercy Catholic Church (founded in 1868), commemorating its predecessor, *La Chapelle de l'Assomption de la Sainte Vierge a la Belle Rivière.*

April 18: A CITY IN ASHES

Just after 5:00 a.m., on **April 18, 1906,** the city of San Francisco, California, started shaking. It didn't stop shaking for a full 45 seconds. Once it did, the entire state of California west of the San Andreas Fault had shifted northward by 16 feet, all thanks to an earthquake believed to have measured 8.4 on the Richter scale.

Once the world stopped shaking, the Paulist Fathers breathed a sigh of relief. Their church, Old St. Mary's, the city's first cathedral, still stood—badly damaged, but whole.

The Paulists didn't breathe easy for long though. Before the priests could assess the damage, the fires began. Severed gas mains and overturned lamps combined to form a fire far more devastating than the quake, as waves of flame and smoke spread rapidly through the city. The earthquake had lasted only seconds. The fires lasted days.

When it was over, three days later, 452 people were dead and thousands injured and homeless. Five hundred city blocks were completely destroyed; 28,000 buildings burned down to ash. Parishes throughout the city were lost, and Old St. Mary's was no more. It was a shell. Even its marble altar was gone, melted by the heat of the blaze.

In the days after the fire, San Francisco's Archbishop Patrick Riordan visited the church's parishioners, newly homeless, living amidst the ruins in tents and temporary shelters. Everywhere he went, he celebrated Mass in the open air, assuring the people, "We will rebuild."

In a homily soon after the quake, he made that same promise.

"'I am a citizen of no mean city,'" he said, quoting St. Paul, "although it is in ashes. Almighty God has fixed this as the location of a great city. The past is gone, and there is no lamenting over it. Let us look to the future and without regard to creed or place of birth, work together in harmony for the upbuilding of a greater San Francisco."

And rebuild they did—completing construction of the new Old St. Mary's just three years later.

April 19: THE MAJORITY REPORT

Le Monde in France, *The Tablet* in England, and the *National Catholic Reporter* in the United States. On **April 19, 1967,** in a coordinated political move, those three newspapers simultaneously released what has come to be known as the "Majority Report." The published statement represented the views of the majority of theologians, clergy, and other experts who served on the Papal Birth Control Commission and endorsed ending the Church's millennia-long prohibition of artificial contraception.

In light of demographic issues and the advent of the hormonal birth control pill, Pope John XXIII formed the 1963 commission to study and articulate why Church teaching could not allow for married couples to use artificial contraception. Three years later, the commission concluded their deliberations and presented its findings to the pope. Along with the "Majority Report," they also presented a "Minority Report," representing the position of commission members who believed that the prohibition should remain.

After a full year, Pope Paul VI was still considering both reports.

In the end, the reports themselves meant little. They didn't represent the authoritative teaching of the Church, nor did either reflect what Pope Paul VI would eventually decide. Nevertheless, those who supported the Church changing her teaching on artificial contraception believed they could influence the pope by making the Majority Report public. Vatican insiders leaked the documents to friendly news outlets, and the friendly news outlets leaked them to the world in the spring of 1967.

To an extent, their plan worked. While the Church waited for the pontiff to speak on the question, numerous theologians and priests assured Catholics that the pope would soon condone birth control. Given those assurances, many began using contraception. By the time Pope Paul VI issued the encyclical *Humanae Vitae* in 1968, it didn't matter that he affirmed traditional Church teaching, siding with the Minority Report. For many Catholics, it was too late, and the confusion sown remained.

April 20: A SPIRITUALLY DEADLY OATH

In March 1777, the New York Assembly gathered in Kingston to hammer out the final details of its State Constitution. Included among those details were the requirements for citizenship in New York.

In the midst of that discussion, statesman John Jay convinced the Assembly to insert a clause requiring anyone seeking citizenship to "abjure and renounce all allegiance and subjection to all and every foreign king, prince, potentate, and state, in all matters *ecclesiastical and civil.*"

The clause seemed harmless to the legislators, but when the final constitution was approved, on **April 20, 1777,** it meant that Catholics not wishing to excommunicate themselves by rejecting the pope's authority could not become New York citizens.

The U.S. Constitution, adopted a decade later, eliminated that problem. But while it superseded New York's citizenship requirements, it had no bearing on the state's Oath of Office, which included similar language:

> *I do solemnly, without any mental reservation or equivocation whatsoever, swear and declare that I renounce and abjure all allegiance and subjection to all and every foreign king, prince, potentate, and state, in all matters ecclesiastical as well as civil, and that I will bear faith and true allegiance to the State of New York, as a free and independent State.*

When Catholics realized that the oath effectively banned them from political office, they were outraged. Not until 1806, however, when Francis Cooper (a New York City Catholic) ran for and won a State Assembly seat, did the situation change.

Upon his election, Cooper refused to take the oath. In turn, the Assembly refused to seat him. Immediately his parish, St. Peter's in lower Manhattan, began collecting signatures to demand a change in the law. When the State Assembly reconvened a month later, it voted to remove "in all matters ecclesiastical as well as civil" from the oath, and Cooper took his seat.

Ever since then, Catholics have in good conscience been able to hold elected office in the State of New York.

April 21: AN ACT OF TOLERATION

In 1634, when Catholic colonists arrived in Maryland, they thought they had found a home where they could freely practice their faith.

Fifteen years later, after briefly losing control of the colony to hardline Protestants, those same colonists realized just how easily that freedom could be taken from them.

In an attempt to guard against that fate, they passed the Maryland Toleration Act on **April 21, 1649**.

The Act stated:

> For the more quiet and peaceable government of this Province, and the better to preserve mutual Love and amity amongst the Inhabitants thereof, Be it Therefore also by the Lord Proprietary with the advise and consent of this Assembly Ordained and enacted . . . that no person or persons whatsoever within this Province, or the Islands, Ports, Harbors, Creeks, or havens thereunto belonging, professing to believe in Jesus Christ, shall from henceforth be any ways troubled, Molested or discountenanced for or in respect of his or her religion nor in the free exercise thereof . . . nor any way compelled to the belief or exercise of any other Religion against his or her consent. . . .

In plain English, what the Act did was secure religious freedom for all Trinitarian Christians, Catholics included.

What the Act did not do was protect those who dissented from Christianity. It prescribed death by hanging for anyone who denied the Trinity or Christ's divinity.

Nor did it tolerate blasphemy. Anyone who slandered the Virgin Mary or the apostles could receive a flogging, and those who lobbed religious insults at their neighbor (such as "heretic," "infidel," or "popish priest") were liable for a hefty fine.

The Maryland Toleration Act remained in force until 1654, when Puritans again took control of the colony and declared the Toleration Act null and void. Four years later, Catholics returned to power and the colonial assembly passed yet another version of the Toleration Act.

This time it remained the law of the land until 1692, when the colony's new Protestant legislature repealed it. Religious freedom did not return to Maryland until the American Revolution began.

History tells us that the stress of shepherding "the City of Brotherly Love" led Philadelphia's first bishop, Michael Egan, to an early grave. His contemporaries' reluctance to fill his shoes indicates that they shared history's opinion. After Egan's death, despite Rome's best efforts, it took five years to find a priest willing to shepherd the see. And the priest they did find, Father Henry Conwell, regretted his decision almost as soon as he arrived.

Bishop Conwell's problems began on December 3, 1820, when Father William Hogan preached the homily for the bishop's installation Mass at St. Mary's Cathedral. Conwell had heard rumors about Hogan—he was contentious and a lady's man—but nothing prepared him for Hogan's rant against the rector of St. Mary's during the homily.

After the Mass, Conwell spoke to Hogan, telling him he needed to apologize to St. Mary's rector. Hogan refused. He then returned to the cathedral and preached against his bishop with equal animosity.

Over the next several months, tensions between priest and bishop escalated. Finally, on **April 22, 1821,** the beginning of Easter Week, St. Mary's elected new parish trustees. Nearly all supported Hogan. He took charge of the cathedral parish, and exiled the bishop to nearby St. Joseph's.

"The Hogan Schism" had begun.

The next two years brought excommunications for Hogan and his parishioners, rioting in the streets, and legal wrangling in the courts. Nothing persuaded Hogan and his supporters to reconcile with his bishop, not even *Non Sine Magno,* the 1822 letter from Pope Pius VII condemning trusteeism.

Hogan walked away from the mess he created in 1823, renouncing Catholicism, leaving the priesthood, and marrying a wealthy widow.

For his part, Conwell got into trouble with Rome for letting parish trustees run roughshod over him, and, after handing over administration of the diocese to a coadjutor bishop, he retired in 1830 to a life of seclusion and prayer.

Only then, when the coadjutor bishop reined in the last of the troublesome trustees, did the Hogan Schism finally end.

April 23: FIGHTING IN THE FIELDS

For Cesar Chavez, social activism was about more than politics, race, or ethnicity. It was about justice and human dignity. It was about helping the world more perfectly live the Gospel of Jesus Christ.

Born in Arizona in 1927, Chavez moved with his family to California during the Great Depression. There, alongside thousands of overworked and underpaid migrant workers, the Chavez family labored long hours in the fields of California's fruit and vegetable growers.

At the tail end of World War II, Chavez joined the U.S. Navy. He hoped the military might provide him with a way out of agricultural labor. But by 1947, he was back in the fields. He soon married and began a family, eventually becoming a father of eight.

Change came for Chavez in the early 1950s, when he met Father Donald McConnell, an Irish-American priest who introduced him to the social encyclicals of Pope Leo XIII and Pope Pius XI. Inspired by the Church's understanding of labor and human dignity, Chavez began working to organize and unionize agricultural laborers.

In the decades that followed, Chavez protested the unjust treatment of farm workers using the same means of peaceful disobedience practiced by Martin Luther King, Jr., while also drawing inspiration from his Catholic faith. Fasting, prayers, and pilgrimages all had a place in Chavez's work, and wherever he and his supporters marched, an image of Our Lady of Guadalupe, the patroness of his movement, led the way.

Chavez's work with the laborers was marked by great successes—including organizing multiple agricultural unions across the country—and by great failures. His most lasting legacy, however, was demonstrating the efficacy of the Church's wisdom and devotions in defending human dignity in the public square.

Fasting for agricultural workers, despite his own ailing health, led to Chavez's death on **April 23, 1993**.

April 24: FROM SLAVE TO PRIEST

On July 17, 1886, the pews of St. Boniface Church in Quincy, Illinois, were packed with white and black Catholics alike. Together, ignoring racial differences, they knelt to receive the blessing of their town's newest priest, a local boy, ordained in Rome, who had arrived back earlier that day.

The priest was Father John Augustine (Augustus) Tolton, the first avowedly African-American priest of the United States.

Born in 1854 to two Missouri slaves, Tolton escaped to freedom with his mother and siblings in 1862. The family then settled in Quincy, where the local priest, Father Peter McGirr, befriended the boy and—despite protests from many parents—enrolled him in St. Peter's Parish School.

Not long afterwards, Tolton, who had been baptized Catholic as a baby, received his First Communion and began serving 5 a.m. Mass for Father McGirr. One day after Mass, McGirr told Tolton that he would make a fine priest. Tolton immediately responded, "Let us go to the Church and pray for my success."

Discerning his vocation, however, proved easier than pursuing it. Despite the support of the local priests, Tolton couldn't find a seminary in the country that would admit him. It took years of searching and praying before McGirr finally convinced a seminary in Rome to take on the young man.

Tolton left for the Eternal City in 1880, and six years later, on **April 24, 1886,** he was ordained to the Catholic priesthood at St. John Lateran Basilica in Rome. He expected to go to Africa, to serve as a missionary, but instead, the Church asked him to return to Quincy.

Father Tolton remained in Quincy until 1889, when the archbishop of Chicago requested that he come north to serve the city's black Catholics, who were building the first Catholic Church in the country constructed exclusively for African-Americans, St. Monica's Catholic Church.

Tolton agreed, pastoring St. Monica's until his unexpected death from sunstroke in 1897. He was 43. His cause for canonization opened in 2011.

April 25: THE EXORCIST

In 1949, Georgetown University was abuzz with rumors. A local priest had attempted an exorcism at the university hospital, and all had not gone well.

William Peter Blatty, then a student at Georgetown, never forgot those rumors, and 20 years later turned them into the bestselling novel *The Exorcist.*

While the country raved about *The Exorcist,* however, one person remained silent: the priest who conducted the exorcism upon which the book was based.

That priest was Father William S. Bowdern, S.J.

In 1949, Bowdern was teaching at St. Louis University in St. Louis, when one of his fellow priests asked him to evaluate a 13-year-old boy who showed signs of demonic possession. The boy, "Roland Doe," had attempted to contact a deceased aunt through a Ouija board. After that, unexplainable events began occurring in Doe's home. Then, the boy himself began to change.

His parents took him to their Lutheran pastor. The pastor attempted an exorcism. When that didn't work, he suggested they call the Catholics. One priest tried, but was injured in the process. That's when Bowdern entered the picture.

Over the course of three weeks, Bowdern and two assistants witnessed beds levitating, Holy Water sizzling, and strange writing mysteriously appearing and disappearing on the boy's body. At times, the boy spoke in unknown tongues. He called himself "legion."

At long last, after three weeks of prayer and fasting, the rite concluded. There was a flash of light, a loud boom, and all signs of the demon disappeared. Nine priests and 39 others witnessed the events.

Years later, when Blatty came looking for help with his book, Bowdern politely declined: he had vowed to remain silent about the exorcism. He may have regretted that vow though by 1973, when he saw the movie. Incensed by the inaccuracies, Bowdern produced such a voluble stream of criticism during the film that the theater almost asked him to leave.

Bowdern passed away 10 years later, on **April 25, 1983**.

Born in Columbia, South Carolina, in 1928, Joseph Bernardin planned on a career in medicine until, as a freshman at the University of South Carolina, he heard God's call to the priesthood. He soon transferred to St. Mary's Seminary in Baltimore, completed his theological studies at The Catholic University of America, and was ordained to the priesthood on **April 26, 1952.**

Recognizing Bernardin's administrative abilities, his bishop soon recruited the young priest for his chancery staff. Father Bernardin then spent the next 14 years serving as chancellor, vicar-general, diocesan counselor, and diocesan administrator for the Diocese of Charleston. Then, at 38 years old, he became an auxiliary bishop for the Archdiocese of Atlanta. Two years later, in 1968, he moved on to the National Council of Catholic Bishops, where he served as general secretary for four years. After that, it was on to Cincinnati as archbishop, in 1972. Ten years later, Bernardin became archbishop of Chicago, and the following year received the red hat.

Through it all, Cardinal Bernardin's unmatched influence helped ensure that his vision for what the post–Vatican II Church should look like—from its toleration of dissent to its support for collegial episcopal governance—spread to other dioceses across the country.

Bernardin's most lasting legacy, however, may be his "seamless garment" metaphor that he popularized while archbishop of Chicago. Arguing that Catholics must approach questions of abortion, euthanasia, capital punishment, and poverty with a "consistent ethic of life," the cardinal's metaphor articulated a core truth of Catholic social teaching: that every human life, from conception until natural death, is sacred and should be treated as such.

Unfortunately (and against the cardinal's protestations), others used the metaphor to relativize the evil of abortion, excusing their support for abortion by noting their support for anti-poverty legislation or their opposition to nuclear war.

After fighting a courageous year-long battle against pancreatic cancer, Bernardin died in 1996.

April 27: A PLEA FOR RELIGIOUS FREEDOM

In 1819, the province of Maine, long a part of Massachusetts, was about to become a state. But first, it needed a constitution.

After assembling in Portland, delegates to the state's constitutional convention drew up a document. They modeled it on the Bay State's constitution and, in an early draft, included the Massachusetts prohibition against Catholics holding public office.

Before the constitution passed out of committee, however, a delegate—one Major Dickey—received an anonymous letter. The letter eloquently made the case for religious freedom, and so impressed Dickey that he read it before the committee. The committee, equally impressed, struck the anti-Catholic language out of the constitution.

Years later, the identity of the anonymous letter writer was discovered when the original draft was found in the private papers of Edward Kavanagh, the first Catholic congressman from New England and Maine's seventeenth governor.

Born on **April 27, 1795,** Kavanagh was the son of Maine's most prominent shipping merchant and a Catholic from birth, who grew up surrounded by missionary priests. Those priests—including Father Jean-Louis de Cheverus, the future first bishop of Boston—used his family's house as their home base while ministering to Maine's far-flung Catholic population.

Kavanagh left home while still a boy to study at Georgetown College and St. Mary's College, and then completed his studies in Europe. When he returned to Maine, he set up a successful law practice and helped his father rescue the family business from bankruptcy.

Not long after his anonymous letter swayed Maine's constitutional convention, Kavanagh began his political career. In 20 years' time, despite rabid anti-Catholicism in New England, he rose from a school committeeman to a state representative and senator, secretary of state for Maine, a two-term U.S. congressman, foreign minister to Portugal, and at last, from 1843 to 1844, governor of Maine.

In 1844, Kavanagh retired from public life. He died less than four weeks later.

In 1728, William Elder, his wife Ann, and a handful of other Catholic families left their home in St. Mary's City, Maryland, and moved west. Like so many other Catholics at the time, they were looking for a new home, a place where they could openly (albeit not legally) practice their Catholic faith.

They found that home near a mountain, and they named it St. Mary's. They built a church, and the little community flourished. By 1793, it had become part of a town, Emmitsburg, with two parishes, St. Mary's and St. Joseph's.

That year, Father John Dubois arrived in nearby Frederick, Maryland, and served as pastor to both parishes. The future bishop of New York had recently come to America from France, where if not for the help of his friend the Marquis de Lafayette, he would have died at the hands of anti-clerical revolutionaries. After his arrival, the priest set about uniting the two parishes and planning for a school.

According to local Emmitsburg records, Dubois purchased the land for what would eventually become Mount St. Mary's Seminary and University, on **April 28, 1807**. Two years later, the school merged with Pigeon Hill Seminary, and a long-tradition of educating future priests began.

Around the same time, Dubois welcomed Mother Elizabeth Seton and her Daughters of Charity to Emmitsburg. The sisters lived in his home while their own house was readied, and every Sunday, for much of the remainder of Mother Seton's life, they traveled to the small mountain church for Mass.

In the centuries that followed, Mount St. Mary's came to be known as "the Cradle of Bishops," with more than 51 future prelates graduating from the school, including some of the giants of the early Church in America such as Archbishop John Hughes of New York; America's first cardinal, Archbishop John McCloskey; and William Quarter, the first bishop of Chicago.

Today, more than 160 men study for the priesthood at the seminary, while an additional 2,000 undergraduate and graduate students are enrolled in Mount St. Mary's University.

Alfred Hitchcock spent the better part of his life focused on death, and yet it took his own impending death to bring his life into focus.

Born in England in 1899 to Catholic parents, Hitchcock went to Mass at the parish pastored by his cousin. He received a Catholic education (thanks to the Salesians and Jesuits), and then began a career as a draftsman.

While working in advertising by day, Hitchcock dabbled in the mysterious and macabre, first writing stories for British magazines, but soon moving into the fledgling motion picture industry. Within five years, he was directing. Within five more, he'd become one of Britain's most popular filmmakers. Along the way, he married writer and editor Alma Reville, who converted to Catholicism upon their marriage.

With Alma as his partner at work and home (which after 1940 was California), Hitchcock established himself as one of the most influential directors of all time. He was a pioneer in cinematic storytelling who made an art out of mystery and suspense.

Through it all, the Catholicism of his youth crept into those stories, with religious imagery and themes both subtly and not so subtly woven into his greatest films: *I Confess, Vertigo, Rear Window, North by Northwest, Strangers on a Train, The Birds,* and more.

Despite that intermingling of religion and art, Hitchcock's own understanding of the Faith was riddled with doubt. He fell away from the Church after the Second Vatican Council and once turned down an audience with the pope. (He said he feared he'd be advised to include less sex and violence in his films.)

In the last months of his life, however, the rift between Hitchcock and the Church healed, and two Jesuits called at his home every Saturday to hear his Confession and offer Mass. As one of those priests later recalled, Hitchcock quietly said his responses in Latin, and cried after he received the Eucharist.

Hitchcock died on **April 29, 1980**. His funeral Mass took place at Good Shepherd Catholic Church in Beverly Hills.

They called it the "Ironclad Oath," for there was no getting around it.

Devised during the American Civil War to guarantee all public servants' loyalty to the Union, the ironclad oath was expanded by the U.S. Congress after the war to prevent former Confederate soldiers and sympathizers from voting or holding public office.

The state of Missouri, however, made their ironclad oath even stricter, writing a post-Civil War constitution that required the oath to apply to teachers, ministers, and lawyers, as well as public servants.

When St. Louis' Archbishop Peter Kenrick learned of the oath, he ordered his priests not to take it. Missouri had sided with the Confederacy during the Civil War, and there was hardly a priest in his diocese who hadn't fed or housed soldiers, prayed with troops, helped families affected by the war, or aided the wounded. Most couldn't take the oath honestly, which meant they also wouldn't be able to legally carry out their priestly duties.

Kenrick's priests obeyed their bishop. Some went to prison for refusing to take the oath. But the Irish-born bishop would not back down. After all, he'd faced greater challenges before.

When Kenrick was ordained as the diocese's coadjutor bishop on **April 30, 1841,** and assumed full responsibility for it shortly thereafter, he inherited a diocese roughly the size of the Louisiana Purchase and laden with debt. Yet he rose to the challenge, transforming St. Louis from a frontier diocese into a major metropolitan see. He also saved the diocese from bankruptcy with shrewd real estate investments made with his personal savings. By 1865, he reasoned that if he could handle angry creditors, he could handle the Missouri government.

Which he did, fighting the oath straight to the U.S. Supreme Court. After two years of legal wrangling, in 1867's *Cummings v. State of Missouri,* the Court sided with the Church, striking down Missouri's provisions regarding ministers and teachers.

Kenrick outlasted the ironclad oath by almost 30 years, dying in St. Louis in 1896.

May

May 1: THE CATHOLIC WORKER

On a December afternoon in 1932, a slightly disheveled vagabond knocked on a young Catholic journalist's door. The vagabond was Peter Maurin, a French immigrant who dreamed of political and social reform. The journalist was Dorothy Day, a convert to Catholicism who couldn't understand why her fellow Catholics weren't more concerned with the plight of the hungry and the jobless.

Before that afternoon, Maurin and Day had never met. The Frenchman was looking for someone who could work with him to bring justice to the poor—a justice grounded in the Gospel and illuminated by Catholic Social Teaching. A mutual acquaintance—*Commonweal*'s editor George Schuster—told Maurin that Day might fit the bill. So, Maurin came knocking.

Schuster was right.

Five months later, on **May 1, 1933,** the world celebrated International Workers' Day and the *The Catholic Worker* went to press. Sold for only a penny an issue, the newspaper sought to educate ordinary workingmen about the social doctrines of the Catholic Church. In that, it hoped to help those most susceptible to Communism's appeal realize that another, better alternative existed.

Within a few months, with Day as its editor, *The Catholic Worker*'s circulation reached 25,000. By 1936, that number had risen to 150,000.

As the newspaper's reach spread, so did its influence and impact. From it sprang an entire movement dedicated to helping the poor and marginalized, a movement whose work ranged from running homes for the dispossessed to operating farms that practiced sustainable methods of agriculture.

Maurin died in 1949. Day passed away 31 years later. But the Catholic Worker Movement they founded and the paper that started it all (still sold for only a penny an issue), endures to this day, proclaiming the Church's social gospel through word and deed.

Years before Hitler rose to power with talk of a "Master Race," early twentieth-century America fell prey to its own eugenics craze. Championed by the likes of Harry Laughlin and Charles Davenport, many of the country's elites started advocating for the forced sterilization of its weakest members, especially the handicapped, believing strict birth control policies held the key to a better tomorrow.

Towards that end, the Commonwealth of Virginia adopted legislation in 1924 that permitted the sterilization of the "intellectually disabled." They based the statute on Laughlin's "model eugenics law," which he designed to withstand constitutional challenges (and which later served as the template for the Third Reich's eugenics laws).

Almost immediately, a state mental institution put the legislation into practice on 18-year-old Carrie Buck. The institution's board claimed that Buck was a promiscuous "imbecile." In truth, Buck had been raped by her foster cousin, become pregnant, and was institutionalized to keep the rape secret.

After her sterilization, the Commonwealth of Virginia challenged the procedure in court—not because it objected, but rather to test the legislation's strength. Because of the collusive nature of the case (including the fact that Buck's lawyer sat on the institution's board), the truth about Buck's situation remained secret.

In 1927, when *Buck v. Bell* reached the Supreme Court, Justice Oliver Wendell Holmes, Jr., supported the Virginia statute, writing, "It is better for all the world, if instead of waiting to execute degenerate offspring for crime, or to let them starve for their imbecility, society can prevent those who are manifestly unfit from continuing their kind."

Seven justices sided with Holmes in his **May 2, 1927,** decision. Only one, Pierce Butler, a Catholic from Minnesota, who sat on the court between 1923 and 1939, dissented. Butler wrote no opinion explaining his vote (which was common then), but his Catholicism was widely "blamed."

Before issuing the decision, Holmes wrote, "I wonder whether [Butler] will have the courage to vote with us in spite of his religion."

To Butler's credit, he had a different kind of courage.

May 3: THE CATHOLIC CROONER

When *Going My Way* was released on its star's 41st birthday, **May 3, 1944,** it gave Bing Crosby one of his biggest box office hits. It also gave him his lone Oscar, winning seven Academy Awards, including Best Actor, the following year.

The film was the perfect vehicle for Crosby, offering him five songs that showcased his legendary bass-baritone voice. Moreover, Crosby's role—a young Irish priest charged with taking the reins of a New York City parish from its aging pastor—solidified the actor's reputation as one of Hollywood's most devout Catholics.

Crosby certainly wasn't a perfect Catholic, but he was serious about his faith, and he lived it more intentionally than many in Hollywood. When he married, he stayed married. He lost his first wife to ovarian cancer in 1952, and his second marriage lasted until his death in 1977. Crosby also gladly welcomed children into the world—seven in total—and raised them in the Church.

Crosby himself was one of seven children and attended the Jesuit Gonzaga University before deciding his future lay in music.

And what a future it was.

As a singer, Crosby put 383 songs onto the charts, including 41 number one hits. His 1942 single, "White Christmas," remains the best-selling single of all time. As an actor, he proved equally successful. For 15 years, he was one of the top 10 box office draws in the country, and for five of those years, he ranked number one.

Crosby was as active behind the camera as he was in front of it, pioneering new techniques in recording and broadcasting. He also was a devoted baseball fan (co-owning the Pittsburgh Pirates from 1946 until his death) and an avid golfer.

It was actually on a golf course in Madrid, Spain, that Crosby died in October 1977. He left strict instructions for his funeral—a low Mass, closed to the public—and he was buried in Holy Cross Cemetery in Los Angeles.

May 4: THE WOMAN

In 1944, the Reverend Fulton J. Sheen received a phone call. On the other end was Connecticut's Congresswoman Clare Boothe Luce.

The Honorable Mrs. Luce, who'd recently lost her only child in a car accident, got right to the point.

"Listen, if God is good, why did he take my daughter?"

"In order that you might be here in the faith," Sheen replied.

Luce didn't like his answer, but she liked Sheen. So, they talked some more . . . and some more, arguing their way through the next two years, until, in 1946, Luce entered the Catholic Church.

Her conversion surprised almost everyone. Luce, after all, wasn't just a congresswoman. In her 41 years, she'd also been a suffragette, millionaire's wife, playwright, journalist, and *Vanity Fair* editor. Her acerbic wit—which gave life to her most famous play, *The Women,* as well as her oft-quoted speeches in Congress—was legendary. It's to Luce the world owes such lines as "No good deed goes unpunished," and "Widowhood is a fringe benefit of marriage."

Luce, however, had known her share of suffering too. Ashamed of her illegitimate birth, she married for money at age 20, only to leave her abusive, alcoholic husband six years later. Despite her relatively happy second marriage to *Time* and *Life* publisher Henry Luce, losing her daughter almost broke her.

In the Church, however, Luce found peace.

After Luce's conversion, one friend noted the change, saying, "Twenty years ago she was like a diamond—beautiful, brilliant and cold. Now she is beautiful, brilliant and compassionate. She has become a kind and remarkably unselfish woman."

Luce retired from Congress in 1946, but returned to political life on **May 4, 1953,** when she became ambassador to Italy under President Dwight Eisenhower. She later served (for four days) as ambassador to Brazil and on the President's Foreign Intelligence Advisory Board under Presidents Richard Nixon and Ronald Reagan.

After her death in 1987, she was laid to rest at the plantation she and her husband gave to the Trappist community years before, South Carolina's Mepkin Abbey.

May 5: CINCO DE MAYO

On **May 5, 1862,** the armies of Mexico and France reenacted the battle of David and Goliath.

France, the number one military power of the day, had sent troops to Mexico the previous year to collect its unpaid debts. When the American Civil War broke out, the country's leader, Napoleon III, decided to leave his troops in Mexico, thinking perhaps the time had come to get back into the North American real estate game.

The events of the fifth of May, however, almost (but not quite) gave him pause. On that day, in the Battle of Puebla, an outmanned and outgunned Mexican Army defeated the far superior French forces. Tactically, the victory meant little. Symbolically, it was a different story. Just four days later, Mexico's president declared the anniversary of the battle an annual national holiday.

Americans of Mexican descent living in California joined in on the celebrations almost as soon as they began. From 1863 onward, *Cinco de Mayo* became an unofficial holiday in the state. In the 1940s, as the Mexican-American population moved northward and westward, so did celebrations of *Cinco de Mayo*. By 2006, more than 150 different cities across the United States hosted official *Cinco de Mayo* celebrations, while countless more hosted unofficial ones.

Many of those unofficial celebrations take place every year in America's Catholic parishes. Latinos now comprise more than 35 percent of U.S. Catholics, while 20 percent of U.S. parishes (and 80 percent of U.S. dioceses) have Latino ministries. With more than 50 percent of Catholics in America under the age of 25 coming from a Hispanic background, those numbers continue to grow.

Although no one knows how such changing demographics will affect the culture of the Catholic Church within the United States, one thing is for certain: more and more Catholics in the coming years will likely find themselves commemorating the long ago victory of the small Mexican Army every fifth of May.

From the start, the young John McCloskey knew getting to Sunday Mass was important. It was important enough to rise before dawn, important enough to walk along the dirt roads of Brooklyn with his parents, and important enough to row across the East River, where the nearest Catholic parish, St. Peter's, waited on the other side.

Perhaps because of what his family went through every Sunday to get to Mass, by the age of 11 McCloskey knew how he wanted to spend his life: offering Mass as a Catholic priest.

That year, 1821, McCloskey left his family and entered minor seminary at Mount St. Mary's College in Emmitsburg. At 23, he was ordained a priest for the Diocese of New York, and at 34, after studying in Rome and pastoring a parish in Greenwich Village, he was consecrated as coadjutor bishop of New York.

Three years later, McCloskey became the first bishop of Albany. There, he established nine religious orders, 19 schools, four orphanages, and nearly 100 parishes, all before **May 6, 1864,** when Rome called the energetic prelate home to become New York's next archbishop.

Back in his native city, McCloskey's energy seemed inexhaustible as he completed the building of St. Patrick's Cathedral, attended the First Vatican Council, established 88 parishes, tripled the number of priests in the archdiocese, founded a hospital for the mentally ill, and helped enroll more than 37,000 children in parochial schools.

Revered for his gentleness, intelligence, and piety (as well as his energy), Catholics across America celebrated, when in April 1875, Archbishop Bayley of Baltimore (who himself had converted to Catholicism through McCloskey's friendship) placed the red biretta on the prelate's head.

That day, America's first cardinal told the gathered crowds, "Not to my poor merits but to those of the young and already vigorous and most flourishing Catholic Church of America has this honor been given by the Supreme Pontiff."

Cardinal McCloskey shepherded New York for 10 years more, dying from fever in October 1885.

May 7: THE FLYING MONK

On **May 7, 1945,** German General Alfred Jodl's unconditional surrender of Nazi forces brought an end to seven long years of fighting in Europe.

For the Allied nations, the day was an occasion for rejoicing. For a small group of American airmen, it was also an occasion to investigate the odd happenings at San Giovanni Rotondo.

Beginning in 1944, the airmen's squadron had repeatedly attempted to bomb the Italian city, where a large cache of German supplies were allegedly stockpiled. But on every bombing run, something went wrong—their planes refused to release the bombs, or their targeting equipment malfunctioned and the bombs hit the nearby forest instead. For the problems, the airmen blamed one person: the flying monk.

"The flying monk" was the name the airmen gave to the mysterious bearded figure who appeared in the sky every time they flew near San Giovanni Rotondo. Sometimes, they just saw his face in the clouds. Other times, the monk appeared as if he were standing in the sky. Usually his arms were raised, like he was issuing a warning . . . or granting a blessing.

Either way, dozens of American airmen and at least one commanding officer saw the monk, and as soon as the war in the European theater ended, they headed back to the scene of the events, wanting to know if the monk was who some believed him to be: the holy Capuchin friar of the city's Our Lady of Grace Monastery, Padre Pio.

Sure enough, when the men arrived, they recognized the future saint as their flying monk. As one witness present at the meeting recalled, Padre Pio greeted the airmen with a friendly, "So you are the ones who wanted to kill us all!"

After his greeting, the Americans knelt and received his blessing. At least one conversion is said to have come from the encounter, perhaps more. Regardless, when they returned to America, the San Giovanni Rotondo they left behind was a city whole and intact . . . all thanks to the flying monk.

Hernando de Soto wasn't what you'd call a "good Catholic."

Unlike some Catholic-born explorers of his age, he didn't come to the New World seeking to spread the Gospel. Instead, de Soto sought fame and fortune. And he attained both—but at a heavy price.

As a young man, de Soto served as a soldier in the conquest of Central America. Ruthless in battle and merciless in victory, de Soto was no kinder once the fighting stopped. In peace, he made a fortune in the Native American slave trade, then used that fortune to finance a military expedition to Peru.

For his loyal service, King Charles V of Spain rewarded de Soto with the governorship of Cuba and another commission. He was to sail to the American mainland and colonize it within four years.

Believing he'd find a land rich with gold, de Soto accepted, and in May 1539, landed in Florida with more than 600 men, 200 horses, 200 pigs, and a boatload of heavy armor.

From there, de Soto and his men traveled as far north as present-day North Carolina, enslaving Native Americans along the way. The party then headed east through Tennessee, Georgia, Alabama, and Mississippi. Everywhere he went, de Soto attempted to intimidate the natives into submission by telling them he was a sun god. Sometimes it worked.

On **May 8, 1541,** de Soto reached the Mississippi River. He named it, "River of the Holy Spirit." Once the river was crossed, the party passed through Arkansas and Texas, going as far as Oklahoma before turning back. No gold had been discovered, and with so many hostile bands of natives, colonization struck de Soto as too difficult.

De Soto never had to explain his decision to the king though. On the return trip to Florida, de Soto contracted a fever and died on the Mississippi's banks. His men, hoping to keep the "de Soto is a god" myth alive, hid his death from the natives and buried his body in an unknown location. They then left in defeat.

May 9: CATHOLICISM IN AMERICA

When the French statesman Alexis de Tocqueville arrived in the United States on **May 9, 1831,** his mission was to examine the American penitentiary system on behalf of the French government. He did that and more, eventually writing a detailed account of his travels through America and his observations of the fledgling nation.

Published in two volumes (in 1835 and 1840) as *Democracy in America,* de Tocqueville's account touches on nearly every aspect of early American life, from economics and politics to religion and the slave trade. It also includes the devout Catholic's thoughts on how his Church was faring in the United States.

In words that offer insight even today, he wrote:

> *America is the most democratic country in the world, and it is at the same time . . . the country in which the Roman Catholic religion makes most progress. At first sight this is surprising.*
>
> *Two things must here be accurately distinguished: equality makes men want to form their own opinions; but, on the other hand, it imbues them with the taste and the idea of unity, simplicity, and impartiality in the power that governs society. Men living in democratic times are therefore very prone to shake off all religious authority; but if they consent to subject themselves to any authority of this kind, they choose at least that it should be single and uniform. . . .*
>
> *At the present time, more than in any preceding age, Roman Catholics are seen to lapse into infidelity, and Protestants to be converted to Roman Catholicism. If you consider Catholicism within its own organization, it seems to be losing; if you consider it from outside, it seems to be gaining. Nor is this difficult to explain. The men of our days are naturally little disposed to believe; but as soon as they have any religion, they immediately find in themselves a latent instinct that urges them unconsciously towards Catholicism. Many of the doctrines and practices of the Roman Catholic Church astonish them, but they feel a secret admiration for its discipline, and its great unity attracts them.*

May 10: THE BIG PRIEST

Father John George Alleman was a giant of a man. Standing well over six feet tall, the broad-shouldered, powerfully built priest seemed ready-made for the American frontier. And for a while, he was.

Born in France in 1804, Alleman came to Ohio in 1832 to complete his formation with the Dominicans. He was ordained in 1834, but just six years later he left the Dominicans for the newly established Diocese of Dubuque.

From his new base in Fort Madison, Iowa, Alleman traveled throughout the Mississippi River Valley, at times by steamboat (the captains granted him free passage), and at other times by foot (legend has it that his gait matched that of any horse's). Between 1841 and 1851, Alleman established over a dozen missions in southeastern Iowa, personally chopping and hewing much of the wood for the churches himself. He also made friends with the Sac and Fox Tribe (who called him "The Big Priest") and the Mormons who lived in nearby Nauvoo, Illinois.

In 1851, with the Church in Iowa flourishing, Alleman left for Rock Island, Illinois. He arrived in the Mississippi River town around **May 10, 1851,** and by August had laid the cornerstone for St. James Catholic Church (now St. Mary's). In Rock Island and the surrounding villages, German and Irish Catholics came to love their generous, gregarious, gardening pastor. He established more parishes, built schools, dined in their homes, and planted flowers in their streets. Always, he wore the same torn cassock. When parishioners gave him money to buy a new one, he just spent it on clothes for local children.

In 1862, however, Alleman took to his bed and refused all visitors. His friends believed that years of constant work and travel had proven too much, even for his strong body. Perhaps. Regardless, a year later, Alleman left Rock Island for St. Vincent's Hospital in St. Louis. There, in 1865, he passed away from what doctors called "melancholia." Far from friends, Alleman was buried in an unmarked grave.

In May 1844, anti-Catholic mobs rioted in the streets of Philadelphia and the city's Catholic churches burned. Yet Bishop Francis Kenrick ordered his flock to stand down. They were not to respond to violence with violence, he explained, adding that it would be better for all the churches to burn to the ground than for Catholics to shed their fellow man's blood.

It was a noble gesture, but New York's Bishop John Hughes was having none of it.

On **May 11, 1844,** a few days after the Philadelphia riots, anti-Catholic Nativists from the City of Brotherly Love threatened to come north and join with Nativist forces in New York for another round of rioting. Upon hearing the news, Hughes called upon the city's Catholic men to take up arms and surround their parishes.

He then issued a warning to the city's Nativist-sympathizing mayor. Evoking the French invasion of Russia in 1812, in which Russians set Moscow on fire rather than see it fall to the French, Hughes declared that "if a single Catholic church were burned in New York, the city would become another Moscow."

The mayor took the bishop's warning to heart and convinced the Nativists to back off.

Hughes later gloated, "There is not a [Catholic] church in the city, which was not protected with an average force of one to two thousand men—cool, collected, armed to the teeth—and with a firm determination, after taking as many lives as they could in defense of their property, to give up, if necessary, their own lives for the same cause."

While historians dispute the "one to two thousand men" claim, Hughes' strategy proved effective. Not a church was burned or a person injured by the Nativists in New York that year.

On the other hand, adherents to the Gospel injunction to "turn the other cheek," did perhaps suffer a heart palpitation or two.

At 20, Perry Como had all he wanted in life: a beautiful girl to marry, a successful barbershop that brought in $125 a week, and his Catholic faith.

Accordingly, in 1932, when the Freddy Carlone Orchestra offered Como a job as one of their lead singers, the Canonsburg, Pennsylvania, native refused. As Como saw it, he had a good thing going with his barbershop, and singing couldn't support a family nearly so well. Only after the girl convinced him that the barbershop would always be there, did Como accept the offer, both marrying the girl and joining the orchestra in 1933.

Seven years passed while Como's fame grew. But by 1940, after he and his wife finally succeeded in having a child, Como knew he wanted more for his young family than constant touring. Soon after, he quit the orchestra and moved back to Canonsburg. Como was working on purchasing a new barbershop there, when a call from New York came. It was CBS Radio, offering him his own show.

Como again refused . . . and was again talked into it by his wife. Together, they moved to New York. Five years later, Como left radio for television. And there he stayed, first with CBS, then with NBC, until 1967.

Despite his success, Como continued to live like the barber he always wanted to be. He was a faithful husband, loving father, and devout Catholic who gave a substantial portion of his earnings to the Church (garnering both him and his wife admission to the Equestrian Order of the Holy Sepulchre of Jerusalem). Fame somehow never managed to change Como—a minor miracle that only added to his popular appeal.

In 1994, Como gave the last concert of his career in Dublin, Ireland. During his stay, he stopped by the Irish barbershop named in his honor—The Como.

He never did get another barbershop of his own though. Soon after his retirement, Como began showing signs of Alzheimer's disease, and died nine years later on **May 12, 2001.**

Gary Cooper was a man who married well. In the end, that made all the difference.

Born in 1901 to British parents, Cooper spent his childhood on the family's ranch in Montana and his adolescence at a boarding school in England. When his parents moved to Los Angeles in 1924, he followed and soon found work in the motion picture industry. Within five years, he was a star.

Over the next three decades, the three-time Academy Award–winning actor moved from hit to hit—*A Farewell to Arms* (1932), *Mr. Deeds Goes to Town* (1936), *Sergeant York* (1941), *Meet John Doe* (1941), *High Noon* (1952), and many more—appearing in nearly 100 films during his 36-year career.

Unfortunately, Cooper also moved from woman to woman, with his leading ladies routinely falling in love with him and Cooper falling back. Even after his 1933 marriage to the Catholic socialite, Veronica "Rocky" Balfe, the love affairs continued, almost without pause.

Rocky, however, bore her husband's wandering eye with patience, always forgiving, always taking him back, and always praying for a change.

Those prayers were answered in the late 1950s, when Cooper became friends with his wife's tough-talking, outdoor-loving parish priest (dubbed "Father Tough Stuff" by Cooper). As their friendship grew, so did Cooper's interest in the Faith, and in 1959, "Father Tough Stuff" received Cooper into the Catholic Church.

Cooper later explained his conversion, saying: "I'd spent all my waking hours, year after year, doing almost exactly what I, personally, wanted to do; and what I wanted to do wasn't always the most polite thing either . . . I'll never be anything like a saint . . . The only thing I can say for me is that I'm trying to be a little better. Maybe I'll succeed."

Cooper learned he had prostate cancer a year after his conversion. He bore the illness with grace, and, as he lay dying, told the world, "I know that what is happening is God's will. I am not afraid of the future."

Cooper passed away on **May 13, 1961**.

On **May 14, 1787,** Daniel Carroll was supposed to be in Philadelphia. The Constitutional Convention was set to begin there that day, and Maryland had elected him to serve as one of its delegates.

But Carroll wasn't there.

The older brother of future bishop John Carroll, Daniel studied in Europe with the Jesuits as a boy, and then returned home to run the family's plantation in Upper Marlboro, Maryland. The estate spanned thousands of acres and demanded his near constant attention.

Because of that estate, Carroll had only reluctantly supported the American Revolution. He favored independence, but also feared the economic consequences of a failed rebellion. Fortunately, his worst fears didn't come to pass, and as the Revolution drew to a close, Maryland sent its reluctant patriot to the Continental Congress. Carroll served there from 1781 to 1784, and during his first year in office, signed the Articles of Confederation.

In late April 1787, Carroll returned to political life when his state sent him to the Constitutional Convention. Before Carroll could leave for Philadelphia, however, he needed to get his affairs in order. Unfortunately, three weeks' notice proved insufficient, which accounted for Carroll's absence on May 14. He wasn't the only tardy delegate, though. So few men arrived in Philadelphia by May 14, that the Convention was delayed by almost two weeks.

When Carroll finally did make it to Philadelphia (in July) and signed the U.S. Constitution (in September), he was one of only two Catholics to do so. He was also one of only five men to sign both the Constitution and the Articles of Confederation.

After the convention, Carroll supported the presidential candidacy of his friend and business partner George Washington. Then, from 1789 to 1791, Carroll represented Maryland in the first U.S. Congress, and, in his last years, he oversaw the site planning for Washington, D.C., a city that was largely built on land that once belonged to Carroll. America's Catholic Founding Father died in 1796, at the age of 65.

May 15: THE CITY OF LITTLE MEN

In 1917, American men headed overseas to fight in World War I. As the migrant laborers who once filled a hostel in Omaha, Nebraska, left to join the fight, homeless drifters filled the hostel instead.

The man who welcomed the new occupants—the hostel's founder, Father Edward Flanagan—didn't understand the world of broken homes and broken promises from which the drifters hailed. His own idyllic childhood had been spent in Ireland, with parents and siblings who loved both him and the Church. In 1904, he came to the United States to join his brother, Father Patrick Flanagan, and eventually followed him into the priesthood. By 1913, he was serving in Omaha with his brother, dividing his time between pastoring a parish and working with the poor.

His life changed, however, after his conversations with the drifters. Flanagan decided he wanted to save troubled boys from following in their footsteps, and believed he could accomplish that with a little love.

In December 1917, Flanagan received his bishop's permission to take in five boys who were wards of the court. Soon, he took in more and moved the growing brood into a rundown Victorian mansion in downtown Omaha. When that grew too small, he bought a farm outside the city and started building Boys Town. Rooted in Flanagan's belief that, "There are no bad boys; there is only bad environment, bad training, bad example, bad thinking," Boys Town strove to give its young men the same experience of love, prayer, and family that Flanagan had in Ireland.

It succeeded. And by the time Spencer Tracy and Hollywood arrived in 1938 to make a movie about Boys Town, Father Flanagan's "City of Little Men" had become a national marvel.

Flanagan died on **May 15, 1948,** while helping the United States assess the problem of war orphans overseas. But his work continues in Boys Town programs in 10 states and Washington, D.C.

The cause for Father Flanagan's sainthood opened in 2012.

When Washington University in St. Louis announced its intention of granting an honorary degree to alumna Phyllis Schlafly, students and faculty alike went wild. But not in the good way.

Fourteen law professors wrote to the administration condemning her "anti-intellectualism," while students staged protests on campus. Then, the press joined in, with magazines such as *The Nation* condemning the university for honoring someone with Schlafly's controversially conservative views.

When the day of the ceremony arrived—**May 16, 2008**—it only got worse. As Schlafly stood up to accept the honorary Doctor of Humane Letters degree, one-third of the faculty and student body stood as well, turning their backs on her in silent protest. A sizable portion of the parents and friends in the 14,000-person crowd did the same.

In her 50-plus years of political activism, however, Schlafly had encountered worse.

Born into a prominent Catholic family in St. Louis, Missouri, Schlafly earned her B.A. and J.D. from Washington University and an M.A. in government from Radcliffe. Her involvement in politics began in the late 1940s, not long after her marriage. Not until the early 1970s, however, when Schlafly successfully led the crusade to defeat the Equal Rights Amendment (arguing that it would "dismantle social security benefits for dependents and open women to the draft"), did she become a walking political lightning rod.

Schlafly's strongly conservative views on the most controversial cultural and political issues of the day—feminism, abortion, same-sex marriage, arms control, and communism—made the mother of six no small number of enemies and friends around the country. Likewise, her effective issue-oriented political organizing through Eagle Forum (the group she founded in 1972), made her a force on Capitol Hill with whom few politicians, Democrats or Republicans, enjoyed reckoning.

For those reasons and more, Schlafly didn't bat an eyelash at the angry protestors on that day in May 2008. She just smiled politely, then returned to her seat, her honorary degree for a lifetime of debate-changing political activism in hand.

Dr. John McLoughlin's General Store was a site thousands of Americans once dreamed of seeing. To arrive at its doors was to arrive at the last stop on the Oregon Trail. McLoughlin, however, was more than just a general store owner in Oregon City.

Born in Quebec and baptized Catholic (but raised Anglican), McLoughlin worked for 11 years as the staff doctor at Fort William in Ontario, before the North West Fur Company, which ran the fort, made him a partner. Ten years later, in 1824, after North West merged with the Hudson's Bay Company (HBC), McLoughlin left Ontario to manage HBC's operations in the Pacific Northwest.

For the next two decades, McLoughlin exercised almost absolute authority over the land west of the Rockies, north of California, and south of Russian America. Friend to natives and pioneers alike, McLoughlin ran the fur trade, inaugurated the salmon and lumber trade, built the Northwest's first lumber mills, and constructed forts throughout the region, including Fort Vancouver.

When Americans began arriving via the Oregon Trail, he welcomed them too, setting up schools and assisting missionaries. Eventually, two of those missionaries—Father Francois Blanchet and Father Modeste Demers—brought McLoughlin back to the Faith of his baptism. Later, in 1847, Pope Gregory XVI thanked McLoughlin for assisting the missionaries by naming him a Knight of the Order of St. Gregory.

Although McLoughlin was arguably the lone reason no armed conflicts broke out between British and American settlers in the Oregon Territory, some resented his power. That resentment showed in 1850, when the Territory's legislature slipped a clause into the Oregon Donation Land Act, stripping McLoughlin of most of his personal land holdings. In 1857, McLoughlin died a financially broken man.

But in the end, he got his due. The Oregon legislature apologized in 1862 and restored the confiscated land to his children. Then, about one hundred years after his death, **on May 17, 1957,** the state officially conferred upon McLoughlin the title he'd more than earned: "Father of Oregon."

Some little boys dream of becoming explorers. Others dream of becoming priests. Father Jacques Marquette was one of the lucky few who grew up to become both.

Born in France in 1637, Marquette first pursued his dream of religious life, entering the Jesuits at 17. Twelve years later, in 1666, Marquette's Superiors sent the newly ordained priest across the Atlantic to evangelize the indigenous peoples of the Americas.

Within two years of his arrival in the Great Lakes region, Marquette fluently spoke six Native American languages. That endeared him to the local tribes and enabled Marquette to make quick work of founding missions in Sault Sainte Marie and LaPointe (in present-day Michigan and Wisconsin).

While serving at LaPointe, Marquette befriended members of the Illinois Tribe, who invited him to travel south along the great *Mesipi* (Mississippi River) and teach their people. Eager to take them up on the offer, Marquette informed his Superiors of both the request and the river.

Recognizing the importance of the river for spreading the Gospel (as well as the fur trade), the Jesuits agreed to a joint mission, allowing Marquette to join his fur trader friend, Louis Jolliet, and explore the river while also evangelizing the peoples they encountered.

In May 1673, with two canoes and five companions, the pair set out from Lake Michigan, went up through Green Bay, and found the rumored river near present-day Prairie du Chien, Wisconsin. For the next month, they traveled south along the Mississippi, befriending numerous tribes as they went.

By mid-July, they came within 435 miles of the Gulf of Mexico. There, however, they learned that Spanish explorers (who didn't care for the French) were close by. Wanting to avoid conflict, they turned around and rowed north.

Although Marquette hoped to return along the same route a second time, his priestly duties proved more perilous than his exploring. He fell ill while establishing a mission in Illinois the following winter. He died on **May 18, 1675.**

Some said it was hubris. Others called it destiny. Either way, on **May 19, 1848,** the U.S. Senate ratified the Treaty of Guadalupe Hidalgo, thereby ending the Mexican-American War, establishing new boundary lines between the United States and Mexico, and adding 525,000 square miles to the nation.

That square mileage was in addition to the 389,000 square miles added when the United States annexed the Republic of Texas three years earlier. The 1845 annexation of Texas had started the war between the United States and its southern neighbor. Mexico, which had never recognized Texas' independence, warned the United States that it would view annexation as an act of war. The United States ignored that warning, and in 1846, Mexican troops attacked. The war didn't last long. Americans controlled California and New Mexico within months, and American troops arrived in Mexico City by early 1847.

Negotiations over the borders and the sale of Mexican territory to America, however, proved more difficult. Not until February 1848 did President James K. Polk have a treaty in hand. The final treaty fixed the Texas/Mexico border at the Rio Grande River and resulted in the United States purchasing all or part of the present-day states of California, Arizona, New Mexico, Nevada, Utah, Colorado, and Wyoming.

The cost?

$15 million, plus $3.5 million in debt assumption.

At the time the treaty was signed, some 80,000 to 100,000 Catholic Mexicans lived in the purchased territory. The treaty offered them the choice of full U.S. citizenship or relocation to Mexico. Over 90 percent chose to become U.S. citizens.

The treaty, which had long-term implications for the geographic, cultural, and religious makeup of the United States, was made public on July 4, 1848.

In 1829, one archbishop and four bishops met in Baltimore for a little meeting—the First Provincial Council of Baltimore—about how to best govern their dioceses in the United States.

Fast forward 23 years and little meetings of the American bishops were no longer possible. The United States had grown exponentially between the 1830s and 1850s, and so had the Catholic Church. The time had come for the nation's first plenary council—a meeting of bishops from all the provinces within a given country.

Baltimore's Archbishop Francis Kenrick (older brother to St. Louis' Archbishop Peter Kenrick) asked the Vatican's permission to hold such a council. The Vatican granted it. And on May 9, 1852, the First Plenary Council of Baltimore convened. Those present included six archbishops, 35 bishops, and nine superiors of religious orders.

Over the course of two weeks, the prelates discussed a host of questions involving Church governance. When they concluded their discussions, on **May 20, 1852,** they issued 25 separate decrees.

Like the discussions themselves, most of those decrees were administrative: every diocese should have a chancellor; bishops should consult with their clergy; chanceries need to audit their parishes annually, etc. A few were hortatory: the Council Fathers pledged their allegiance to the Holy Father and solemnly swore to believe everything the Church believes. A few more were evangelical: all Catholics should pray for the conversion of non-Catholics.

Other decrees from the Council touched on the sacramental and juridical problems created by Catholics marrying non-Catholics (the Council Fathers strongly recommended against it), as well as education and handing on the Faith (every diocese should have a seminary; every parish should have a school).

With only minor changes and additions, Rome subsequently approved the Council's decrees, making them binding on all Catholics in the United States and her territories.

On **May 21, 1990,** television history was made. That night, the last episode of *Newhart* aired.

Later declared the best series finale of the twentieth century by *TV Guide,* the episode's now legendary closing scene featured Bob Newhart waking up in bed with his wife. Nothing unusual there. Save for the fact that the woman in the bed wasn't his TV wife from *Newhart,* Mary Frann. It was his TV wife from *The Bob Newhart Show,* Suzanne Pleshette.

The latter show had been off the air for 12 years, but Newhart recruited Pleshette to help him end his second hit sitcom in unforgettable style: The entire eight-season run of *Newhart* had been a dream . . . brought on by eating Japanese food before bed.

The episode was classic Bob Newhart: a confounded, stammering everyman taking everyone by surprise.

Born and raised in Chicago, the life-long Catholic attended Loyola University, tried and failed at a career in accounting, then turned to comedy in 1959. After a year of playing local clubs, the everyman routine took his debut comedy album, *The Button-Down Mind of Bob Newhart,* to the top of the charts for 38 straight weeks (a record at the time and for 30 years afterwards). The record also won the 1961 Grammy for Album of the Year.

Although Newhart never left the comedy club circuit, in 1972 he made his successful move to television, starring in four shows over the next 25 years (*The Bob Newhart Show, Newhart, Bob,* and *George and Leo*).

Along the way, he married, raised four children (who, like their father, attended Catholic grade school, high school, and college), and served on the Board of Trustees at Loyola University.

An active member of his parish in Beverly Hills (and brother to a Catholic religious sister), Newhart was once asked how his faith influenced his work. His reply?

"When I work, I work clean . . . I get more satisfaction from that than getting a cheap laugh." Judging by Newhart's enduring popularity, so do his audiences.

James Farl Powers wanted to write stories that "even God would like."

"I think it's possible to write something . . . that is worthy of God's attention," he explained. "Not as a soul seeking salvation, but just as entertainment for God."

That quest resulted in one of the mid-twentieth century's most acclaimed bodies of fiction. Flannery O'Connor described Powers as "one of the country's finest story writers," and his first novel, *Morte d'Urban,* beat out books by John Updike and Katherine Anne Porter to win the 1963 National Book Award.

A self-taught writer, Powers was born into a devout Catholic family in 1917 and was educated by Franciscans in high school, but never graduated from college. Instead, the Illinois native worked odd jobs, while honing his craft.

During World War II, the pacifist Powers spent 20 months in jail for refusing to fight. Professionally, the time was well spent. He met other artists and had ample time to write. Personally, it was challenging. In a **May 22, 1944,** letter he wrote, "There is a justice, hardly poetic, in the way I find myself tied up in destiny with millions of people when what I want most is to be separated from them."

Echoes of that sentiment run throughout Powers' work, which focused largely on Catholic priests struggling with their vocations. Neither saints nor devils, Powers' priests grapple equally with the demands of holiness and the trivialities of parish life. Those trivialities leave some spiritually bankrupt; others humbled.

After publishing his first short story collection in 1947, Powers wrote two novels and another 19 short stories. He also taught writing at Saint John's Abbey in Collegeville, Minnesota. His 42-year marriage to writer Betty Wahl ended with her 1988 death. Losing her tested Powers' faith, but didn't break it.

"I figure you have to make a bet," he said. "You can't go through this life and just be a spectator without ever laying it on the line. I'm betting on God to win, not to show."

Powers died in 1999.

Stories—by the early nineteenth century, that's all that remained of the early French Jesuits and their missions among the Iroquois. Some tribes hadn't seen the men they called "Black Robes" for more than a century. But they still told stories about the priests and the God they proclaimed.

In 1823, some of those Iroquois married into the Salish tribe and repeated the stories of the Black Robes to their new brothers. After eight years of listening to the stories, the Salish decided to look for a Black Robe who could come teach them about God.

Due to sickness and hostile tribes, it took four tries and seven years before a Salish delegation successfully made the trip from modern-day Wyoming to St. Louis. When they arrived, the Jesuits they found promised to send Father Pierre-Jean DeSmet back with them.

At the time, the Belgian-born DeSmet had just returned from establishing a mission for the Potawatomi Indians. Although DeSmet arrived in America in 1821, while still a seminarian, poor health and other responsibilities had limited his contact with Native Americans. From 1838 on, however, he devoted the entirety of his priestly ministry to serving them.

As for the Salish, in 1840 DeSmet found the tribe in present-day Wyoming. There, 1,600 Native Americans awaited him. Some had traveled nearly 800 miles to meet him. Within a month, he baptized two great chiefs and 350 others.

After establishing St. Mary's Mission in southern Montana, DeSmet entrusted its care to others. He then spent the next 33 years on the move—negotiating treaties for the federal government, crossing the Atlantic 16 times to raise money for Native American missions, and traversing more than 180,000 miles ministering to tribes spread across the West.

Through it all, however, St. Mary's Mission remained his favorite. And before his death, on **May 23, 1873,** he attempted to pay the Salish one last visit.

He found the mission abandoned, his friends dead, and their children the victims of a government perpetually unfaithful to its promises.

The bishops of the United States wanted a school, but not just any school. They wanted a research university, where both clergy and laity could pursue advanced studies in theology, philosophy, and other fields of knowledge that intersected with faith and morals.

The bishops discussed the idea for such a university at the Second Plenary Council of Baltimore in 1866. They approved the idea at the Third Plenary Council in 1884. In between Councils, supporters secured a generous donor willing to underwrite the endeavor and sought (then later obtained) Pope Leo XIII's blessing.

Once the bishops agreed to move ahead with the plan, they picked a location—Washington, D.C.—and a name—The Catholic University of America. They also picked the man to take charge of the university, appointing the bishop of Richmond, the Most Reverend John J. Keane, as the school's first rector.

Less than four years after the Council's decision, on **May 24, 1888,** the bishops gathered to lay the cornerstone for Catholic University's first building: Caldwell Hall. President Grover Cleveland, members of Congress, and members of the president's cabinet also turned out for the event, which took place not far from the Capitol, in the city's Brookland neighborhood.

Although the university's early decades weren't always the most financially stable (at one point, bad investments by its administration led the bishops to take up a nationwide collection for the school), Catholic University grew in other ways at a rapid pace. Before its first year was out, the university added a program in canon law. By 1904, it welcomed undergraduates.

The community around the university grew as well, with religious orders and institutions from across the nation acquiring property, building homes, and setting up their novitiate houses in the surrounding neighborhood. Between 1900 and 1940, more than 50 orders rented or owned property in the vicinity, earning the neighborhood the nickname, "Little Rome."

Today, more than 6,000 students—graduate and undergraduate—are enrolled in the school the bishops built.

When Stephen Badin entered seminary in his native France, he didn't know that revolution soon would come to his country and, along with it, a hatred for the Catholic Church. Nor did he know that in 1791, while still a seminarian, he would flee to America with two companions—the Fathers (and future bishops) Joseph Flaget and J. B. David. And he most certainly didn't know that on **May 25, 1793,** he would receive the Sacrament of Holy Orders from Bishop John Carroll, becoming the first priest ordained in the United States.

If he had known, perhaps he would have followed a different path. But, most likely not. For in the decades that followed, America's proto-priest served his adopted homeland faithfully and well.

First, Father Badin served it from a base in Kentucky, riding more than 100,000 miles in the 26 years he ministered to Catholics in the Northwest Territory. Then, for a short while, he served the Church in America from France, where he raised money for the American missions. Finally, he served it as vicar-general for the Diocese of Cincinnati. There, he grew old on horseback, regularly traveling as far north as Chicago to minister to Native Americans and European immigrants.

On one of those trips, Badin spotted 524 acres of land that he thought well suited for a mission. He paid $655 for the land, and built a small log chapel there, by the lake he named "St. Mary's." A few years later, when the Diocese of Vincennes was created, he sold it to the new bishop for $1. The bishop in turn sold it to the Holy Cross Fathers. There, they founded the University of Notre Dame.

Badin hung up his saddle in 1850, at age 82, and retired to the bishop's residence in Cincinnati. He died three years later. His remains, however, found their final resting place by St. Mary's Lake in a replica of the chapel Badin built there long ago.

It's never a good idea to get on a Puritan's bad side. Just ask the Jesuits, who, in 1647, found themselves evicted from the Massachusetts Bay Colony on penalty of death.

The Puritans, of course, had their reasons. They took matters of religion quite seriously, and as far as they were concerned, the Jesuits were a threat to the eternal salvation of everyone in their colony. The Catholic missionaries not only believed doctrines that the Puritans saw as heretical—such as the Real Presence—but they preached those doctrines well. The natives were converting to Catholicism at alarming rates, as were English men and women captured by the natives.

The Puritans also saw the Jesuits as a political threat. In the century after the Anglican Church separated from the Catholic Church, rumors of malicious "popish" plots to restore Catholicism ran rampant in England. Most Puritans believed that the Jesuits were dangerous emissaries of Rome and would stop at nothing to destroy the safe haven they'd built for themselves in the New World.

Lastly, the Jesuits in and around the Massachusetts Bay Colony were French. And the Puritans, like most Englishmen, were none too fond of the French.

Clearly something had to be done.

In late 1646, as they considered the problem, a French ship arrived in Boston's harbor with two priests on board. The colony's governor invited the priests to dine at his house. Surprisingly, the rioting in the streets was minimal. Nevertheless, it moved the people to action. On **May 26, 1647,** the Massachusetts Bay Colony voted to ban all Jesuits from Massachusetts. They also swore to summarily execute anyone who defied the ban.

Their ban proved successful. No Jesuit ever was summarily executed, but the Puritans did manage to keep their colony almost 100 percent Catholic-free until sometime in the mid-eighteenth century. Likewise, the practice of Catholicism (including attending or saying Mass) remained illegal in Massachusetts as late as 1772, and not a single priest permanently settled there until after the American Revolution.

In February 1776, Father John Carroll received a letter from his cousin, Charles Carroll.

The Continental Congress had commissioned Charles Carroll to travel north to Quebec, along with Benjamin Franklin and Samuel Chase, in an attempt to secure Canadian support for the American Revolution. Carroll thought their mission to the largely Catholic country might benefit from having a priest along, so he invited Father Carroll to accompany them.

Father Carroll consented, albeit reluctantly, writing, "I have observed that when the ministers of religion leave the duties of their profession to take a busy part in political matters, they generally fall into contempt and sometimes even bring discredit to the cause in whose service they are engaged."

The priest also knew that the Canadians would never support their cause. In the years leading up to the American Revolution, anti-Catholic prejudices ran high in the American colonies, and Great Britain's 1774 decision to grant Canadian Catholics religious freedom only made matters worse. Since then, every town hall and colonial assembly in America—including the Continental Congress— had been denouncing the British Crown and Canadian Parliament as popish heretics.

Now that same Continental Congress wanted Father Carroll to convince Canadian Catholics that they had nothing to fear from America?

It wasn't going to happen.

The mission was over in a month, a disaster from first to last. Then, on the way home, Franklin fell ill, and the party split: Charles Carroll and Chase continued on to Philadelphia, while Father Carroll stayed with Franklin, nursing him back to health.

Franklin expressed his gratitude for that in a letter dated **May 27, 1776,** writing, "I could hardly have got so far but for Mr. Carroll's friendly assistance and tender care of me."

He expressed the same gratitude seven years later when the Papal Nuncio consulted Franklin (then serving as America's ambassador in Paris) about the matter of appointing America's first bishop. Franklin, without hesitation, endorsed his friend John Carroll, helping ensure Carroll's appointment and bring about perhaps the only good thing to come of the otherwise ill-fated Canadian mission.

Jim Thorpe had never run a competitive race in his life. Nor had he participated in any other track and field events. But that didn't stop him from attempting the high jump one afternoon in 1907 and beating everyone on his school's team.

Thorpe jumped on a whim. He was walking past the team as they practiced and thought he could do better. When he proved himself right, the team's coach, Glenn "Pop" Warner, recruited him on the spot. Soon, Warner also recruited Thorpe for just about every other sports team at Carlisle Indian Industrial School in Carlisle, Pennsylvania.

Thorpe, who was born on **May 28, 1888,** to Catholic parents of mixed European and Native American ancestry, excelled at every sport he tried. Years later, his old football rival President Dwight Eisenhower said of Thorpe, "He never practiced in his life, and he could do anything better than any other football player I ever saw."

That didn't just apply to football. At the 1912 Olympics, Thorpe received the gold medal in both the pentathlon and decathlon. Prior to his Olympic trials, he'd never competed in over half the individual events of which the pentathlon and decathlon comprised.

After the Olympics, Thorpe turned pro and spent the next 20 years playing football, baseball, and basketball. He also married three times and divorced twice.

With the Great Depression came Thorpe's retirement from professional athletics, and then his second divorce. Outside of the arena, Thorpe was less adept, and for the rest of his life bounced between jobs, always broke, and drinking heavily.

Jim Thorpe died in 1953. Despite his checkered past, he received a Catholic funeral and was buried in Jim Thorpe, Pennsylvania (a town renamed in his honor). Near his tomb stands a memorial bearing the words allegedly spoken to him by King Gustav of Sweden at the 1912 Olympics, "You sir, are the greatest athlete in the world."

On **May 29, 2004,** Father Henry Timothy (Tim) Vakoc celebrated the twelfth anniversary of his ordination to the priesthood. Had Vakoc been at home that day, he might have marked the occasion by going out to dinner or enjoying cake with the parish staff. But Vakoc wasn't at home. He was in northern Iraq, serving as chaplain for the 44th Corps Support Battalion.

In his eight years as a military chaplain, the Minnesota native had traveled with American troops to Germany, Bosnia, and Korea. By May 2004, he'd served in Iraq for six months. Despite the danger, he dismissed his family's concerns, explaining to his sister, "The safest place for me to be is in the center of God's will, and if that is in the line of fire, that is where I will be."

And so, instead of eating cake to celebrate his 12 years as a priest, Vakoc celebrated by leaving the safety of his base to say Mass for a group of soldiers serving in the field.

The drive out that morning was uneventful. But on the return journey, the Humvee in which Vakoc and his two military escorts traveled struck a roadside bomb. The two soldiers were fine. The priest was not.

Vakoc's companions knew they couldn't wait for medical assistance. They administered first aid, then drove back to the base on two flat tires. From there, Vakoc was airlifted to Baghdad, then Germany, before returning to the United States.

For six months, Vakoc lay in a coma, his brain badly damaged. Once he awoke, he could only communicate with the help of a computer. Yet all who visited him in the years he lay immobilized in a hospital bed, say that he bore his cross with humor, patience, and grace.

Awarded the Purple Heart and the Bronze Star for his service, Father Vakoc died of complications from his injury in 2009. He was the only military chaplain to give his life in Operation Iraqi Freedom.

Mark Twain—born Samuel Clemens—loved little about Christianity. He loved even less about the Catholic Church. He didn't like her priests. He didn't like her sacraments. And he didn't like her scriptures.

"It's ain't those parts of the Bible that I don't understand that bother me; it is the parts that I do understand," he once quipped.

Yet, for all that Mark Twain disliked about the Church, there was one Catholic he loved: Saint Joan of Arc.

As Twain tells it, he first came across an account of the warrior-maiden's martyrdom as a teenager. He then spent the next three decades dreaming of writing a book about her, and another decade researching her life. That research included traveling to France's National Archives to read through the transcripts of the trial that ended in her martyrdom on **May 30, 1431**.

When Twain's research was complete, the writing began. Two years later, in 1895, *Personal Recollections of Joan of Arc* went to press.

Then, as now, the book surprised Twain's readers. Absent from it were the sharp wit and broad humor which characterized most of his work. In their place was some fairly serious scholarship, as well as a reverence for the saint bordering on devotion.

"Whatever thing men call great, look for it in Joan of Arc, and there you will find it," he wrote, adding, "She is easily and by far the most extraordinary person the human race has ever produced."

Although few critics found much to praise in the book, Twain couldn't have been happier.

"I like *Joan of Arc* best of all my books," he said in his last years, "and it is the best; I know it perfectly well. And besides, it furnished me seven times the pleasure afforded me by any of the others; twelve years of preparation, and two years of writing. The others needed no preparation and got none."

The Catholic Church celebrates the feast day of Twain's favorite saint on May 30. Hopefully, through her intercession, Twain now does the same.

From the start, the partnership formed by Father James Anthony Walsh and Father Thomas Frederick Price was an unlikely one.

Father Walsh was from the North, born in 1867, and raised in the Boston suburbs. Father Price, born in 1860, was from the South, the son of Catholic converts living in Wilmington, North Carolina. Father Walsh was educated at two of the best schools in the country—Boston College and Harvard. Father Price went straight to the local seminary after high school, and then finished his formation in Baltimore. The urbane Father Walsh had traveled the world. Father Price spent most of his priestly life in the backwoods of North Carolina.

Despite all that divided the pair, however, the two men shared a common desire: to send American Catholics abroad to proclaim the Gospel. They discovered their shared interest after a chance encounter at the 1910 Eucharistic Congress in Montreal. Immediately, they began devising a plan to make their dream a reality. The following year, they took that plan to the U.S. bishops, who wholeheartedly endorsed it on the condition that the pope also approved.

On **May 31, 1911,** Fathers Walsh and Price sailed for Rome seeking his approval. A month later, Pope Pius X granted them his blessing, and the Catholic Foreign Mission Society of America officially began.

Before the year was out, the two priests had begun building a seminary on a small hill in New York known as "Mary's Knoll." From the hill, the fledgling society took its name.

In 1912, the order welcomed its first seminarians, and six years later, the first Maryknoll missionaries departed for China. Price was among them. Walsh remained behind to run the seminary.

At that point, the two priests' paths once more diverged. Price never came home, dying in Hong Kong in 1919. Father Walsh became Bishop Walsh, shepherding the growth of the Maryknoll Fathers and Sisters until his death in 1936.

Today, however, both men share the same title: Servant of God.

June

"Nice try. But no dice." That, in a nutshell, sums up the U.S. Supreme Court's response to the State of Oregon in *Pierce v. Society of Sisters.*

The case originated two years earlier, in Oregon's 1922 revision of its Compulsory Education Act. Prior to that revision, Oregon required all children between the ages of eight and 16 to attend public schools, but it also allowed certain exemptions, including private school education.

The problem with that exemption, as Oregon saw it, was that it prevented all children from receiving an equally "American" education. And by "American," it meant "Protestant." The state didn't like Catholic immigrants and children of Catholic immigrants attending Catholic schools. As far as the voters of Oregon were concerned, those schools taught "foreign values" and prevented children from assimilating into American culture. In 1922, Oregon solved that problem by outlawing private schools.

Not surprisingly, the private schools didn't take kindly to that solution, and the Society of Sisters of the Holy Names of Jesus and Mary quickly filed suit.

First in an Oregon District Court, then later in the U.S. Supreme Court, justices unanimously sided with the sisters, ruling that the state's compelling interest in educating children was neither threatened by private schools nor more important than a parent's right to guide their child's education.

The decision was a decisive win for Catholic schools. The grounds upon which the U.S. Supreme Court based its **June 1, 1925,** decision, however, had long-term implications that went far beyond education.

Rather than address the First Amendment arguments made by the sisters' attorneys, the Court instead invoked the Fourteenth Amendment's Due Process Clause, applying its protections for the first time to groups, not just individuals, and expanding the types of liberties it guaranteed. That established a precedent now cited in more than 100 Supreme Court Cases, including *Roe v. Wade,* and set the stage for the expansion of constitutionally protected rights to include the right to abortion.

The law of unintended consequences strikes again.

Father Thomas O'Reilly came to Atlanta, Georgia, from Ireland in 1857. War came four years later.

In the American Civil War's first years, Father O'Reilly prayed for peace and comforted the grieving parishioners of Immaculate Conception Church, Atlanta's first (and at the time only) Catholic parish. Then, when the fighting moved closer, he went to the battlefields to tend to the bodies and souls of the wounded. Soon known to officers on both sides of the conflict, O'Reilly moved freely across the lines, administering the sacraments to Union and Confederate soldiers alike.

For that reason, in 1864, when Union General William Tecumseh Sherman ordered all non-combatants out of Atlanta, he asked O'Reilly to stay. The priest was too important to both armies' soldiers for Sherman to allow him to leave.

Sherman, however, hadn't accounted for O'Reilly's reaction to the Northern army's plans to burn Atlanta.

When the priest discovered what Sherman had in store for his city, he went to one of the Union commanders he'd befriended, General Henry Slocum, and demanded that Sherman spare the city's churches, as well as the court house and the city hall. O'Reilly also threatened to excommunicate any soldiers who participated in the burning of his church.

Slocum conveyed the message to Sherman, along with his belief that the general would see mass defections from his army if he ordered them to go against the priest's will. Sherman conceded. When Atlanta Catholics returned to their burned-out city, their parish, civic buildings, numerous churches, and the surrounding neighborhoods still stood.

After the war, Immaculate Conception was intact but badly damaged. Father O'Reilly lived long enough to begin building a new church in 1869, but not long enough to see the church completed in 1873.

Following a major restoration, the church was rededicated on **June 2, 1954,** as the Catholic Shrine of the Immaculate Conception. On the lower level of the refurbished church, next to Father O'Reilly's tomb, a small museum was created to honor the priest who helped his adopted city rise again.

June 3: THE ROSARY PRIEST

In 1941, Father Patrick Peyton needed to honor a bargain.

Thirteen years earlier, Peyton left his native Ireland for America. While he completed his high school education, he worked as a janitor in Scranton, Pennsylvania's cathedral. Then, in 1932, he entered the novitiate for the Holy Cross Fathers. All was going well until Peyton started coughing up blood. The diagnosis came in 1939: advanced tuberculosis.

The prognosis was grim. Peyton, however, struck a deal with the Blessed Mother: if she healed him, he would dedicate his life to promoting peace through the Rosary.

She accepted the deal. All signs of tuberculosis disappeared, and on June 15, 1941, Peyton became a Catholic priest.

To uphold his end of the bargain, Father Peyton turned to the mass media, which he used to help those devastated by war understand that peace in the world begins with peace in individual hearts and homes. As he explained in the slogan he popularized, "The family that prays together stays together. A world at prayer is a world at peace."

To help people put that slogan into action, Peyton launched the Family Theater and Family Rosary Crusade.

Over the course of seven decades (and counting), Family Theater has produced a long-running hit radio program, as well as television specials and films, that, in earlier decades, featured A-list Hollywood stars—such as Bing Crosby, Grace Kelly, and Loretta Young—promoting faith, prayer, and family values.

For its part, the Family Rosary Crusade sought to popularize the idea of a nightly family Rosary and continues to sponsor Rosary rallies around the world. During Peyton's lifetime, the movement spread to Europe, Asia, and Latin America (the latter with the help of the CIA, who decided the Rosary was as good a weapon as any in the fight against communism).

Before his death, those efforts earned Father Peyton the nickname, "The Rosary Priest." After his death, on **June 3, 1992,** they also earned him the title "Servant of God."

June 4: THE FATHER OF AMERICA'S NAVY

It was madness. That was clear from the start. American Naval Captain John Barry had 27 men. The British had hundreds of sailors and possession of every ship in Philadelphia's harbor.

Yet that didn't stop Barry in 1778 from rowing up the Delaware River in the dead of night, pulling alongside two British transports, and swarming over the gunwales. Within minutes, the Americans had possession of the transports, as well as a schooner.

Nobody but Barry would have attempted such a mission. And nobody but Barry could have pulled it off. He was—from the time he received his first captain's commission in the American (Continental) Navy in 1775 until his death in 1803—the country's greatest seaman.

Born in Ireland in 1745, Barry began his career as a cabin boy on a merchant ship. By 1766, he had his first command, the *Barbados,* which sailed out of Philadelphia. While there, Barry took a liking to the city, and made it his homeport.

When the American Revolution came, Barry offered his services to General Washington, receiving command of the USS *Lexington* and the task of helping outfit a navy for the colonies. Within months, Barry gave the Continental Navy its first victory at sea and captured America's first British prize. He would do the same repeatedly throughout the war, capturing more than 20 British ships, as well as large sums of prize money, oftentimes through acts as bold as his 1778 escapade on the Philadelphia waterfront.

After the war, Barry returned to commercial shipping. A decade later, however, President Washington asked him to defend American ships from the Barbary pirates. He agreed, and as of **June 4, 1794,** the date of his commissioning as Commodore, was the highest-ranking officer in the American Navy.

Accounts of Barry's naval prowess abound, but so too do accounts of his virtue—of his deep Catholic faith, devotion to Scripture, love for his wife, honor in battle, and fatherly concern for all who served under him.

Lauded as "the father of America's Navy," Commodore Barry died in 1803 in Philadelphia.

June 5: MOYLAN'S HORSE

Stephen Moylan had only lived in America for seven years when the American Revolution began, but that was long enough for him to catch independence fever.

The son of a wealthy Irish shipping merchant, Moylan studied with the Jesuits in Paris, then lived for a short while in Lisbon, before coming to Philadelphia to open a branch of the family business.

Soon after his 1768 arrival, Moylan recognized the advantages of independence for his shipping interests. More fundamentally, as an Irishmen, he delighted in the prospect of the British losing their colonial "crown jewel."

Accordingly, in the years leading up to the Revolution, Moylan helped found the Friendly Sons of St. Patrick, a fraternal organization of Protestant and Catholic Irishmen in Philadelphia, which eventually supplied one-third of the initial capital for the Bank of the United States. The Bank, in turn, funded the Continental Army.

Not content to simply finance the war, Moylan enlisted as soon as fighting began. Assigned to General Washington's personal staff, he first held the post of muster-master general, then aide-de-camp, and finally, as of **June 5, 1776,** quartermaster general.

The following January, Washington asked Moylan to organize and command a regiment of light dragoons. Although Washington intended the regiment to be an elite cavalry force, there was nothing elite (or even forceful) about Moylan's dragoons in the beginning. Fighting in stolen British red coats, the men chaffed at discipline and caused confusion in battle. But after more than a year of training and practice, the men finally evolved into an effective fighting force. Now sporting green coats, the regiment was known as "Moylan's Horse."

After the winter at Valley Forge, Moylan assumed command of the entire Continental cavalry and became the highest-ranking Catholic officer in Washington's army. He commanded his troops in battle with distinction until 1781, when ill health forced him to return to Philadelphia.

After the war, Moylan received the title of brigadier general, but his military days were over. He spent the next three decades as a private citizen and merchant, dying in 1811 in Philadelphia.

June 6: CHICAGO'S FOUNDING FATHER

Jean-Baptiste Point du Sable might have been Haitian. Or he might have been French-Canadian. He might have been black. Or he might have been white. He might have lived at the mouth of the Chicago River as early as 1774. Or, he might not have settled there until **June 6, 1790,** the date most often listed by Chicago sources as the city's official founding by Point du Sable.

When it comes to Chicago's first permanent resident, separating fact from fiction is a near impossible task. So little was written about the man during his lifetime, and so much was invented after his death, that few details are certain.

What is known is that Point du Sable was a French-speaking Catholic who built both a successful trading post and a home for his wife (a Potawatomi Indian) on the site of present-day Chicago, and that he did so well before any other Europeans settled there.

It's also known that during the American Revolution, the British captured Point du Sable, a known colonial sympathizer, and imprisoned him in Fort Michilimackinac. Depending on which source you consult, the British may have held on to him for the entirety of the war . . . or they may have released him early on good behavior.

Either way, by 1790, historical records agree that Point du Sable lived in Chicago, running a trading post and assisting new settlers as they arrived.

The historical records likewise agree that in 1800, for reasons unknown, Point du Sable sold his substantial holdings in Chicago, and moved his family to St. Charles, Missouri . . . or Peoria, Illinois. Everybody has a different opinion.

By 1810, however, the man was in St. Charles for certain, where he lived until his death in 1818 . . . or 1819. Again, few can agree. Although the Archdiocese of St. Louis' records show that he received a Catholic funeral and burial in St. Charles Borromeo Cemetery, his grave has never been found.

June 7: WESTWARD, HO!

When the barons of American industry looked at the immigrants arriving from Ireland in the nineteenth century, they saw one thing: cheap labor. That's what they wanted from the Irish, and that's what they got.

Although the majority of those immigrants came to America hoping to continue the farming life they'd led in their homeland, most never made it past the great cities of the East Coast. The jobs were in the cities, as was the money. Some still dreamed of a farm in the country, far away from overcrowded tenements, but few factory jobs paid enough to make that dream a reality.

Then, in 1879, the Irish Catholic Colonization Association (CCA) of the United States was born.

Championed by Bishop John Spalding of Peoria and Bishop John Ireland of St. Paul, the CCA wanted to help Catholic immigrants escape the dangers of city and factory life. To that end, it bought large tracts of land in Illinois, Minnesota, and Kansas, then subdivided it into family farms. It next built homes, parishes, and schools on the land, and assigned a pastor to the community. Finally, it subsidized Catholic immigrants' travel out West and sold them the farms at a price well below market value.

Many, including the editorial board of the *New York Times,* doubted the scheme could work. When the editors of America's most esteemed newspaper learned of the plan, they asked in a **June 7, 1879** editorial, "Will they succeed?"

They then answered:

> *We doubt it. An Irish Catholic population is not the best for pioneer work or for founding institutions. They make a capital working population, where Yankee brain and Protestant character lead them. But by themselves we should apprehend many difficulties . . . An isolated colony of Irishmen and Romanists would learn nothing new and keep all that was bad in the old; the priestly influence would be excessive, and education very limited.*

In the years that followed, all the Irish immigrant farmers that the CCA successfully relocated had a delightful time proving the *New York Times* wrong.

June 8: MOURNING BOBBY

At 12:30 p.m., on **June 8, 1968,** a train left New York's Grand Central Station. On board were the friends and family of Senator Robert F. Kennedy.

Earlier that morning, thousands filled St. Patrick's Cathedral for Kennedy's Requiem Mass. Black and white, rich and poor, Congressmen and migrant laborers—all came to pay tribute to the slain presidential candidate, who, as a U.S. attorney general and senator, fought against organized crime, championed civil rights, and advocated for the fair treatment of workers.

Kennedy, like his older brother John, was assassinated in his prime. Shortly after midnight on June 5, he finished celebrating his victory in the California presidential primary, and headed off to meet the press. As he passed through the hotel's kitchen the assassin fired. Kennedy died the following day.

By the time the funeral train left Grand Central Station on June 8, tens of thousands had paid tribute to Kennedy while he lay in state at St. Patrick's Cathedral. As his body made its way to Washington, D.C., perhaps a million more people lined the tracks to do the same.

Inside the train, Kennedy's wife Ethel, pregnant with the couple's eleventh child, held her rosary tightly and slowly made her way through the long line of 20 cars, thanking the mourners for their support. As for the mourners, journalist Frank Mankiewicz recalled that the Catholics drank and told stories, the Protestants sat in silence (scandalized by the Catholics drinking and telling stories), and the Jews wept.

"They'd have torn their clothes if they'd thought of it," he wrote.

Although the journey should have taken four hours, it took more than eight, with the crowds of mourners along the way slowing them down. Not until 9 p.m. did the train pull into Union Station and Bobby Kennedy's funeral procession begin.

Wending its way through the capital's dark streets, the procession moved towards Arlington National Cemetery. And there, with Washington's Archbishop Patrick Cardinal O'Boyle officiating, they laid Kennedy to rest beside the brother he served so well.

June 9: WHITE-WINGED ANGELS

Satterlee U.S.A. General Hospital in Philadelphia set out to be the biggest and best of the Union Army's hospitals, employing the most modern means of sanitation, treatment, and care. For that reason, Dr. Isaac Israel Hayes—the Arctic explorer turned Civil War doctor running the newly built facility—would not compromise when it came to his nursing staff. He wanted nothing less than the best. And the best meant Catholic religious sisters.

Although the world applauded Catholic religious for their service in the Crimean War, Americans had not yet adjusted to having women, let alone habited Catholic women, working in their hospitals. Hayes, however, believed that women made the best nurses, and women religious made better nurses still. As he saw it, their life of discipline and self-denial lent itself well to the constant discipline and self-denial called for in wartime hospitals.

Despite a few objections, Hayes won the day. And soon after Satterlee opened its doors, on **June 9, 1862,** Mother Mary Gonzaga and 22 Sisters of Charity arrived to minister to its patients. Over the next three years, more than 100 sisters and 20,000 wounded men would pass through Satterlee, including more than 5,000 wounded in the Battle of Gettysburg.

Of the care the sisters provided, Satterlee's chaplain wrote, "It is proper now to state that it is most firmly believed that better nurses, better attendants on the sick, more noiseless, ceaseless performers of service in the hospital could not be found."

For their part, the soldiers adored the sisters and wrote home praising them as "white-winged" angels. Hayes shared their admiration. When a group of Protestant women from Philadelphia suggested it would be more appropriate if they cared for the men, he laughed them out of the room.

Hayes' biographer, Douglas Wamsley, explained, "He considered the Sisters of Charity the only women in the world capable of nursing the sick properly."

When the Civil War ended, so did the sisters' work. They left Satterlee on August 3, 1865, the day the hospital closed its doors for good.

Father William Judge, S.J., had never gone to sea before, so he didn't know how he would fare. But within hours of boarding the Alaska-bound ship, on **June 10, 1890,** he knew the answer was, "Not well."

The journey from San Francisco to the Jesuits' northern-most mission on the Yukon River, however, was a long one. And by the time his ship made landfall 34 days later, Judge had adjusted to the sea.

In fact, Judge excelled at adjusting. He had been adjusting ever since he was 15, when ill health forced him to leave seminary and go to work in a Baltimore lumber mill. Ten years later, when the Jesuits accepted him, he adjusted to religious life, despite being significantly older than his fellow novices.

In the years since, Judge had left his parents and 11 siblings behind to serve in the Jesuit missions in Washington and Idaho. He adjusted to life there too, and he had no doubt he would adjust to life in Alaska.

He was right.

As the Yukon (Klondike) Gold Rush brought tens of thousands of miners north, Judge personally constructed churches and hospitals, putting to use the building and blacksmithing skills he had acquired in that Baltimore lumber mill. He said Mass for the miners, nursed the sick, and consoled the dying. He also, almost always, did it alone, with no companions by his side for much of the nine years he ministered in Alaska and the Yukon.

Judge never complained though. He knew his purpose and pursued it gladly.

As he explained in a letter home, "You would be astonished to see the amount of hard work that men do here in the hope of finding gold . . . if men would only work for the kingdom of heaven with a little of that wonderful energy, how many saints we would have."

In 1899, at only 49, the man they called "The Saint of Dawson" died from exhaustion and pneumonia at his Yukon mission.

Six hundred people lived in Detroit in 1805. For a frontier town, that was no small number.

But Detroit was also an old town—at least by New World standards. People had lived there for more than a century, ever since the city's first Catholic church was built in 1701. Then, the population primarily consisted of a few French-speaking artisans and farmers. Now there were families and businesses, with both Catholics and Protestants living alongside one another in relative harmony.

Detroit was a good city, with great promise. And when fire broke out on the morning of **June 11, 1805,** it had much to lose.

The fire began as most do: by accident. The local baker, John Harvey, didn't properly extinguish the ashes from his pipe tobacco. First his barn caught on fire, then his house, then another house, and before people quite knew what had happened, whole blocks were ablaze.

As fast as they could, men and women of the town formed long lines, beginning at the river and winding through town. They filled buckets with water and passed them quickly along. But their homes and businesses, all made of wood, were built close together. No amount of water could stop the fire's spread.

By that afternoon, all that stood in Detroit was one stone fort and the brick chimneys of the houses that burned. The blaze leveled the entire city, from first building to last. Yet, almost miraculously, not one person died.

After the fire, some people left, but most stayed. Those who remained found hope in the new city motto crafted for them by the pastor of St. Anne's Catholic Church, Father Gabriel Richard: *Speramus meliora; resurget cineribus.*

In English: "We hope for better things; it shall arise from the ashes."

In the centuries since, as Detroit's fortunes have ebbed and flowed, the city's motto has remained unchanged, proclaiming the hope of resurrection to each new generation.

The Virginia Declaration of Rights was, in a sense, a template for American liberty. Penned by George Mason (with a little help from James Madison) and ratified on **June 12, 1776,** at the Virginia Constitutional Convention, the Declaration of Rights was the first constitutional guarantor of individual freedoms in North America. It presented a vision of government that functions as a servant of the people, and articulated both the inherent rights enjoyed by a free citizenry and the moral principles which undergird just government.

Among its 16 sections, the Declaration of Rights defended man's "inherent" right to the "enjoyment of life and liberty, with the means of acquiring and possessing property, and pursuing and obtaining happiness and safety." It likewise defended the right to rebel against an unjust government and supported a well-armed militia, freedom of the press, and the separation of powers within the government.

Regarding the freedom of religion, it said:

"That religion, or the duty which we owe to our Creator, and the manner of discharging it, can be directed only by reason and conviction, not by force or violence; and therefore all men are equally entitled to the free exercise of religion, according to the dictates of conscience . . . "

Within weeks of its passage, Thomas Jefferson drew on the document to write the Declaration of Independence, imitating parts of it in both style and substance. Later, James Madison would use Virginia's Declaration as the model for the U.S. Bill of Rights, as would French revolutionaries for their *Declaration of Rights of Man and of the Citizen.*

For all its egalitarian liberal-mindedness, however, the Declaration of Rights fell short in one crucial way: it limited its application by asserting that men only possess the enumerated rights "when they enter into a state of society"—meaning that slaves, who had not entered into "society," enjoyed none of the articulated rights and privileges.

June 13: THE BABE

George Herman Ruth, Jr., was, as his admission papers to St. Mary's Industrial School for Boys testified, "incorrigible."

Just what "incorrigible" entailed is a little fuzzy. But whatever the boy who would become "the Babe" was up to, it wasn't good. And on **June 13, 1902,** it earned the seven-year-old Ruth a one-way trip to St. Mary's. The Baltimore reformatory didn't help much though. During Ruth's 12 years there, the future slugger found himself in constant trouble for fighting, insubordination, and general mischief making.

Despite misbehaving (or perhaps because of it), Ruth developed an abiding affection for the school's chief disciplinarian, Brother Matthias Boutlier. It was Boutlier who encouraged the boy to play baseball, and it was Boutlier who helped him develop his signature power swing. Ruth eventually came to think of Boutlier as a father figure. And even though the religious brother didn't succeed in reforming Ruth, he planted seeds that gradually took root.

Ruth left St. Mary's in 1914, after a major league scout saw him play baseball at a game against a team at Mount St. Mary's College. In the years that followed, Ruth's power hitting changed baseball. It also won three World Series for the Boston Red Sox and four World Series for the New York Yankees. Of the dozen plus records Ruth broke in his 21-year career, several—including his .690 slugging percentage—still stand.

Off the field, Ruth was as notorious for his drinking and womanizing as he was generous to St. Mary's and the poor. Teammates likewise recalled Ruth painting the town red on Saturday night, then heading off to Mass on Sunday morning.

By 1946, however, when Babe fell ill with cancer, the wild days were over and the seeds planted at St. Mary's came into full bloom. As death approached, Ruth explained, "Once religion sinks in, it stays there—deep down. The lads who get religious training, get it where it counts—in the roots. They may fail it, but it never fails them."

Ruth died a penitent, practicing Catholic in 1948.

June 14: I CONFESS

In 1813, Father Anthony Kohlmann, S.J., had a secret. And he wasn't telling. Two penitents had entrusted the secret to him during the Sacrament of Confession. When the penitents confessed their crime (receiving stolen goods), they also mentioned the names of the thieves who brought them the goods.

After hearing their confession, Kohlmann made the penitents return the items to their rightful owner. The local magistrate, however, wasn't satisfied. He wanted to know who stole the goods in the first place. Accordingly, he summoned Kohlmann, then vicar-general of the Diocese of New York, to court and demanded that he reveal the thieves' names. Kohlmann protested. He couldn't do that. The seal of the confessional bound him to silence.

For his silence, the magistrate charged the priest with contempt of court.

As word of Kohlmann's secret leaked out, anti-Catholic New York rose up in protest. To them, the priest's refusal to cooperate looked like further proof that American democracy and Catholic "superstition" were incompatible. The threat of violence loomed.

To keep the peace, local authorities convinced the magistrate to drop the charges. By then, however, Catholics didn't want that. They recognized that the inviolability of the confessional in legal proceedings needed to be addressed sooner or later.

It took the Court of General Sessions six days to decide the case, and on **June 14, 1813,** they delivered their verdict: Not guilty.

In a statement issued afterwards, New York's Mayor DeWitt Clinton defended the court, saying:

> *Although we differ from the witness and his brethren in our religious creed, yet we have no reason to question the purity of their motives, or to impeach their good conduct as citizens. They are protected by the laws and constitution of this country in the full and free exercise of their religion, and this court can never countenance or authorize the application of insult to their faith, or of torture to their consciences.*

June 15: A MODEL FOR DISSENT

Catholics serving in the public square have wrestled with the extent to which their faith should influence their politics since America's founding. In the wake of *Roe v. Wade* and the legalization of abortion, however, that wrestling took on an even greater urgency.

This was evident in 1984, when New York's Catholic governor, Mario Cuomo, visited the University of Notre Dame. Cuomo, who was born on **June 15, 1932,** was a cradle Catholic, lifelong Democrat, and committed supporter of abortion rights. Many questioned how he could reconcile his faith and abortion politics. At Notre Dame, Cuomo attempted to answer that question. He explained:

> *Almost all Americans accept some religious values as a part of our public life. We are a religious people, many of us descended from ancestors who came here expressly to live their religious faith free from coercion or repression. But we are also a people of many religions, with no established church, who hold different beliefs on many matters.*
>
> *Our public morality, then—the moral standards we maintain for everyone, not just the ones we insist on in our private lives —depends on a consensus view of right and wrong. The values derived from religious belief will not—and should not—be accepted as part of the public morality unless they are shared by the pluralistic community at large . . .*
>
> *As a Catholic, I have accepted certain answers as the right ones for myself and my family . . . As a Governor, however, I am involved in defining policies that determine other people's rights in these same areas of life and death . . .*
>
> *Approval or rejection of legal restrictions on abortion should not be the exclusive litmus test of Catholic loyalty. We should understand that whether abortion is outlawed or not, our work has barely begun: the work of creating a society where the right to life doesn't end at the moment of birth.*

Widely criticized by clergy and laity alike, Cuomo's speech nevertheless continues to serve as a model for dissent among pro-choice politicians.

On a gray February day in 1939, Avery Dulles went for a walk along the Charles River. Dulles was a junior at Harvard that year, and great things were expected of him.

Great things were, in fact, the family business: Dulles' grandfather was an eminent Presbyterian theologian. His great-grandfather and great-uncle both had served as U.S. secretary of state. Soon, his father would do the same, while his uncle would become director of the Central Intelligence Agency (CIA). Dulles was different from his family though. He couldn't share their Presbyterian faith—he'd long doubted God's existence—and wasn't committed to a career in politics. He became even more different after that February stroll.

As he walked, Dulles spotted a tree in bud. In a moment, his doubts about God disappeared.

"The thought came to me suddenly, with all the strength and novelty of a revelation, that these little buds in their innocence and meekness followed a rule, a law of which I as yet knew nothing," he later explained. "That night, for the first time in years, I prayed."

Much to his family's chagrin, Dulles entered the Catholic Church within a year. Six years later, he joined the Society of Jesus, and on **June 16, 1956,** he was ordained a Catholic priest.

In the decades that followed, Dulles would become America's preeminent Catholic theologian—teaching at Woodstock Seminary, The Catholic University of America, and Fordham University; serving as president of the Catholic Theological Society of America; and authoring hundreds of articles and books.

Through it all, Dulles defended Catholic orthodoxy in an age of dissent, saying once, "Christianity would dissolve itself if it allowed its revealed content, handed down in tradition, to be replaced by contemporary theories."

For his theological contributions, Pope John Paul II bestowed upon Dulles the cardinal's red hat in 2001. He was the first American theologian to receive such an honor.

Cardinal Dulles died in 2008, having become every inch the great man his family expected him to be.

June 17: THE POLES' PRIDE

Paul Peter Rhode was only nine years old when he arrived in the United States. He came with his mother, Krystyna, who had been widowed years before in their native Poland. Like countless other Poles who came to America in the late-nineteenth century, Krystyna and her son settled in Chicago.

There, while still a boy, Paul heard the call to the priesthood. He attended minor seminary in Kentucky, then returned to Chicago to study with the Jesuits at St. Ignatius College (today's Loyola University). He completed his theological studies in Wisconsin and was ordained to the priesthood for the Archdiocese of Chicago on **June 17, 1894**.

Two years later, at only 25, Rhode became the first pastor of Sts. Peter and Paul Parish in Chicago's McKinley Park. Like many parishes built by Polish immigrants in the major metropolitan centers of the Midwest, the church was an imposing structure—a marvel not only for its size, but also for the poor immigrants' ability to finance such a church.

Already proud of their parish, those same Polish-Americans grew even prouder on July 29, 1908, when 37-year-old Father Rhode was consecrated an auxiliary bishop for the Archdiocese of Chicago. He was the first Polish-American bishop in the country. Polish-Americans grew prouder still in 1915, when Bishop Rhode became the bishop of Green Bay, Wisconsin, a see he would shepherd for 30 years.

When Bishop Rhode died in 1945, at the age of 73, he left behind a legacy of 10 new parishes, 19 Catholic schools, and the diocese's first office of Catholic Charities.

In 1892, despite the urgings of Pope Leo XIII, many French Catholics refused to embrace their constitutional government, believing instead that the future of the Faith depended on the restoration of the monarchy. To convince them otherwise—and alleviate mounting tensions between Church and State in France—Pope Leo asked the archbishop of Saint Paul, Minnesota, to pay the French a visit.

Archbishop John Ireland was the perfect man for the job. Born in Ireland, raised in America, and educated for the priesthood in France, the archbishop's French was fluent and his manners were polished. More important, he'd spent much of his priestly career confronting the problems the Church faced in a pluralistic society.

Although some accused Archbishop Ireland of going too far in his efforts to make Catholicism palatable to Protestant America, he was nevertheless well versed in what Catholics brought to democracy and what democracy brought to Catholics. He learned those lessons as he partnered with his state to relocate thousands of immigrants to Minnesota farmland, helped secure the rights of laborers through unions, and found creative ways to educate children in the Faith while still working through the public schools.

Archbishop Ireland brought that experience with him when, on **June 18, 1892,** he went before the elites of Catholic Paris to make Pope Leo's case.

"In America," he reassured his audience, "we have a free church in a free country, and the Church is happy in her freedom."

He continued:

> *Of all the forms of civil government which the Church has recognized, and of which she has made trial, she cannot say from which she has received more harm or more good. Just now, she is resolved to make trial in France of the republic, and I, as a citizen of a republic, say to the Church, "In this experiment, thou shall succeed."*

His words had their desired effect. Lauded for swaying at least some royalists to the constitutional cause, Archbishop Ireland returned to Minnesota to shepherd his see for another 26 years.

June 19: THE BEER MONKS

At 10 a.m. on **June 19, 1855,** an anxious Father Boniface Wimmer, O.S.B., sat in a Vatican antechamber, awaiting an audience with Pope Pius IX.

A German Benedictine priest, Father Wimmer had immigrated to America almost 10 years earlier. Upon his arrival, at the invitation of Pittsburgh's Bishop Michael O'Connor, he founded America's first Benedictine monastery, St. Vincent's Abbey.

Like all German abbeys, St. Vincent's raised its own crops, ground its own flour, and brewed its own beer.

O'Connor didn't mind the crop growing or flour grinding, but as an early adherent of the temperance movement, he was none too pleased with the beer-brewing. After reflecting upon the scandal of monks in his diocese brewing (and selling) alcohol, he decided the best course of action was to order them to stop. The Benedictines obeyed, but then pled their case to Rome.

Once Wimmer's audience began, he explained to the Holy Father that, out of obedience, the monks had drunk nothing but water since they ceased brewing. He then added, "Whether we can keep it up is another question."

The pope agreed, saying, "Water alone would never do on a permanent basis."

The two men reached a compromise: the monks could brew beer for themselves, but would avoid the retail trade for a time. The monks abided by the decision, and, when they later resumed distributing beer, sold only small amounts.

Even that compromise, however, proved insufficient. As the temperance movement grew in popularity, increasing numbers of the Catholic clergy and hierarchy in America criticized the monks. One Buffalo-area priest even devoted a series of pamphlets to the infamous "beer monks" of St. Vincent's.

"Instead of laboring for the cause of sobriety, on which the welfare of the church in this country so greatly depends," he wrote, "the beer monks . . . are actually gaining revenue from the spread of intemperance."

The monks stopped selling beer in 1898, then, following Prohibition, closed the brewery for good.

Today, they sell coffee instead.

June 20: PREACHING EQUALITY

On June 11, 1963, Americans turned on their television sets to watch President John F. Kennedy speak about the Civil Rights Movement.

In what some consider his most important national address, Kennedy said:

> . . . *We preach freedom around the world—and we mean it—and we cherish our freedom here at home. But are we to say to the world, and much more importantly, to each other, that this is a land of the free except for the Negroes; that we have no second-class citizens except Negroes; that we have no class or cast system, no ghettoes, no master race except with respect to Negroes?*
>
> . . . *The fires of frustration and discord are burning in every city, North and South, where legal remedies are not at hand. Redress is sought in the streets, in demonstrations, parades, and protests, which create tensions and threaten violence and threaten lives.*
>
> *We face, therefore, a moral crisis as a country and as a people. It cannot be met by repressive police action. It cannot be left to increased demonstrations in the streets. It cannot be quieted by token moves or talk. It is a time to act in the Congress, in your State and local legislative body and, above all, in all of our daily lives.*
>
> . . . *Those who do nothing are inviting shame as well as violence. Those who act boldly are recognizing right as well as reality.*
>
> *Next week I shall ask the Congress of the United States to act, to make a commitment it has not fully made in this century to the proposition that race has no place in American life or law.*

Two weeks later, on **June 20, 1963,** Kennedy submitted his proposed legislation to Congress. Although it quickly stalled, the bill found new life after Kennedy's assassination, when President Lyndon B. Johnson asked Congress to pass the bill as a tribute to the fallen president.

Johnson signed the Civil Rights Act into law the following July.

In early-nineteenth-century Ireland, English penal laws barred Catholics from the country's schools. An uneducated populace, the laws' authors reasoned, could never pose a threat to the ruling class.

In early-nineteenth-century America, a similar line of thinking held sway, with Protestant America undermining the education of Catholics at every turn. In some places, they prohibited Catholics from building schools. In others, the public schools served as the arm of Protestant congregations, with Protestant doctrine preached in the classroom and anti-Catholic propaganda incorporated into the curriculum.

Such was the situation in 1838 New York, when the Irish-born priest John Hughes became the see's coadjutor bishop. Hughes had not forgotten anything about his boyhood in Ireland and the laws banning Catholics from schools. He knew the city's poor, immigrant Catholics could never succeed without an education, and he also knew he couldn't depend upon the public schools to provide that education.

"We shall have to build the schoolhouse first, and the church afterwards," he said.

To that end, Hughes opened more than a hundred Catholic schools in New York during his tenure. Included among those schools was the first Catholic institution of higher education in the Northeast: St. John's College.

Within weeks of his consecration, Hughes began searching for a suitable location to build a college and seminary. He found one a year later, purchasing Rose Hill Manor in 1839 and immediately beginning construction.

It took another two years before classes could commence, but on **June 21, 1841,** St. John's College opened its doors, with a future cardinal, Father John McCloskey, at its head. Although financial and faculty difficulties immediately followed, Hughes solved those problems in 1846 by transferring the teaching and administrative duties to the Society of Jesus.

A year later, confident at last in the school's future, Hughes wrote, "It was a daring and dangerous undertaking, but now it is successfully provided for."

The Jesuits have provided for Bishop Hughes' school ever since. Today, however, it goes by another name: Fordham University.

June 22: A BLESSING IN DISGUISE

In 1915 Anna Zervas was only 15 —much too young, as far as her family was concerned, to enter the convent. But Zervas knew what God wanted of her, and with the help of her parish priest, convinced her parents to allow her to enter St. Benedict's Monastery in St. Joseph, Minnesota, that year. As a novice, she took the name Sister Mary Annella, and on **June 22, 1922,** professed her final vows.

All was unfolding as she believed it would. Then, God threw her a curve ball.

One year after she made her final vows, a rash started spreading across Sister Annella's skin. Soon, it covered her entire body. Her hair fell out, her immune system weakened, and secondary infections set in. But try as they might, the doctors couldn't diagnose her condition.

Eventually, the Mayo Clinic recognized the rash as *Pityriasis Rubra Pilaris,* a skin disease so rare only six people in the United States suffered from it at the time.

With her superior's permission, Sister Annella returned home to Moorhead, Minnesota, where her mother could nurse her. In time, the rash receded. But Sister Annella feared she hadn't born her sufferings well. So, she asked for another chance, telling God, "If he wanted me to have it all over again, I would carry it as he wanted me to."

God gave her that opportunity the following summer. The rash returned, and no reprieve came.

As death approached, Sister Annella wrote:

> *What He has in store for me, I do not know, but all He does is well, so there is no need to worry. God has given me the grace to be resigned, and I thank him heartily for this, but also for all else He has given me with my illness . . . I often wonder what great harm of body or of soul I may have suffered had not God given me this "blessing in disguise."*

Sister Annella died on August 14, 1926. She was declared a Servant of God the following year.

June 23: THE APOSTLE OF THE UPPER MIDWEST

The house, despite its generous proportions, was full past overflowing. Canadian trappers perched in the windows. Native Americans filled the lawn outside. Even the Protestants of Sault Sainte Marie came out on **June 23, 1833,** eager to hear the baby-faced man in black preach the Gospel and offer the Mass.

Properly speaking, as a Dominican, the man in black—Father Samuel Mazzuchelli—should have worn white. But when Mazzuchelli arrived in Wisconsin three years before, he discovered that the natives still spoke reverently of the "Black Robes"—the Jesuits who left the region decades earlier. With the permission of his bishop, Edward Fenwick of Cincinnati, the priest exchanged his white robes for black, thereby enhancing his credibility with the Chippewa, Menominee, Winnebago, and Potawatomi Indians he'd come to evangelize.

Mazzuchelli was only 23 then. He arrived in America still a deacon, was quickly ordained by Fenwick, then sent north, by himself, to serve as the lone priest in a territory half the size of his native Italy.

In the three years since his arrival, he'd kept busy—rebuilding an abandoned church in Mackinac, building a new church in Green Bay, translating textbooks into Menominee, and opening schools for Native Americans and European immigrants. He also traveled thousands of miles to catechize Catholics who hadn't seen a priest since their baptism, perform marriages, hear confessions, say Mass, and baptize new converts.

Administering the sacraments would eventually take Mazzuchelli across Wisconsin, Iowa, and Illinois. Over the next 30 years, he would build more than 20 churches, design the Iowa Old Capitol Building in Iowa City, found more schools, teach oil painting and astronomy, advocate for the rights of Native Americans, and bring untold numbers into the Church.

The Apostle of the Upper Midwest contracted pneumonia in 1864, while caring for the sick of his Wisconsin parish. He died that February. Pope John Paul II, 129 years later, conferred upon Mazzuchelli the title, "Venerable."

June 24: THE KNIGHT OF LABOR

May 4, 1886, was the beginning of the end for Terence V. Powderly and the Knights of Labor.

The week had started out well enough. In coordination with other groups, the Knights—led by Powderly—initiated a nationwide strike for their signature issue: the eight-hour workday. Although the Knights generally avoided strikes, preferring peaceful arbitration instead, they made an exception in this case.

All went according to plan until May 3, when conflict arose between strikers and police in Chicago. The following day, in retaliation, an anarchist protestor threw a bomb at police in Haymarket Square. The police responded with gunfire. By the end of the day, seven policemen and at least four workers were dead. More than 100 were injured.

Although the Knights eschewed violence and had nothing to do with the bombing, the public blamed them. Powderly was devastated.

Born into a large Irish-Catholic family in Carbondale, Pennsylvania, Powderly began working as a machinist at 13, joined the Knights of Labor at 27, and was its national leader within three years.

With him at the helm, the organization grew rapidly, admitting both skilled and unskilled workers, as well as women and African-Americans. By 1886, it had become the country's largest labor union, with more than 700,000 members. It also had the favor of increasing numbers of Catholic bishops.

Although Powderly was a poor organizer, he was an excellent politician—a skill that earned him three terms as Scranton's mayor and the trust of the Church's hierarchy, much of which initially viewed the Knights with suspicion. Powderly, however, recognizing the compatibility of Catholicism and unions, worked closely with Archbishops Gibbons and Ireland to make the organization more palatable to prelates, eventually securing the Vatican's permission for Catholics to join the Knights.

Unfortunately, after the Haymarket Affair, few did. Membership plummeted, and by 1893, Powderly himself left the union. He later worked for the U.S. Bureau of Immigration under Presidents William McKinley and Theodore Roosevelt.

Powderly died on **June 24, 1924.**

June 25: THE CATHOLIC COURT

Usually one. Maybe two. No more.

From 1836, when President Andrew Jackson appointed Chief Justice Roger B. Taney to the U.S. Supreme Court, until late in the Reagan Administration, that was the unspoken rule about how many Catholics could serve on the Court at the same time.

In fact, only twice between the country's founding and 1986, was there ever more than a single Catholic on the country's highest bench: Justices Edward White and Joseph McKenna served concurrently between 1898 and 1921, as did McKenna and Justice Pierce Butler between 1923 and 1925.

More often, Catholic justices tended to follow each other in steady succession. As one Catholic stepped down from the Court, another was appointed: Justice Frank Murphy succeeded Butler in 1940, Justice Sherman Minton followed Murphy in 1949, and Justice William J. Brennan, Jr., replaced Minton in 1956.

For good reason, court watchers and legal scholars came to speak of the "Catholic seat" on the Court, a seat given almost as a courtesy to the nation's single-largest religious group.

That began to change, however, during the Reagan Administration, when two Catholics—Justices Antonin Scalia and Anthony Kennedy—joined Brennan, bringing the Court's Catholic numbers to three. Brennan retired in 1990, but the following year another Catholic, Justice Clarence Thomas, joined the court. Then, in 2005 and 2006, in rapid succession, Chief Justice John G. Roberts and Justice Samuel Alito came on board.

Three years later, a sixth Catholic, Justice Sonia Sotomayer, joined the court. Born on **June 25, 1954,** Sotomayer was not only the first female Catholic Justice, but also the first Latina Justice. For observers of both court and culture, her appointment in May 2009 exemplified just how much had changed since the days when Catholics were granted only a token seat, and then, usually, begrudgingly, with anti-Catholic smears invariably surfacing.

With six Catholic justices serving on the Court under Roberts, the "Catholic seat" had become the "Catholic Court."

June 26: DEFENDING MARRIAGE

In 2013, six Catholics sat on the U.S. Supreme Court.

Nevertheless, on **June 26, 2013,** the Court ruled in a 5–4 decision that the Federal Government must recognize same-sex marriages when the couples' home states do so. Anything less, asserted Catholic Justice Anthony Kennedy, was a violation of the Fifth Amendment.

In a statement released that day, the United States Conference of Catholic Bishops said:

> *Today is a tragic day for marriage and our nation. The Supreme Court has dealt a profound injustice to the American people by striking down in part the federal Defense of Marriage Act. The Court got it wrong. The federal government ought to respect the truth that marriage is the union of one man and one woman, even where states fail to do so. The preservation of liberty and justice requires that all laws, federal and state, respect the truth, including the truth about marriage . . .*
>
> *Marriage is the only institution that brings together a man and a woman for life, providing any child who comes from their union with the secure foundation of a mother and a father.*
>
> *Our culture has taken for granted for far too long what human nature, experience, common sense, and God's wise design all confirm: the difference between a man and a woman matters, and the difference between a mom and a dad matters. While the culture has failed in many ways to be marriage-strengthening, this is no reason to give up. Now is the time to strengthen marriage, not redefine it.*
>
> *When Jesus taught about the meaning of marriage—the life-long, exclusive union of husband and wife—he pointed back to "the beginning" of God's creation of the human person as male and female (see Matthew 19). In the face of the customs and laws of his time, Jesus taught an unpopular truth that everyone could understand. The truth of marriage endures, and we will continue to boldly proclaim it with confidence and charity.*

On **June 27, 1944,** a 20-year-old girl from Texas drove to Camp Bennett, and enlisted in the Woman's Army Corps (WAC). She thought serving in World War II would be the bravest thing she would ever do.

She was wrong.

After the war, the girl—Nellie Gray—would become Catholic, earn her law degree from Georgetown University, and work for 28 years in the U.S. Departments of State and Labor. Not until the age of 49, however, would her bravest moment come.

That was in the wake of *Roe v. Wade* and *Doe v. Bolton,* the two 1973 Supreme Court rulings that legalized abortion. Horrified by the decisions, Gray partnered with the Knights of Columbus to organize a pro-life protest march. On the one-year anniversary of *Roe* and *Doe*—January 22, 1974—more than 20,000 people participated in the event.

When the march concluded, $400 remained in the organizers' coffers. As they debated what to do with the extra cash, one Knight suggested they save the money and do the whole thing over again the next year. So they did.

Gray quit her job and devoted the rest of her life to planning that annual march. As the years passed, more and more people joined her.

By the time of her death in 2012, hundreds of thousands of men, women, and children were traveling to Washington, D.C., every January to walk in the March for Life. Included among those travelers were the two women whose Supreme Court cases rebooted Gray's life: Norma McCorvey ("Jane Roe") and Sandra Cano ("Mary Doe"), both converts to the pro-life cause.

Near the end of her life, Gray reflected on the two great evils she combatted in her lifetime, saying, "After fighting against evil in World War II, I get very upset that we have Americans trying to justify abortion. Somehow a juggernaut of evil has grown in this country . . . We will never win this fight until this juggernaut is exposed and eliminated."

History remembers Thomas Jefferson as the author of American liberty. He earned that title for penning the Declaration of Independence, which he submitted to the Continental Congress on **June 28, 1776**.

But as then-Senator John F. Kennedy wrote in his 1958 book, *A Nation of Immigrants,* "No one man can take complete credit for the ideal of American democracy."

History agrees and has given at least some credit for the Declaration to Jefferson's editors, John Adams and Benjamin Franklin. George Mason, George Washington, and Thomas Ludwell Lee, who authored other founding documents from which Jefferson drew inspiration, have also received thanks.

In his book, however, Kennedy argued that history still needed to acknowledge one other man: Philip Mazzei.

Born in Tuscany and educated in Florence, Mazzei moved to London as a young man. There, he ran a successful import business for almost two decades, until in the early 1770s he met Franklin. At his urging, the Catholic Mazzei came to America in 1773, and taught Virginia's planters how to cultivate vineyards.

While in Virginia, Mazzei settled on a plantation near Jefferson's. The two became friends and corresponded regularly about politics and philosophy.

In Mazzei's letters, Jefferson found a phrase he would later borrow for the Declaration of Independence: "All men are created equal."

Although not an exact quote—which would be difficult as he and Jefferson corresponded in Italian—both Kennedy in his 1958 book and the U.S. Congress in 1994, recognized that fundamental phrase as originating in Mazzei's writing.

Those words weren't Mazzei's only contributions to the cause of liberty. He later served as an emissary for Virginia in Italy and helped smuggle arms to the Continental Army. His words to Jefferson, however, remain his most enduring contribution.

To honor him for that, the U.S. Government issued a commemorative stamp in 1980, which bore Mazzei's image and the words he first wrote to Jefferson: "All men are by nature equally free and independent."

> *My name is Marie Justine Cirnaire. I was born in Guinea. When*
> *I was perhaps seven years of age I was carried to St. Domingue. I*
> *am as a result not aware of the name of my father or my mother,*
> *nor do I know my age. I was married to Bernard Couvent, free*
> *Negro, whose widow I now am. We have had no children . . .*
>
> *I bequeath and order that my land at the corner of Grand*
> *Hommes and Union Streets be dedicated and used in perpetuity*
> *for the establishment of a free school for the colored orphans of the*
> *Faubourg Marigny . . . Also, I declare that said lands and build-*
> *ings shall never be sold under any pretext whatsoever.*
> *Signed,*
> *Madame Marie C. Couvent,*
> *Native of West Africa, Former Slave, Free Woman of Color*

Shortly before her death, on **June 29, 1837,** Marie Couvent dictated those words to her priest, Father Constantine Maenhault of St. Louis Cathedral, New Orleans.

Couvent had come to New Orleans decades earlier, in the wake of the great Haitian slave uprising. In Louisiana, she found freedom, and through her hard work and the work of her husband, New Orleans' preeminent Afro-Creole carpenter Bernard Couvent, she built up a substantial fortune.

Although it took more than 10 years of legal wrangling after her death, that fortune eventually gave rise to the *Institute Catholique,* a private Catholic school that made it possible for thousands of the city's free black children to learn what their patroness never did: how to read and write.

At the time of the school's founding, New Orleans prohibited free black children from attending public schools. In order to educate their children, the city's wealthier African-Americans hired private tutors or sent their children to school in France. Couvent's legacy, once secured, helped to provide for the rest.

Although the *Institute Catholique* was destroyed by a hurricane in 1915, a steady succession of Catholic schools have operated on the property ever since, ensuring that the wishes of a former slave are honored to this day.

June 30: FROM SLAVE TO SAINT

He could have been free, but he chose slavery. He could have been wealthy, but he chose generosity. He could have been a saint, and that's what the Archdiocese of New York contends Venerable Pierre Toussaint was.

Born into slavery in 1766, Toussaint traveled from Haiti to New York in 1787, with his owners, the Bérards. The Bérards planned to return to their Haitian plantation, but then Haiti's slaves rebelled. After the violence ended, Toussaint's master, Jean Bérard went home to assess their losses. He died while there. Back in New York, his wife was left almost penniless . . . but not alone.

Shortly before the rebellion, the Bérards had sent Toussaint to learn the trade of hairdressing. He proved talented, and New York's finest clamored for his services. Soon Toussaint earned enough to buy his freedom.

When news came of Jean Bérard's death, however, Toussaint chose to remain a slave. He loved the Bérards. They treated him like a son, taught him to read, and raised him in the Catholic Faith. He didn't want to abandon his mistress in her poverty. So, he stayed with her, supporting her from his earnings until her death in 1807.

After that, as a free man, Toussaint continued his work and found a wife, Juliette, who shared both his Catholic faith and charitable inclinations. Together, the couple used Toussaint's earnings to found a school for orphaned African-Americans, purchase freedom for dozens of slaves, provide food and housing for whites and blacks alike, aid refugees, and support the Catholic churches of New York. Numbered among those churches were St. Patrick's Old Cathedral and Touissant's own parish, old St. Peter's, where he attended daily Mass for 66 years. Toussaint also took in orphans, nursed the sick, and provided spiritual counsel to clergy and laity alike.

When he died, on **June 30, 1853,** his pastor told the huge crowd of mourners, "There were very few left among the clergy superior to him in devotion and zeal for the Church and for the glory of God; among laymen, none."

July

July 1: AN HONORARY IRISHMAN

The Confederate artillery barrage began around 1 p.m. Not until the evening of **July 1, 1862,** however, was the Fighting Irish Brigade—the 69th New York Infantry—of the Union Army ordered to proceed to Malvern Hill, where General Robert E. Lee had launched yet another frontal assault at retreating Union forces.

As the men marched toward the battle, their chaplain, Father Thomas Ouellet, S.J., marched with them.

Born and raised in Canada, the French-Canadian Jesuit completed his seminary studies at St. John's College, then remained in New York until his order sent him to Europe in 1857. Once the American Civil War began, Ouellet returned to New York to volunteer for the military chaplaincy. There, the French-Canadian was appointed to a unit composed exclusively of Irish-Americans.

The Irishmen, however, grew to respect their French priest. Although he was a martinet about religion, he was an egalitarian martinet, who would chastise a colonel for swearing as quick as he'd chastise a private. More important, Ouellet was fearless in battle, standing always in the line of fire so he could be closest to the men who needed him most. When others urged him to fall back, he dismissed them. "I'm more than a soldier in McClellan's army," Ouellet would say. "I'm a soldier of Christ."

Ouellet proved that at the Battle of Malvern Hill. As night fell and men fought by the light of bursting shells, Ouellet waged into open fire. With a lantern in hand, he moved from wounded man to wounded man, asking, "Are you Catholic? And do you wish absolution?"

One badly injured man answered, "No, but I would like to die in the Faith of any man who has the courage to come and see me in such a place as this."

Captured by the Confederates before the battle's end, but soon released, Ouellet continued to serve as a chaplain until 1865. He then spent the remainder of his life working in American and Canadian parishes, as well as Native American missions.

July 2: THE BLACK SISTERS OF BALTIMORE

Mary Elizabeth Lange had the dark skin of her mother, a native of San Domingo. Thanks to her wealthy French father, however, she knew nothing but comfort and privilege in her native Havana.

That changed after 1812, when unrest among Cuba's slaves drove Lange away from her homeland. A year later, Lange settled in Baltimore, where regardless of her fortune, her skin color put her at the bottom of the city's social ladder.

Lange, however, didn't accept the limitations placed on her. Rather, she defied them, and used her money to open a school in her home for the children of other Caribbean immigrants—free blacks still banned from Baltimore's schools.

More than a decade passed. Lange's fortune dwindled. Then, she met a Sulpician priest, Father James Joubert.

Joubert had been attempting to catechize Baltimore's free African and Caribbean-Americans, but so few could read or write that he found the work nearly impossible. Lange, for her part, dreamed of entering a religious order, but found her black skin made it nearly impossible. Together, Lange and Joubert came up with a plan to make the impossible possible. Lange would found the first religious order for black women in America, and Joubert would help her finance Catholic schools for black children. Their plan became reality on **July 2, 1829,** when four women, including Lange, made their vows as Oblate Sisters of Providence.

Success, however, came slowly for the Oblates. Black religious opening Catholic schools for black children scandalized many, and the sisters were mocked, insulted, and threatened for their work. For similar reasons, as Baltimore's bishops came and went, support for their work waxed and waned. At times, the sisters survived only by begging in the streets.

Nevertheless, despite overwhelming opposition, the Oblates eventually founded more than a dozen schools in Baltimore and beyond. And by the time the 88-year-old Mother Lange died in 1882, the order's future was secure. Its work continues in Baltimore and elsewhere to this day.

July 3: AFTER GETTYSBURG

At first, the sisters saw only a thin blue line on the horizon. But within minutes, blue was everywhere. The date was June 27, 1863, and the Union Army was coming to St. Joseph's Academy in Emmitsburg, Maryland.

When the soldiers' commanding officer finally arrived, he promised that his troops would remain only a short while at the Sisters of Charity's motherhouse and school. In the meantime, he requested food for his men and urged the sisters to invoke St. Joseph's protection over their house and grounds.

The sisters complied on both counts.

Three days later, the Union Army packed up camp and moved north to Gettysburg. The next day, the bloodiest battle of the American Civil War began.

For three days, as guns roared in the distance, the sisters remained in the chapel, praying without ceasing. The guns fell silent late on **July 3, 1863**. Soon afterwards, the sisters set out for the battlefield.

One of the women, Sister Matilda Coskery, described what they found:

> *Houses burnt, dead bodies of both Armies strewn here and there, an immense number of slain horses, thousands of bayonets, sabres, wagons, wheels, projectiles of all dimensions, blankets, caps, clothing of every color covered the woods and fields. We were compelled to drive very cautiously to avoid passing over the dead. Our terrified horses drew back or darted forward reeling from one side to the other. The farther we advanced the more harrowing was the scene; we could not restrain our tears.*

Rain soaked the battlefield, but that didn't prevent the sisters from tending to the wounded. As more help arrived, they moved everyone they could to farmhouses, businesses, churches—any place the women could find to nurse the soldiers.

The sisters spent the following weeks traveling between 113 makeshift hospitals, caring for Union and Confederate soldiers alike. No officer dared refuse their requests for supplies. And by summer's end, thousands of men, who otherwise would have perished, returned home.

All told, nearly 300 Sisters of Charity served as nurses during the American Civil War.

Every man who signed the Declaration of Independence had something to lose. In putting their name to the document, they committed treason. If their bid for independence went wrong, everything they had—their property, their livelihoods, their freedom—would disappear.

Charles Carroll of Carrollton, however, had more to lose than most.

The only son of Maryland's richest planter and cousin to the future Archbishop John Carroll, Charles Carroll was one of the wealthiest men in America at the time. But that didn't stop him from signing the Declaration after the Congress passed it on **July 4, 1776.** When it came to revolution, fortune or no, he was all in.

Carroll had been all in for nearly a decade. Although he spent 16 years on the far side of the Atlantic studying in France and London, he began agitating for independence soon after he returned to Annapolis in 1765. In the pages of the *Maryland Gazette* (under the pseudonym "First Citizen") and on various committees of correspondence, he championed American self-governance and railed against British taxation policies.

By the early 1770s, Carroll anticipated armed conflict, telling his friend Samuel Chase that it would ultimately require "the bayonet" to resolve the colonies' dispute with the British. "Our arguments will only raise the feelings of the people to that pitch, when open war will be looked to as the arbiter of the dispute," he predicted.

In 1776, Carroll became one of Maryland's delegates to the Continental Congress. Although he wasn't present to vote on Jefferson's Declaration, he signed it gladly and proudly, giving the document its lone Catholic signature.

In later years, Carroll served as both a state senator and U.S. senator, advocated (unsuccessfully) for the gradual abolition of slavery in Maryland, and sought to resettle former slaves in Liberia.

When Carroll died on November 14, 1832, he was the last surviving signer of the Declaration of Independence—an act that, in the end, cost him little and gained him much.

Rafael Cordero dreamed of teaching the children of Puerto Rico. Despite his family's poverty, his parents—the artist Lucas Cordero and his wife, Rita—provided their three children with a good education at home. Cordero saw no reason why other poor children shouldn't have the same opportunity, and believed he could give it to them.

There was only one problem: Cordero was black, which meant in 1810 Puerto Rico he couldn't hold a teacher's license.

The 20-year-old Cordero weighed his options. In the end, he decided that teaching children mattered more than obeying an unjust law, and opened his home to any and all children, black or white, who wanted an education. He asked for no payment, so even the poorest of the poor could afford to learn.

For 58 years, Cordero personally instructed all the students who came to his home on Luna Street in San Juan. The school day, as he designed it, began with a *Salve Regina*. Lessons in reading, writing, mathematics, and catechetics followed. After the children left, Cordero set his books aside and worked late into the night, making shoes and cigars so that he could support himself and the school.

Over time, Cordero's reputation as a teacher spread, attracting the notice of Puerto Rico's governor, Juan Prim y Prats. Wanting to investigate the city's black teacher of the poor, Prats paid the school a visit. He left so impressed that not a word was said about Cordero lacking a teaching license.

Before Cordero's death, on **July 5, 1868,** he taught some of Puerto Rico's greatest heroes, including abolitionist Román Baldorioty de Castro and the "Father of Puerto Rican Literature," Alejandro Tapia y Rivera.

Cordero himself is known as the "Father of Public Schools in Puerto Rico." And since December 2013, when Pope Francis moved the Puerto Rican teacher one step closer to sainthood, he is also known as Venerable Rafael Cordero.

July 6: CHAOS IN PHILADELPHIA

The Nativists were at it again. On July 3, 1844, Father John Dunn, pastor of St. Philip Neri Church in Philadelphia, learned that the anti-Catholic group planned to go on parade and burn his church to the ground. Only two months before, the same crowd had torched multiple Catholic churches and homes, as well as a school and convent. During the riots, Catholic Philadelphia followed Bishop Francis Kenrick's orders to avoid conflict and let the buildings burn.

But this time, regardless of what the bishop wanted, Dunn was determined to protect his church.

To that end, the priest sought permission from the governor to stockpile weapons in the parish. Dunn assured the governor that he would use them only if the Nativists attacked. He received permission and the weapons. A few of the muskets were faulty, though, so Dunn returned those and requested replacements.

Trouble started when the replacements arrived.

On July 5, a few Nativists saw the muskets delivered. They spread the word that Catholics were arming themselves, and soon thousands of Nativists stood outside St. Philip's, demanding that the sheriff seize the weapons. Hoping to calm the crowd, the sheriff reclaimed a few muskets and asked everyone to disperse.

Instead, the mob demanded a second search, this time with their men. Seventeen Nativists forced their way into the church. There, they found the stockpile of weapons and gunpowder. Knowing the chaos such a discovery would unleash, the sheriff refused to let the search party leave the church and ordered the crowd to disperse.

Tensions only escalated. By the evening of **July 6, 1844,** three cannons and a large group of city guards had arrived outside St. Philip's. The next day, the guards started firing those cannons. Soon after, the Nativists had cannons of their own and fired them at the church. Chaos reigned yet again.

That reign continued until July 9. By that point, at least 15 people were dead and 50 injured. This time, however, the city's churches still stood.

July 7: CARROLL'S CATHEDRAL

One might think that President Thomas Jefferson was too busy running the federal government in 1806 to take an interest in the design of a Catholic cathedral in Baltimore.

If so, one would be wrong.

Jefferson, himself a student of architecture, had previously hired his friend Benjamin Henry Latrobe to build the U.S. Capitol. When he learned Latrobe had volunteered to design the first Catholic cathedral in the United States, he grew curious. That curiosity only increased when he learned of Bishop John Carroll's plans.

Those plans were for a cathedral distinctly American in style. Carroll wanted the design of his church to reflect the country he shepherded, so he asked Latrobe to eschew the Gothic and Romanesque designs of the Old World and build something more in accord with the neoclassical lines favored in the New World. At the same time, he also wanted a cathedral as magnificent as any cathedral in Europe, announcing in marble and glass that, at long last, Catholics in America could worship as they wished.

While Latrobe drew up his design, Jefferson looked on, occasionally suggesting alterations. Finally, the plans were complete, and on **July 7, 1806,** Carroll laid the cornerstone for the Cathedral of the Assumption of the Blessed Virgin Mary. It would take 15 more years, with frequent stops and starts, before construction ended. Once complete, however, no building in America, save for the U.S. Capitol, rivaled Baltimore's proto-cathedral in size or architectural sophistication. Even today, many consider it Latrobe's greatest work.

America's first cathedral was elevated by Rome to a basilica in 1937 and designated a national shrine by the U.S. bishops in 1993. Ten years later, the Archdiocese of Baltimore undertook a $34 million renovation of the basilica. That renovation restored Baltimore's proto-cathedral to its original splendor, ensuring that pilgrims for centuries to come can marvel at the architectural masterpiece that captured the imagination of America's third president.

July 8: ARCHBISHOP KENRICK, THE ELDER

It's a rare family that produces one archbishop. Yet Thomas and Jane Kenrick of Dublin, Ireland, produced two: Peter, archbishop of St. Louis, and Francis, archbishop of Baltimore.

Francis was the elder son. Born in Ireland in 1796 and educated in Rome, he was ordained a priest in 1821. Soon afterwards, he volunteered for the mission fields and joined Bishop Joseph Flaget in Bardstown.

In Kentucky, when not teaching theology and Greek, Father Francis traveled throughout the diocese, defending the Church in a series of apologetics lectures. Nine years later, his intelligence and administrative skills earned him a trip to Philadelphia, where the weary Bishop Henry Conwell still struggled with fallout from the Hogan Schism. Ordained coadjutor bishop for the diocese, Kenrick took over Conwell's administrative duties and soon brought the rebellious parishioners of St. Mary's Cathedral back into line.

Kenrick ran the diocese for 12 years before Conwell died and he became Philadelphia's third shepherd. In those first 12 years and the nine he served as bishop, he helped nurse the city through a cholera epidemic, established a free Catholic school in every parish, resolved the last of the problems wrought by trusteeism, and began translating the Old and New Testaments into English.

He also convinced his brother Peter to come to America, founded Philadelphia's first Catholic newspaper, and dealt with an anti-Catholic riot . . . or two. Despite losing churches to the Nativist riots, the number of parishes in Philadelphia grew from 22 to 92 during Kenrick's tenure.

After 21 years in Philadelphia, Francis Kenrick moved to Baltimore to serve as the archdiocese's sixth archbishop. There, he presided over the First Plenary Council of Baltimore, restored administrative order to a chaotic chancery, instituted the 40 Hours' Devotion, and, in 1854, traveled to Rome for the promulgation of the Dogma of the Immaculate Conception.

Kenrick's 42 busy years as a priest and bishop came to an abrupt end on **July 8, 1863**. That morning, word reached him of the bloodshed in nearby Gettysburg. Grief-struck, he didn't live to see the sun set.

As a child, Rose Hawthorne lived a charmed life. Adored by her famous father, author Nathaniel Hawthorne, she spent her childhood in Europe and grew up surrounded by the literary elites of the day.

As an adult, however, she endured a difficult marriage to an alcoholic, the loss of her only child, and a stalled career as a writer.

Hawthorne found the strength to endure those trials in the wake of her and her husband's 1891 conversion to Catholicism. Her husband did not find the same. As his drinking grew worse, Hawthorne obtained her bishop's permission to separate. She then created a new life for herself, caring for cancer patients in the slums of New York.

In the early days of her work, she explained that choice, writing:

> *The distance up Fifth Avenue sometimes seems as far and as frozen as the road to the famous mines of Alaska. Or so it seems when I stand in my little rooms, very nearly at the end of my money for the time being, and ask myself: What am I trying to do down here among the poor? To make impossible the homeless condition of incurable cancer patients; to make impossible their semi-neglect in homes that are unfit for them; to take the lowest class we know, both in poverty and suffering, and put them in such a condition, that if our Lord knocked at the door we should not be ashamed to show what we have done.*

Following the death of her husband in 1898, Hawthorne took the Dominican habit. With her friend Alice Huber, she founded a religious order, the Servants of Relief for Incurable Cancer (now the Dominican Sisters of Hawthorne). And in 1901, as Mother Mary Alphonsa, she opened a home for cancer patients in Hawthorne, New York.

There, on **July 9, 1926,** she died, and there, as well as in Philadelphia and Atlanta, her order continues her work, providing free care to terminally ill cancer patients.

Mother Alphonsa's cause for canonization opened in 2003.

The French Revolution, with its rabid anti-clericalism, brought untold suffering to the Church in France. But to the Church in the fledgling United States, it brought untold blessings in the form of Sulpician priests.

In 1790, when Father John Carroll traveled to London for his episcopal consecration, he met the Sulpician's superior-general, Father Jacques-André Emery. Father Emery needed to find a new mission field for his French priests and seminarians before the guillotine found them. The papal nuncio suggested he consider Baltimore. Carroll, desperate for help in his vast diocese, seconded the suggestion, and Emery agreed to send four priests to America to found a seminary.

Those four priests, along with five Sulpician seminarians, arrived in the United States on **July 10, 1791**. Almost immediately, they purchased One Mile Tavern in Baltimore and opened the first seminary in the United States: St. Mary's.

The following year, more Sulpicians and seminarians arrived. By 1795, the order comprised nearly a third of the 35 priests then serving in the United States and her territories.

The list of those first Sulpicians reads like a "Who's Who" in the Church in early America, including luminaries such as Benedict Joseph Flaget, the first Bishop of Bardstown; Gabriel Richard, missionary to Detroit; Stephen Badin, the first priest ordained in America; Louis William DuBourg, bishop of Louisiana and the Two Floridas; and Ambrose Maréchal, the third archbishop of Baltimore.

With such giants at the helm, it's not surprising that the Sulpicians became the fathers of seminary formation in America. In addition to St. Mary's in Baltimore, the Sulpicians founded or administered nearly a dozen other seminaries, including St. John's Seminary in Boston, St. Joseph's Seminary in New York, St. Patrick's Seminary in San Francisco, St. Edward's Seminary in Washington, and the Theological College in Washington, D.C.

Throughout the nineteenth and early-twentieth centuries, those Sulpician-run seminaries formed thousands of faithful priests for parishes across the United States. That made the French Revolution, at least for the Church in America, the gift that kept on giving.

July 11: NO QUARTER

On **July 11, 1839,** the American Protestant missionaries stationed in Hawaii sent a letter to the U.S. consulate, requesting sanctuary. The French frigate *Artémise* had sailed into port the day before, and the missionaries feared for their lives.

No other Americans, however, shared their fear.

The *Artémise*'s captain, Cyrille Laplace, came with orders to "commence hostilities" if Hawaii's King Kamehameha III didn't reverse the decade-old prohibition of Catholicism. After Laplace delivered the warning to the king, he invited all Americans residing on the island to board his ship, where they could wait out the conflict in safety. That is, he invited all Americans to board *except* for the islands' Protestant missionaries. As far as Laplace was concerned, those missionaries were on their own.

Laplace's seeming lack of charity stemmed from his belief that the missionaries had brought the danger upon themselves.

Eight years earlier, many of those same missionaries convinced Hawaii's newly converted Protestant queen regent Ka'ahumanu to ban Catholicism from her son's kingdom. The Catholic priests then serving in the islands were rounded up and deported, via ship, on December 24, 1831. Once the priests left, Hawaiian officials went after the islands' native Catholics, imprisoning and torturing them until they renounced their faith and embraced Protestantism.

The Church attempted to resolve the matter peacefully, but those attempts stalled in 1836. Finally, France took charge of the situation, and commissioned Laplace to "make it well understood that it would be to the advantage of the chiefs of those islands of the Ocean to conduct themselves in such a manner as not to incur the wrath of France."

King Kamehameha III knew he didn't stand a chance against Laplace and quickly conceded, issuing the Edict of Toleration on July 17, 1839. By means of reparation, he gave the Church a substantial piece of land on which to build a church.

As for the Protestant missionaries, they were less than pleased that Catholicism had returned to Hawaii, but quite pleased to escape "the wrath of France."

July 12: ON DYING WELL

In 53 years, Tony Snow accomplished much. He served as press secretary to two President Bushes, hosted his own television and radio shows, and was a widely published journalist. But in the end, none of those accomplishments could keep cancer at bay.

Still, for all the suffering the cancer caused, it also became an occasion of grace. Years earlier, while still in college, Snow assessed the state of the world and found it wanting. He became Catholic and threw himself into the practice of his newfound faith. But then he fell in love with an evangelical Protestant. She wanted to marry in her church. He wanted to marry in his. The bride won, and after the wedding, Snow continued to worship with his wife in her church.

In 2005, however, after learning he had cancer, Snow resumed the practice of his faith. He had his marriage regularized, returned to the sacraments, and began studying Catholic teachings with the same enthusiasm of his college days.

Through it all, Snow learned to make sense of his suffering. Shortly before his death, he explained how he did that in an essay for *Christianity Today.*

He wrote:

> *God relishes surprise. We want lives of simple, predictable ease—smooth, even trails as far as the eye can see—but God likes to go off-road. He provokes us with twists and turns. He places us in predicaments that seem to defy our endurance and comprehension—and yet don't. By his love and grace we persevere. The challenges that make our hearts leap and stomachs churn invariably strengthen our faith and grant measures of wisdom and joy we would not experience otherwise.*

Snow died on **July 12, 2008.**

July 13: TAKING THE PLEDGE

In 1849, thousands of cheering New Yorkers greeted Father Theobald Mathew, the famous temperance priest, when he first arrived in the United States from Ireland. The same held true in Boston, Philadelphia, and everywhere else Father Mathew visited.

But not Pittsburgh. When the steamship *Cornplanter* docked there, on **July 13, 1851,** only a few people stood on the docks.

That's not to say the city wasn't eagerly awaiting Father Mathew's arrival. Pittsburgh, like most of America, was enraptured with the priest. They knew that after he founded the Cork Total Abstinence Society in 1836, it took him only six months to convince 150,000 Irishmen to do the unimaginable: Give up the drink. Now that he'd come to America, temperance advocates hoped he could do the same here.

Mathew didn't disappoint. As he traveled the country, he persuaded hundreds of thousands of Catholics to take his famous temperance pledge. Lauded by bishops and politicians alike, he dined at the White House with President Zachary Taylor and became the second non-U.S. citizen admitted to the Senate floor (the first was the Marquis de Lafayette). The only people who didn't love the priest were German immigrants (who had no intention of giving up their beer) and abolitionists angered by his silence regarding slavery.

For his first two years in America, Pittsburgh Catholics cheered those successes and waited anxiously for Mathew to visit them. So, why the empty docks when he finally came?

That was Mathew's fault. The busy priest only sent word of his arrival the day before his ship docked, which gave his supporters no time to spread the news. During Mathew's two-week stay in Pittsburgh, however, his fans came out in force, with more than 11,000 people in the city taking the pledge.

Four months later, in November 1851, Father Mathew sailed home to Ireland. He left behind a nation with 600,000 fewer drinkers. America wasn't dry yet, but after Father Mathew's visit, it was on its way.

Saints aren't prone to moderation—at least, not when it comes to show-ing their love for Christ. And Saint Kateri Tekakwitha was no exception.

Born in 1656 in what is now upstate New York, Kateri Tekakwitha was the daughter of a Mohawk chief. When she was only four, however, smallpox came to her village, killing her father and the rest of her family. Tekakwitha survived, but the disease left her face badly scarred.

Later adopted by her uncle, the Mohawk princess lived a quiet life, avoiding others and hiding her face from view. When Jesuit missionaries came around, however, curiosity trumped vanity. Tekakwitha ventured out to meet them, eager to learn more about Jesus. Faith came quickly. It did not, however, come cheap.

First, Tekakwitha's uncle opposed her baptism. Later, after he con-sented, both her family and her fellow villagers opposed her efforts to practice the Catholic Faith, mocking her for not working on Sundays and criticizing her decision to remain celibate.

Eventually, with the help of her brother-in-law, Tekakwitha escaped her uncle's house and traveled north to modern-day Canada, where a community of Mohawk Christians and Jesuit missionaries lived. There, Tekakwitha made a vow of perpetual virginity and embarked on a life of extreme penance—frequently fasting, praying for long hours in a freez-ing chapel, and even sleeping on a bed of thorns.

Tekakwitha's extreme devotion most likely contributed to her early death at the age of 24. But it also earned her the admiration of all who knew her, and led to her veneration by Catholic Americans, Native Americans, and Canadians for centuries after her death.

Beatified by Pope John Paul II in 1980 and canonized by Pope Bene-dict XVI in 2012, the "Lily of the Mohawks" is America's first Native American saint. Catholics around the world celebrate her feast day on **July 14**.

July 15: THE CRIME OF KNOWING LATIN

John Ury may have been a Catholic priest. Or he may have been nothing more than a schoolteacher. But he taught Latin. And, in 1741 New York, that was enough to send him to the gallows.

The man himself is clouded in mystery, with little known about Ury before the spring of 1741. That's when he moved to New York, supposedly from New Jersey, and took a job as a private tutor instructing children in Latin and Greek.

Unfortunately for Ury, he arrived in the city just as rumors of a possible slave rebellion started circulating. When a series of fires broke out, frightened New Yorkers believed rumor had become fact, and began rounding up suspects. By early summer, more than half the city's slave population was in jail. A fair number of poor whites were with them.

The suspects multiplied by the day as the accused indicted others, hoping to better their position, and as neighbors turned in neighbors, seeking revenge for small spites. The situation had escalated beyond all reason, when the lead investigator, Daniel Horsemanden, learned that a Catholic priest might be in town. That priest was (or maybe was) Ury.

Convinced that no slave could have concocted such a grand "plot," Horsemanden decided that if a priest resided in New York, a priest must be responsible. He had no evidence, but that didn't stop him from arresting Ury in mid-June. Ury's trial began a month later, on **July 15, 1741**. With anti-Catholic sentiment in New York at fever pitch, no attorney would defend Ury. So, he defended himself.

Although Ury never admitted to being a priest, he never denied it either. He did deny, however, that he had any knowledge of or involvement in fomenting rebellion. His testimony was credible. The testimony of the other witnesses (who were paid to speak against him) was riddled with contradiction and error. The only thing no one disputed, including Ury, was his knowledge of Latin.

Nevertheless, that proved sufficient. He swung on August 29, 1741.

For more than 70 years, Mortimer J. Adler's writing served as a gateway to the Catholic Church, helping both Protestants and secularists find their way home. Yet Adler himself refused to join the Church until it was almost too late.

Born in 1902 to a secular Jewish family, Adler had little interest in God or religion until, as a student at Columbia University, he discovered the writings of Thomas Aquinas. Enamored with the Angelic Doctor's clear, precise thinking, Adler soon became part of the early twentieth century's neo-Thomistic revival.

In 1930, Adler's work in Thomistic philosophy secured him a professorship at the University of Chicago School of Law. There, he embarked upon the project that would define his professional life: making classic works of philosophy and literature accessible to the common man.

Along with the school's president, Robert Hutchins, Adler launched the Great Books of the Western World series through Encyclopedia Britannica. He also served on the Board of Editors for Encyclopedia Britannica, eventually becoming its chairman, and published his own series of popular books on philosophy, religion, education, and more.

As early as the 1940s, that work led people to assume that Adler had left his secular Judaism behind and entered the Catholic Church. But in life, as opposed to work, Adler struggled to embrace the Church's moral teachings. He verged on the edge of conversion for years, but he still wavered as late as **July 16, 1980,** the date he published his apologia on God's existence, *How to Think About God: A Guide for the 20th-Century Pagan.*

When Adler finally did embrace Christianity, it was as an Episcopalian, the faith of his second wife, Caroline. Only after her death in 1998, did Adler complete the journey that began nearly 80 years before, entering the Catholic Church at the age of 97. He died less than two years later.

When Father Joseph Alemany, O.P., immigrated to the United States from Spain in 1840, fewer than 400 people lived in the village of Yerba Buena, California. By 1851, when Alemany arrived as bishop, the village had been renamed San Francisco and was home to almost 40,000 residents.

Both events—Alemany's appointment to the newly created Diocese of Monterey and the city's mushrooming population—stemmed from the 1848 discovery of gold nearby. In the wake of that find, men and women from around the world came pouring into the city. Along with them, came saloons, gambling halls, and brothels.

To that mission field, Rome sent Alemany.

While the bishop established schools and hospitals, he also made plans for a cathedral—a beautiful, centrally located building that bore silent witness to God in a city filled with debauchery and dissipation.

To put those plans into action, he hired two architects, who modeled the new cathedral's design on a church in Alemany's hometown. They then contracted with granite suppliers in China and brick makers in New England to ship the necessary materials across the Pacific and around Cape Horn.

On **July 17, 1853,** Bishop Alemany laid the cornerstone for the future St. Mary's Cathedral. Seventeen months later, on Christmas Eve, the church opened its doors for Mass. Above those doors was a message, carved in stone for those who walked the city's streets: "Son, Observe the Time and Fly from Evil."

Unfortunately, few listened, and by 1884, when Alemany retired as archbishop of San Francisco, brothels and saloons flanked the cathedral on all sides. For that reason, his successor, Archbishop Patrick Riordan, built San Francisco a new cathedral in a better neighborhood.

Old St. Mary's, however, still stands. Fire gutted her in 1906, but the Paulist Fathers quickly rebuilt and carried on the work begun by Archbishop Alemany: proclaiming Christ to the wounded and weak.

On **July 18, 2007,** strains of Bach filled Loretto Chapel in Santa Fe, New Mexico. The music couldn't have found a more fitting home. The Gothic chapel's acoustics were perfect for Bach, just as they were once perfect for the voices of the Sisters of Loretto, who chanted the Church's Office in the chapel daily for nearly a century.

By 2007, however, the sisters' voices hadn't sounded in the chapel for decades. Deconsecrated in 1971, the only people who'd filled Loretto Chapel in the years since were wedding guests, concert-goers, and curiosity seekers come to hear the tale of the Miraculous Staircase of Loretto.

According to legend, in 1878, as the chapel neared completion, the sisters realized the architect (who died months earlier) hadn't included a staircase to the choir loft. Confused, they consulted several carpenters. The carpenters, however, were no help. They told the sisters that adding a staircase was impossible and advised them to use a ladder instead.

As the choir loft towered 20 feet above the church floor, the sisters didn't like that suggestion much. So, they began a novena to St. Joseph and entrusted the problem to him. On the final day of the novena, a carpenter riding on a donkey appeared at the chapel. He asked if the sisters had any work for him. They showed him to the chapel.

The man labored for months. Then, as soon as he finished, he disappeared, lingering neither for thanks nor pay. The sisters searched for him, but in vain.

The staircase he left behind, however, was a marvel of engineering and construction. Ascending 20 feet, without the use of nails or a central support beam, it includes two 360-degree turns and is made of non-native wood. To this day, engineers agree that building such a staircase would be difficult now, but in an age of hand tools, near impossible.

The sisters, however, didn't wonder at their miracle. They expected St. Joseph to deliver, and he did.

July 19: TROUBLE COMES FOR THE ARCHBISHOP

When Bishop Jean-Baptiste Lamy arrived in Santa Fe in 1851, a few problems awaited him: corrupt priests openly living with their mistresses; a bizarre fraternal sect practicing ritualized crucifixions; and a laity almost completely unschooled in Catholic doctrine. In the midst of the mess, the last thing Bishop Lamy needed was a Vatican clerical error. But that's what he got.

Lamy, who was born in France, came to Ohio as a missionary in 1839. Eleven years later, the Church created the Apostolic Vicariate of New Mexico, and appointed Lamy its leader.

Thanks to a shipwreck and other disasters, it took Lamy 10 months to reach Santa Fe. When he did arrive, he found the local Church in shambles, having been ignored by previous bishops for more than a century. To make matters worse, his clergy refused to recognize his authority. Their bishop, they claimed, was Bishop Zubiría of Durango.

Hoping to nip the trouble in the bud, Lamy hopped on a horse and rode the thousand miles to Durango. There, he discovered the Vatican clerical error: Rome forgot to tell Zubiría that his diocese had been redrawn and a new bishop appointed.

Neither bishop was happy about the situation, but when Lamy returned to Santa Fe, he carried with him a letter from Zubiría, ordering clergy to obey their new bishop. Obedience didn't come in a day; Lamy wrestled with rebellious clergy for years. And when he wasn't wrestling, he was either on horseback—traversing a diocese that at one point spanned today's New Mexico, Arizona, and Colorado—or building parishes, hospitals, and schools.

Nevertheless, in the end, patience won the day, and by the time Lamy retired on **July 19, 1885,** the Archdiocese of Santa Fe was flourishing.

Archbishop Lamy died three years later. His legend, however, lives on in the novel he inspired, Willa Cather's *Death Comes for the Archbishop.*

July 20: A DIFFERENT DECLARATION OF INDEPENDENCE

In July 1776, the United States declared its independence from Great Britain. In July 1967, Catholic universities in America similarly declared their independence from Rome.

That declaration of independence came in the wake of three days of meetings in Land O'Lakes, Wisconsin. In attendance at those meetings were 26 Catholic educators, primarily from America's preeminent Catholic institutions of higher education. The conference began on **July 20, 1967,** and ended on July 23, when all 26 men signed the "Statement on the Nature of the Contemporary Catholic University"—now more commonly known as "The Land O'Lakes Statement."

Those who drafted the document argued that it wasn't so much freedom from Rome that they were asserting, but the importance of academic freedom to any university, Catholic or otherwise. They believed that Vatican II's call to engage the modern world demanded that Catholic universities up the ante for academic excellence. To their view, this couldn't be achieved when their every move was answerable to bishops and religious superiors who were not professional academics or administrators.

To the authors' credit, their statement recognized the preeminence of theology to a Catholic university, as well as the mission of Catholic universities to serve the universal Church. In the years that followed, however, as many Catholic schools pursued the goals laid out by The Land O'Lakes Statement, Catholic identity often fell by the wayside. Dissent became the norm in most theology departments, and the Catholic Faith ceased to inform many schools' curricula or campus life. Academic "freedom" flourished, but often at the cost of faith.

By 1990, the situation in some universities was so problematic that Pope John Paul II attempted a course correction, outlining the proper mission and objectives of Catholic higher education in the apostolic constitution *Ex Corde Ecclesiae.*

Despite that attempt, Catholic colleges and universities still remain divided about the place of academic freedom and the meaning of Catholic identity in higher education.

Father Wilhelm Grutza, pastor of Milwaukee's St. Josaphat Catholic Church, was determined to not let a good building go to waste.

His parish, composed mostly of Polish immigrants, had grown rapidly since its founding in 1888. And by 1896, Grutza realized a new church was necessary.

That year, he hired preeminent church architect Erhard Brielmaier to build a second St. Josaphat's, preferably something much larger and modeled on St. Peter's Basilica in Rome. Brielmaier's design was almost complete when Grutza threw a wrench in the works.

The priest had just learned that the Federal Building in Chicago was scheduled for demolition. It was a magnificent building, with walls of stone, pillars of granite, and doors of bronze. To Grutza, it seemed a shame to waste all that stone and granite. It seemed equally shameful to spend a fortune on new materials for the church when old materials could be had for a song. Perhaps, the priest proposed, if Brielmaier made some changes to his design, neither materials nor money would go to waste.

Brielmaier agreed. While the architect reverse-engineered the church's design to accommodate new materials, the priest struck a deal to purchase the salvage material from the Federal Building for a mere $20,000. He then arranged to have all 200,000 tons of it shipped to Milwaukee on 500 railroad flatcars.

When it arrived, builders measured and numbered the blocks of stone to determine their place in the church. They then fit the blocks together, jigsaw puzzle-style. Amazingly, the builders made almost no cuts to the stone, and they wasted almost nothing. Along with the stone, six granite columns from the Federal Building, as well as bronze railings, doors, and light fixtures, found a home in the church.

After four years of construction, Archbishop Francis Katzer dedicated the church in a Solemn High Mass on **July 21, 1901**. Twenty-eight years later, in 1929, St. Josaphat's became America's third minor basilica. It remains, however, its only recycled basilica.

On the shelves of the Special Collections Division of the Georgetown University Library, you'll find a box filled with the letters of Archbishop John Carroll. You'll also find boxes filled with the letters and papers of other early Catholic American greats, such as New York's fiery archbishop, John Hughes; the first American-born saint, Elizabeth Ann Seton; and pioneering missionaries Frederic Baraga and Pierre Jean DeSmet.

All those papers belong to the John Gilmary Shea Collection: 26 boxes containing some of the most important primary records of Catholic American history. Shea spent more than half his lifetime tracking down those documents, and without his work, much of what Catholics know about the Church in early America would long ago have been forgotten.

Born in New York on **July 22, 1824,** the future historian got his first taste of writing about the Church's past at age 14, when the *Young People's Catholic Magazine* published his essay on the cardinal-soldier Gil Álvarez Carrillo de Albornoz.

History then took a backseat for more than decade while Shea studied law and tried out (but decided against) a vocation as a Jesuit priest. After leaving the Society of Jesus in 1852, he married and began studying the history of the Church's missions to Native Americans. After that, Shea moved on to studying the lives of the first explorers in America, followed by Catholic founding fathers and patriots, and then early bishops and religious giants, all while working as an editor for various Catholic publishing houses and periodicals.

Shea published dozens of books and hundreds of essays, articles, and pamphlets on U.S. Catholic history. With almost no secondary sources to help him in his work, Shea personally tracked down countless primary documents, in the process ensuring that those priceless pieces of paper were preserved and catalogued. Historians still rely on those papers, as well as Shea's writings, for their work on the Church in early America.

The father of U.S. Catholic history died in February 1892.

July 23: THE POLISH COUNT

Count Casimir Pulaski was not a model Catholic. He lacked prudence, engaged in some questionable political plots, and at least dabbled in Freemasonry. He was, however, a first-rate soldier, and Benjamin Franklin recognized as much when he met the Polish count in Paris, in the spring of 1777.

Only 32 at the time, Pulaski had already spent more than a decade fighting the Russians in Poland and the Ottoman Empire. In both places, his reckless disregard for his and his men's safety earned him a reputation as equal parts daring and crazed. Exiled from Poland in 1773 (for one of those half-daring, half-crazed exploits), Pulaski was a soldier without an army in Paris. Franklin solved that problem by sending him off to America, recommendation letter in hand.

Pulaski arrived in Massachusetts on **July 23, 1777**. Thanks to some fancy horseback riding and saving General Washington's life in the Battle of Brandywine, the Pole was a brigadier general by September.

For the next six months, as commander of the Continental Army's four cavalry regiments, Pulaski acquitted himself well in battle, but made few friends among his men and fellow officers. An aristocrat to the core, he was arrogant with his inferiors and insubordinate with his superiors.

By March 1778, Pulaski was fed up with the Continental Army's egalitarian ways and resigned his commission. Then, largely at his own expense, he formed an independent cavalry corps: the Pulaski Legion.

The Legion saw battle first in New Jersey, before moving to South Carolina and Georgia. In Savannah, on October 9, 1779, its commander made his last foolhardy charge.

While attempting to rally fleeing French forces, Pulaski rode straight into cannon fire. Grapeshot felled him from his horse, leaving him mortally wounded. Impressed by his bravery (or madness), the English broke protocol and allowed Pulaski's men to carry him to safety.

He died two days later.

July 24: THE WONDERWORKER

First people lined up in Yonkers. Then in Harlem, Detroit, and Brooklyn. Always those lines led to the same man: Father Solanus Casey, the Capuchin wonder-worker.

Born Bernard Casey in 1870, the future priest grew up in a three-room log cabin with his parents and 15 siblings. With Morning and Evening Prayer said daily, a Rosary prayed nightly, and regular chores, life in that Wisconsin cabin wasn't all that different from life in a monastery. Yet not until he was 21 (and had worked as a lumberjack, hospital orderly, prison guard, and streetcar operator) did Casey consider religious life.

At first, he pursued the diocesan priesthood. But the seminary he entered offered classes in only German and Latin. Speaking neither, Casey fell behind academically. When the rector suggested monastic life, Casey went to Detroit to study with the Capuchins.

He was finally ordained to the priesthood on **July 24, 1904,** but due to his ongoing academic struggles, his ordination was an *ordinatio simplex,* meaning he could say Mass, but not preach publicly or hear confessions. Casey, however, was happy: He was a priest.

That fall, Casey took up his first assignment as sacristan and doorkeeper at Sacred Heart Parish in Yonkers, New York. There, the miracles began.

People would come to the monastery with some sort of trouble. Casey, as the doorkeeper, would greet them and talk with them. He would then enroll them in the Capuchin's Seraphic Mass Association. With remarkable frequency, healing followed. Some days, the people who lined up to see Casey numbered more than 200.

In every city he served, the priest met with them all. For 53 years, Casey spent his days talking with visitors and his nights in prayer. By the time of his death in 1957, the Capuchins had filled seven notebooks with accounts of cancers cured, kidneys healed, limbs made whole, and infertility vanquished, all through the intercession of the man now honored as "Venerable."

July 25: OPEN DISSENT

Dissent among Catholics is hardly unprecedented. In every age, some doctrine or discipline fails to garner the universal assent of clergy or laity. The dissent that followed Pope Paul VI's promulgation of *Humanae Vitae,* however, was like nothing the Church had seen since, perhaps, the days of Martin Luther.

The encyclical, which explained and reasserted the Church's prohibition of artificial contraception, was published on **July 25, 1968**. Immediately, bishops' conferences, priests, theologians, and ordinary Catholics began voicing their disagreement.

In the United States, opponents of the encyclical found their voice early, thanks to The Catholic University of America's Father Charles Curran. Within two days of *Humanae Vitae's* publication, Curran rallied more than 600 theologians and academics to sign a letter of open dissent, asserting that "spouses may responsibly decide according to their conscience that artificial contraception in some circumstances is permissible and indeed necessary . . . "

Defenders of the encyclical, however, had a champion of their own: the philosopher Germain Grisez.

Raised in a large Catholic family, Grisez didn't fully embrace the Church's traditional teaching on contraception until the early 1960s. After that, however, he wrote extensively on the topic, including the book *Contraception and the Natural Law.* He also spent time in Rome, advising one of the members of the Papal Birth Control Commission, Father John C. Ford, S.J.

In the wake of *Humanae Vitae,* defending the encyclical became almost a fulltime job for Grisez. He took a leave of absence from his teaching position at Georgetown and joined forces with Archbishop Patrick Cardinal O'Boyle of Washington (who had more than 50 openly dissenting priests on his hands and feared he might soon have a schism as well) to explain and defend the Church's teaching.

Although Grisez was mostly "a lone voice, crying out in the wilderness" in those early years, his work paved the way for a new generation of priests, theologians, and philosophers who are slowly changing the contraception conversation from one of dissent to one of assent.

The French who settled Detroit in 1701 had their priorities straight. On July 24 of that year, Antoine de La Mothe, sieur de Cadillac, and a group of French artisans, farmers, soldiers, and tradesmen arrived at the straits of Lake Erie, where they planned to build a fort and a city. Two days later, on **July 26, 1701,** they began building St. Anne's Catholic Church, the second oldest continuously operating parish in the United States.

St. Anne's was the first building constructed in what became Fort Ponchartrain du Détroit. It also was the most frequently constructed, burning to the ground three times in its 200-plus year history (including once by the settlers themselves), and falling under the wrecking ball a few more times.

In the early years, though, perpetual construction wasn't the parish's primary concern. That honor belonged to the local Native Americans who seemed to enjoy shooting flaming arrows at the church and who kidnapped St. Anne's first pastor, Father Nicholas Constantin del Halle, in 1706. Although the French settlers successfully negotiated del Halle's release from the Ottawas, another Native American shot and killed the priest as he walked back to the fort.

As the eighteenth century passed, so too did French control of Detroit, first to the British, then to the Americans. The parish itself carried on the French Catholic traditions of its founders, continuing to offer at least one Mass with a French sermon, until 1942. Soon after, St. Anne's priests began preaching some sermons in Spanish, in order to serve the parish's growing Hispanic population.

The current St. Anne's Church is the eighth building the parish has occupied. Completed in 1886, the Gothic Revival church bears traces of its colorful past, with remnants of its former incarnations—including an altar, communion rail, statues, bells, and even a cornerstone—incorporated into its design, and one of her former pastors—Father Gabriel Richard, U.S. congressman and University of Michigan co-founder—entombed within.

Charity isn't always its own reward. Just ask Charles Calvert, the third Lord Baltimore.

Calvert, like his father before him, governed the colony of Maryland in the late-seventeenth century with a mind towards religious tolerance. Yes, he tended to favor Catholics and concentrated political power in Catholic hands. But Calvert never established Catholicism as the colony's official religion, nor did he make life difficult for Protestants. Rather, he welcomed them to Maryland, especially those, like the Quakers, who were less than fond of the Church of England.

Unfortunately for Maryland's Catholics, the Calverts were perhaps a little too welcoming. By 1688—the year of England's "Glorious Revolution"—Protestants far outnumbered Catholics in Our Lady's colony. And when Maryland's government was slow to celebrate the victory of England's new Protestant monarchs—William and Mary—over the deposed Catholic King James II, more than a few of the colony's subjects took offense.

Chief among those was John Coode. In 1681, Coode attempted to overthrow Calvert by spreading tales of a Jesuit and Indian plot to eliminate Protestants from Maryland. It was nonsense, and everyone, Protestants included, recognized it as such. In 1689, however, Coode tried it again, this time with greater success.

In July of that year, Coode formed the Protestant Associators, ostensibly to defend Maryland's Protestants from more fictional Indian attacks. Seven hundred men joined with him, and on **July 27, 1689,** they seized the colony's state house. They then convinced the pro-Calvert officers and colonial officials, who were holed up in the nearby fort, to surrender without a fight.

By August 1, 1689, Coode and the Protestant Associators controlled the colony. In short order, successive governments passed laws banning the practice of Catholicism and public Masses, and forbidding Catholics to vote or hold public office. Across the pond, the Calverts lost their royal charter and the British crown took charge of the colony.

Not until the American Revolution could Catholics again openly practice their faith and exercise the full rights of citizenship in the colony they had founded.

July 28: A MARTYR FOR THE POOR

On the morning of **July 28, 1981,** Sister Linda Wanner was on her knees, scooping blood off the floor and into a mason jar.

The blood came from Father Stanley Rother, a missionary priest gunned down in his library hours earlier. Rother's executioners belonged to a death squad that did the dirty work of the Guatemalan Army. They killed Rother, like they killed others, because he loved Guatemala's poor. And he loved them even though he suspected this day would come.

Rother didn't necessarily suspect his martyrdom in 1968, when, as a newly ordained priest, he arrived in the remote mission of Santiago Atitlán to serve the Tz'utujil Mayans. Nor did he suspect it in the 12 years that followed, years where he worked alongside the Tz'utujil, farming the land, repairing the church, and building a hospital.

But he did have his suspicions by 1980, when those who worked among the poor began disappearing. The country's right-wing extremists had placed their names on death lists, labeling them all as communists. Rother was no communist, nor did he care for liberation theology, which often advocated violent political responses to poverty. His concern was for Christ, the sacraments, and his people. But he knew that would make no difference to the military. And it didn't.

In January 1981, Rother's name appeared on a death list. Before military assassins could carry out their orders, he escaped to his parents' farm in Oklahoma. He remained there for four months. Then, in April, after learning that his name had been removed from the list, he returned to Guatemala.

But his source was wrong. In the early hours of July 28, assassins found Rother in his office. He was dead in minutes.

Rother's family transported his body back to Oklahoma, where the Archdiocese of Oklahoma City opened his cause for canonization. His heart, however, and that mason jar filled with blood, remained in death where they belonged in life: with the people of Santiago Atitlán.

July 29: CHINA'S AMERICAN BISHOP

On July 10, 1970, a frail, white-haired American walked across the Lo Wu Bridge, leaving Communist China behind. When he arrived at Hong Kong's border, he identified himself as Bishop James Edward Walsh, a Maryknoll missionary, held captive for 12 years in a Chinese prison.

Bishop Walsh first arrived in China 52 years earlier, in 1918. He was a newly ordained priest then, the second for the Maryknoll order and one of its first four to arrive in China.

Between 1918 and 1927, Father Walsh ran the Maryknoll mission in Yeungkong (now Yangjiang). From 1919 on, he also served as Superior of the Maryknoll Mission in China, and in 1927, he was ordained Bishop of the Diocese of Kongmoon (now Jiangmen).

Bishop Walsh remained in China until 1936, when his order elected him its second Superior General. At the end of his term in 1948, the Vatican requested Walsh return to China to head up the Catholic Central Bureau in Shanghai and coordinate the Church's missionary work throughout the country.

A year later, the communists came to power.

In their quest to purge China of foreign and Christian influences, the government demanded that foreign clergy leave. Walsh, however, refused to go, telling his order, "To put up with a little inconvenience at my age is nothing. Besides, I am sick and tired of being pushed around on account of my religion."

In 1958, after nine years of sparring with Walsh, the Red Army finally came for him. For the next 12 years, they held him captive. In all those years, they allowed him one visitor, one time—his brother in 1960. They permitted no other contact with the outside world.

Then, in 1970, without warning, the 79-year-old priest was taken to the Lo Wu Bridge and released.

Walsh spent the last 11 years of his life at the Maryknoll seminary in New York. So great was his love for the Chinese people, that not once did he speak an ill word of his captors. He died on **July 29, 1981**.

For 30 years, Archbishop Francis Cardinal Spellman was the most powerful churchman in America. Some loved him. Some despised him. But no one doubted his influence.

Born in 1889 and raised in Massachusetts, the future cardinal attended Fordham University before heading to Rome to study for the priesthood. There, he proved good at his studies but even better at making friends. In later years, as those friends became bishops, that skill served him well, ensuring that the instant dislike his own bishop (Boston's William Cardinal Henry O'Connell) felt for him, didn't affect his rise through the clerical ranks.

Ordained in 1916, Spellman began his priesthood as a lowly proofreader for Boston's archdiocesan newspaper, but by 1925 he had become the first American attaché for the Vatican Secretariat of State. Seven years later, on **July 30, 1932,** Pope Pius XI appointed him auxiliary bishop of Boston. By 1939, he was archbishop of New York.

More than just the influence of Spellman's friends, however, accounted for that meteoric rise. He was also a gifted administrator and fund-raiser. Spellman demonstrated those skills soon after his arrival in New York. He quickly erased the archdiocesan debt, launched a massive building campaign, and made strides in improving Catholic health care.

Not content to confine himself to Church affairs, Spellman also waded into political waters. He used his influence to silence Catholic critics of President Franklin Roosevelt in 1936 (thereby ensuring the president's reelection); worked closely with Joseph Kennedy to further Catholic interests in Washington, D.C., throughout the forties and fifties; and championed the Vietnam War during the 1960s. Spellman likewise garnered attention for his vociferous criticism of lax morality in Hollywood films.

A theological and liturgical conservative, Spellman participated in the Second Vatican Council but viewed those who championed radical change with suspicion. As the cardinal left for the Council, he reportedly promised, "No change will get past the Statue of Liberty." Spellman didn't live long enough to keep that promise. He died two years after the Council's close, in December 1967.

July 31: WHERE OTTAWANTA PRAYED

It may be nothing more than a legend. No one knows for sure. But for centuries, Catholics in Maryland spoke of Our Lady of the Fields.

As the story goes, in 1642, the Jesuit priest Father Andrew White brought a Piscataway chief and his family to the Catholic Faith. Persecuted by other tribes for their beliefs, the chief, Ottawanta, moved his family north, near modern-day Emmitsburg.

Decades passed. One family member after another died. Eventually, the "Black Robes," as the Indians called the Jesuits, stopped coming. But Chief Ottawanta lived on, clinging to his faith and praying the Rosary daily, just as the Black Robes taught him.

One day, Ottawanta knelt in prayer near his children's graves. As always, his beads were with him. Suddenly, a lady in white appeared and spoke to him, saying, "Know that in these fields, where you have for so many years prayed to me, there shall one day gather many virgins who will sound the praises of God."

Legend or not, just over a century later, near that very place, on **July 31, 1809,** the future Saint Elizabeth Ann Seton and her companions began their life together as Sisters of Charity.

In a small stone house, the Sisters of Charity started a school for girls, which eventually grew into a college. They also established their motherhouse there and formed thousands of young women for religious life. As the Church in America grew, those women left Emmitsburg to found America's first Catholic orphanages and hospitals, nurse soldiers on battlefields and the high seas, and travel across the Rockies to teach pioneers' children.

Throughout the nineteenth century, no religious order was more in demand than Mother Seton's Sisters of Charity. It was the first women's religious order founded in the United States and six separate communities grew out of it.

To this day, near the field where legend says Ottawanta prayed, the consecrated women who live in the motherhouse of Seton's order continue to sound the praises of God.

August

August 1: THE MOST DANGEROUS WOMAN
IN AMERICA

Before *Mother Jones* was a news magazine, she was a teacher, a dress-maker, a union leader, a strike organizer, an occasional Socialist, and a self-proclaimed "hell-raiser." She also was a pro-life Catholic, baptized Mary Harris on **August 1, 1837,** who believed women belonged at home with their children and that the suffrage movement was foolishness itself. "You don't need the vote to raise hell," she once proclaimed.

A native of Ireland, Harris immigrated to Canada as a teenager. She then moved south to teach at a Catholic school in Michigan and eventually settled in Memphis as the bride of Mr. George E. Jones. Life for Mrs. Jones was nothing but ordinary until 1867, when yellow fever killed her husband and four children. After that, she moved to Chicago and opened a dress shop, only to lose it in the Great Chicago Fire of 1871.

From that point forward, Jones devoted her life to improving the working conditions of America's laborers. Urging people to "Pray for the dead and fight like hell for the living," she led strikes and planned marches that championed eight-hour work days, the end of child labor, fair pay for workers, and safer mines and factories.

Standing barely 5 feet tall and always dressed in widow's black, Jones grew old fighting unjust labor practices. By the time she was 60, the country knew her as Mother Jones, a persona Jones carefully cultivated, knowing it worked in her favor.

But those who opposed her weren't fooled. As a West Virginia prosecutor once said of Jones in court, "There sits the most dangerous woman in America . . . She comes into a state where peace and prosperity reign . . . crooks her finger [and] twenty thousand contented men lay down their tools and walk out."

Jones continued raising hell until 1930, when at the age of 93, shortly after receiving Last Rites, she passed away.

Simon Miller and Hannah Huber wanted to marry. Unfortunately, their priest, the elderly German Jesuit Frederick Farmer, was too ill to make the journey from Philadelphia, where he lived, to New Jersey, where the couple lived. Another priest would soon inherit Father Farmer's missionary circuit. But Farmer had been Miller and Huber's spiritual father all their lives, and they didn't want to be wedded by anyone other than him. So, since Farmer couldn't come to them, Miller and Huber went to him instead, making the two-day journey on foot.

When the couple arrived in Philadelphia, on **August 2, 1786,** they found the priest in the rectory of Old St. Joseph's, his home of 28 years.

Born in Germany and christened Ferdinand Steinmeyer, Farmer studied mathematics and astronomy before joining the Jesuits. He was ordained around 1750, and two years later came to America to minister to German immigrants in Pennsylvania.

Soon after his arrival, the priest adopted the English last name Farmer. He first spent six years in Lancaster, then moved to Philadelphia, all the while riding a missionary circuit that gradually expanded beyond Pennsylvania to Delaware, New Jersey, and (secretly) New York, where until the American Revolution, being a priest remained a hanging offense.

In his spare time, as a member of the American Philosophical Society and founding trustee of the University of Pennsylvania, Farmer corresponded with leading philosophers and scientists in Europe. And in 1783, when George Washington came to Philadelphia, his signature topped the list of eminent clergy and citizens who signed a congratulatory letter welcoming the nation's first citizen.

In 1786, Farmer made one last trip to Manhattan, where a year earlier he'd founded Old St. Peter's Parish, the first Catholic parish in New York. Then, illness struck. No more trips were made. He did, however, marry Simon Miller and Hannah Huber from his bed, on August 2. That was the last of the 568 marriages he blessed as a priest in America.

He died 15 days later.

August 3: MYSTERY AND MANNERS

When visitors arrived at the small farm in Milledgeville, Georgia, a host of rare birds came out to greet them—mostly peacocks, but also ostriches, emus, toucans, and more. None of the birds, though, were as rare as their owner, the celebrated writer Flannery O'Connor.

O'Connor had retreated to the farm, Andalusia, in 1951, after she began showing signs of the same form of lupus that killed her father 10 years earlier. She was 15 at the time of her father's death, an only child living with her parents in Savannah.

After losing her father, O'Connor earned her bachelor's degree at the Georgia State College for Women and her master's degree through the University of Iowa's renowned Writers' Workshop program. From there, she went to Yaddo—an artists' colony in Saratoga Springs, New York—and afterwards to the Connecticut home of poet Robert Fitzgerald and his wife Sally, all the while working on her first novel, *Wise Blood*.

Once she fell ill, however, O'Connor left Connecticut for Georgia. She believed her budding literary career was over before it began.

But she was wrong. Her career wasn't over. It just unfolded differently.

Back in Georgia, rather than living broadly, O'Connor instead lived deeply, embracing a quiet life of suffering and prayer, study and work. A faithful Catholic living in what she described as the "Christ-haunted" Protestant South, O'Connor's writing drew on the mystery of her Catholic faith and the manners of her Southern culture. That combination produced tales of startling grace and even more startling redemption. Each story, in its own way, depicted the soul's struggle with what O'Connor called "the stinking mad shadow of Jesus." Each also reflected its author's sharp wit and keen intelligence.

Those tales were crafted slowly, with O'Connor working only a few hours a day to conserve her strength. Yet by the time of her death, on **August 3, 1964,** she produced one of the twentieth century's most honored bodies of work, including two novels, 32 short stories, plus over a hundred book reviews, essays, and talks.

August 4: VIBIANA

In 1876, the newly built Cathedral of St. Vibiana's was the most beautiful building in Los Angeles. Modeled on the boyhood parish of the diocese's Spanish bishop, Thaddeus Amat y Brusi, the Baroque-Italianate church was named by Pope Pius IX. He chose the name to honor the third-century virgin and martyr, whose remains were discovered in Rome in 1853. The pope also entrusted Saint Vibiana's remains to Amat, who enshrined them above the high altar.

More than a century later, Los Angeles still considered the cathedral an architectural treasure, and Los Angeles Catholics considered the cathedral their spiritual home. But the archdiocese considered the cathedral a problem.

As then-Archbishop Roger Cardinal Mahony maintained, the 1,200-seat cathedral was too small for the archdiocese's rapidly expanding population and ill-suited for contemporary liturgies. He wanted to raze the building and build a new cathedral in its place. Because St. Vibiana's was on the National Register of Historic Places, however, he needed a better reason than size limitations. The 1994 Northridge earthquake didn't give him a reason. But it at least gave him an excuse.

After the earthquake, although city inspectors declared the cathedral structurally sound, Mahony claimed the damage was too costly for the archdiocese to repair. He closed the cathedral and prepared it for demolition. That's when city preservationists stepped in, offering to save the cathedral. But Mahony wasn't interested.

For two years, preservationists fought Mahony's plans. The cardinal fought back, pressuring legislatures to change laws, claiming religious freedom violations, and even beginning demolition without authorization. Finally, as an **August 4, 1996,** Associated Press article announced, Mahony cried "Uncle" and agreed to build the new cathedral elsewhere. The archdiocese gave the city St. Vibiana's, and the city gave the archdiocese land for its new cathedral.

Soon afterwards, Los Angeles sold the property to a private developer, who turned the former cathedral into a special events venue called Vibiana. Structural repairs and renovations cost $6 million. Cardinal Mahony, in turn, built the new Cathedral of Our Lady of the Angels. Construction cost the archdiocese over $200 million.

Who was the first African-American priest?

Many say Father Augustine Tolton, the first priest to admit to the honor and look the part.

In truth, however, that title belongs to Bishop James Healy.

Born in 1830, Healy was the eldest son of Michael Healy—a Georgia planter who sent all his children by his mixed-race wife to live in the North, rather than risk them becoming slaves in the South. James Healy was the first of the children to go.

In 1837, when he was just seven years old, Healy left Georgia for a Quaker school in New York. He later transferred to The College of the Holy Cross in Worcester, Massachusetts, and graduated as the school's inaugural valedictorian in 1849.

While still in school, Healy dreamed of becoming a Jesuit, but because the Jesuits' formation house was in Maryland—a slave state—he pursued the diocesan priesthood instead. After studying in Canada and Europe, Healy was ordained in 1854, and then returned to the Diocese of Boston.

There, only a few close friends and mentors knew that Healy wasn't the full-blooded Irish priest he appeared to be. That helped him rise quickly through the clerical ranks, and by 1866, he was pastor of Boston's largest parish.

In 1875, America's first (unofficial) African-American priest became her first (equally unofficial) African-American bishop, when Pope Pius IX named Healy the second bishop of Portland, Maine.

Healy shepherded his see for 25 years, and as new immigrants flowed into Maine, he oversaw the construction of 60 parishes, 68 missions, 18 convents, and 18 schools.

Bishop Healy died on **August 5, 1900**. Although he never publicly talked about his African ancestry, the Archdiocese of Boston nevertheless honors its most notable black Catholics with the Bishop James Healy Award.

August 6: BLOODY MONDAY

In 1855, Louisville, Kentucky, was Know-Nothing territory. The anti-Catholic, anti-immigrant party controlled the mayor's office, city hall, and both major newspapers. It also controlled the school board, a fact that became apparent in July of that year when the school board fired every Catholic teacher in the city, save one.

Louisville's Know-Nothings liked controlling their city and had no intention of letting the growing population of Irish and German Catholics (who mostly voted Democrat), take that control away from them. Accordingly, when the city's polls opened for Election Day on **August 6, 1855,** more than 1,500 Know-Nothings stood outside polling place doors. The city's police stood alongside them. Heavily armed, the Know-Nothings refused entry to any voters not identifying with their party.

In most places, the Catholics who came to vote left peacefully, recognizing defeat when they saw it. But by 6 p.m., tensions in two of the Irish and German wards had escalated. Shots were fired (no one knows by whom), and then the real rioting began.

Angry Know-Nothings, itching for a fight, stormed through the city's streets, attacking any Catholic they could find. They smashed windows and looted businesses. They broke into homes, dragging sleeping Catholics from their beds and beating them in the streets. They burned other homes to the ground, with whole families still inside. Angry mobs likewise surrounded the cathedral, but Bishop Martin Spalding had wisely entrusted the cathedral's keys to the city's mayor, who stopped the mobs from setting it alight.

By the time the rioting ended, several days later, over 100 business and homes were gone and as many as 100 people were dead, with many more injured. Immediately, Catholics began packing up their belongings and moving to friendlier climes. The city they left behind soon became a shell of its former self and struggled economically for years.

Nevertheless, not one individual was ever charged or prosecuted for the events of what history calls Bloody Monday.

August 7: LIKE LEAVEN

When the first edition of the *American Catholic Tribune* went to press in 1886, it announced:

> *We will do what no other paper published by colored men has dared to do—give the great Catholic Church a hearing and show that it is worthy of at least a fair consideration at the hands of our race, being as it is the only place on this Continent where rich and poor, white and black, must drop prejudice at the threshold and go hand in hand to the altar.*

The brainchild of Daniel Rudd, a former slave then living in Ohio, the *American Catholic Tribune* condemned segregation, supported civil rights, and called on black Catholics to be like "leaven" among their race by bringing more blacks into the Church.

Rudd himself was born into slavery 32 years earlier, on **August 7, 1854,** in Bardstown, Kentucky. He was baptized Catholic as a baby and attended Mass with his parents in the same church where his owners worshipped.

In that church—St. Joseph's—Rudd experienced his first taste of racial harmony. Convinced that the Catholic Church was the answer to America's race problem, Rudd moved to the North after the Civil War to complete his education. He then started a successful business and launched his newspaper to form, encourage, and evangelize African-Americans.

Three years after the newspaper's launch, Rudd organized the first National Black Catholic Congress in Washington, D.C. Prominent black Catholics, including Father Augustine Tolton, came from across the country to discuss pressing problems of education and evangelization. They also met with President Grover Cleveland, who invited them to the White House.

Rudd would host four more such gatherings before his newspaper folded in 1897 and he returned to the South. In Arkansas, he worked as a businessman and civil rights leader until his health failed in 1932. He died in Bardstown a year later.

In the late 1980s, the National Black Catholic Congress re-formed. Today, it has a nationwide membership committed to carrying on Rudd's original mission.

August 8: EXTRA ECCLESIAM NULLA SALUS

In 1949, in a small building on the corner of Bow and Arrow streets in Cambridge, Massachusetts, heresy was fomenting.

The building was the Saint Benedict Center, a small Catholic educational institution established in 1940 to provide ongoing formation to Catholic students at Harvard, Radcliffe, and other nearby colleges. The chief fomenter was Father Leonard Feeney, a popular Jesuit author, speaker, and radio host who came to the Center in 1942 to serve as its chaplain.

At that time, Feeney was a true son of the Church, orthodox to the core. But by 1949, he and his bishop were at odds over the question of whether or not non-Catholics could be saved. Boston's Archbishop Richard Cardinal Cushing taught what the Church teaches: that although no salvation exists outside the Church, one doesn't have to be a baptized, card-carrying Catholic to be considered "inside the Church."

Feeney, however, thought that position to be modernist nonsense. As he saw it, the gates of Heaven were closed to anyone who died before receiving a Catholic baptism—from newborn babies and virtuous, Jesus-loving Protestants to natives in the most remote African jungles and every man, woman, or child who lived before the Incarnation.

The Church tried explaining to Feeney that *extra Ecclesiam nulla salus* ("outside the Church there is no salvation") didn't mean what he thought it meant. Pope Pius XII even weighed in, personally editing a letter saying as much. The Vatican sent that letter to Cushing on **August 8, 1949**.

But Feeney refused to budge. For his persistent refusal, the Church excommunicated him in 1953. Unfazed, Feeney and his followers continued to defend his position, and set up a religious community—the Slaves of the Immaculate Heart of Mary—devoted to their heretical interpretation of the doctrine.

In the end, Church officials took pity on Feeney and allowed him to reconcile with the Church before his 1978 death. Unfortunately, the limits of that reconciliation are evident in the four words carved upon his tombstone: *extra Ecclesiam nulla salus*.

On **August 9, 1680,** Tiwa Indians rode north towards Santa Fe to warn the Spanish of a brewing revolt.

For months, led by a Native American named Popé, the Pueblo peoples had been plotting rebellion. They'd lived for nearly 100 years under Spanish rule—100 years in which they saw their numbers decimated and their culture crippled. By 1680, they'd had enough.

The Tiwa in the south, however, were fond of the Spanish and the agricultural innovations they'd introduced. They had no intention of co-operating with Popé, and when they found Spanish settlers on August 9, they warned them that revolt was coming in two days' time.

But before the settlers could prepare, Popé learned of the southern Tiwas' betrayal. He sent word to 46 Pueblo settlements: begin now.

By August 10, violence had erupted in 42 of the 46 pueblos. Hundreds died, including 21 Franciscan missionaries. Hundreds more fled to the largest Spanish settlements—Santa Fe and Isleta. There, they held out only a little while longer. Within two weeks, any Spaniards who survived fled to El Paso.

After the Spanish exodus, Popé ordered the Pueblo peoples to destroy all traces of the Spanish and Christianity. One of those traces was the San Miguel Mission in Santa Fe, which had served as a parish for Spanish laborers and artisans since at least 1620.

The natives, however were somewhat lax in their destruction of San Miguel, and in 1692, when the Spanish returned to re-conquer the pueblos and reoccupy Santa Fe, they quickly restored the chapel to working order.

Eighteen years later, the old chapel was demolished and a new one was built. In the centuries that followed, locals renovated, repaired, and embellished the church—including adding a bell in 1856, engraved with the date August 9, purportedly to commemorate the Tiwas' ride north.

Nevertheless, for all those changes, the same adobe walls laid in 1710 still stand, making the church the Pueblo peoples couldn't destroy the oldest parish church in the United States.

August 10: THE URSULINE CONVENT RIOT

Young women held against their will. Dungeons. Torture chambers. Sexual improprieties of every sort.

In 1834, that was the average Bostonian's opinion of the happenings inside Catholic convents. It was wild fantasy, fueled by animosity towards the city's growing Irish population. Yet fantasy and prejudice were enough to send an angry mob knocking on the door of the Ursuline Convent and School in Charlestown, Massachusetts, in August of that year.

The trouble had started days earlier, when a young sister left the convent, but returned just hours later. Rumors about the sister quickly spread, and on **August 10, 1834,** placards appeared in Boston, calling upon the city's men to "rescue" the woman.

By 8:00 p.m. the following evening, a mob had gathered outside the convent. When a sister appeared in the window, the mob demanded they release the "mysterious lady" imprisoned within.

The sister told them to stop talking nonsense, then went back to her work. When the nonsense only grew louder, Mother Superior Mary St. George, came outside. She explained that the sisters weren't in the business of keeping prisoners and that all the noise was waking sleeping students.

She then added, perhaps imprudently, "The bishop has twenty thousand of the vilest Irishmen at his command, and you may read your riot act till your throats are sore, but you'll not quell them."

That did the trick . . . but only temporarily. The crowds dispersed, then reconvened at 11 p.m., this time with fire.

As the sisters and students snuck out the back, the fire company pulled up in front. Rather than help the sisters though, they joined the rioters. By midnight, two thousand people stood on the convent's grounds. Within the hour, the convent was in ashes.

No recompense was ever made to the sisters or diocese, and of the 13 men arrested, all but one—a friendless boy—were acquitted. Soon afterwards, the ringleader of the riots placed an ad in the newspaper, thanking greater Boston for the many kind gifts sent his way.

As a child, Eunice Kennedy knew how beautiful children with special needs could be. She saw that beauty everyday in her big sister, Rosemary, who was born with a developmental disability.

In 1941, however, after a botched lobotomy took away Rosemary's ability to walk, speak, and interact with the world, Eunice learned that not everyone recognized the beauty of her sister and those like her. Eunice—the fifth of Joseph and Rose Kennedy's nine children—was just 20 years old at the time, and could do nothing to help her sister, whom her parents institutionalized. But she could help others. And that's what she resolved to do when she took charge of the Joseph P. Kennedy, Jr. Foundation 16 years later.

Founded in 1946, after the eldest Kennedy brother's death in World War II, the Foundation first focused on general charitable giving. But with the recently married Eunice at its head (she'd wed Robert "Sargent" Shriver, Jr., in 1953), it switched its focus to advocating for those with intellectual disabilities.

In the years that followed, the Foundation spurred groundbreaking advances in research and care for those with special needs—helping launch the National Institute for Child Health and Human Development, establishing intellectual disabilities research centers at major universities and hospitals, and creating centers for the study of medical ethics at Harvard and Georgetown. Kennedy Shriver herself helped found Special Olympics International, which grew out of an annual summer camp for special needs children that she started in the early 1960s on her Maryland farm.

A devout Catholic and committed friend of the pro-life movement, Kennedy Shriver brought five children into the world and supported pro-life organizations such as Feminists for Life and the Susan B. Anthony List. She also vociferously opposed the inclusion of the pro-abortion plank in the 1992 Democratic Party platform.

Made a Dame of the Order of St. Gregory the Great by Pope Benedict XVI, Kennedy Shriver died on **August 11, 2009.**

August 12: SON OF THE SOUTH

William Elder was a kindhearted priest and exemplary bishop—devoted to his flock and prudent in his governance of church affairs. He just wasn't a fan of President Abraham Lincoln.

It's not that Elder had anything personal against Lincoln. But the bishop was a son of the South, born in Baltimore, educated in Emmitsburg, and, when the Civil War broke out, bishop of Natchez, Mississippi.

In the months leading up to the Civil War, Bishop Elder prayed for peace. When Mississippi decided to secede, however, he defended the decision. He then did his best to assist the Confederacy's soldiers, asking his priests to pray for the soldiers' safety and asking his parishioners to donate clothes, religious articles, and other necessities to the men.

When the war eventually came to Mississippi, Elder cared for wounded soldiers from both the North and the South. He made no distinction. Nevertheless, he had his limits. Brigadier General James Madison Tuttle, commander of the occupying Union Army, discovered those limits in 1864 when he ordered Mississippi clergy to pray for Lincoln in all religious services.

Elder refused, telling Tuttle that the government had no business mandating the prayers of the Catholic Mass. He then wrote the president, restating that opinion. Lincoln agreed, and Tuttle backed down.

Tuttle, however, never mentioned the exchange to his successor, General Mason Brayman, and when Brayman arrived, he insisted officials in Washington had never rescinded his predecessor's order. He again commanded Elder to pray for Lincoln. Elder again refused. This time, the general had the bishop arrested and sent to a Louisiana prison. There, he was tried for treason and convicted.

Elder remained in prison for three weeks, until officials in Washington got wind of the situation and ordered Elder's release. The bishop went home on **August 12, 1864**. Elder almost died 14 years later, when nursing Mississippi's sick through a yellow fever epidemic. He recovered, however, and lived to become coadjutor bishop of Cincinnati in 1880 and archbishop in 1883. The 85-year-old archbishop died, still shepherding Cincinnati, in 1904.

August 13: A NEW EVANGELIZATION

"It won't work."

"No one will come."

"America's young people don't care about religion."

In the months leading up to the 1993 World Youth Day, skeptics about the event's success abounded. No sooner did the Vatican announce that Denver would host the first World Youth Day in North America than did people in the media, the City of Denver, and even the Church begin voicing their doubts. Most everyone expected the event to be a failure, attracting 20,000 young people at best.

But Pope John Paul II had personally made the call. After much prayer and discernment, he concluded that the Holy Spirit wanted to do something great in Denver, both for the Church in America and for the world.

The throngs of young people who greeted him on August 11, when he entered Mile High Stadium, proved him right. And as those crowds continued to swell—topping 500,000 by the closing Mass on August 15—it became clear to everyone watching that something monumental was unfolding in Denver. In the middle of the festivities, on **August 13, 1993,** hundreds of thousands of young people listened to the Holy Father's words as they prayed the Way of the Cross.

He said:

> *Young people, you are a special part of Christ's inheritance, the people won by the love of the Redeemer. Take courage in the face of life's difficulties and injustices. Commit yourselves to the struggle for justice, solidarity, and peace in the world. Offer your youthful energies and your talents to building a civilization of Christian love. Be witnesses of God's love for the innocent and the weak, for the poor and the oppressed.*

They obeyed. Hundreds, if not thousands of religious vocations began that week. Countless other young people went on to pursue studies in theology and philosophy; become catechists, youth ministers, and missionaries; start faithful Catholic families; and found apostolates committed to spreading the Gospel. The week that experts said would be a disaster proved to be the week that the New Evangelization in America officially began.

The men weren't coming to Church. Father Michael J. McGivney could see that clearly enough from the pulpit every Sunday. In 1882, in the pews of his Connecticut parish, women and children abounded, but men were few.

McGivney knew the danger for families and communities that would follow as men drifted away from the Faith. He also recognized the danger for the men themselves, who were instead gravitating towards saloons and anti-Catholic fraternal societies such as the Freemasons. At the same time, McGivney was also concerned with the parish's widows and children, who were often left impoverished by the sudden death of the family breadwinner.

As a young man, that same fate had nearly been McGivney's. His father's death in 1873 forced him to leave seminary to care for his mother and six younger siblings. If not for the generosity of his sister's new husband, who helped pay Mrs. McGivney's bills after their wedding, and the Diocese of Hartford, which paid his way through seminary (something rarely done at the time), McGivney never could have pursued the priesthood.

To both bolster the declining faith of men and help the impoverished bereaved, McGivney decided his parish needed to form its own fraternal society, something which could connect men more closely to the Church through brotherhood and faith formation, while at the same time offering life insurance and sick benefits to its members.

With a small group of parishioners by his side, the 29-year-old assistant pastor founded the Knights of Columbus in the basement of St. Mary's Church, New Haven, in March 1882. The term "Knights" was meant to call the men on to greatness, while "Columbus" celebrated America's Catholic roots.

Slowly but surely, the popularity of the Knights spread—first at St. Mary's, then throughout New Haven, and finally across Connecticut and the United States.

By the time McGivney died of pneumonia, on **August 14, 1890,** the Knights of Columbus had grown to 6,000 members. Today, it has more than 1.8 million members, and McGivney's cause for sainthood is under way.

August 15: MARTYRED AT MASS

The Colorado assignment was meant to give Father Leo Heinrichs a rest—that is, as much rest as any priest can have in a large parish. And Heinrichs needed rest.

Heinrichs was born in Germany on **August 15, 1867,** and entered the Franciscan novitiate in Fulda as a teenager. When Otto von Bismarck's campaign against the Catholic Church began, Heinrichs' order fled to America. Five years later, in 1891, Heinrichs was ordained. One challenging assignment after another followed: nursing victims of a smallpox epidemic; disciplining novices in his order's seminary; and rebuilding a church, school, and monastery in the wake of a devastating fire.

Finally, in September 1907, the Franciscans sent him west. Before he left, Heinrichs hoped to return to Germany for the first time in 20 years and see his family. But St. Elizabeth's in Denver couldn't wait for its new pastor, so Heinrichs decided to delay the trip until the following spring.

He never made it.

Five months after his arrival at St. Elizabeth's, on Sunday, February 23, 1908, Heinrichs left the rectory shortly before 6 a.m. and unlocked the church doors. At 6:30, he began offering Mass. By 7:30, he was dead.

That morning, a Sicilian anarchist intent on assassinating any priest he could find, seated himself in the third pew. During Communion, he knelt at the altar rails with the other parishioners. When Heinrichs approached, he pulled out a gun. An altar server tried to warn the priest, but it was too late. The anarchist shot Heinrichs in the heart.

Stunned but not yet unconscious, the priest began gathering up the spilled Hosts. His last act was to place them on the steps of the Marian altar. There he died moments later, at rest at last.

As for the assassin, parishioners tackled him before he could escape. He went to the gallows unrepentant, lamenting that he'd killed only one priest that day and wishing he'd killed more.

August 16: ALLEVIATING SUFFERING

They were in Europe when World War II left millions displaced and millions more without food or clothing. They were in India and Pakistan when the formerly united states divided, resulting in widespread violence and mass migration. They were also in Ethiopia during the time of famine, in Rwanda during a time of genocide, and in Kosovo during a time of ethnic cleansing. Then they went to Thailand when a tsunami struck and Haiti when an earthquake left the country in rubble.

For more than 70 years, wherever hunger or war or natural disaster has struck, Catholic Relief Services has been there too, providing material assistance to all God's children, regardless of race, nationality, or creed.

Their mission of ministering to those in need began on **August 16, 1943,** when the United States Bishops appointed Father Patrick O'Boyle—the future archbishop of Washington—as the first executive director of War Relief Services.

As war raged in Europe, the American bishops founded War Relief Services to provide immediate material aid to the refugees then flooding America's cities, in addition to the needy and displaced persons in war-torn Europe. At the time, they saw the undertaking as short-term, something simply for the duration of World War II and its immediate aftermath. By 1947, however, the endeavor had proved so successful that, with the assistance of U.S. government grants, the bishops expanded its mandate to assist in other troubled parts of the globe.

Seven decades later, the re-named Catholic Relief Services provides both emergency aid and long-term development programming to more than 130 million people in approximately 90 countries and territories. Guided by Catholic Social Teaching, CRS's 5,000 employees worldwide address immediate needs for food, shelter, and medical care in places ravaged by war and natural disaster. They also assist communities in sustainable development efforts, including agricultural initiatives, community banking, health education, and clean water projects.

For good reason, the United States Conference of Catholic Bishops said of CRS in 2013, "Its service around the world makes us all proud."

In 1970, a troubled, pregnant 22-year-old Norma McCorvey signed her name to an affidavit. Two lawyers then took that affidavit, gave McCorvey the pseudonym Jane Roe, and made her the plaintiff in *Roe v. Wade.*

That case eventually made it to the U.S. Supreme Court, which in its 1973 ruling on *Roe v. Wade* declared abortion a fundamental right.

McCorvey spent the next two decades supporting abortion rights. But in 1995, while working at a Dallas abortion clinic, she encountered the group Operation Rescue. Soon afterwards, her thinking about the case tried in her name dramatically changed.

She described that change in her 1998 book, *Won by Love:*

> *I was sitting in [Operation Rescue's] offices when I noticed a fetal development poster . . . I kept seeing the picture of that tiny, 10-week-old embryo, and I said to myself, "That's a baby!" . . . I felt crushed under the truth of this realization. I had to face up to the awful reality. Abortion wasn't about "products of conception." It wasn't about "missed periods." It was about children being killed in their mother's wombs. All those years I was wrong. Signing that affidavit, I was wrong. Working in an abortion clinic, I was wrong. No more of this first trimester, second trimester, third trimester stuff. Abortion—at any point—was wrong. It was so clear. Painfully clear.*

Three years after that experience, on **August 17, 1998,** McCorvey entered the Catholic Church. Today, she remains a committed pro-life activist, working to overturn the Supreme Court case she helped launch.

August 18: THE TROUBLED BISHOP

Bishop Louis William DuBourg never had it easy.

In 1792, the Reign of Terror forced the Sulpician priest to flee his native France. Once in America, Father DuBourg's troubles continued during his three years as president of Georgetown University. There, trustees continually complained that he hired too many Frenchmen and eventually forced his resignation. After that, DuBourg tried (and failed) to establish a Catholic school in Havana, and then moved on to St. Mary's Seminary in Baltimore, where financial difficulties plagued the school throughout his 13-year tenure as rector.

But all those troubles paled in comparison to the trouble that afflicted DuBourg after **August 18, 1812,** when Rome announced his appointment as apostolic administrator of the Diocese of Louisiana and the Two Floridas.

Under normal circumstances, the Vatican would have named DuBourg a bishop, not an apostolic administrator. But because Pope Pius VII was Napoleon's prisoner in 1812, the Vatican couldn't issue the right papers. That proved problematic when DuBourg arrived in New Orleans to take up his see.

There, the rector of the cathedral, who'd long headed up the local Church, only grudgingly recognized DuBourg's authority. The rest of the city took its lead from him and gave DuBourg the cold shoulder.

In 1815, a frustrated DuBourg sailed for France, hoping the now free Pope Pius VII would resolve the dispute. He did receive his crook and mitre, but soon discovered that made little difference to New Orleans' Catholics.

To spare himself some trouble, Bishop DuBourg took up residence in St. Louis instead and invested his energy in building up the Church outside New Orleans. To that end, he recruited Jesuit and Vincentian priests, as well as the Christian Brothers and the Religious Sisters of the Sacred Heart of Jesus to serve his diocese.

Although DuBourg also tried to send religious to New Orleans and visited the city annually, the cathedral priests thwarted most of his efforts. He finally admitted defeat in 1826. He resigned his see and returned to France, where he died seven years later as Archbishop of Besançon.

Bishop Simon Bruté was remarkable in most every way.

As a child, Bruté smuggled the Eucharist into French prisons during the Reign of Terror. As a young man, he graduated at the top of his class from the University of Paris' Medical School (then the best college of its kind in the world). And as a newly minted doctor, he declined a prestigious hospital appointment and chose to enter seminary instead. There, he was a remarkable scholar and a favorite of Napoleon Bonaparte, who wanted Bruté to serve as his personal chaplain after ordination. Again, Bruté said no, choosing to come to America as a Sulpician missionary instead.

In America, Father Bruté served as the spiritual director to the equally remarkable Elizabeth Ann Seton. He carried out that task during the 20-plus years he served at Mount St. Mary's College in Emmitsburg, Maryland. Described by John Quincy Adams as one of the most brilliant men in America, Bruté was also described as the most devoted of priests, who, quite remarkably, never tired of his duties. One day, after ministering from morning until night, he wrote, "How wonderful the day of a priest . . . God, God, God, all day long!"

In 1834, Father Bruté became Bishop Bruté of the newly created Diocese of Vincennes. In just five remarkable years, he built 20 parishes, established 30 missions, recruited dozens of priests, and founded multiple schools.

Most important, however, Bruté was a remarkable lover of Christ, humble, patient, pious, and poor. After his death, in June 1839, he was buried in borrowed clothes. His own were thought unfit for the occasion.

On **August 19, 1839,** in a memorial service for Bruté, Mount St. Mary's president, Father John McCaffrey, summed up Bruté's priestly genius:

> *His exhortations to virtue and piety could scarcely fail of effect, because he recommended what he himself practiced. No standard of Christian or priestly excellence to which he pointed could appear too high, since he was himself a living instance of its attainment.*

The remarkable bishop's cause for canonization opened in 2005.

On **August 20, 1636,** Father Isaac Jogues wrote to his mother. In the letter, the recently ordained French Jesuit recounted his arrival in Quebec a month earlier and spoke of his hopes for evangelizing the natives.

At the end, he attached a simple postscript: "I have just received orders to get ready to start for the mission among the Huron."

Four days later, Jogues began his journey north. He then spent the next six years ministering to the Huron, as well as other tribes throughout modern-day Ontario and Michigan.

His mission changed abruptly in 1642, when the Iroquois, who had no love for the French, ambushed Jogues and his companions in the middle of a supply run. Those they didn't kill, they took captive, including Jogues.

During the first days and weeks, the Iroquois beat, tortured, mutilated, and starved their prisoners. A few were burned alive. Jogues' fellow Jesuit, René Goupil, was tomahawked to death.

But as weeks turned into months, the captors relaxed their grip on Jogues, allowing him to minister to the other captives and talk about God. Some even asked for baptism. For that reason, when the chance to escape presented itself, in August 1643, Jogues hesitated . . . but not for long.

Aided by the Dutch, he traveled first to New Amsterdam, then to France, where he informed his superiors of his escape. Although many urged him to remain in France, he sailed once more for the missions in the spring.

For the next two years, Jogues served in Montreal, proclaiming the Gospel, celebrating the sacraments, and attempting to negotiate peace with the Iroquois.

During one of those attempts, near modern-day Auriesville, New York, Jogues endured his second martyrdom, again at the hands of angry Iroquois. This one he didn't survive. Both Jogues and his companion, Father Jean de Lalande, lost their heads to the Indians' tomahawks.

Along with six other North American Jesuit martyrs, Jogues and de Lalande were canonized in 1930.

August 21: THE GERMAN SISTER

Mother Pauline von Mallinckrodt never planned to come to America. She loved her native Germany and saw the religious order she founded, the Sisters of Christian Charity, as a German order. God, however, had different plans.

In 1817, Mallinckrodt was born to a Catholic mother and Protestant father. Her father, a prominent politician, allowed his wife to raise his daughter and her siblings as Catholics. But when, as a young woman, Mallinckrodt started showing inclinations to religious life, he put his foot down.

For years, Mallinckrodt contented herself with doing charitable works in her local community—visiting the poor and the sick, opening a day care for the children of working mothers, and eventually founding a school for the blind. She also helped raise her sister and two brothers after her mother's early death.

By her 32nd birthday, however, her father had also died, her siblings were married, and her charitable works had grown so numerous that her local bishop urged her to found a religious community. She complied, and on **August 21, 1849,** finally realized her dream of becoming a religious.

Over the next two decades, the Sisters of Christian Charity flourished, growing to 250 sisters running 20 different charitable enterprises.

Then the German *Kulturkampf* began. The sisters had to choose: disband or leave their country. They chose to leave, with one group of sisters heading to Chile, another to Belgium, and the rest to America.

The first group to arrive in the United States went to New Orleans. The second, which included Mother Pauline, settled in Wilkes-Barre, Pennsylvania. There, in 1873, they established the order's new American motherhouse.

After that, Mother Pauline was perpetually on the move, spending the remaining eight years of her life traveling between Chile, Belgium, and the numerous houses springing up across America.

Eventually, her order had houses in 16 dioceses, including Baltimore, Chicago, New York, and Detroit. Today, although smaller in numbers, Sisters of Christian Charity in New Jersey, Pennsylvania, and Illinois continue the work first begun by the now Blessed Pauline von Mallinckrodt.

August 22: MIRACLE HILL

Legend says the first European to visit Holy Hill was Father Jacques Marquette. It's believed (but not verified) that the famous French missionary climbed the miniature Wisconsin mountain in 1673, on his way home from exploring the Mississippi River Valley.

Nearly two centuries later, a man haunted by some past misdeed heard of the hill and Marquette's alleged climb. As penance, the man—Francois Soubrio—traveled from Quebec to southeast Wisconsin, hiked up the 1,350 foot hill, and decided to stay.

Eventually, local farmers befriended Soubrio, who had been living on the hill as a hermit. The farmers helped him build a home and chapel there in 1863. Twelve years later, in 1875, the men erected the Stations of the Cross along the hillside. Around the same time, the hill began acquiring a reputation for mysterious healings: The sick and the lame who climbed it in faith became well and walked. Not surprisingly, the number of pilgrims to the chapel grew.

In 1880, to accommodate those pilgrims, the Diocese of Milwaukee began constructing a large new shrine on the now officially named Holy Hill. Twenty-six years later, in 1906, they recruited the Discalced Carmelites to run the shrine. The Carmelites built an inn and retreat center on the mountain, then tore down the old shrine to make way for a new one. They laid the cornerstone for the current Holy Hill National Shrine of Mary, Help of Christians on **August 22, 1926**.

Today, nearly a century later, the Shrine welcomes 500,000 pilgrims annually. Some come for the view and the glimpses it affords of Milwaukee's skyline. Others come to make a retreat or marvel at the Romanesque-Revival basilica. Others still come for healing, hoping that a climb up Marquette's mountain will reward them as it has so many others, with some miraculous cure or spiritual grace.

It's because of those last pilgrims that Holy Hill is sometimes called by another name: Miracle Hill.

Who was Father Sébastien Rale? It all depends on whom you ask.

If you ask the French, Rale was a faithful Jesuit, who came to the New World in 1689 and spent 35 years in Quebec and Maine, ministering to the Abenaki. If you ask the English, Rale was a rabid French partisan who went about the woods of Maine using British soldiers for target practice.

As the French tell his story, Father Rale knew that if the British controlled Maine, all priests would be exiled and Catholic practices forbidden. So, understandably, he encouraged the Abenaki to oppose British encroachment.

As the English tell it, Father Rale was "a bloody incendiary," who fought side by side with the natives. For that, the British put a price on his head, repeatedly tried to capture him, and even named their skirmishes with the French and Abenaki between 1722 and 1725, "Father Rale's War."

The French say Father Rale died a martyr on **August 23, 1724,** when British and Mohawk raiders invaded Rale's parish in Norridgewock, Maine. Attempting to draw attention away from his flock so more could escape, a wounded Rale crawled to the center of the village and died there at the foot of a cross. The English say Father Rale died a villain, shot in his cabin while reloading his pistol.

Both, however, agree that after Father Rale died, his body was mutilated, his scalp was taken to Boston, and the English-Abenaki dictionary he wrote was given to Harvard.

So, who was the real Father Rale?

Although the English account dominated American history books, the enduring faith of the Abenaki people suggests that the truth lies elsewhere.

Even after the tribe lost their pastor, the Abenaki refused to allow Protestant preachers or Protestant Bibles in their villages. Fifty years later, they only agreed to support the American Revolution after George Washington promised to send them a Jesuit. And as recently as 1986, they gave America her first Native American bishop—Bishop Donald Pelotte of the Diocese of Gallup, New Mexico.

In 1792, Thomas Jefferson anonymously entered the design competition for his future home—the U.S. presidential mansion. What Jefferson didn't realize, however, was that before the competition even began it was as good as won by the Catholic architect James Hoban.

Born to a poor tenant farmer in Ireland, Hoban worked as a carpenter until the age of 20, when he secured admission to Ireland's most prestigious architectural school. After completing his studies, he set up a successful practice in Ireland, and then a more successful practice in America, his home after 1785.

Hoban settled in Philadelphia, before moving to South Carolina. There, while completing work on the Charleston County Courthouse in 1791, he met President George Washington, who knew talent when he saw it.

The following spring, the president summoned Hoban to Philadelphia and asked him to enter his design competition. Hoban complied. When the time came for Washington to choose the winner, he didn't linger long over the decision. Construction began, according to Hoban's proposed designs, that October.

Jefferson never forgot his loss though. Nor did he accept it. In 1800, when he moved into the recently completed presidential mansion, he quickly redesigned it with elements of his earlier plans.

Fourteen years later, on **August 24, 1814,** the British torched the now popularly named White House. After the war, President James Madison called on Hoban to oversee the reconstruction. Proving himself a more gracious loser than Jefferson, Hoban replicated the third president's modifications in his restoration.

When he wasn't working at the White House, Hoban kept busy raising a large family (including one son who became a Jesuit priest), designing other buildings across the new nation, and helping found Catholic institutions in his adopted home of Washington, D.C., including Georgetown University, St. Patrick's Parish (the city's first Catholic church), and St. Peter's Parish on Capitol Hill.

He died in Washington in 1831.

August 25: THE ROYAL HYDROGRAPHER

Louis Jolliet thought, at first, that God had called him to the priesthood. But God had a different plan in mind.

Born in 1645, in a French settlement near Quebec, the young Jolliet grew up in a bustling community of fur traders, Jesuits, and Native Americans. While still a boy, Jolliet enrolled in the Jesuits' small school in Quebec and spent his adolescence studying theology, philosophy, and music. He showed talent as an organist and harpsichordist, and took minor orders in 1662. But five years later, he decided the priesthood wasn't for him, and left the community.

After that, Jolliet pursued the fur trade. He also befriended a young Jesuit missionary, Father Jacques Marquette, who, in 1673, joined Jolliet on an expedition to explore the *Mesipi*—a possible water route to the Pacific Ocean—and bring the Gospel to Indian tribes along the river.

Throughout the spring and summer, the pair conducted the first extensive exploration of the Mississippi River Valley by Europeans. Although it disappointed them to learn that the river emptied into the Gulf of Mexico, not the Pacific, their findings still proved invaluable.

On their return journey, Jolliet and Marquette paddled north along the Mississippi for six weeks until, on **August 25, 1673,** they turned east and entered the Illinois River, which Jolliet described as, "the most beautiful, and most suitable for settlement."

"The river is wide and deep, abounding in catfish and sturgeon," he wrote. "Game is abundant there; oxen, cows, stags, does, and turkeys are found there in greater numbers than elsewhere."

After that first legendary expedition, Jolliet married, became a father of four, and continued his explorations of the waterways of Eastern Canada. His reward for his work was an appointment as New France's Royal Hydrographer and an expansive island in the St. Lawrence River.

In 1700, while returning to that island from Quebec, Jolliet disappeared. Presumed dead, he was never seen again.

Michael Portier was studying for the priesthood in his native France, when Bishop Louis William DuBourg came calling.

Recently consecrated as bishop of the Diocese of Louisiana and the Two Floridas, DuBourg needed priests for his massive diocese, where only a handful of ordained men served its largely Catholic population. Moreover, with the priests in New Orleans, the diocese's largest city, staging a quiet rebellion, DuBourg was desperate for allies.

He found one in Portier.

Without completing his studies, Portier sailed for America with Du-Bourg in July 1817, arriving in Annapolis that September.

While DuBourg continued on to St. Louis, Portier traveled to Baltimore. He finished his formation, then joined his bishop in the spring.

Ordained to the priesthood in May 1818, Father Portier served the frontier diocese for seven years, until Rome divided it into more manageable parts and entrusted one of those parts—the Vicariate of Alabama and the Floridas—to the 30-year-old Portier. He was consecrated in St. Louis on **August 26, 1825,** and then left for Mobile, Alabama.

More than a century earlier, in 1703, the bishop of Quebec established the Gulf Coast's first parish in Mobile. Eight years later, in 1711, the parish built a new church, a small building 20 feet wide and 50 feet deep. Originally named Our Lady of Mobile, it was renamed Immaculate Conception Parish during the Spanish occupation. This was the "cathedral" awaiting Portier. He had two other parishes in his diocese—one in Pensacola and one in St. Augustine—and no other priests.

That changed after his vicariate became a diocese in 1829, and Portier, imitating DuBourg, traveled to Europe to recruit young men eager for adventure.

Over the next 30 years, Portier, with the help of his European recruits, built the present-day Cathedral Basilica of the Immaculate Conception on the site of Mobile's first parish. He also founded the first Catholic college in the South (Spring Hill College), two orphanages, a hospital, and multiple parishes and schools.

Portier passed away on the eve of the American Civil War, in 1859.

The Know-Nothings may have stopped running candidates for office in the mid-nineteenth century, but in 1949, anti-Catholicism in America was still alive and well. Protestant preacher turned secularist agitator Paul Blanshard proved as much that year when, to widespread acclaim, he published the bestselling anti-Catholic screed, *American Freedom and Catholic Power.*

Born in Ohio on **August 27, 1892,** Blanshard inherited the seeds of his anti-Catholicism from his Methodist grandmother and Protestant pastor father. Those seeds grew during his years at Harvard Divinity School, where he became a socialist and befriended eugenicist Margaret Sanger.

Eventually apostatizing from Christianity and leaving the Congregationalist church he pastored in Florida, Blanshard moved to New York, where he earned a degree in law. There, his anti-Catholicism came into full flower.

Much of Blanshard's original animosity towards the Church was rooted in his support for abortion. Determined to weaken what he saw as the Catholic influence on obstetric practices, Blanshard began writing a series of articles for *The Nation,* which depicted the Church as a money-hungry foreign power, determined to control the U.S. government.

Outraged, New York's archbishop at the time, Francis Cardinal Spellman, called upon Catholics to cancel their subscriptions to the magazine and demanded (fruitlessly) that the city's public schools stop carrying it as well. When Blanshard published the articles in book form in 1949, the accusations it made against the Church were so outlandish that even the *New York Times* refused to advertise it.

Yet somehow, a book that claimed Catholics wanted to seize the government, repeal the First Amendment, and make the pope "the president's official superior" still earned the praise of John Dewey and Albert Einstein. It also sold 240,000 copies in its first printing.

In later years, Blanshard made a successful living as a professional anti-Catholic, including representing the predecessor to Americans United for the Separation of Church and State—Protestants and Others United for the Separation of Church and State.

Blanshard died in 1980. His book went out of print four years later.

Land. It was a sight Pedro Menéndez de Avilés had long waited to see. Months earlier, in the spring of 1565, the Spanish admiral set sail from Cadiz, along with more than 800 men and women. They'd seen almost nothing but ocean ever since.

On **August 28, 1565,** however, the cry went up. A sailor had glimpsed land on the horizon.

A week later, Menéndez's fleet sailed into Matanzas Bay. A small landing party disembarked soon afterwards to build temporary fortifications, which would allow Menéndez to unload both his people and their supplies in safety. On September 8, Menéndez himself disembarked. Immediately, he knelt and kissed the crucifix presented to him by Father Francisco López de Mendoza Grajales, chaplain of his expedition. He then claimed the land for Spain and named it St. Augustine, in honor of the saint whose feast the Church celebrated on the day his crew spotted land.

After that, 500 soldiers, 200 sailors, 100 settlers, and three more Franciscan friars disembarked to join the admiral for Holy Mass.

After Mass, the men quickly set about unloading their goods and building a small fort to protect their party, both from the country's native inhabitants and from the French, who had settled up the coast (on present-day Parris Island, South Carolina) and were none too happy about the Spanish moving in.

Ongoing conflict with both the French and the English eventually forced the Spanish of St. Augustine to abandon their initial landing spot and move to more defensible ground. The Spanish settlers, however, continued to honor the place where Menéndez first knelt: they built Mission Nombre de Dios there in the mid-sixteenth century, and in the early seventeenth century, they constructed the first Marian shrine in the United States—Our Lady of La Leche—at the mission.

Both the mission and the shrine still stand today. And there, where the first residents of St. Augustine celebrated Mass 450 years ago, Mass is celebrated still.

August 29: CHURCH HILL

On **August 29, 1862,** as the Second Battle of Bull Run raged, volunteers began pulling the pews out of St. Mary of Sorrows Catholic Church in nearby Fairfax Station, Virginia.

The pews were new, installed just a few years earlier when the small mission church was built. Within days, however, they would look decades old, their polish worn off and the wood soaked with blood. Volunteers placed the pews outside, lining what the locals called Church Hill. There, they would serve as beds for a makeshift field hospital.

After the battle ended the following day, trains full of food and supplies began arriving at the local station. On one of those trains was Clara Barton, a young clerk in the U.S. Patent Office. When news of the mounting casualties (more than 21,000 by battle's end) reached Washington, D.C., Barton convinced several friends to go south with her to care for the wounded.

Upon arriving at St. Mary's, Barton helped organize the chaos unfolding outside and inside the church, which after the rain began to fall, became an operating room.

It rained for days, but Barton and her small group of nurses worked without pause. Eventually, trains came to collect the wounded. Barton remained until the last soldier was gone.

After she left Fairfax Station, Barton founded a volunteer corps to provide similar help for soldiers throughout the war: the American Red Cross.

For their part, St. Mary's parishioners received new pews courtesy of the American government and continued to tend the graves of the Union and Confederate soldiers who died there. Several years later, the War Department arranged to have the bodies transported to Arlington National Cemetery. But one family, the Kidwells, wanted their son to remain on Catholic ground and conspired with the priest to hide his grave when officials came. They succeeded, and his grave remains there today, a perpetual reminder of all the boys who died long ago on Church Hill.

Boston needed a cathedral. In 1866, that was priority number one for Bishop John Williams, the newly consecrated shepherd of "Beantown."

The original Holy Cross Cathedral—designed by famed Boston architect James Bullfinch, funded by both Catholic and Protestant Bostonians (including John Adams), and decorated with the help of Henry Sargent—had grown too small for Boston's exploding Catholic population. In September 1860, Bishop John Fitzpatrick offered one final Mass there, and then had the building demolished.

Unfortunately, before construction on a new cathedral could commence, the American Civil War began. For the next six years, with money, materials, and men in short supply, Fitzpatrick celebrated Mass in an abandoned theater and former Unitarian church.

As soon as Williams succeeded Fitzpatrick, he set out to change that.

Boston born and bred, Williams knew his diocese well. The diocese's second bishop, Benedict Joseph Fenwick, taught him as a child, and later sent him to Montreal and Paris for seminary. Upon returning to Boston, in 1845, Williams served for 12 years as curate (and later rector) of the cathedral, then as pastor of St. James Church, one of the city's largest parishes. While there, he also acted as vicar-general for the diocese, administering Boston's financial affairs for the ailing Fitzpatrick.

With that much knowledge of his diocese, Williams hit the ground running, laying the new cathedral's cornerstone one month after his consecration. Nine years later, he dedicated the new Cathedral of the Holy Cross.

Williams would dedicate many more buildings in his 41 years as bishop and (after 1875) archbishop of Boston. During his tenure, he consecrated eight to ten new parishes almost every year. New hospitals and charitable institutions also opened, the diocese's parochial school system began, St. John's Seminary was founded, and more than a dozen religious orders, personally recruited by Williams, came to town.

When Archbishop Williams died, on **August 30, 1907,** he left behind an archdiocese and a city transformed. Where just over a century earlier priests were outlawed and the Mass banned, Catholicism had become the dominant cultural force.

August 31: BULL FEENEY

In the late 1960s, director John Ford sat down with a reporter for an interview. As they spoke, the reporter described himself as an atheist. Ford responded by pulling out his rosary beads and pressing them into the young man's hands.

Such a public display of faith was atypical for Ford, to say the least. For as long as anyone could remember, Ford, who was christened John Feeney, cared almost as much about his reputation as a tough guy as he did about his films. In his Portland, Maine, high school, his classmates called him "Bull" Feeney and as a director, he bullied stars and studio executives in equal measure. He was, said character actor Henry Brandon, "the only man who could make John Wayne cry."

Besides his temper, Ford had problems that put him at odds with his Church, including his marriage to a Protestant divorcee, a wandering eye, and an addiction to alcohol.

Yet Ford never left the Church; he just didn't obey her.

Regardless of his personal struggles, Ford's private charity was as legendary as his public gruffness. As one story goes, during the Depression he publicly rebuked a man who asked him for $200 (to pay for his wife's surgery), then privately gave the man $1,000, flew in a specialist to perform the operation, and bought the couple a house.

Ford also brought a distinctly Catholic vision to his films, which depict redemption unfolding within a community and where grace abounds in the midst of everyday life.

With roughly 150 films to his credit, Ford was one of Hollywood's most prolific Catholic directors, and, arguably, its greatest. His work includes the monumental World War II documentaries shot for the U.S. Navy, and the films that earned him Academy Awards for Best Director: *The Informer, The Grapes of Wrath, How Green Was My Valley,* and *The Quiet Man.*

Ford died on **August 31, 1973**. His funeral Mass took place in his parish, Hollywood's Blessed Sacrament Church.

September

September 1: RIGHT REASONING

In 1894, everything was coming up roses for the American Protective Association (APA). Founded only seven years earlier, the rabidly anti-Catholic political organization boasted 2.5 million members by 1894 and with a hefty campaign war chest, expected major victories at the polls in November.

Catholics, meanwhile, weren't sure how to respond. Some within the American episcopal hierarchy urged their flocks to ignore the APA's rhetoric, not wanting to legitimize the group by disputing their baseless assertions. Others, such as the first bishop of the Diocese of Peoria, John Spalding, took a different tack.

As a poet, historian, prolific author, editor of the "Baltimore Catechism," and one of the chief founders of the Catholic University of America, Bishop Spalding had powerful friends in the publishing world. With the help of those friends, he convinced the prestigious journal *North American Review* to run his essay rebutting the APA's claims. He was sure that sound reasoning would bring the American electorate to its senses.

The essay, which ran in the **September 1, 1894,** issue, reminded America that:

> *[Catholics] founded one of the thirteen colonies and were the first in the New World, the first, indeed, in all the world, to make freedom of conscience an organic part of the constitution of the State. Their action marks an era in the progress of mankind. When the hour came to break the bond which united the colonies to England and which had become a fetter, none more generously than the Catholics hearkened to the trumpet call, and in the darkest days of the struggle, Catholics from Europe mingled their blood on our battlefields with that of our fathers. If long tenure, if fidelity, if honorable deeds, have aught of efficacy, Catholics have the right to be here, nor has this right ever become forfeit by any act or attempt of the Catholic Church in America.*

It was an intelligent and stirring defense—but, unfortunately, not stirring enough to prevent nearly 100 APA-backed candidates from winning seats in the U.S. House of Representatives two months later.

September 2: THE ROAD TO ROME

In 1908, William Henry Hope moved his wife and seven sons from England to Cleveland. He was looking for work. He found women and booze.

While the elder Hope drank, his fifth son, Leslie, put food on the table by singing and dancing on street corners. Eventually, the busking led to Vaudeville, Vaudeville led to Broadway, and Broadway led to Hollywood.

By the early 1940s, the one-time busker went by the name "Bob" and was one of Hollywood's most bankable stars. He also was one of its most generous. Bob Hope gave his time to America's soldiers—headlining 57 USO (United Service Organization) tours in his lifetime—and he gave his money to the Catholic Church. For the first gift, the U.S. government rewarded the entertainer with the USNS *Bob Hope,* commissioned on **September 2, 1993**. For the second gift, Hope's wife, Dolores, rewarded him with a smile.

Hope, who was raised Presbyterian, married the devoutly Catholic Dolores in 1934, and throughout their marriage generously supported her Church. That support included large-scale gifts to parish building campaigns for parishes, hospitals, and religious orders. It also included more personal gifts, such as funding one priest's outreach to the homeless in Los Angeles and letting local Catholic school children use his yard as a playground. Hope likewise donated the funds to build Our Lady of Hope Chapel at the Basilica of the National Shrine of the Immaculate Conception in Washington, D.C.

Unfortunately, despite his generosity, what Hope couldn't do for most of his 69-year marriage was share Dolores' faith. A notorious philanderer, Hope seemed incapable of embracing the teachings of the Church for which he did so much. Dolores, however, never walked away. Rather, she endured years of humiliation by growing in her faith and praying for Hope to find his.

God answered those prayers in the last decade of the couple's married life. Bob Hope spent his final years as a faithful Catholic convert, dying at the age of 100 in 2003.

September 3: LOMBARDI'S LEGEND

In Green Bay, Wisconsin, and wherever else Packers fans reside, Vince Lombardi's legend looms as large today as it did in 1967, the year he coached his final season with Green Bay.

Every loyal Packers fan can tell you that Lombardi saved the franchise from an almost certain demise when he became the team's head coach in 1959. They all know that he led Green Bay to five National Football League (NFL) championships in nine years (three of them consecutive). And they also know that Lombardi's Packers won the first two Superbowls, that Lombardi never had a losing season as an NFL head coach, and that he is the reason every Packers home game has been sold out since 1960.

Most Green Bay fans also can tell you a little about Lombardi's past: he was born in 1913 to first generation Italian-Americans, grew up in Brooklyn, and coached high school and college football before entering the NFL in 1954 as assistant coach to the New York Giants.

But what many younger Packers fans couldn't tell you is that before Lombardi dreamed of coaching in the NFL, he dreamed of serving God as a priest and spent several years in seminary. Later, while coaching football at St. Cecilia Catholic High School in New Jersey, Lombardi earned the bulk of his salary teaching Latin. Later still, when he made the move to Green Bay, he did so in large part because of the city's reputation as a bastion of Catholicism.

Other lesser known facts include Lombardi's lifelong habit of attending daily Mass (which he did in Green Bay at St. Willebrord's); his willingness, even as an NFL coach, to assist at the altar during the Liturgy; and his membership in both the Knights of Columbus and Knights of Malta.

Death came for the football legend on **September 3, 1970**. Felled by colon cancer, the 57-year-old Lombardi was survived by his wife of 30 years, Marie, their two children, and six grandchildren.

September 4: THE GRUNT PADRE

The attack came before dawn on **September 4, 1967,** while most of the 1st Battalion 5th Marines' Delta Company still slept. The evening before, the Americans had set up a nighttime defensive perimeter, but with 2,500 North Vietnamese soldiers aligned against them, it didn't help. D Company was outnumbered and outgunned.

The battle raged for hours. The gunfire was relentless. So too, however, was the D Company's chaplain, Father Vincent Capodanno.

Under heavy artillery fire, the Staten Island native administered Last Rites to the dying and pulled the wounded to safety. The injured men were heavy, but Father Capodanno had grown accustomed to carrying heavy loads.

For the past 17 months, ever since he had arrived in Vietnam, the former Maryknoll missionary had carried his own gear—over 40 pounds' worth—through the Vietnamese jungles, where temperatures regularly climbed to 125 degrees. Capodanno could have handed off his burden to another Marine, but he didn't think his priesthood should exempt him from the trials his men faced. That's why the Marines called him "The Grunt Padre." And that's why, when battle began on September 4, he didn't retreat to safety.

As the morning progressed, Capodanno's decision to remain in the thick of the fighting earned him shrapnel wounds in the right arm, hand, and leg. But he refused medical attention and went on administering Last Rites with his one good hand. Nothing seemed to stop him.

Then, something did.

Hours into the battle, Capodanno spotted a wounded Marine pinned down yards away from a machine gun. Venturing forward was a risk. Capodanno took it. He made it safely to the Marine's side, but as soon as he did, the enemy soldier manning the gun opened fire. The 38-year-old priest died instantly.

Capodanno was posthumously awarded the Medal of Honor, the Purple Heart, and the Bronze Star, and in 1971, the U.S. Navy named a ship in his honor, the USS *Capodanno*. It later became the first American ship to receive a papal blessing.

Father Capodanno's cause for canonization opened in 2002.

September 5: A MISSIONARY OF CHARITY

On **September 5, 1997,** the world said goodbye to one of its living saints—Mother Teresa of Calcutta.

The tiny Albanian sister, who spent nearly 50 years laboring among the poorest of the poor in India's slums, traveled to America many times in her long life. She came to establish Missionaries of Charity communities in major metropolitan centers, including New York, San Francisco, and Dallas. She also came to open AIDS hospices and homeless shelters, receive honorary degrees, and meet with politicians. During those visits, she unfailingly addressed what she saw as America's greatest spiritual struggles: loneliness, materialism, and abortion.

But perhaps on no other occasion did she confront those struggles as bluntly as she did at the 1994 National Prayer Breakfast.

During her address, Mother Teresa reminded President Bill Clinton and other U.S. political leaders present at the event that because "it hurt" Jesus to love us:

> . . . it is very important for us to realize that love, to be true, has to hurt. I must be willing to give whatever it takes not to harm other people and, in fact, to do good to them. This requires that I be willing to give until it hurts. Otherwise, there is no true love in me and I bring injustice, not peace, to those around me.

Mother Teresa concluded her remarks by focusing on the topic of abortion, saying:

> But I feel that the greatest destroyer of peace today is abortion, because it is a war against the child, a direct killing of the innocent child, murder by the mother herself.
>
> . . . Any country that accepts abortion is not teaching its people to love, but to use any violence to get what they want. This is why the greatest destroyer of love and peace is abortion.

In November 1996, a year before her death, the United States granted Mother Teresa honorary citizenship. Eight years later, in 2003, Pope John Paul II declared her "Blessed."

September 6: THE *NIÑA*, THE *PINTA*, AND THE *SANTA MARIA*

On **September 6, 1492,** three ships prepared to set sail from the harbor town of San Sebastian de la Gomera. For days, the *Santa Clara* (nicknamed the *Niña)*, the *Pinta,* and the *Santa Maria* had rested in the Canary Islands' port, while their captains and crew completed repairs on the ships and restocked their supplies.

A month earlier, under the command of the Genoan sailor Christopher Columbus, the three ships had departed Spain, en route (they hoped) for China. Columbus believed he could reach Asia by sailing west as well as east, and made that claim to the crowned heads of Portugal, Venice, Genoa, England, and Spain. Most dismissed his plan. They shared his conviction that the journey was theoretically possible, but believed (rightly) that Columbus underestimated the westward distance between Europe and Asia.

But after much persuading, King Ferdinand II of Aragon and Queen Isabella I of Castile decided the idea might have merit. In early 1492, they agreed to sponsor Columbus' expedition and, if he succeeded, reward him generously with titles, authority, and wealth.

For most men, that would have been motivation enough. But Columbus' interests weren't entirely mercenary. The devoutly Catholic Columbus believed God wanted him to bring the Gospel to foreign lands. Isabella shared his passion for evangelization, and in sponsoring the voyage, believed she was fulfilling the Great Commission of Matthew 28: to make disciples of all nations.

That motivation sustained Columbus during the five long weeks that followed his fleet's September 6 departure from the Canary Islands. At the time, no European ship in living or recorded memory had sailed so far from land for so long, and Columbus expected the journey to be much shorter than it turned out to be. His men shared those expectations, and on October 10 came close to mutiny.

Just two days later, when all seemed lost, they spotted an island on the horizon. Columbus christened the island *San Salvador* or "Holy Savior."

And the world was forever changed.

September 7: THE CHAPEL CAR PRIESTS

In the first decades of the twentieth century, no regular Sunday Mass took place in Florence, Oregon. Instead, Catholics in Florence and the surrounding towns contented themselves with a monthly liturgy or spent hours traveling to distant parishes in distant towns. Some simply stopped going to Mass altogether.

That changed in 1958, when the Catholic Church Extension Society funded the construction of St. Mary's Mission Church. Nine years later, on **September 7, 1967,** St. Mary's, Our Lady of the Dunes Catholic Church, was officially established as a parish in the Archdiocese of Portland.

The Society that made St. Mary's possible began six decades earlier, when Father Francis Kelley—a Vatican diplomat and priest for the Archdiocese of Detroit—realized that despite the Church's growth in urban America, the Church in rural America was dying for lack of priests.

To correct that problem, Kelley founded the Catholic Church Extension Society. Beginning in 1905, missionaries traveled the country in "Chapel Cars"—railroad cars purchased for the Society that went wherever the trains would take them. When the train stopped, the Chapel Car priests preached missions. They also distributed food, clothing, money, and other material goods to the rural poor.

As the Society grew, it began building churches, sponsoring missionaries, and underwriting ministry programs. Kelley's increasingly high profile as a diplomat and writer helped the Society's work as well.

Kelley became the second bishop of Oklahoma in 1924. By the time of his death, in 1948, the Catholic Church Extension Society had grown to become one of the largest Catholic charitable organizations in the United States. Today, as Catholic Extension, it continues to provide over $20 million in support each year to people, ministries, and parishes in 33 states. Forty-six percent of all U.S. dioceses receive some form of aid from the Society, with one in six Catholics benefiting from its efforts.

As for St. Mary's, if you ever find yourself along the central Oregon coast on a Sunday, Holy Mass begins at 11 a.m.

Some have called Rafael Guastavino "the best architect you've never heard of." But in the late-nineteenth century, few in the construction business didn't know the Spaniard's name.

Born in Valencia in 1842, Guastavino was still in his twenties when he developed an interest in ancient Moorish construction techniques. He became particularly fascinated with the Moors' expansive but unsupported archways and domed ceilings. He practiced replicating those techniques while in Spain, and then perfected them after he immigrated to America in 1881.

Typically working in partnership with other architects, Guastavino built floors, stairs, and curved roofs and ceilings by placing layers of thin, interlocking terra-cotta tiles in mortar. Strong, enduring, and fireproof, Guastavino's work endures in more than 1,000 churches, private homes, and public buildings, including: Carnegie Hall, Grand Central Station, St. Patrick's Cathedral, the Great Hall at Ellis Island, Grant's Tomb, the Plaza and St. Regis hotels, the Cloisters, and more.

In the mid-1890s, while working on the Biltmore Estate, Guastavino decided to relocate to North Carolina. He first built a large estate for himself outside Asheville and later built a large church for local Catholics inside Asheville. As the story goes, Guastavino couldn't find a seat at Mass one Sunday because the town's original Catholic church was overcrowded. After that, he approached the parish priest and offered to design a new church, provide the tile, and oversee the construction. He also volunteered to subsidize a large part of the cost. Without hesitating, the priest accepted Guastavino's offer.

That church eventually became the Basilica of St. Lawrence. It was the first Guastavino-designed Catholic Church in North Carolina to receive the papal honor. Gustavino designed the second, St. Mary's Catholic Church in Wilmington, shortly before his 1908 death. Just over a century later, the Vatican elevated St. Mary's to a basilica, and on **September 8, 2013,** Bishop Michael Burbidge of the Diocese of Raleigh celebrated a Mass of Thanksgiving for the newly received designation.

Guastavino is buried in Asheville, in the crypt of the first North Carolina basilica he built.

September 9: THE SWAMPOODLE CHURCH

In 1857, a reporter covering the groundbreaking ceremony for St. Aloysius Catholic Church in Washington, D.C., surveyed the Irish immigrants surrounding him and the swampy, puddle-riddled topography on which they stood. He then coined a name for the area: "Swampoodle."

The name stuck. For more than 50 years, Swampoodle comprised the blocks immediately surrounding North Capitol and I Streets. During the late-nineteenth century, those blocks were known as the most lawless and poverty-stricken streets in the District. But Swampoodle still had its charms. Cows, chickens, and other livestock grazed in wide, open yards. Neighbors looked after neighbors. And St. Aloysius stood in its midst.

When construction on the Jesuit-run parish ended in 1859, President James Buchanan ventured into Swampoodle for the dedication. In the paintings above the main altar, he saw the handiwork of Constantino Brumidi, whose frescoes decorated the Capitol's rotunda. In those same paintings, he saw the wife of Senator Stephen A. Douglas, whom Brumidi used as the model for St. Aloysius Gonzaga's mother.

The people of Swampoodle were proud of their beautiful parish. And when the District's military governor attempted to requisition the church on **September 9, 1862,** they didn't take the news well.

The governor, however, had good reason for the attempt. With Civil War casualties pouring into the city, he needed a hospital in which to put the soldiers. He thought St. Aloysius would do nicely. The parishioners thought otherwise. So, their pastor made the governor a counter-offer: If the parish built the Union Army a hospital, would the city leave the church alone?

The governor accepted the offer, and in eight days' time he had a new 250-bed hospital, courtesy of every able-bodied man, woman, and child in Swampoodle.

Swampoodle ceased to exist as a neighborhood after 1907, when the District destroyed 300 homes in the neighborhood's center to make room for Union Station. St. Aloysius hung on for a century more, closing its doors in 2012. It still remains in occasional use, however, as part of the adjacent Gonzaga College High School.

September 10: THE AJACÁN MISSION

On **September 10, 1570,** a Spanish ship sailed into the Chesapeake Bay and deposited two Jesuit fathers and six Jesuit brothers on shore. The men brought no weapons and no soldiers with them. They had but one mission: evangelization. Likewise, the only valuable belongings they possessed were the tools of the missionary's trade: vestments, Mass vessels, and the Scriptures. One servant and an Algonquian guide named Don Luís traveled with them.

The Spanish had captured Don Luís 10 years earlier on those same shores (known then as Ajacán). When they returned to Spain, the Algonquian boy went with them. He met the king, became Catholic, and received a Jesuit education. He appeared to embrace the Faith enthusiastically, and after the Jesuits announced their plan to take the Gospel to Ajacán, Don Luís asked to come along, seemingly eager to share his faith with his people.

But Don Luis' tune changed after their arrival. Explaining that he wanted to recruit catechumens for the Ajacán mission and secure food for the Jesuits, the Algonquian asked the party's leader, Father Juan Segura, for permission to travel to his family's village. The priest readily agreed. When several weeks passed, however, with no sign of Don Luís, the Jesuits grew concerned.

Twice, Father Segura sent novices to fetch their guide. With each failed attempt, the missionaries' fears grew. Finally, in February 1571, a third search party ventured out. Don Luís met them on the way and fired arrows into their hearts. The Jesuits' former guide and several of his tribesmen then continued to the encampment. Segura met him with a smile, crying out, "Don Luís! You are most welcome!" Don Luís struck the priest's head with an axe.

The remaining priests and brothers were dead in minutes. Only the servant boy escaped. A supply ship found him a year later, and learned of the missionaries' fate. With the ship's departure, Spanish colonization attempts along America's mid-Atlantic seaboard ended.

The Diocese of Richmond opened the Jesuits' cause for canonization in 2002.

For over 225 years, Old St. Peter's Catholic Church in New York City has held a backstage pass to American history.

In the 1770s, New York Catholics still worshipped in secret—usually in a German family's house on Wall Street. The end of the American Revolution, however, brought religious freedom, and in 1786, they built St. Peter's Catholic Church on Barclay Street. It was the first Catholic church in the state.

Almost immediately, the problem of trusteeism reared its head. In 1787, parish trustees fired their first pastor—the holy Irish Franciscan, Father Charles Whelan—because they didn't like his preaching. To replace him, they hired the more eloquent (but less holy) Father Andrew Nugent. Trustees quickly changed their minds, but Nugent proved difficult to remove. So much so, that when Father John Carroll, then provisional Superior of America's priests, visited St. Peter's, a disgruntled Father Nugent crashed his Mass and shouted Carroll out of the sanctuary.

In 1805, Saint Elizabeth Ann Seton became a Catholic at St. Peter's. In 1806, anti-Catholics rioted at St. Peter's. And in 1810, the baby that grew up to become New York's first cardinal, John McCloskey, was baptized at St. Peter's. By 1836, however, the first St. Peter's had become too small. So, parishioners took it down and built a second St. Peter's.

As the twentieth century began, St. Peter's said goodbye to the families moving away from the once rural neighborhood and hello to an influx of commuters. Sixty years later, the parish witnessed the rise of the World Trade Center's Twin Towers across the street. And on **September 11, 2001,** it watched those towers fall.

That day, for two hours, the body of the fallen chaplain Father Mychal Judge, lay in the church's sanctuary. Later, for almost two months, the parish served as a staging ground for rescue and recovery operations.

In honor of all the history Old St. Peter's has witnessed, the United States, New York State, and New York City governments have all declared the church a historic landmark.

September 12: THE AMERICANIST BISHOP?

In October 1896, rumors about The Catholic University of America's rector, Bishop John J. Keane, filled the pages of America's newspapers. Or, more accurately, rumors about Catholic University's *former* rector filled those pages.

That month, news broke that Pope Leo XIII had requested Keane's resignation and called him to Rome. There, the pope planned for him to reside at the Basilica of St. John Lateran and serve as a consultant for the Congregation for the Propagation of the Faith. The press knew nothing more.

The press speculated, however, that Keane's summons to Rome had more to do with his progressive views than it did with any pressing need at the Vatican for another consultant.

Born on **September 12, 1839,** Keane spent 12 years as a priest in Washington, D.C., and nine as bishop of Richmond before becoming the first rector of The Catholic University of America in 1887. A master fund-raiser and skilled administrator, his tenure there should have been secure. Many of Keane's fellow bishops, though, frowned upon his support of the Knights of Labor and his participation in the controversial World's Parliament of Religions of 1893. Likewise, rightly or wrongly, many associated Keane with the heresy of Americanism—wanting to update the Church to bring it more in line with American ideals. Given all that, it took no great stretch of the imagination for the press to suspect that the summons to Rome was more punishment than reward.

Their suspicions were likely correct. But by 1899, the Vatican had enough confidence in Keane to re-task him with fund-raising for The Catholic University. Only a year later, it named him archbishop of Dubuque. Once installed, Keane focused his energies on promoting temperance and Catholic education. During his tenure in Iowa, he established 12 academies for girls and two for boys. He also doubled the faculty and buildings of present-day Loras College.

Archbishop Keane resigned his see in 1911 due to ill health. He died in Dubuque seven years later. To this day, his association with the Americanist heresy clouds his legacy.

Some claim the soldiers deserted because of the hatred Protestant officers had for Catholics. Others think the promise of money and land in Mexico lured the Irish-American soldiers south.

In truth, no one knows for certain why nearly 200 Irish Catholic immigrants deserted the U.S. Army in 1846 and joined cause with Mexico at the outset of the Mexican-American War. Although, had American officers not forced Catholic soldiers to attend Protestant services in the war's early days, they might have had fewer deserters on their hands.

Regardless, enough Irish-American soldiers switched sides in those first several months that the Mexican Army organized them into a battalion. The men called their unit St. Patrick's Battalion. The Mexicans called them the *San Patricios*. Despite the name, other foreigners fought in the unit as well, including immigrants from Germany, France, Poland, Italy, Scotland, Spain, and Switzerland.

For more than a year, the *San Patricios* commanded heavy artillery for Mexico. And the heavy casualties they inflicted on American troops at the Battles of Monterey, Buena Vista, and Cerro Gordo made their defeat a priority for U.S. Commander Zachary Taylor.

That defeat came on August 20, 1847, at the Battle of Churubusco. Knowing that surrender would mean capture and certain death, the *San Patricios* forcibly stopped Mexican officers from raising the white flag three times. Then, when their ammunition ran out, they turned to hand-to-hand combat. Nevertheless, by the end of the day, more than 35 *San Patricios* were dead and upwards of 75 were taken prisoner. Just days later, an American military court found nearly all the men guilty of desertion and treason, and then sentenced them to death by hanging. The last of those sentences was carried out on **September 13, 1847.**

The U.S. Army denied the existence of the *San Patricios* until 1915. But both in Mexico and Ireland, the *San Patricios* were and are celebrated as heroes, with statues, streets, and even towns named in their honor.

As they say, one man's hero . . .

September 14: THE FIRST AMERICAN SAINT

In 1805, Elizabeth Ann Seton left the Episcopal Church and became Catholic. In the mind of the world, that decision made little sense.

Three years earlier, in 1802, the business of her husband, William, failed, leaving the once wealthy and prominent couple nearly destitute. The following year, William died of tuberculosis. At 29 years old, Seton was a widow with five young children to support and no means to do so. She did have prosperous friends and relatives to whom she could turn, but she knew she would lose their support if she became Catholic. Conversion meant alienating those in the best position to help her.

But Seton was convinced of the Church's claims. After her husband's death, she spent nearly a year with friends in Italy and came to love the Catholic Faith. Motherless since childhood, Seton found comfort in her new relationship with the Virgin Mary, and she longed to receive the Eucharist. So, she risked everything and converted, trusting that God would provide.

At first, it was rough going. Friends cut her off. Family members isolated her. And rampant prejudice prevented her from founding a school in New York. She did succeed in opening a boardinghouse for schoolboys, but as word of her conversion spread, parents removed their children and the enterprise failed.

In 1808, however, at the invitation of the Sulpician priest (and future bishop) Father Louis William DuBourg, Seton moved her young family to Baltimore to open a Catholic school for girls. There, with DuBourg's help, Seton devised a plan to both keep her children and live the religious life for which she longed.

She embarked on that plan in 1809, leaving Baltimore for Emmitsburg, Maryland, where she founded the first American religious order for women—the Sisters of Charity—and opened the first free Catholic school in the country. Her order grew rapidly, eventually giving rise to six separate congregations.

Mother Seton died of tuberculosis in 1821. When Pope Paul VI canonized her 154 years later on **September 14, 1975,** she became America's first native-born saint.

Where does conversion begin? More specifically, where does conversion for a communist-supporting, Western Civilization-hating, openly bisexual, black Harlem Renaissance poet begin?

For Claude McKay, it began in Europe's cathedrals.

Born in Jamaica on **September 15, 1889,** McKay immigrated to America in 1912. Just seven years later, he left his adopted home of Harlem for England. From there, he journeyed across Europe, North Africa, and Russia. Although only a few years earlier, McKay had written poems blaming "the Christian West" for ravaging the "Black Land" of Africa, something in the ancient holy places he visited during his travels made him question his agnostic views.

"What jeweled glory fills my spirit's eye," he wrote after visiting a church in St. Petersburg, Russia. "What golden grandeur moves the depths of me!"

In 1940, with four acclaimed books of poetry, three successful novels, and a short story collection under his belt, McKay returned to New York and became a U.S. citizen. Soon afterwards, both his health and finances failed. A Catholic acquaintance came to McKay's rescue and took him to Friendship House, where the staff provided him with food, shelter, and medical care.

In their charity, McKay found another reason to rethink his opinion on Christianity. And the more he learned about the Church's social teachings, the more convinced he became that Catholicism held the answer to racial and economic injustice. Having already rejected communism, McKay decided to devote his energies to the Church's work among the marginalized. He moved to Chicago in 1944, and took a job at Friendship House's headquarters. He also became an advisor to Auxiliary Bishop Bernard Sheil of Chicago on black affairs and communism.

By that point, McKay was studying the Church's doctrine and contemplating conversion. But beautiful cathedrals and social teachings weren't enough. In a June 1944 letter to a friend he explained that before he could convert he had to make sure his belief was "intellectually honest and sincere." Conviction came before summer's end, and in October 1944 McKay entered the Catholic Church. He died four years later.

September 16: SEEKING TRUTH

Orestes Brownson was, by his own description, an old man before he entered his teens.

Born on **September 16, 1803,** and raised by an elderly Protestant couple in rural Vermont, Brownson had neither toys nor children to play with during his childhood. Instead he had the Holy Bible, which so preoccupied Brownson's young mind that by the time he turned eight, religion was the only topic that interested him. By the time he turned 12, the great question of his life was what religious sect he should join. In Vermont, Brownson's options included the Methodists, Baptists, Congregationalists, and "Cristyans." The trouble was that he didn't like those options. In 1822, a chance encounter with Presbyterians led him to seek baptism in their community, but that too failed to satisfy. After two years, he moved on, rejecting traditional Christianity in the process.

Over the next two decades, Brownson's search for a spiritual home led him to become a Universalist minister and Unitarian preacher, a prominent Transcendentalist, a militant atheist, and a subscriber to the utopian schemes of Robert Owen and Fanny Wright. Brownson even founded his own church in 1836—the Society for Christian Union and Progress. All the while, as Brownson searched, he also wrote, lectured, and dabbled in politics. His prose was forceful and his pen prolific, so by 1843, America considered him one of its greatest intellectuals.

Then, rumors started circulating that Brownson might convert to Catholicism. Rumor became fact in 1844. Most critics believed this was just another phase. But Brownson surprised them all. For the next 32 years, until his death in 1876, Brownson remained one of the Church's most ardent apologists, writing more on Church, culture, and politics than perhaps any other Catholic—ordained or lay—in the nineteenth century.

In honor of his lasting contributions to Catholic intellectual life in America, the University of Notre Dame granted Brownson a final resting place in the crypt of its Basilica of the Sacred Heart.

September 17: THE GEORGIA MARTYRS

In the sixteenth century, long before the definition of marriage as the permanent union of one man and one woman came under attack in the United States, five Franciscan friars gave their lives defending that truth in the New World.

The friars were missionaries, living along the coast of present-day Georgia. They came from Spain, arriving first in St. Augustine, and then striking out on their own sometime after 1587, with no soldiers accompanying them.

At first, they needed no soldiers. Many of the Guale to whom they preached eagerly embraced the Gospel. But others balked when it came to the Church's teachings on marriage. The Guale practiced polygamy, and the friars' demand that men live in a permanent marriage with only one wife seemed unreasonable to them. The friars refused to baptize those Guale, accepting only converts who promised to embrace the Catholic understanding of marriage.

In 1597, a convert named Juanillo broke that promise. Father Pedro de Corpa, the friar in charge of the mission where Juanillo lived, called him to repent. Instead, on September 14, Juanillo and a Guale war party broke into de Corpa's cabin and severed the priest's head with the *macana*—the Guale tomahawk.

The war party then proceeded to the next mission along the coast. There, they took Father Blas de Rodríguez captive, and two days later clubbed him to death.

The next day, **September 17, 1597,** Juanillo and his companions landed on St. Catherine's Island. Before they arrived, they sent a message to the island's chief and ordered him to kill Father Miguel de Añon and Brother Antonio de Badajóz, the two Franciscans stationed there. Instead, the chief begged the Franciscans to flee. They refused and died that day.

One more Franciscan, Father Francisco de Veráscola, was martyred later that month, when he returned to St. Simon's Island from St. Augustine.

Although reports from the martyrs' contemporaries testified to the graces and conversions that followed the massacre, their cause for beatification didn't move forward until 1984. It remains open still.

September 18: THE SUFFOLK RESOLVES

In December 1773, the good citizens of Boston threw a little party and dumped 342 chests of tea into Boston Harbor. That "party" cost the East India Trading Company £9,000, or $1.6 million in today's dollars.

Not surprisingly, Great Britain was none too happy about the incident, and responded by passing a series of laws known as the Intolerable Acts.

First, they closed Boston Harbor in March 1774 with the Boston Port Act. Two months later they passed the Massachusetts Government Act and the Administration of Justice Act, which limited colonists' ability to govern themselves and try British officials in court. The Quartering Act followed on June 2; that allowed colonial governors to requisition housing for troops as they saw fit. Lastly, on June 22, they passed the Quebec Act. Among other things, the act granted religious freedom to Catholics in Canada.

For the colonists already inclined to rebellion, the Quebec Act was the proverbial last straw. Outraged, the people rioted in the streets and denounced the Crown from the steps of every town hall in the land. Meanwhile, their leaders called for a more organized response. The response—the First Continental Congress—convened that September in Philadelphia.

There, on **September 18, 1774,** 56 delegates from 12 colonies unanimously endorsed the Suffolk Resolves, a resolution that enumerated colonists' grievances with Great Britain and spelled out the rights and privileges to which they believed themselves entitled.

The Suffolk Resolves also made clear that:

> *[T]he late Act of Parliament for establishing the Roman-Catholic religion and the French laws, in that extensive country now called Canada, is dangerous in an extreme degree to the Protestant religion, and to the civil rights and liberties of all America; and there-fore, as men and Protestant Christians, we are indispensably obliged to take all proper measures for our security.*

Less than two years later, Congress sent Charles Carroll, Samuel Chase, and Ben Franklin to Catholic Canada in the hopes of enlisting their support for revolution. To no one's great shock, Catholic Canada said No.

September 19: THE SISTERS OF MERCY

In 1835, Father Michael O'Connor, a recently ordained priest in Ireland, learned about his country's newest religious order, the Sisters of Mercy. "Someone really should establish that order in the United States," he said to himself.

Eight years later, O'Connor took his own advice. After his consecration in Rome as the first bishop of Pittsburgh, O'Connor went straight to Ireland. There, he met with the order's Superior and pleaded with her to send sisters with him to Pittsburgh. She agreed, entrusting the mission to her predecessor, the 36-year-old Mary Frances Xavier Warde.

Bishop O'Connor, Mother Warde, and six young Sisters of Mercy set out for America in November 1843. For the duration of their journey (and their first years in the United States) the sisters shed their habits and wore secular clothing instead. Given the anti-Catholic prejudices of the time, O'Connor thought it safer that way.

Weeks later, when their ship arrived in New York, a small welcoming party greeted them at the docks. Included in that party was Chicago's bishop-elect Father William Quarter. Warde had barely stepped off the boat when Quarter asked if she could spare a few sisters for his diocese.

"Not yet," she replied.

Three years later, though, the Sisters of Mercy were prepared to extend their work beyond Pittsburgh. On **September 19, 1846,** Warde and six sisters, set out for the frontier city of Chicago. There, they took up residence in the bishop's house (described by Warde's biographer as "a small, miserable cottage"), while the bishop moved into a "wretched hovel" with another priest.

In short order, the Sisters of Mercy had a school up and running. Warde remained in Chicago several months before returning to Pittsburgh.

Over the next 38 years, Warde repeated her successes in Pittsburgh and Chicago dozens of times, with some cities even volunteering to build the schoolhouses and pay the sisters' salaries. By 1884, the year of Warde's death, nearly 50 Sisters of Mercy communities served the country's Catholic population.

September 20: WALLS OF STONE

On **September 20, 1863,** the Battle of Chickamauga ended, and the Catholics of Chattanooga, Tennessee, couldn't have been happier.

Catholics had lived in the Chattanooga area for at least 20 years by the time the American Civil War began. Throughout the 1840s, they gathered for Mass in individual homes. By 1852, however, they had their first resident pastor, the Presbyterian convert Father Henry V. Brown, and within a few years of his arrival, they raised sufficient funds to begin building a proper church.

In 1863, Saints Peter and Paul Catholic Church was nearly complete when Union Major General William S. Rosecrans began his disastrous pursuit of Confederate General Braxton Bragg's Confederate Army of Tennessee.

After routing Bragg's troops in the Tullahoma Campaign, Rosecrans' superiors ordered him to solidify the Union's victory on the western front by cutting off the fleeing Confederate general and forcing his surrender. Unfortunately for Rosecrans, due to a badly written order sent to one of his officers, that pursuit backfired, and soon Union forces were retreating to Chattanooga.

With the Confederate troops bearing down on the city, Rosecrans—himself a convert to Catholicism—ordered his men to demolish Saints Peter and Paul Church. He desperately needed the stone for fortifications and culverts that could protect his troops. In the church's walls, he found stones aplenty.

Nobody knows how many lives the church's stones spared—some for certain, but not enough for Rosecrans to win the day. He lost the battle in the most humiliating defeat of his career, and Washington relieved the general of his duties in the war's western theater.

After the Battle of Chickamauga ended, it took 25 years before Saints Peter and Paul's parishioners could build again. Their second pastor, Father William Walsh, laid the cornerstone for a new church in 1888. Two years later, the bishop dedicated the new building, a brick and stone Gothic structure featuring stained glass windows designed by Louis Tiffany. Now known as the mother church of East Tennessee, Saints Peter and Paul Catholic Church became a minor basilica in 2011.

It's not every day that an American cardinal offends both Nazi leaders and the International Brotherhood of Painters, Paperhangers, and Decorators. In May 1937, however, Archbishop George Cardinal Mundelein of the Archdiocese of Chicago did just that.

The fury arose when the cardinal delivered an address condemning Nazi persecution of the Catholic Church in Germany. As he spoke, he wondered aloud, "[H]ow is it that a nation of sixty million people, intelligent people, will submit in fear to an alien, an Austrian paperhanger, and a poor one at that I am told . . . ?"

Within days, the Nazis responded by denouncing Mundelein at a massive rally and demanding that the Vatican censure the cardinal. When the Vatican refused, attacks against Catholics in Germany intensified. At the same time, in Philadelphia, outraged decorators denounced Mundelein for including "paperhanger" in the disparaging remarks he leveled against Hitler. They took no comfort in the fact that the cardinal qualified his statement by noting that Hitler wasn't a very good paperhanger.

The controversy generated by Mundelein's remarks was colorful, but not unusual. The Manhattan-born prelate tended to generate controversy wherever he went.

Ordained to the priesthood in 1895, Mundelein was consecrated auxiliary bishop of New York on **September 21, 1909,** and installed as archbishop of Chicago in 1916. An outspoken political liberal and theological conservative, Mundelein championed labor unions, President Franklin Roosevelt, and the New Deal with the same vigor that he opposed contraception, divorce, and the film star Mae West.

Mundelein's liberal politics, however, didn't stop a Chicago-based anarchist from lacing his soup (and the soup of a hundred other city leaders) with arsenic at a 1916 event celebrating his installation. Only the quick thinking of a doctor present at the dinner saved the whole party from sudden death.

Besides his well-aired opinions, Mundelein's most lasting legacy was his work renewing priestly vocations in Chicago, a renewal he made possible by founding Quigley Memorial Preparatory Seminary and re-opening Saint Mary of the Lake Seminary. Although Cardinal Mundelein lived loudly, he died quietly, passing away in his sleep in 1939.

One afternoon in the late 1920s, Katherine Burton stood outside a Catholic church, desperate and overwhelmed. Her husband of almost 20 years had recently suffered a nervous breakdown and left. With three children still at home, Burton didn't know how she would make ends meet. She also wanted to help her husband, but he didn't want her help.

Exhausted and unsure of what to do next, the nominal Episcopalian went inside the church and prayed. She later described what happened next:

> *As I knelt I was suddenly aware of a new sensation. For weeks and weeks I had had the feeling of falling and falling nowhere. Now of a sudden something seemed to be holding me up. It too came from outside; it was not anything I had conjured up to comfort myself. Somehow I had been caught and lifted high above my own pain and loss. They were still there, heartbreakingly real, but the sense of being alone with them was gone.*

For two years, while working as an assistant editor at *McCall's,* Burton contemplated conversion. In 1930, she made up her mind and entered the Catholic Church. Burton then spent the next three years working as an editor at *Redbook,* until she worked up the confidence to venture out on her own.

When she did, Burton became one of the most prolific Catholic writers of the mid-twentieth century, penning more than 40 books (mostly biographies of prominent Catholics and institutions), as well as writing essays and news stories for Catholic periodicals. Her column, "Woman to Woman," published in the Passionist Fathers' magazine *The Sign,* was the first regular column written by a Catholic woman in America.

Although Burton wrote widely on questions of both Church and culture, much of her work focused on the role of women. Long before Pope John Paul II spoke of "the feminine genius," Burton helped Catholic women understand and navigate their place at work and home in a changing world.

Burton continued writing until her death on **September 22, 1969.**

September 23: A SHRINE FOR MARY

Bishop Thomas J. Shahan, The Catholic University of America's fourth rector, wanted to build a Marian shrine. But before he could do that, he needed Pope Pius X's approval. He also needed to convince Catholic University's Board of Trustees to donate the entire southwest corner of its campus to the project.

Shahan secured his first objective in August 1913. That month he traveled to Rome and met with the Holy Father, who enthusiastically signed off on the idea. The pope then pulled the Italian equivalent of $400 out of his desk and handed it to Shahan.

Once Shahan returned to the States, the university's trustees proved equally accommodating, and the bishop turned his focus to fund-raising. Within seven years, he raised enough money to begin construction, and on **September 23, 1920,** Baltimore's Archbishop James Cardinal Gibbons laid the cornerstone for the National Shrine of the Immaculate Conception. Ten thousand people attended the ceremony, including much of President Calvin Coolidge's cabinet.

After that, building began in earnest. The first phase of the project focused on the Crypt Church. By Easter 1924, the shrine's first public Mass took place in the nearly completed Crypt. But five years later the U.S. stock market crashed and the Great Depression began. With no funds to move forward, all major construction on the Shrine halted. The outbreak of World War II delayed the project even further.

Finally, in 1953, *Our Sunday Visitor*'s founder, Archbishop John Noll, made it his personal mission to raise enough money to complete the Shrine. One year later, building resumed. It took five years more, but in November 1959, the Upper Church opened. Minor construction—including on the Shrine's 70 chapels honoring the Blessed Virgin Mary—has continued ever since.

Designated as a basilica in 1990, the Basilica of the National Shrine of the Immaculate Conception is the largest church in North America and the eighth largest church in the world. Only one person, however, is entombed within its walls: Bishop Thomas Shahan, who died in 1932 without seeing his shrine complete.

September 24: THE LITTLE SISTERS

Sister Jeanne Jugan, the aged foundress of the Little Sisters of the Poor, loved her American postulants best. Or so the postulants living at the French formation house in the 1870s believed.

"She always favors the Americans," they grumbled. "Why do the Americans get special treatment?"

Jugan invariably replied that the Americans needed the extra attention because they were "the first missionaries of the little family." She also told the postulants that it was "heroic for young girls to come from so far away . . . It needed a double vocation."

Judging by the rapid growth of Jugan's community in the United States, double vocations abounded in late-nineteenth-century America.

In August 1868, the first group of Little Sisters arrived in New York. With the help of Father Isaac Hecker, founder of the Paulist Fathers, the Little Sisters set up a home in Brooklyn and took in the elderly poor, providing them with food, shelter, and medical care. The Little Sisters had no endowment and wanted none. They begged for every dollar and every bed.

After that, the order exploded in America. In less than three years, the Little Sisters of the Poor established nine houses across the country. In every city people asked, "What are you going to do in a house where there is nothing?" "Wait a few days," they replied. Sure enough, something always came. By the 1950s, the order had 52 homes in America, all solely funded by begging. New nursing home regulations in the 1960s made it more difficult for the Little Sisters to operate, but even as the health care environment changed, they kept 30 homes open.

Passage of the Affordable Care Act in 2010, however, has called into question the future of those homes. The Little Sisters today face millions in fines because they cannot, in good conscience, comply with federal rules that mandate they provide employees with free access to contraception, sterilization, and abortion-inducing drugs. Hoping to avert closing their doors, the Little Sisters of the Poor filed a class-action lawsuit on **September 24, 2013.**

September 25: CALIFORNIA'S CATHOLIC FATHER

The Franciscans of Spain had great plans for Junípero Serra. Soon after the 17-year-old Serra came to them in 1730, they decided the unusually bright novice had the makings of a great theologian. For 14 years, they sent him to their best schools, and when the young priest completed his education, they honored him with a chair in philosophy at the Lullian University in Palma, Majorca. His future as a great scholar and teacher seemed secure.

Father Serra, however, didn't want to be a great scholar and teacher. He wanted to be a missionary. And, after much prayer, Serra got what he wanted. In 1749, his superiors reluctantly granted his request to sail for the Americas. Months later, Serra and his companions arrived on the shores of Mexico.

For the next 19 years, Serra taught and preached at missions throughout Mexico. His reputation as an enthusiastic proclaimer of the Gospel was unmatched. For that reason, in 1768, Serra's superiors asked him to go north and evangelize the Native Americans of Alta California. Despite suffering from asthma and painful ulcers in his legs, the 55-year-old Serra enthusiastically embarked upon his new task. Within 15 years, he personally founded nine missions: San Diego, San Carlos at Monterey, San Antonio, San Gabriel, San Luis Obispo, San Francisco, San Juan Capistrano, Santa Clara, and San Buenaventura.

During those years, Serra traveled over 24,000 miles up and down California's coast, not only laying the foundations for California's first cities, but also teaching the region's people how to successfully farm their land. As a chief defender of the rights of Native Americans in their disputes with Spanish colonists, Serra regularly pressured his government to adopt more native-friendly policies. For similar reasons, when he learned of the war for independence taking place on the other side of North America, he took up a collection in his missions and sent it to General George Washington.

Considered the Father of Catholicism in California, Father Junípero Serra died in 1784. Pope John Paul II beatified the Franciscan on **September 25, 1988**.

While editing the letters of Charleston's Bishop John England, his successor—Bishop Ignatius A. Reynolds—described the Diocese of Philadelphia in its early days as "a deranged mess." The description was apt.

First, in 1822, the Hogan Schism exiled Philadelphia's second bishop, Henry Conwell, from his own cathedral. Then, in July 1828, two troublesome Dominicans stationed at the cathedral dragged the federal government into the mess.

The second bout of trouble began in early 1828, when Pope Leo XII called Bishop Conwell to Rome and ordered the Dominicans to Cincinnati, with hopes of defusing tensions in Philadelphia.

Conwell complied immediately. The priests, however, wrote to President Andrew Jackson protesting the order. In their letter, they contended that a "sovereign ruler" like the pope should have no say over where American citizens live or work. They also suggested that Jackson should view any attempt by the pope to exercise such authority as an infringement upon America's national sovereignty.

The president referred the matter to the U.S. State Department. The State Department sided with the Dominican priests. And a U.S. envoy warned the Vatican to back off and let the priests do as they pleased.

Meanwhile, back in America, the priest left in charge of Philadelphia, Father William Matthews, tried explaining to the State Department that while the men were bound by oath to obey the pope, any punishments they incurred for their disobedience would be spiritual. Pope Leo XII had no plans of sending troops to Philadelphia. The men were free to stay or go. Only, if they stayed, they couldn't remain in good standing with the Church.

The State Department didn't budge. Finally, Bishop England intervened. On **September 26, 1828,** England wrote to President Jackson, reiterating Father Matthews' arguments and reminding him that the federal government could not interfere in ecclesial affairs.

The next day, Jackson personally assured England that he would take no further action. By that point, however, the question was somewhat moot, as the troublesome Dominicans had already fled to Ireland, never to be heard from again.

Her enemies called her "Prohibition Portia" and "Deborah of the Drys." Her admirers called her the "First Lady of Law." And in 1928, all but her closest friends called Mabel Walker Willebrandt "anti-Catholic."

The accusations came in the wake of Willebrandt's vigorous campaigning against the Catholic Democratic presidential nominee, Al Smith.

For eight years, beginning with her **September 27, 1921,** appointment as assistant attorney general, Willebrandt led the federal enforcement of prohibition. At the time of her appointment, she was only 32 years old and neither a teetotaler nor a fan of prohibition. But Willebrandt believed the law was the law and understood that accepting the appointment meant agreeing to enforce the laws, whether she liked them or not.

And enforce them she did. Describing her job as "attempting to dry up the Atlantic Ocean with a blotter," Willebrandt oversaw more than 50,000 prosecutions of prohibition violators, all while cleaning up massive corruption in federal law enforcement.

Ambitious, intelligent, and disciplined, Willebrandt did nothing halfway, which explains why she publicly went on the offensive against Smith, who as governor of New York made no secret of his disdain for prohibition. In addition to arranging raids in New York perfectly timed to humiliate the Governor, Willebrandt also denounced him in Scripture-laced speeches before prohibition's strongest supporters: Protestants. In one such speech, delivered to a Methodist ministers' conference, she urged her audience to, "Take to your pulpits! Preach the message! Rouse your communities!"

Almost everyone in America, Smith included, accused Willebrandt of playing the religion card. She denied it, but to no avail.

After President Herbert Hoover's victory, Willebrandt expected him to reward her with a promotion. When he didn't, she left the Department of Justice and returned to private practice. Her first client was California Fruit Industries, which specialized in providing grapes to home winemakers. Willebrandt's new alliance with the industry she'd worked against shocked America. Her conversion to Catholicism, many years later, shocked the country even more.

Willebrandt died of lung cancer in 1963.

Just weeks after the signing of the *Declaration of Independence,* two Spanish Franciscans became the first Europeans to enter present-day Utah. The priests, Fathers Francisco Dominguez and Silvestre Velez de Escalante, came north from Santa Fe in July 1776 to establish missions among the Ute and Laguna. Political changes in Spain, however, soon forced the friars to abandon their work and the few converts they made.

Catholics wouldn't return to the region until the end of the American Civil War, when prospectors discovered silver and gold in Utah's mountains. Catholic immigrants came to work in the mines, and missionary priests followed. One of those priests persuaded Brigham Young to sell him land in Salt Lake City, and in 1871, his successor used the land to build Utah its first Catholic Church, St. Mary Magdalene.

Two years later, Father Lawrence Scanlan arrived to serve as pastor.

Born on **September 28, 1843,** Scanlan had come to San Francisco from Ireland in 1869 as a newly ordained priest. Four years later, convinced that Catholics needed to establish a foothold in a territory fast becoming known as "Mormon country," he volunteered for the Utah missions.

To that end, Scanlan spent most of his first decade in Utah on horseback, visiting even the most far-flung mining camps every month. The priest also persuaded the Sisters of the Holy Cross to come to Salt Lake City. Together, they built a hospital, school, and orphanage.

Rome recognized Scanlan's accomplishments in November 1886, when they named the 43-year-old priest Vicar Apostolic of Utah. Then, when Salt Lake became a diocese in 1891, Scanlan became its first bishop.

Almost immediately, Scanlan began planning for a cathedral. He already had the land—just five blocks away from the Mormon's Temple Square—but, at the time, Utah's wealth was concentrated in Mormons' hands and raising the money proved nearly impossible. Not until 1899 could Scanlan lay the cornerstone for the Cathedral of the Madeleine.

Sixteen years later, with the interior still unfinished, Scanlan was laid to rest inside his cathedral's walls.

September 29: SAN MIGUEL DE GUALDAPE

In 1521, Lucas Vázquez de Ayllón, a wealthy Spanish sugar planter in Santo Domingo, grew curious about the land that lay to the north of Hispaniola. So, he hired a captain, outfitted a ship, and funded a scouting expedition that sailed up along the coast of the present-day United States. Once the expedition returned with favorable reviews of the land, climate, and people it encountered, Ayllón began preparing his own expedition. This time, however, the objective wasn't exploration. It was colonization.

Five years after the first expedition sailed, Ayllón left his home and sailed north. With him, he took three ships, 600 settlers, and 100 horses. He also took a large group of African slaves, recently brought by the Spanish to the New World. After losing one ship en route, what remained of Ayllón's party landed near present-day Georgetown, South Carolina, on **September 29, 1526**. Not long after the landing, their Native American guide abandoned them. Disoriented, the group proceeded another 45 leagues—some by land, some by sea—until on October 8 they reunited and began plotting the settlement of San Miguel de Gualdape.

Today, the location of that original settlement is unknown. Early historians placed it as far north as the Chesapeake Bay. Most modern scholars, however, believe the disoriented landing party proceeded south instead of north, stopping on the southern Georgia coast, near Sapelo Island. Regardless, the enterprise was short-lived.

Almost as soon as the settlers began building, the Africans doing most of the work staged the first documented slave rebellion in North America. The colonists then endured a brutal winter, marked by terrible illness and ongoing problems with the Guale Indians. Ayllón died before the winter ended, and at the first sign of spring, the colony's 150 survivors returned to Hispaniola. One ship foundered on the way, taking her passengers down with her.

After Ayllón's failure, it would take another 38 years before Europeans successfully established a colony in the present-day United States—the Spanish St. Augustine, Florida, in 1565.

Father James Cox knew what work meant to a man. Before his ordination in 1911, the Pittsburgh native drove a cab and worked in the city's steel mills. Later, he labored in the trenches of France as a chaplain in World War I. Through it all, Cox came to see work as God's way of helping men grow in holiness. Then, when the Great Depression began, he saw how the lack of work could have the opposite effect and lead men astray.

In the Depression's first years, while unemployment in Pittsburgh quadrupled, Cox did what he could to aid the jobless. He opened up a soup kitchen and medical clinic near his parish, Old St. Patrick's Catholic Church. He also set up a distribution center for coal, clothing, and milk. The help was meant for everyone, not just parishioners. "If you turn one person away, Mary, I'll strangle you," he told his housekeeper.

As the months passed, Cox grew increasingly frustrated with the government's seeming lack of concern. So, to draw more attention to the plight of the unemployed, he organized a march on Washington, D.C. The march began on January 5, 1932, with Mass at Old St. Patrick's. By the time Cox reached the District, 25,000 people marched with him.

Speaking to reporters covering the event, Cox explained, "It's not charity these men want but jobs." He had the same message for President Herbert Hoover when they met later that day. The priest, however, left the meeting dissatisfied. Soon afterwards, Cox took matters into his own hands. He organized a new political party—the Jobless Party—and launched his own presidential campaign.

That campaign lasted less than nine months. After arriving in California on **September 30, 1932,** for a barnstorming tour, Cox suddenly changed his mind and decided Franklin Roosevelt would make a better president than him. He endorsed the Democrat and exited the race.

Cox then returned to Pittsburgh, where he spent the next 29 years serving his parish and Pittsburgh's poor. He passed away in 1951.

October

October 1: A SEVERE MERCY

They met "angrily in the dead of winter." Sheldon "Van" Vanauken was a college student, home for Christmas break. Jean "Davy" Davis was a clerk at a department store, working her way through school. Ten months later, on **October 1, 1937,** they married. Seventeen years later, on January 17, 1955, she died. And 22 years after her death, he attempted to make sense of their story—of their love, his loss, and the grace that surprised them both—in the bestselling book *A Severe Mercy.*

In the decades that followed, thousands of people "met" Van through that account of his life with Davy. Readers knew of their service in Pearl Harbor during World War II and of their sailing adventures on the schooner *Grey Goose.* They also knew of the couple's time at Oxford, where C. S. Lewis' friendship helped lead the former agnostics to Christ. Most of all, they knew of Van and Davy's all-consuming love, a love they protected with what they called "a shining barrier," shutting out anything that could pull them apart.

What many fans *of A Severe Mercy* don't know, however, is the rest of the story, the story that followed Davy's 1955 death from liver disease.

They don't know that as an English professor at Lynchburg College, Van spent the 1960s and 1970s championing civil rights, opposing the Vietnam War, and supporting the feminist movement. They also don't know that in 1981, Van converted to Catholicism and subsequently penned hundreds of essays for Catholic periodicals. Nor do they know of his other books, including two that reflected upon life "after Davy": *Under the Mercy* in 1985 and *The Little Lost Marion and Other Mercies* in 1996.

After Vanauken's death in late 1996, friends scattered his ashes where he had scattered Davy's ashes four decades earlier—at the foot of a cross near St. Stephen's Episcopal Church in Forest, Virginia, and in a churchyard in England.

Daniel Barber's journey to the Catholic Church began with a book.

The book came to Barber—who was born on **October 2, 1756**—by way of a friend. Written by an Anglican, it intimated that the Congregationalist sect to which the 27-year-old Barber belonged didn't have valid ecclesial orders. Barber found the book persuasive and entered the Episcopal Church, eventually becoming an Episcopal priest.

The next 30 years passed peacefully, with Barber pastoring an Episcopal congregation in Claremont, New Hampshire. Then, Barber discovered another book. This one questioned the validity of Anglican orders. Confused, Barber set out for Boston, determined to find a Catholic priest and put his questions to him.

The priest Barber found was Jean-Louis Lefebvre de Cheverus, Boston's first bishop. Cheverus' kindness and learning impressed Barber, and when the Episcopal minister returned to New Hampshire, he took a stack of the bishop's books with him.

While still tending to his congregation, Barber read and reread those books. So did his wife, children, and siblings. In 1817, after much reading, the family produced its first converts: Barber's son, Virgil (an Episcopal minister like his father), and Virgil's wife, Jerusha. A year later, Barber's wife, Chloe, plus his sister, niece, three more children, and several grandchildren, entered the Church. That November, Barber resigned his parish and, with his brother-in-law, nieces, and nephews, followed suit.

Eventually, Virgil joined the Jesuits, and Jerusha entered a Visitation convent. Their four daughters became Ursuline Sisters and their son a Jesuit. Likewise, Daniel Barber's four nieces entered the Sisters of Charity and his nephew, William Tyler, was ordained a priest for Boston (later becoming the first bishop of Hartford, Connecticut).

For months, the country buzzed over the conversion of New Hampshire's most prominent Episcopalians. When the fuss died down, Virgil returned to Claremont to found New Hampshire's first Catholic parish. Daniel assisted his son until Chloe's death in 1825. He then went to live with Jesuit friends, dying in Maryland in 1834. Daniel Barber's last words to his family were, "I have lost nothing."

October 3: THE BOY BISHOP

Near the end of James Cardinal Gibbons' long life, an admirer asked Baltimore's Archbishop how he managed to reach his advanced age.

"Acquire an incurable ailment in your youth," he replied.

Gibbons "incurable ailment" was the lingering effects of malaria. The Baltimore-born prelate contracted the disease as a seminarian, just prior to the American Civil War. The disease nearly cost him his life and, when his superiors expressed misgivings about ordaining someone so sickly, almost cost Gibbons his vocation as well.

Persistence, however, won the day. In 1861, Gibbons became a priest. Seven years later, he became bishop of the Vicariate Apostolic of North Carolina. Only 34 years old at the time, Gibbons was then the world's youngest Catholic bishop, a fact that earned him the nickname "boy bishop."

After North Carolina, Gibbons served five years as bishop of Richmond, Virginia, before becoming coadjutor bishop of Baltimore in May 1877. Five months later, on **October 3, 1877,** he became the Archdiocese of Baltimore's ninth archbishop.

From that point forward, Gibbons exercised unmatched authority in the late-nineteenth and early-twentieth-century American Church. His influence ensured the creation of The Catholic University of America and forged an alliance between Catholics and labor unions. It also thwarted Cahenslyism, which aspired to establish separate, ethnic Catholic Churches in America. A cardinal after 1886, Gibbons was a friend or advisor to nearly every president from Andrew Johnson to Woodrow Wilson and wildly popular with the American Catholic public, who knew him largely through his writing. His most popular work, the apologetics handbook *The Faith of Our Fathers,* sold more than 1.4 million copies by 1917.

At times a pacifist (he opposed the Spanish-American War) and at other times an ardent nationalist (World War I had no greater champion), Gibbons was frequently accused of being more American than Catholic. When Pope Leo XIII penned two letters condemning the Americanist heresy, many considered Gibbons guilty as charged.

Despite those allegations (and his incurable ailment), Gibbons reigned supreme among America's Catholic bishops until his death at the age of 86 in 1921.

October 4: THE CATHEDRAL OF THE PLAINS

In 1912, William Jennings Bryan traveled to Victoria, Kansas. As he approached the remote farming community, the first thing he spied was St. Fidelis Catholic Church. Larger and more impressive than many of America's grandest cathedrals, the limestone Romanesque church rose up from the Kansas prairie, dwarfing all that surrounded it. Awestruck, Jennings dubbed St. Fidelis, "The Cathedral of the Plains."

The story behind that unlikely "cathedral" began in the eighteenth century, when Catherine the Great invited European farmers to immigrate to Russia. In exchange for introducing new agricultural methods, she promised cultural and political autonomy. A group of German Catholic peasants accepted her offer and moved to Russia, settling along the Volga River.

A century later, when the Russian czars began reneging on Catherine's promises, many Volga Germans left for America. One group arrived near Victoria, Kansas, in 1876. Although the area's original British settlers struggled to farm the Kansas prairie, the Germans found the conditions similar to what they'd known in Russia. Soon, hundreds more Volga Germans joined them.

When they first arrived, despite limited resources, the Catholic community constructed a small church. Within a few years, they outgrew it and built another. History repeated itself twice more before 1900, when the parish began planning for a grand new church building that could seat up to 1,200 people—approximately the community's entire population, then and now.

In 1905, St. Fidelis' Pittsburgh-based architect completed his designs, and every man in the parish over the age of 12 was assessed $45 per annum, an enormous sum for Kansan farmers at the time. Every man was also required to haul six loads of stone and four loads of sand each year until construction ended. But not one parishioner protested. For them, little mattered more than their church.

On **October 4, 1909,** the parish laid the cornerstone for St. Fidelis Catholic Church. Only two years later, they celebrated the dedication Mass.

Dubbed "one of the eight wonders of Kansas," The Cathedral of the Plains became a minor basilica in February 2014.

In 1953, Michael Scanlan thought he knew what the future held. First, he would serve as a commissioned officer in the U.S. Air Force. After that, he would marry the girl who wore his ring.

That spring, however, government budget cuts changed the first part of his plan, putting the New York native's ROTC commission on hold. While he waited, Scanlan entered Harvard Law School. There, the second part of his plan changed when Scanlan heard God ask, "Will you give me your whole life?"

Scanlan said yes. He broke off his engagement, completed his studies, and served out his commission as a lawyer in the Judge Advocate Corps (JAG). Soon after he left the military, he entered the Franciscans Third Order Regular (T.O.R.), and in 1964, became both a Franciscan priest and academic dean at the College of Steubenville. Father Scanlan served at the Ohio college until 1969, when his order transferred him to St. Francis Seminary in Loretto, Pennsylvania. In 1974, however, Scanlan returned to Steubenville's campus to interview for the job of college president.

Beset by economic and cultural troubles, the College of Steubenville was on the verge of extinction that year. Most suspected the trustees simply wanted to hire someone who could close the college down gracefully. Scanlan, however, had a different plan. As he explained to the trustees, he didn't want the school to close, nor did he think it needed to become less Catholic to stay open. Rather, he said, the college needed to become more Catholic and center every activity on Jesus Christ.

The trustees took a risk, and on **October 5, 1974,** Scanlan became the school's fourth president.

The Franciscan friar led the school for 26 years, transforming it from a regional college into Franciscan University of Steubenville—a major center of renewal for both the Catholic Church and Catholic higher education in America. For his work, the Vatican honored Scanlan with the *Pro Ecclesia et Pontifice* medal in 1990.

Now retired, Scanlan holds the title *President Emeritus* of Franciscan University.

October 6: THE RUNAWAY TRAILBLAZER

On **October 6, 1826,** the *Missouri Intelligencer* ran the following ad:

> *Notice is hereby given to all persons, That Christopher Carson, a boy about 16 years old, small of his age, but thick-set; light hair, ran away from the subscriber, living in Franklin, Howard County, Missouri, to whom he had been bound to learn the saddler's trade. One-cent reward will be given to any person who will bring back the said boy.*

Perhaps no one saw the runaway apprentice or, more likely, the $.01 reward proved insufficient motivation to secure his return. Either way, by the time Christopher "Kit" Carson resurfaced in Missouri, he had become a living legend.

In the intervening decades, Carson worked as a successful fur trader and even more successful guide, leading soldier-explorer John C. Frémont through Oregon, California, and much of the Central Rocky Mountains. Carson also married three times—first to an Arapaho woman who died, then to a Cheyenne woman who abandoned him, and lastly to a Mexican woman, who lived to bear him eight children. It was for his third wife that Carson entered the Catholic Church in 1842.

Few Americans in the nineteenth century, however, knew about Carson's religion or his close friendship with Santa Fe's Archbishop Jean-Baptiste Lamy. Frémont's accounts of their travels, newspaper stories about Carson's service in the Mexican-American War and the American Civil War, and the popular series of Kit Carson books (which Carson loathed) didn't mention God or bishops. Rather they told of Carson's adventures—some factual, most fictional—exploring the West and defending settlers from Native Americans.

Reality was more complicated and tragic than fiction, but as one modern biographer, Harvey L. Carter, wrote, "If history has to single out one person from among the Mountain Men to receive the admiration of later generations, Carson is the best choice. He had far more of the good qualities and fewer of the bad qualities than anyone else in that varied lot of individuals."

Carson died one month after his wife, in 1868.

October 7: A SHOW OF UNITY

The American Civil War fractured more than the North and South. It fractured families, communities, and churches. Afterwards, many doubted whether those breaks could heal. But not Baltimore's Archbishop Martin Spalding.

As Spalding saw it, what the nation needed was hope. Moreover, he believed the best way to give it hope was to provide a demonstration of unity, to show the country that men from North and South, East and West could come together and speak as one. And so, a year after the war ended, the Second Plenary Council of Baltimore convened.

On **October 7, 1866,** thousands of onlookers stood in the streets of Baltimore to watch seven archbishops, 38 bishops, three abbots, and 120 theologians—all dressed in full regalia—solemnly process into the Cathedral of the Assumption of the Blessed Virgin Mary. The bishops came from Alabama and New York, Georgia and Ohio. Some, such as Natchez, Mississippi's William Elder, had championed the Confederate cause. Others, such as Cincinnati's John Baptist Purcell, supported the Union with equal fervor. But they marched side by side into the cathedral.

Once inside, the bishops tackled an agenda equally shaped by the war.

If not for the onset of fighting in 1861, the bishops would have met as scheduled in 1862, and discussed questions of doctrine, liturgy, and ecclesiastical policy. They still had those questions to discuss. But they also had to address the problems created by millions of newly freed slaves who needed work, education, and spiritual care. Additionally, the bishops had to find ways to provide for devastated families, parishes, and communities on both sides of the Mason-Dixon Line.

For 14 days, America's bishops examined those problems and more. In the end, they resolved to pursue some solutions privately and address others publicly. They then closed the Second Plenary Council as solemnly as they began it. Only this time, as the last bishop processed into the cathedral, President Andrew Johnson processed in behind, putting his stamp of approval on both the much-needed show of national unity and the bishops' concern for post-war America.

October 8: THE FLYING CARDINAL

The Holy See needed allies. In 1936, as Soviet Russia and Nazi Germany expanded their reach, the situation for Catholics across Europe grew increasingly perilous. On its own, the Vatican realized it could do little to protect those Catholics. It needed partners.

That need led Archbishop Eugenio Cardinal Pacelli to board a ship bound for the United States in October 1936. Ostensibly, the then-Secretary of State for the Vatican (and future Pope Pius XII) came to America for vacation. But his real objective was to secure the appointment of a U.S. diplomatic representative to the Holy See, a post that lingering anti-Catholicism had kept vacant since 1867.

Fortunately for Pacelli, President Franklin D. Roosevelt needed something from Rome as well. A Catholic priest in Michigan, Father Charles Coughlin, was using his popular radio show to attack Roosevelt's politics. With Roosevelt's first bid for reelection upon him, the president feared Coughlin's potential effect on Catholic voters. A visit from Pacelli and the appearance of friendly relations between the White House and Rome seemed like just the thing to neutralize the Michigan priest.

With both sides prepared to deal, Pacelli arrived in New York on **October 8, 1936**. He spent a week on the East Coast, and then boarded a plane that took him to nearly a dozen cities across the Midwest. His fast-paced, city-hopping tour led the American press to dub him "The Flying Cardinal."

As Pacelli traveled, stories and rumors about his visit—the first ever for such a high-ranking Vatican official—filled the press. Chief among them was that he had come to silence Coughlin. No record exists of what, if anything, transpired between Pacelli and Coughlin during the visit. But on November 4, Roosevelt won his reelection and Coughlin fell silent.

The following day, Pacelli traveled to Roosevelt's home at Hyde Park, New York. He congratulated the president on his victory and secured his promise of a U.S. envoy to the Holy See. Pacelli sailed for Rome 24 hours later, his "vacation" successfully complete.

October 9: OUR LADY OF PROMPT SUCCOR

War was coming to New Orleans. For weeks, British ships sat anchored in the Gulf of Mexico, not far from Lake Pontchartrain, while British troops camped south of the city. American forces tried once to repel them, but failed. So, they strengthened the city's fortifications instead and waited for the British to attack. Before dawn on January 8, 1815, the waiting ended.

On the eve of the Battle of New Orleans, the city's women fled to the Ursuline Convent on Chartres Street. There, they joined the sisters and priests keeping vigil before the statue of Our Lady of Prompt Succor. As the day wore on, the Ursuline Prioress vowed to have a Mass of Thanksgiving offered every year, if only Our Lady would spare their city.

Just moments later, the sisters learned that the British were beating a fast retreat. U.S. Commander General Andrew Jackson had routed them successfully. American casualties numbered 71. British casualties surpassed 2,000.

When hostilities ended, weeks later, Jackson went to the convent and thanked the sisters for their prayers, crediting his victory to "heavenly intercession." For the rest of Jackson's life, whenever he came to New Orleans, he never failed to visit the Sisters on Chartres Street.

The Battle of New Orleans, however, was only one of many times the Ursulines came to the city's aid. They were the first order of women religious to settle in the present-day United States and arrived in New Orleans in 1727. Immediately, they began caring for the city's poor at the Royal Hospital and opened a school for girls. They welcomed all students—black, white, and Native American.

Nearly 300 years later, the Ursuline Sisters continue their mission of educating the young women of New Orleans through Ursuline Academy. Likewise, their convent on Chartres Street still stands, although it no longer houses the Ursuline Sisters. Today it belongs to the Archdiocese's Catholic Heritage Center.

Declared a National Historic Landmark on **October 9, 1960,** the old Ursuline Convent is purportedly the oldest existing building in the Mississippi River Valley.

October 10: AN ACT OF OBLATION

Francis J. Parater was born on **October 10, 1897**. He died on February 7, 1920. In the intervening 22 years, the Virginia native graduated at the top of his class from Benedictine High School in Richmond, became an Eagle Scout, discerned a vocation to the priesthood, and began his formation at Belmont Abbey Seminary.

In 1919, the Diocese of Richmond sent Parater to Rome, to continue his seminary studies at the Pontifical North American College (NAC). He began his classes at the college on November 25, 1919. Less that eight weeks later, the pious, popular, easy-going seminarian contracted rheumatism. That led to rheumatic fever and, by early February, his death.

Just days later, a seminarian friend sorting through Parater's belongings, discovered an Act of Oblation to the Sacred Heart that the seminarian wrote shortly after he arrived at the NAC. It read:

> *I have nothing to leave or give but my life and this I have consecrated to the Sacred Heart to be used as he wills. I have offered my all for the conversion of non-Catholics in Virginia. This is what I live for and in case of death what I die for . . . Since my childhood, I have wanted to die for God and my neighbor. Shall I have this grace? I do not know, but if I go on living, I shall live for this same purpose; every action of my life here is offered to God . . . I shall be of more service to my diocese in Heaven than I can ever be on earth.*

Somehow the Act of Oblation made its way to Pope Benedict XV, who asked the Vatican's newspaper, *L'Osservatore Romano,* to publish it. The future Pope Pius XI then saw it, and copied it out so he too could pray Parater's oblation.

As the years passed, the Diocese of Richmond held up Parater as a model for all seminarians, and in 2001, it officially opened his cause for sainthood.

The Irish worried about former slaves taking their jobs. The Irish worried about provoking their anti-Catholic neighbors. The Irish worried about appearing unpatriotic. And for those reasons and more, few Irish immigrants in 1840s America worried about slavery. Instead, the majority distanced themselves from the Abolitionist Movement. They also distanced themselves from prominent politicians in their homeland who decried America's "peculiar institution."

Chief among those politicians was Daniel O'Connell, one of the first Irishmen to sit in Great Britain's House of Commons. A respected leader, both in Ireland and abroad, O'Connell was a close friend of Frederick Douglass' and a committed abolitionist, who used his political platform to condemn American slavery. Irish-Americans revered O'Connell for his work on behalf of Irish independence. But in 1843, they sent him a letter, asking him to please mind his own business when it came to the slavery question.

O'Connell replied with a letter of his own, writing on **October 11, 1843**:

> [Y]ou speak of man being the property of man—of one human being the property of another, with as little doubt, hesitation, or repugnance, as if you were speaking of the beasts of the field. It is this that fills us with utter astonishment. It is this that makes us disclaim you as countrymen. We cannot bring ourselves to believe that you breathed your natal air in Ireland . . . Ireland, that never was stained with negro slave-trading—Ireland, that never committed an offense against the men of color—Ireland that never fitted out a single vessel for the traffic in blood on the African coast.

His words didn't go over well. In fact, they cost O'Connell almost every Irish-American friend he had. But, two decades later, when the American Civil War began, newspapers in the North repeatedly reprinted the letter, using O'Connell's words to rally Irish support for the Union cause. In large part, the tactic worked, and whole regiments of Irish volunteers fought as O'Connell dreamed they would.

O'Connell, however, never lived to see that fight. He died in 1847.

Mother Mary Magdalen Bentivoglio bore a striking resemblance to the "Little Engine That Could." She chugged and she chugged up a veritable mountain of obstacles, all to establish the first order of contemplative religious women in nineteenth-century America.

The Poor Clare nun arrived in New York from Rome on **October 12, 1875.** Her sister Constanza, several other Poor Clares, and their spiritual director, Father Paulino de Castellero, traveled with her. The women originally came to America to run a girls' school in Minnesota, but soon after their ship docked Castellero had second thoughts and advised against it.

Unsure of how to proceed, Bentivoglio approached New York's Cardinal John McCloskey about establishing a monastery in his diocese. But McCloskey told them that a contemplative order wasn't compatible with the American way of life. So, Bentivoglio approached Archbishop John Baptist Purcell of Cincinnati. He said the same. After that, the nun went to almost every other diocese on the Eastern Seaboard. The answer was always no.

Finally, New Orleans said yes. The nuns arrived in March 1877 and welcomed their first postulants almost immediately. Before the summer ended, however, the Franciscan Minister Provincial ordered the women to Cleveland. Once they arrived, the same Minister Provincial ordered them to abandon their rule, take in a group of German Poor Clares, and start speaking German.

It was too much for Bentivoglio. With her sister and several novices, she packed up and moved on. Finally, a wealthy Catholic from Omaha, John A. Creighton, offered to build the nuns a convent. Omaha's bishop, James O'Connor, agreed, and a papal bull establishing the Poor Clares in America sealed the deal.

All was not yet well, though. In the years that followed, the Bentivoglio sisters endured two years of exile from their community due to false allegations of impropriety, and when Bentivoglio established a new convent in Indiana, the nuns nearly starved for lack of money. But today, more than 20 Poor Clare monasteries in the United States and Canada owe their beginnings to the "Venerable" Little Abbess Who Could.

October 13: THE CONVERTED BISHOP

One evening in the late 1850s, Father Charles Pise invited a former Episcopal bishop, Levi Silliman Ives, and a former Episcopal priest, Donald McLeod, to dine in his rectory. The rectory was attached to St. Charles Borromeo Catholic Church in Brooklyn, New York, which Pise had purchased from the Episcopalians in 1849.

After dinner, the men went into the church to pray, and McLeod asked Ives if he remembered the last time they stood there together. Ives paused, and then exclaimed, "Oh, the mercy of God! The last time I was here was when I, as a Protestant Bishop, ordained you an Episcopal minister, and now bishop, minister, and church are all Catholic!"

At the time of the second meeting, Ives taught at St. John's College and ran New York's Society of St. Vincent de Paul. Both were unlikely jobs for a one-time Protestant bishop, but the conversion of a Protestant bishop was an unlikely thing.

Ordained in 1823 and consecrated as the first Episcopal bishop of North Carolina in 1831, Ives came from one of America's oldest families and married the daughter of New York's Episcopal bishop John Henry Hobart. As an Episcopalian, Ives' life was happy, prosperous, and secure. In the 1840s, however, John Henry Newman's work captured his attention and led him to the Church Fathers. In both, Ives said he found "something in religion more real than I had hitherto experienced."

In 1852, the 55-year-old Ives traded security for the Eucharist and resigned his office. He then traveled with his wife to Rome, where Pope Pius IX received him into the Church. Ives was the first Protestant bishop to convert in nearly 200 years. Soon afterwards, his wife converted as well.

While still in Rome, Ives wrote his conversion story. With its 1854 publication, the couple returned to America, where the Catholic bishops took up a collection to support them and later helped Ives find work.

When Ives passed away on **October 13, 1867,** his last words were, "Oh, how good God has been to me."

October 14: TARRED AND FEATHERED

In 1848, when the Swiss Jesuit Father Johannes Bapst arrived in the United States and received his first assignment—pastoring the Penobscot in Maine—he had two concerns. First, he spoke neither English nor Penobscot. Second, 10 of his predecessors, including the most recent, had been killed in the course of their duties.

As it turned out, though, Bapst quickly mastered both languages and passed three peaceful years with the Penobscot. Those were his last peaceful years in Maine.

In 1851, Boston's Bishop John Fitzpatrick expanded Bapst's mission territory to include numerous cities with Catholic immigrants. In one city, Ellsworth, Protestant leaders forbade Catholic children from using Catholic Bibles in public schools. They were only permitted to use Protestant Bibles. When Bapst couldn't change their minds, he built a Catholic school. Then, the Know-Nothings intervened.

In June 1854, the anti-Catholic group hatched a plot to kidnap Bapst. They only failed because the priest was in Bangor. A few months later, the same party blew up the Catholic school in Ellsworth and tried (but failed) to blow up the Catholic church as well. Finally, on **October 14, 1854,** a large mob successfully kidnapped Bapst and attempted to burn him alive. When damp weather prevented the fire from catching, they instead beat the priest, then tarred and feathered him, leaving him for dead.

He wasn't dead though, and local Catholics soon found him and nursed him back to health. After that, Bapst could have left. But he didn't. He remained in Maine five years more, building churches and schools in defiance of Protestant objections.

After Maine, Bapst went to Boston, where in 1863, he became the founding president of Boston College. He served there until 1869, when the Jesuits named him Superior of New York and Canadian Missions. Ten years later, the 64-year-old priest suddenly developed dementia. He spent the last eight years of his life mentally reliving the night of his kidnapping.

Peace came with death in 1887.

In 1822, when Michigan Territory elected its new representative for the United States Congress, most agreed only one man would do: Father Gabriel Richard.

Born in France on **October 15, 1767,** Richard fled to America with his fellow Sulpicians in 1792. Upon his arrival, he briefly taught at St. Mary's Seminary in Baltimore, then spent six years ministering in the Illinois Territory, before moving to Detroit in 1798.

There, as pastor of St. Anne's Catholic Church, Richard built the frontier town some of its first schools, secured Detroit its first printing press, started its first newspaper, and gave the city its first library. When fire destroyed Detroit in 1805, Richard organized the rebuilding efforts and wrote the city's new motto. Likewise, when the local Protestant congregation lacked a minister, they turned to Richard, who preached sermons for them every Sunday. Once the congregation found a proper Protestant minister, he and Richard convinced the Territory's government to open the school that later became the University of Michigan. Father Richard served the school as a professor, founding vice president, and trustee.

The priest's kindness and integrity won over the local Native Americans as well, who came to Richard's aid when the British captured Detroit during the War of 1812. After the redcoats arrived, they demanded Richard swear an oath of loyalty to the British Crown. The priest refused. He'd already sworn an oath to uphold the U.S. Constitution and would swear no other. Immediately, the soldiers imprisoned him. But when the Shawnee chief Tecumseh got wind of Richard's capture, he made the Shawnee's continued alliance with the British conditional on Richard's release. Richard soon walked free.

Dubbed "Detroit's Second Founder," Richard seemed a logical choice to represent the Michigan territory in the 18th U.S. Congress. He served for two years, secured funding for the first major road to Detroit, and then returned to full-time ministry.

Richard died nursing the sick during a cholera epidemic in 1832. They say the crowd at his funeral outnumbered the entire population of Detroit.

October 16: DETROIT'S FIRST FOUNDER

Antoine Laumet excelled at three things: telling tales, making money, and influencing powerful friends.

The tales Detroit's founder told were many, starting with his name. Although history remembers him as Antoine Laumet de La Mothe, sieur de Cadillac, his noble titles were a fiction, manufactured by Laumet after his 1683 arrival in New France. Around the same time, Laumet also manufactured his military record in order to obtain a post in New France's Navy.

Some saw through Laumet's lies. Nevertheless, his schemes for expanding New France's reach and shoring up profits from the fur trade won him the friendship of the chancellor of France, Louis II Phélypeaux, comte de Pontchartrain, as well as Quebec's governor and other officials close to King Louis XIV. Those friendships, in turn, earned Laumet several prestigious government appointments and made it possible for him to found Fort Pontchartrain du Détroit, in 1701.

In Detroit, Laumet told more tales, mostly to hide how much money he made conducting trade with the English, selling brandy to Native Americans, and extracting exorbitant fees from Detroit's tradesmen. After outraged Jesuit missionaries protested Laumet's dealings with local tribes, it became impossible for the Pontchartrain to ignore the other complaints he'd received. He launched an investigation, which ultimately unmasked Laumet for the scoundrel he was. Unwilling to admit to his own poor judgment, the chancellor removed the troublemaker from Detroit by appointing him governor of Louisiana in 1710.

In Louisiana, history repeated itself. Laumet lied, bribed, and schemed in pursuit of profit. When his abuses of power came to light in 1716, the Duke of Orleans, Philippe II, deposed Laumet, and ordered him back to France, where the disgraced former governor was tossed into the Bastille.

Yet, even after all that, Laumet still had friends. Those friends secured his release the following year, as well as an apology and financial restitution. Laumet then used that money to buy himself the governorship of Castelsarrasin. He died there on **October 16, 1730,** and was buried at the local Carmelite Monastery.

October 17: STAGECOACH MARY

Mary Fields was a sharp-shooting, whisky-drinking, cigar-puffing, pants-wearing, punch-throwing, six-foot-tall former slave. She also loved the Ursuline Sisters.

Born around 1832, Fields spent the first three decades of her life as a slave in Tennessee. After the war, she remained in domestic service, eventually moving to Florida with the family of Judge Edmund Dunne. Although sources conflict on the details, most agree that when Dunne's sister, Sarah, left to join the Ursuline Sisters in Toledo, Fields eventually followed her and found work doing odd jobs for the sisters.

Then, in 1884, the Ursulines received a letter from a Jesuit mission in Montana, asking their community to take over a school outside Cascade. The Sisters of Providence had begun the school 20 years earlier, on **October 17, 1864,** but the Jesuits thought the Ursulines more suited to the task. Sarah Dunne (by now Mother Mary Amadeus) left with a small group of Ursulines, but Fields remained behind, serving the community in Toledo, Ohio.

Before the year was out, another letter arrived at the Cleveland convent: Mother Amadeus was dying from pneumonia. Immediately, Fields packed up and headed west to nurse her former mistress back to health. Once Amadeus recovered, she convinced Fields to stay. And stay she did, helping the Ursulines build their new convent, tending their garden, and doing their laundry.

The resident Jesuits, however, did not take kindly to Fields' hard-drinking, cigar-smoking ways. After she got into yet another brawl (with a man), they ordered the Ursulines to let her go. The sisters reluctantly obeyed, but privately gave Fields enough money to open a restaurant in town.

When that failed (because Fields gave away food for free), the Ursulines convinced the government to give her the stagecoach mail route from Cascade to the convent. In 1903, as "Stagecoach Mary" Fields approached 70 years of age, she retired from her route and set up shop as a laundress in Cascade. When she died 11 years later, the townspeople buried her alongside the winding road that led to the Ursulines.

Father Michael O'Connor wanted to teach theology, and he wanted to teach it at Ireland's Maynooth College. But after the Irish priest applied at the college, a friend—Philadelphia's coadjutor bishop, Francis Kenrick—urged him to reconsider. Kenrick didn't doubt O'Connor's scholarly abilities. But he knew O'Connor had all the makings of an effective missionary, and he wanted his friend to join him in Pennsylvania.

Kenrick's arguments won the day. In 1839, the 29-year-old O'Connor left Ireland for Philadelphia, where he served as rector of St. Charles Borromeo Seminary. Two years later, Kenrick asked O'Connor to accept the post of vicar-general for Philadelphia and assume responsibility for the Church in Western Pennsylvania.

O'Connor agreed, but didn't plan to hold the post for long. Unbeknownst to many of his fellow priests, O'Connor wanted to join the Society of Jesus. In 1843, however, the Fifth Provincial Council of Baltimore interrupted those plans when it decided that Pittsburgh should become a diocese and O'Connor its bishop.

O'Connor learned the news directly from Pope Gregory XVI. The priest had traveled to Rome that summer to ask the pope's permission to join the Jesuits. But when O'Connor knelt and made his request, Pope Gregory replied, "You shall be a bishop first and a Jesuit afterwards. I will not let you rise from your knees until you promise to accept the Diocese of Pittsburgh."

O'Connor obeyed. For 17 years, he faithfully served Pittsburgh, founding 44 parishes, a seminary, five colleges, two orphanages, a hospital, and numerous schools. Trusting he'd honored his end of the bargain, O'Connor submitted his resignation in 1860. Pope Pius IX accepted it. Two years later, O'Connor made his solemn profession of the four Jesuit vows. The order exempted him from another decade of formation owing to his experience. Afterwards, O'Connor taught at Boston College and became the Jesuits' provincial Superior in the United States.

The only American bishop to ever leave his see for religious life died at the age of 62 on **October 18, 1872.**

October 19: THE CONSERVATIVE MIND

On **October 19, 1918,** the man who would create the history of Conservatism was born. The man was Russell Kirk and the history he created began as his doctoral dissertation for the University of St. Andrews in Scotland. In 1953, he published it as *The Conservative Mind.*

In his book, Kirk traced the conservative underpinnings linking the likes of Edmund Burke, John Adams, Nathaniel Hawthorne, Benjamin Disraeli, and a host of other thinkers, writers, and statesmen. What emerged was a political philosophy essentially rooted in Catholic tradition that sought to do more than simply oppose Liberalism. Rather, it attempted to balance the competing claims of freedom and order.

According to Kirk's philosophy, a conservative . . .

1. Believes in "an enduring moral order";
2. "Adheres to custom, convention, and continuity";
3. Recognizes that modern man is unlikely "to make any brave new discoveries in morals or politics or taste";
4. Is guided by prudence and judges measures by their "probable long-run consequences, not merely by temporary advantage or popularity";
5. Recognizes that the "only true forms of equality are equality at the Last Judgment and equality before a just court of law";
6. Knows that because all men are imperfect "no perfect social order ever can be created";
7. Understands that "freedom and property are closely linked";
8. Upholds "voluntary community" and opposes "involuntary collectivism";
9. "Perceives the need for prudent restraints upon power and upon human passions";
10. "Understands that permanence and change must be recognized and reconciled in a vigorous society."

As Kirk's fame grew, he moved to his ancestral home in Mecosta, Michigan. There, he authored dozens of books, both fiction and nonfiction, and at the age of 45, he converted to Catholicism and married. Near the end of his life, The Heritage Foundation recognized Kirk's invaluable contributions to Conservatism by naming him a distinguished fellow. Kirk died in 1994.

In 1960, Hollywood starlet Dolores Hart flew to Italy to film *St. Francis of Assisi.* While there, she met Pope John XXIII.

"I am Dolores Hart, the actress playing Clare," she said to him.

"No, you are Clare!" he replied.

Thinking he misunderstood her, Hart repeated, "No, I am Dolores Hart, an actress portraying Clare."

The pope looked at her intently and again said, "No. You are Clare!"

Hart eventually understood. At the time, the 22-year-old actress was wrestling with her own vocation and wondered if she, like St. Francis' friend, could give up everything for Christ. The pope's words, in some sense, answered that question.

Hart was an unlikely candidate for religious life. Born on **October 20, 1938,** neither Hart's parents nor grandparents were Catholic. Nevertheless, they sent her to a Catholic school, and at the age of nine, Hart asked her family if she could become Catholic like her classmates. They agreed.

As the years passed, Hart's faith grew, but her vision for the future never included a religious habit. After Hollywood producers discovered the 19-year-old Hart and cast her alongside Elvis Presley in *Loving You,* religious life seemed even more improbable. But in 1959, while acting on Broadway, the starlet visited the Benedictine nuns at the Abbey of Regina Laudis in Bethlehem, Connecticut. After a few more visits, her vision for the future began to change. When she raised the possibility of a religious vocation, however, the Prioress responded with a strong, "No."

To the world, that answer made sense. With the talent and looks of Grace Kelly, Hart had her choice of roles. She also had a loving fiancé. If she wanted, she could have a successful career and a happy Catholic family. But Hart only wanted God.

By 1963, both Hart and the Abbey's Prioress were convinced of that, and Hart left Hollywood for Bethlehem. There she has remained, serving as Prioress since 2001. Hart wrote a book about her experience, *The Ear of the Heart,* in 2013.

Thomas Merton has been called the man with a thousand lives. The number is an exaggeration. The sentiment is not.

Born in 1915 France to an American mother and a New Zealander father, Merton's early life was that of a troubled child. First, his family fled to America to escape World War I. Then, on **October 21, 1921,** his mother died. After that, Merton bounced between schools, homes, and countries. By his sixteenth birthday, his father had died too.

Merton's next life was that of a hard-drinking, womanizing, agnostic. As a student at Cambridge University, he fathered a child out of wedlock. Later, as a student at Columbia University, he joined the Young Communist League. Religion, of any sort, held no attraction for him.

Then, it did. Merton's life changed yet again in 1937, when he encountered the work of the Catholic philosopher Étienne Gilson. One Catholic book led to another, and in November 1938, Merton entered the Church. Three years later, on December 10, 1941, he entered the Abbey of Our Lady of Gethsemani in Kentucky and became a Trappist monk.

Merton's quiet monastic life, however, was also short-lived. Soon after his arrival, the monastery's abbot encouraged him to pursue his writing. Merton's literary reputation grew, and in 1948, Merton published his spiritual autobiography, *The Seven Storey Mountain.* Widely acclaimed, the book sold over 100,000 copies in its first year. For the next two decades, Merton (who became Father Merton in 1949) was one of the most influential intellectuals in America, writing more than 70 books and helping thousands find their way to the Church.

By the late 1960s, however, Merton had transformed once more, embodying the angst and questioning that defined the early post-conciliar years. Increasingly discontented with his life at Gethsemani, Merton spoke out on Vietnam, fell in love with a woman half his age, and became fascinated with Zen Buddhism. In 1968, that fascination took him to Asia. There, 27 years to the day of his entrance to Gethsemani, Merton died in an accident.

The last of his "thousand" lives had begun.

Sister Théodore Guérin did not normally question her Superior's orders. But in 1839, she was sorely tempted to do so. Earlier that year, Vincennes' Bishop Célestine Hailandière asked the French Sisters of Providence of Ruille-sur-Loir to come to Indiana. The order's Superior agreed and entrusted the mission to Guérin. But Guérin didn't want the assignment. Frail, sickly, and unable to eat anything but soft foods, the 41-year-old sister thought she would make a very poor missionary.

Then, Guérin remembered a line from her order's rule: "Being obliged to work with zeal for the sanctification of souls, the sisters will be disposed to go to whatsoever part of the world obedience calls them."

That stayed her doubts. In July 1840, Mother Guérin and five other sisters left France for America.

Within days, Guérin discovered that her health would be the least of her difficulties. During their Atlantic crossing, a thief with unusually low scruples stole nearly all the sisters' money. They had barely enough to complete their journey, let alone start a school. And when they arrived in Indiana, on **October 22, 1840,** they discovered that their home was in a densely wooded wilderness, not the diocesan see as the bishop had promised. In the woods, they had one room and a corn loft to call their own.

After that discovery, the sisters endured a fire, a famine, and bitter cold, leading Guérin to write: "If ever this poor little Community becomes settled, it will be established on the Cross; and that is what gives me confidence and makes me hope."

Her hope was well placed. Within a year, the sisters opened St. Mary-of-the-Woods College, America's oldest Catholic women's college. Within 10 years, they opened nearly a dozen more schools. And by the time Guérin died, in 1856, the original community of six sisters numbered 67 professed members, nine novices, and seven postulants. More than 5,000 women would eventually join the order, and in 2006, the Church declared the frail sister who thought herself ill-equipped for missionary life, "Saint" Théodore Guérin.

"Catholic," wrote James Joyce, "means 'Here comes everybody.' "

Nevertheless, in 1935, much of America was surprised to learn that "everybody" included the notorious mobster Dutch Schultz.

Born Arthur Flegenheimer to German-Jewish immigrants in the Bronx, New York, Schultz terrorized the country during the last years of Prohibition and the first years of the Great Depression. Rising in less than a decade from bootlegger to crime boss, Schultz's ability to turn an illegal profit was surpassed only by his savagery. One victim he hung by a meat hook. Another he shot in the mouth over lunch, and then cut out his heart with a knife.

"Dutch Schultz did that murder just as casually as if he were picking his teeth," said one observer.

That was the Dutch Schultz America knew. And in the last year of his life, as he plotted the assassination of U.S. Attorney Thomas E. Dewey, he didn't seem inclined to change. But as he plotted, Schultz also read all he could about the Catholic Church.

Months earlier, Schultz inexplicably dodged a conviction for tax evasion. He decided Jesus had spared him, and the reading was his way of learning more about the Jewish Carpenter. No one who knew Schultz believed he'd become Catholic—possibly not even Schultz believed it. But when the gangster found himself mortally wounded in a shoot-out on the night of **October 23, 1935,** he immediately called for a Catholic priest.

Father Cornelius McInerney answered the call. He arrived at the hospital to find Schultz lucid but weak. At Schultz's request, the priest heard his confession, baptized him, and administered Last Rites. McInerney then remained by Schultz's side until he passed away.

News of the conversion leaked out days later, when Schultz received a Catholic funeral. Horrified that the Church would allow the killer into its fold, the public demanded an explanation. The only one McInerney gave was to remind people that three crosses stood on Calvary, and on one hung a penitent thief destined for paradise.

Sebastian Wimmer lacked direction.

Born in 1809 in Bavaria, the son of a tavern keeper, Wimmer contemplated careers in the military and law, before pursuing the priesthood. After his 1831 ordination, however, Wimmer decided the diocesan priesthood wasn't for him and entered St. Michael's Abbey at Metten. There, the newly professed Benedictine priest took the name "Boniface." With the name, came direction.

Just as the first Boniface believed God had called him to evangelize pagan Germany, his Bavarian namesake became convinced that God wanted him to evangelize Protestant America. When his fellow monks laughed at the idea, Wimmer insisted that Benedictine spirituality—with its emphasis on manual labor, prayer, and hospitality—would appeal to Americans. And when his Superiors expressed their misgivings, he told them, "If I cannot work in America as a Benedictine, I will go in another habit . . . I can be delayed and retarded, but not stopped. I can be persecuted with suspicion and distrust . . . but I will go my way because I freely believe that God wills it."

It never came to that. The Benedictines sanctioned Father Wimmer's mission in 1846, and that July, he and 18 aspirants left for America. Upon their arrival Bishop Michael O'Connor offered them a parish in Latrobe, 40 miles southeast of Pittsburgh. Wimmer accepted, and on **October 24, 1846,** became pastor of St. Vincent's Catholic Church. With his installation, the first Benedictine monastery in the United States was officially established. Ten years later, more than 200 monks called St. Vincent's Abbey home.

Although Wimmer spoke only German when he arrived, he soon picked up enough English to say, "I understand English now to the extent that I can preach just barely, hear confessions, catechize, and argue with the Protestants." In later years, he did much more, founding five abbeys, two priories, 152 parishes, and multiple schools. St. Vincent's eventually became America's first archabbey and Wimmer, the most successful evangelist of the late-nineteenth century.

Archabbot Boniface Wimmer died in 1887, having more than lived up to his name.

"The Catholics are coming! The Catholics are coming!"

In 1868, a frightened cry went up and down Hillhouse Avenue in New Haven, Connecticut. At the time, Hillhouse was New Haven's most prestigious address, home to Yale University's president, several professors, and numerous millionaires. The only Catholics on the street were the millionaires' maids and gardeners. But then, an inventor in financial straits decided to teach Hillhouse residents a lesson.

The inventor owned the only empty lot on the street. He had bought it years before, intending to build his home there. But after his fortunes changed, he needed to sell. At first, he offered the lot to his neighbors. When no offers came, he threatened to sell the property to undesirable characters, hoping that would spur someone to action. And when that didn't work, he made good on the threat, selling the lot to St. Mary's Parish, which needed a bigger church for its growing congregation.

As news of the sale spread, panic struck Hillhouse Avenue. Residents begged the city to stop the sale, and convinced it to offer the parish another piece of land elsewhere. St. Mary's almost accepted the city's offer, until the mayor substituted a less desirable lot at the last minute. At that point, the parish's frustrated pastor, Father Edward O'Brien, refused the city's offer and made plans to build on Hillhouse.

The parish laid the cornerstone in 1870. Two years later, on **October 25, 1874,** they dedicated the new St. Mary's Church.

Twelve troubled years followed that initial triumph. The parish struggled with the debt it acquired building the church, and the burden of repayment purportedly sent more than one St. Mary's pastor to an early grave. In 1886, however, the Dominicans took over the parish (where the Knights of Columbus began in 1882), and its troubles ended.

More than 125 years later, most of the street's millionaires have left, but the Dominicans and St. Mary's remain, serving nearby Yale University and the surrounding community.

Joseph Warren Revere, grandson of the American patriot Paul Revere, was no stranger to war. After joining the U.S. Navy in 1828, at the age of 16, Revere combatted the African slave trade in the Pacific, and witnessed the Spanish Carlist War in the Atlantic. He also served with the Mosquito Fleet along Florida's coast during the Seminole War, and raised the American flag above Sonoma during the Mexican-American War.

Through the years, shipwrecks, disease, and death became routine for Revere. But nothing prepared him for the bloody battles of the American Civil War.

Revere had retired from the U.S. Navy in 1850, and naval politics made a return to the sea difficult. So when the Civil War began he enlisted in the Union Army instead, receiving the rank of colonel. In the war's first year, Revere saw action with the 7th New Jersey Volunteer Infantry in the Peninsula Campaign, the Seven Days Battles, and the Second Battle of Bull Run. The Union Army commended him for his bravery, but the brutality he encountered left Revere badly shaken.

In the fall of 1862, as Union troops regrouped, Revere went to Washington, D.C. One day, still struggling with all he'd experienced that year, Revere happened upon a Catholic Church and went in to pray. Although Revere was familiar with the Church's teachings, he was neither a Catholic nor a particularly religious man. That day, however, something changed. Soon, he found a priest, and told him he wished to become Catholic. After talking the matter over, the priest agreed. He baptized Revere on October 19, and gave him his First Holy Communion on **October 26, 1862**. Revere then returned to battle for another year as a brigadier general.

After the war, General Revere joined Assumption of the Blessed Virgin Mary Parish in Morristown, New Jersey. An accomplished painter, he gave the parish one of his best works, *Espousal of the Blessed Virgin and St. Joseph*. It hung for more than a century in the church's Marian aisle.

Revere died in 1880.

Father Charles Coughlin had the best of intentions when he began his radio broadcasts in 1926. That year, the Ku Klux Klan came to Royal Oak, Michigan, where Coughlin served as pastor of the newly built Shrine of the Little Flower Church. The Klan burned a cross on the parish grounds, and the priest took to the airwaves to condemn the act.

Coughlin's broadcasts were an immediate hit, and within four years, CBS picked up his show. Around the same time, the focus of the show began shifting from faith to politics, with Coughlin denouncing communism and championing Franklin D. Roosevelt's "New Deal." "The New Deal is Christ's deal," he proclaimed.

By 1935, however, Coughlin's support of Roosevelt turned to condemnation. Roosevelt wasn't doing enough to please "the Radio Priest" (as America called him), nor was he doing it fast enough. The following year, Coughlin gave his full support to the National Union for Social Justice (which he helped create), and called for the nationalization of major industries, the redistribution of wealth, and limitations on private property rights.

With more than 40 million Catholics tuning in weekly to hear Coughlin's broadcasts, Roosevelt feared for his reelection prospects. A well-timed visit from Archbishop Eugenio Cardinal Pacelli—the future Pope Pius XII—neutralized that problem and Coughlin fell silent, but only for a short while.

When Coughlin returned to the air in 1937, anti-Semitism colored his broadcasts. Praise for Italy and Germany's fascist governments soon followed. The Vatican wanted him silenced. So too did the Roosevelt Administration. But the only person who could make that happen was Coughlin's bishop, Michael Gallagher, and he refused to take action.

Finally, the approach of World War II led the Roosevelt Administration to drastically curtail broadcast freedoms, which made it possible for them to force Coughlin off the air. Detroit's new bishop, Edward Mooney, helped matters along by forbidding Coughlin from engaging in political activity. Coughlin obeyed and quietly pastored the Shrine of the Little Flower Church until 1966. He died 13 years later.

October 28: THE APOSTLE OF THE ALLEGHENIES

On **October 28, 1792,** the 21-year-old "Augustine Smith" walked off a ship in Baltimore's harbor and encountered a new country where Catholics were few and priests even fewer. Within weeks, he decided to become a priest and serve the Church in America.

But when Bishop John Carroll learned of the young man's intentions, he had his doubts. Although Carroll desperately needed priests, he knew that "Smith" wasn't who he pretended to be. In truth, he was Prince Demetrius Gallitzin, son of one of the wealthiest noblemen in Russia, traveling in disguise. Carroll appreciated that gesture of humility, but doubted that the Prince had the makings of a missionary. Gallitzin grew up in the courts of Europe. His childhood playmates were future kings. Carroll couldn't envision him roughing it on the American frontier.

Gallitzin, however, knew his own mind. Five years earlier, over the strong objections of his father, he had joined his mother in the Catholic Church. With that same determination, Gallitzin convinced Carroll of his vocation. Three years later, in 1795, the Prince became a priest.

Still using his pseudonym, Father Gallitzin spent four years ministering in Maryland, Virginia, and Pennsylvania, before discovering a small community of Catholics near the summit of the Alleghenies. With Carroll's permission, Gallitzin built a church there. He also built a town, borrowing on the prospects of his immense inheritance to buy farmland for Catholic families, and construct saw mills, gristmills, and tanneries. He named the city Loretto. As Gallitzin's reputation as a preacher and apologist grew, so did the town.

Although the inheritance never came (mostly because Russia wanted to punish him for becoming a Catholic priest), Gallitzin's friend King William of the Netherlands, Pope Gregory XVI, and others helped the Prince settle his debts. And while that indebtedness somewhat tarnished his reputation, in retrospect Gallitzin spent money wisely. By the time of his death, in 1840, more than 10,000 Catholics lived in and around Loretto, and the Church in southwestern Pennsylvania was flourishing.

Gallitzin's cause for canonization opened in 2005.

Father John Dubois needed to leave France. Radical revolutionaries, including his former classmate Maximilien de Robespierre, were out for Catholic blood, and the 26-year-old Dubois risked death if he stayed. Fortunately, Dubois had powerful friends who smuggled him onto a ship bound for America.

When Dubois arrived in Norfolk in 1791, he brought with him a letter of recommendation from the Marquis de Lafayette. That won him the immediate friendship of Virginia's governor, Beverley Randolph, who allowed Dubois to celebrate Mass in the State House, and Patrick Henry, who taught him English. A year later, Bishop John Carroll sent Dubois to Frederick, Maryland. His new mission territory reached from Frederick to St. Louis, Missouri.

During those early years, Dubois' energy was legendary. One story tells of his hearing confessions until 9 p.m., riding 50 miles and swimming the Monocacy River twice to administer Last Rites, and still arriving back at his parish in time for 9 a.m. Mass.

By 1807, however, Dubois' missionary days were over. That year, he bought land in Emmitsburg, Maryland, and opened Mount St. Mary's College. Dubois believed he would spend the rest of his life at the Mount. Rome thought differently.

On **October 29, 1826,** Dubois became the third bishop of New York. Unfortunately, his mostly Irish flock didn't want a French bishop, and parish trustees thwarted him at every turn, refusing to pay priests he recruited and firing teachers he hired. When they refused to pay him, Dubois replied, "I am an old man, and do not need much. I can live in a basement or in a garret. But whether I come up from the basement or down from the garret, I shall still be your bishop."

Dubois' troubles continued through the 1830s, when Nativists burned his seminary and threatened his cathedral. Finally, before his death, in 1842, he asked to be buried under the sidewalk at the entrance to Old St. Patrick's Cathedral, in New York, so that "people could walk on me in death, as they did while I was living."

His flock complied.

In 1685, England had a Catholic king, and New York had a Catholic governor. The King, James II, had appointed the Colonial Governor, Thomas Dongan, in 1682, before receiving his crown. At the time, James was simply the Duke of York and the colonial proprietor of New York. Dongan was the son of an Irish baronet, whose family had long supported the claims of James' family (the Stuarts) to the throne. The two became friends during the years Oliver Cromwell ruled England and the Stuarts and their supporters lived in exile.

By 1682, however, Cromwell was long gone, James' brother Charles II sat on the throne, and James was free to appoint anyone he wished as governor of his colony. After he selected Dongan, he tasked the Irishman with calling an assembly and drawing up a colonial charter.

The assembly met in October 1683. Guided by Dongan, they drafted a charter that declared New York's Assembly co-equal to Britain's Parliament, prohibited taxation without representation, and forbade the quartering of soldiers without the people's consent. Described as the "Magna Charta of American Liberty," the charter also guaranteed freedom of conscience in religious matters to all who "profess faith in God by Jesus Christ."

Dongan signed the New York Charter of Rights and Liberties on **October 30, 1683**. James signed it the following year. When he became king in 1685, however, he realized that the charter granted a bit too much authority to the people. So, he decided not to confirm it.

Even without the original charter, Catholics enjoyed religious liberty in New York for several years. But in 1688, James lost his crown in England's Glorious Revolution, and the following year, New York's Jacob Leisler staged a revolution of his own. Leisler overthrew New York's government, ordered the arrest of all "reputed papists," and disenfranchised Catholics. Further legislation banned Catholic priests from the colony and made the practice of Catholicism illegal.

Within a few years' time, hardly a Catholic remained in New York.

October 31: ALL HALLOWS EVE

On November 1, Catholics honor the souls in Heaven with the Feast of All Saints. On November 2, Catholics pray for the souls in Purgatory with the Feast of All Souls. But what about the souls in Hell? How should Catholics remember them?

In medieval Ireland, simple peasants pondered that question and worried that the damned, if neglected, might seek revenge. They solved the problem by banging pots and pans on **October 31**. Noisemaking became their way of letting the eternally lost know that they weren't forgotten.

A couple of hundred years later, the Bubonic Plague swept through France, killing untold millions. Those who survived prayed for the dead and meditated on their own mortality by staging elaborate All Souls' Day parades. These "Dances of the Dead" featured people dressed up in the garb of princes, popes, and paupers, all following the devil to the grave, side by side.

Meanwhile, on October 31 in Catholic England, people walked from house to house, promising prayers for the inhabitants' dearly departed on All Souls' Day in exchange for tasty cakes, dubbed "soul cakes." Years later, after England became a Protestant country, every November 5 the revelers celebrating Guy Fawkes Day visited the houses of known (or suspected) Catholics and demanded food or drink for their merry-making. If the Catholics didn't want to see their homes or business vandalized, they supplied what the revelers demanded. The choice was simple: trick or treat.

Many of those traditions eventually died out in their country of origin. In early-nineteenth-century America, however, they found new life and new purpose on All Hallows Eve. As immigrants from England, Ireland, and France poured into the United States, they brought their ways of celebrating the triduum of Hallowtide with them. The arrival of more Catholic immigrants from elsewhere in Europe brought more traditions. And eventually all those traditions mingled together to form the very American (and very Catholic) holiday of Halloween.

November

American Naval Commander Jeremiah Denton, Jr., was blinking, rapidly. In 1966, as American intelligence officers watched a televised interview with the prisoner of war, orchestrated by his North Vietnamese captors, they noticed that straightaway. At first, they attributed Denton's blinking to bright television lights. But soon, they recognized it as Morse code. Quickly and deliberately, Denton blinked *T-O-R-T-U-R-E*. That encoded message gave the United States its first confirmation that the North Vietnamese Army was torturing its American prisoners.

Days after the propaganda broadcast, Denton's captors realized what he'd done and tortured him yet again. Later, Denton would spend four years in solitary confinement. Two of those years he would pass in a cell the size of a refrigerator.

Yet through it all, the U.S. Naval Academy graduate never broke and never despaired. His secret, as he later explained, was the Rosary and the simple phrase, "Sacred Heart of Jesus, I give myself to you." Denton prayed those prayers repeatedly during his time in captivity, finding strength, consolation, and even joy as a prisoner, through his relationship with Christ.

"Jesus did so many miraculous things," Denton said of his years as a POW. "On a number of occasions I turned my life over to him and miraculous things happened."

In 1973, almost eight years after Denton's plane went down over Thanh Hóa, the North Vietnamese released him. Awarded the Navy Cross for heroism in captivity, Denton went on to become commandant of the Armed Forces Staff College. He served there until **November 1, 1977,** when he retired with the rank of rear admiral. Afterwards, Denton wrote a book about his time in captivity—*When Hell Was in Session*—and represented his native Alabama in the U.S. Senate from 1981 to 1987. He was the first Catholic elected to statewide office in Alabama.

After leaving politics, Denton devoted himself to helping veterans, his wife, Jane, their seven children, and his parish—Saint Bede Catholic Church, in Williamsburg, Virginia. Denton died in 2014, at age 89.

War can be the making of a man. It also can be the making of a saint. Such was the case with Servant of God Emil Kapaun.

Born in Kansas to Czech immigrants, the young Kapaun never struck anyone as all that special. His classmates in school and seminary remember him as pious and studious, but not extraordinary. Even in his first years as a military chaplain— serving at an army base in Georgia in 1944, and in India from 1945 to 1946—Father Kapaun didn't stand out among his peers. He was just a good chaplain, who did his job and loved his Church.

That changed after Kapaun re-enlisted in 1948. He accompanied troops to Japan in 1949, and Korea in 1950, arriving only one month after North Korea invaded South Korea. The fighting in Korea was like nothing Kapaun had yet encountered. But he rose to the challenge, ministering to the wounded and the dying, bringing men into the Faith through baptism, and celebrating Mass as often as possible, usually on the hood of his military jeep. When the fighting was too intense for sacraments, he carried men to safety, risking his own life in the process.

In September 1950, the U.S. Army rewarded Kapaun's bravery with the Bronze Star. Little did they know that his bravest hour still lay ahead.

That hour came on **November 2, 1950,** when the North Koreans captured Kapaun during the Battle of Unsan. He spent the next six months in a prisoner of war camp near Pyoktong, North Korea. There, he cared for his fellow prisoners both physically and spiritually—going without food so others could eat, stealing drugs for dying soldiers, and helping them endure the psychological warfare within the camp.

Hungry and weak, Kapaun succumbed to pneumonia and dysentery in May 1951. His cause for canonization opened in 1993. Twenty years later, in 2013, the U.S. government posthumously awarded Kapaun the Medal of Honor.

November 3: FATHER DUFFY OF THE FIGHTING 69TH

In New York's Times Square, where Broadway and 7th Avenue meet, stands a statue of a man wearing a soldier's uniform. The man, however, was no soldier. He was Father Francis P. Duffy, chaplain to the "Fighting 69th."

A well-known theologian in the first years of the twentieth century, Duffy left academia in 1912 for pastoral work. Two years later, on the eve of World War I, he volunteered to serve as chaplain for the 69th New York Infantry Regiment. Made up mostly of Irish Catholics, the regiment left America in October 1917, to join the fight in Europe. Their chaplain went with them.

On the crossing, Duffy offered Mass daily. He heard Confession just as often, and the poet Joyce Kilmer, who fought with the Fighting 69th, wrote that the line of soldiers for Confession was "as long as the mess line." By **November 3, 1917,** the men reached France. Soon afterwards, they left for the trenches.

After observing Duffy in action, one newspaper described him as "covered with mud and grime . . . cheering on the living, administering the last rites of his Church to the dying, filling the place of a stretcher bearer who had been struck down by a bullet, assisting the wounded, darting hither and yon . . . For 117 hours, he was under fire without rest."

The soldiers respected no one more than Duffy, and General Douglas McArthur made the unprecedented move of recommending him for regimental commander. McArthur's superiors didn't take that recommendation, but by war's end, Duffy was the most highly decorated chaplain in U.S. Army history.

When Duffy returned to New York, he became pastor of Holy Cross Church. He remained there until his death in 1932. Because his gift for friendship was as legendary as his bravery, more than 25,000 people came to his funeral, among them one wealthy woman who tried to jump the lines. When a police officer stopped her, she protested, "But I was a friend of Father Duffy."

"Lady," he replied, "everyone in New York was a friend of Father Duffy."

On October 19, 1781, General Lord Charles Cornwallis surrendered more than 7,000 British troops to General George Washington. With Cornwallis' surrender, more than just the Battle of Yorktown ended. On that day, the American Revolution was as good as won.

Two weeks later, on **November 4, 1781,** members of the Continental Congress filled Old St. Mary's Catholic Church in Philadelphia to give thanks for the Yorktown victory and the coming end of America's fight with Great Britain.

Before the war began, such a gathering would have been almost unthinkable. The first Continental Congress had declared Catholicism a religion "fraught with impious tenets" and wondered how Great Britain could permit its practice in Canada when the Church had "deluged England in blood and dispersed impiety, bigotry, murder, and rebellion."

That, however, was in 1774, before years of hard fighting and near defeat led America into an alliance with France. With the alliance, came greater tolerance of Catholics. And by 1781, when the French Minister invited the Congress to join him at Old St. Mary's for the *Te Deum* (an ancient Catholic hymn of praise), most members saw nothing improper in saying yes.

The American leaders who came that day heard the Church's priests chant the hymn. They also heard a stirring sermon on the virtues of America's soldiers. And according to Dr. James Thatcher, the Continental Army's Protestant surgeon who attended the event, they liked what they heard.

Thatcher wrote:

> *The occasion was in this hemisphere, singular and affecting; and the discourse itself is so elegant and animated . . . so warm with those sentiments of piety and gratitude to our Divine Benefactor, in which good men of all countries accord . . . as must give pleasure to every serious and candid friend to our glorious cause.*

Afterwards, British loyalists decried Congress as "papists" and declared that an American victory "would mean the triumph of popery." But by then, such talk had little effect. America was too busy celebrating to worry about a little *Te Deum.*

November 5: POPE'S NIGHT

In 1605, a small group of English Catholics devised a singularly bad plan to blow up the British Parliament and restore the Catholic monarchy. Although other Catholics helped foil the plot, the Church of Rome was blamed, and the anniversary of the plot's discovery— November 5—became an annual occasion for anti-Catholic riots in Great Britain. The English called it "Guy Fawkes Night," in honor of the first conspirator discovered.

In the beginning, the evening's celebrations included burning effigies of Fawkes. In later years, the rioters also took to burning effigies of the pope. British immigrants to America continued that tradition and renamed the festivities "Pope's Night." Especially in anti-Catholic Boston, the fifth of November became synonymous with rioting, drunkenness, and vandalism.

George Washington, however, put an end to all that on **November 5, 1775**. At the time, Washington was working to secure French-Canadian Catholics' support for the American Revolution. Recognizing that burning the pope in effigy wouldn't help his cause, he put a stop to Pope's Night, ordering:

> *As the Commander in Chief has been apprized of a design form'd for the observance of that ridiculous and childish custom of burning the Effigy of the pope, He cannot help expressing his surprise that there should be Officers and Soldiers in this army so void of common sense, as not to see the impropriety of such a step at this Juncture; at a Time when we are solliciting, and have really obtain'd, the friendship and alliance of the people of Canada, whom we ought to consider as Brethren embarked in the same Cause . . . At such a juncture, and in such Circumstances, to be insulting their Religion, is so monstrous, as not to be suffered or excused; indeed instead of offering the most remote insult, it is our duty to address public thanks to these our Brethren, as to them we are so much indebted for every late happy Success over the common Enemy in Canada.*

After that, Pope's Night in America was no more.

In 1783, with the signing of the Treaty of Paris, the American colonies won their independence from Great Britain. The following year, the Catholic Church in America did the same.

Before the American Revolution began, the Church in America had long answered to a bishop in London. Once the American Revolution ended, however, Catholic colonists wanted an American bishop. To them, it seemed inappropriate for a British bishop to serve as their shepherd. It also seemed dangerous. Animosity for the Catholic Church may have waned during the American Revolution, but it hadn't died, and American Catholics didn't want anyone questioning their national loyalties.

Recognizing the need for independence, about two dozen Jesuit priests—representing almost the entirety of the country's Catholic clergy at the time—gathered at Whitemarsh Plantation in Maryland in the fall of 1783. After days of discussing the needs of American Catholics, the priests decided not to ask Rome to appoint an American bishop. Rather, believing they'd have more success with a smaller request, the Jesuits drafted a petition seeking permission to nominate a superior who could exercise some of a bishop's powers. They sent the petition to Rome in November 1783. The following year, Rome agreed to their proposal, creating the Apostolic Prefecture of the United States and certifying the Jesuits' nomination of Father John Carroll as Superior of the Missions.

Four years later, the American Jesuits decided the time had come to ask for more. After holding another meeting at Whitemarsh, they asked Pope Pius VI to appoint a bishop for the United States. On **November 6, 1789,** the pope agreed, elevating Baltimore to a diocese and naming Carroll as its first bishop.

The following summer, Carroll traveled to England for his episcopal consecration. At long last, America's 40,000 Catholics had a bishop of their own.

When Katharine Drexel's father died in 1885, he left her a great fortune—more than $250 million in today's dollars. Drexel, however, understood that the money didn't belong to her. It belonged to God.

Drexel learned that from her parents. Throughout Drexel's childhood, her family opened their Philadelphia mansion to the city's poor three times a week, providing those in need with food, clothing, and rent money. When Drexel's parents passed away, she resolved to follow in their footsteps and began supporting a school for Native Americans in South Dakota.

In December 1886, a year after her father's death, the 29-year-old heiress traveled to Rome. A month later, she met with Pope Leo XIII, and she told him about the South Dakota school. When she asked him if he knew of any missionaries who could serve there, he replied, "Why not, my child, become a missionary yourself?"

The question surprised Drexel. She knew she wanted to enter religious life, but she wanted to become a contemplative nun, not an active sister. The pope's question led her to reconsider. On **November 7, 1889,** Drexel received the novice habit from the Sisters of Mercy. Then, in 1891, just as originally planned, Drexel struck out on her own and professed her vows as the first Sister of the Blessed Sacrament. Thirteen other women joined her and committed themselves to educating Native Americans and African-Americans.

For the next 44 years, with Mother Drexel at the helm and her fortune at their disposal, the Sisters of the Blessed Sacrament opened 145 missions, 49 elementary schools, and 12 high schools. Not everyone appreciated white women teaching black and red students, though, and threats of violence followed the Sisters wherever they went.

After suffering a near-fatal heart attack in 1935, Drexel entrusted the task of leading the order to another and spent her last decades in the Sisters' Mother House, living the contemplative life for which she'd always longed. Drexel died in 1955. Forty-five years later, the Church declared the Philadelphia heiress "Saint Katharine Drexel."

In 1889, as Father Damien de Veuster lay dying in the leper colony on Molokai, a woman sat by his side. The woman was Mother Marianne Cope, a Franciscan sister from New York who had come to share the "Leper Priest's" burden.

Born Maria Anna Barbara Koob in Germany, but raised as Barbara Cope in America, Cope was no stranger to the sick. As a young girl growing up in Utica, New York, the work of nursing her invalid father fell primarily to her. Later, as a Sister of St. Francis, Cope helped found two hospitals in central New York and governed one of them—St. Joseph's Hospital in Syracuse—for nearly a decade.

By 1883, Cope had become Superior General of her order and a pioneer in hospital administration and nursing education. But that year, she left behind all that she'd built in New York and took on a task that 50 others religious orders had refused: establishing a system of hospital nursing for Hawaii's poor. Along with six other sisters, Cope arrived in Hawaii on **November 8, 1883**. There, the Sisters of St. Francis founded Maui's first hospital and took over the main hospital on Oahu, where they cared for the Hawaiian lepers who had not yet left for Molokai.

The Sisters of St. Francis continued that work until 1888, when the Hawaiian government began enforcing a strict deportation policy for all victims of leprosy. Cope and her companions then left their work on the other islands and joined Father Damian on Molokai. Cope remained there until her death in 1918. Neither she nor any of the sisters who served in the colony ever contracted leprosy.

Pope Benedict XVI canonized the Franciscan sister in 2012.

November 9: A MORE CERTAIN PATH

The Gilded Age brought tremendous economic growth to America. It also brought skepticism, greed, and rapid social change.

Charles Bonaparte believed his Church could help with those problems. The prominent Baltimore attorney (and future U.S. secretary of the navy and U.S. attorney general) knew the Catholic Church possessed what the culture increasingly lacked—truth. And when the American bishops convened on **November 9, 1884,** for the Third Plenary Council of Baltimore, Bonaparte greeted them with a plea: offer the country a more certain path than the robber barons. Bonaparte delivered that plea during a reception at the Council's outset, saying:

> *In our day and country two classes of thinking men contemplate [the times] with ever-increasing anxiety. Many see, with alarm and distress fast deepening into silent despair, religious faith in themselves and others fading into a dim uncertainty . . .*
>
> *[Others] note in the American people a blunting of the sense of justice; a growing dimness of moral sight; an inability to distinguish clearly and promptly between right and wrong; a tendency to resolve ethics to blind sentiment; in short, a distortion and maiming of the national conscience . . .*
>
> *To your assembly are turned, now when our wants are most sorely felt, the eyes of those who seek . . . They leave with confidence to your wisdom the means by which the good cause may be made to prosper; but they ask with earnestness and humility . . . that through this Council. [God] may make the American people more worthy of His priceless gift—their civil and religious liberty.*

Before the close of the Council, the bishops answered Bonaparte's plea. Convinced that the solution to America's (and Catholics') confusion lay in clear teaching and sound catechesis, they passed resolutions to author a national Catholic catechism, found a national Catholic university, and build Catholic schools in every one of the nation's parishes.

In the years that followed, the prelates and their priests enacted all three resolutions, which, in turn, helped give rise to the Catholic intellectual, literary, and social justice revival that flourished in the first half of the twentieth century.

For decades, most Americans believed that the first Carmelites in the United States arrived in 1790, when four nuns came from Holland to establish the Carmel of Port Tobacco in Maryland. The Carmelites' American roots, however, actually date back to 1602, when Sebastián Vizcaíno set out from Acapulco to explore California's coastline. With him, he brought three Spanish Discalced Carmelites: Father Andres de la Asuncion, Father Antonio de la Ascension, and Father Tomas de Aquino.

After sailing north from Mexico, the Spaniards made landfall on **November 10, 1602,** near present-day San Diego. There, Father Andres offered what some claim was the first Mass in California. Ten days later, they resumed sailing north. They arrived in Monterey by mid-December, and the fathers named the area in which they celebrated Mass, *Carmelo* (present-day Carmel Valley). With its wide fertile valley overlooking the sea, they thought it resembled Mount Carmel in Palestine. During their stay, the Carmelites made several converts among the natives. But duty soon called them back to their ship, and the new Catholics were left to their own devices.

A century later, in 1720, another group of Carmelite Fathers, this time from France, attempted to found a mission in present-day Mobile, Alabama. Unfortunately the sudden death of their Superior ended that mission almost as soon as it began.

Seventy years later, though, the Carmelites became a permanent presence in North America with the arrival of the Carmelite nuns in Maryland. Three of the original four women grew up in Maryland, but moved to Europe to pursue a religious vocation. Because no orders of women religious existed in the British colonies prior to the American Revolution, they had no other options. With the advent of religious liberty in the newly formed United States, however, the women returned home to establish the first monastery (Carmelite or otherwise) in the country.

A century later, the Carmelite Fathers joined the Sisters, establishing their first mission in Manhattan in 1889. This time, they not only stayed, but also went on to found dozens of Carmelite monasteries across America. Many continue to flourish today.

The Russian Orthodox Church was dying. By 1929, Soviet Communists had killed more than 157,000 priests. Fewer than 4,000 remained. Wanting to help, Pope Pius XI issued a call for Catholic missionaries. Almost immediately, Walter Ciszek volunteered.

The son of Polish immigrants, Ciszek was born in Pennsylvania on **November 11, 1904.** He joined the Jesuits in 1928, and a year later, asked to go to the Soviet Union. His superiors agreed, and sent him to the Pontifical Russian College in Rome to complete his studies.

Ordained in 1937, Father Ciszek went first to Poland. Then, after the outbreak of World War II, he snuck into the Soviet Union. Posing as a layman, Ciszek found work as a logger and offered Mass after hours in the forest. In 1941, however, the Soviet police discovered his secret and arrested him. For the next five years, they held Ciszek in Moscow's Lubyanka prison, torturing him relentlessly. Later, they sent him to Siberia to serve out the rest of his sentence in the gulag prison system.

For nine years, Ciszek worked 12-hour days in subzero temperatures, mining coal and shoveling it onto freighters. With no running water, he washed with snow. But Ciszek was happy. In the gulag, unlike Lubyanka, he could offer Mass, albeit with wine made from raisins and a shot glass for a chalice.

"I thanked God daily for the opportunity to work among this hidden flock, consoling and comforting men who had thought themselves beyond His grace," he wrote.

Released from the gulag in 1955, Ciszek spent eight more years under government observation in Siberia. He nevertheless managed to found numerous parishes and ministered to thousands of Russians, all while working as an auto mechanic. Around the same time, the government permitted Ciszek to contact his family; they'd heard nothing from him since 1939 and believed him dead. Eight years later, in 1963, the priest went home in a prisoner exchange.

Ciszek spent the remainder of his life at Fordham University. He died in 1984. His cause for canonization opened in 1990.

In 1837, Father Mathias Loras learned he would become the first shepherd of the Diocese of Dubuque, Iowa. Loras was humbled by the honor, but also at a loss. He knew nothing about his diocese or its people.

Loras' ignorance was understandable. Born into a noble French family in 1792 and ordained a Catholic priest on **November 12, 1815,** Loras spent the first years of his priesthood as a seminary professor and rector near Lyon, France. He came to America in 1829, but never strayed far from Alabama's Gulf Coast. To Loras, Iowa might as well have been Africa.

Accordingly, before setting out for his diocese, Bishop Loras sent a letter to Bishop Joseph Rosati of St. Louis, who'd formerly overseen the territory. The letter contained a detailed list of questions about his see's size, population, climate, and missionary history. Near the end, he added, "How does one reach there?"

Unfortunately, Rosati had few answers. Not until Bishop Loras arrived in Dubuque did he learn that his diocese—initially comprising present-day Iowa and parts of Minnesota and the Dakotas—had fewer than 3,000 Catholics and just one priest. After exploring the region, Loras decided that if he didn't do something fast, Rome would suppress the see for lack of Catholics.

Rather than become Dubuque's last bishop, as well as its first, Loras sought out German and Irish immigrants from the East Coast and urged them to buy farmland in Iowa. As an added incentive, he used his connections in France to find money for schools, recruit priests and religious orders, and build parishes. In the process, Loras helped lay the secular as well as the sacred foundations for the State of Iowa.

Tensions between the Germans and the Irish frequently flared (twice forcing Loras to flee Dubuque), but by the time of Loras' death, in 1858, the diocese was thriving and his flock considered him a saint. Wrote one priest, "Everyone here venerates him . . . and many are disputing over pieces of his cassock and of his hair."

Fanny Allen didn't care about God. Nor did the people she loved and respected. Her father, the American Revolutionary War hero Ethan Allen, opposed organized religion. Her mother and stepfather thought it unimportant.

Allen, who was born in Vermont on **November 13, 1784,** didn't necessarily have anything against God. She just didn't consider him worthy of her time. Known for her wit and beauty, Allen cared about parties and conversation, not questions of faith.

Then, in 1805, Allen decided she wanted to learn French. She asked her parents' permission to go to Montreal, where she could study with the Sisters of the Congregation of Notre Dame. Fearing that the Sisters might convert her, Allen's parents consented on one condition: that she be baptized an Episcopalian. Allen agreed, although she thought the request ridiculous and laughed her way through the ceremony.

Allen stopped laughing after she arrived in Montreal. One day in 1807, a sister asked Allen to place flowers on the altar in the Blessed Sacrament chapel. The sister also asked Allen to pray before entering the chapel. Three times Allen tried to enter without saying a prayer, and three times she found herself unable to move. At last, she fell on her knees in adoration, convinced that Christ was present before her.

Soon afterwards, Allen entered the Catholic Church and told her parents she intended to become a nun. They did everything they could to change her mind, even throwing elaborate parties populated by handsome young men. Their hopes that romance would dissuade her, however, proved fruitless. In time, they relented.

On May 18, 1811, in a chapel filled with the first families of New England (including some who would one day become Catholic themselves), Allen professed her vows as a Religious Hospitaller of St. Joseph. For the next eight years, the first known woman from New England to become a Catholic nun served at the order's hospital, Hôtel-Dieu, in Montreal. There, she contracted lung disease, which ended her life at the age of 34 in 1819.

"I have here in my hand . . . a list of names that were made known to the Secretary of State as being members of the Communist Party and who nevertheless are still working and shaping policy in the State Department."

With those words, spoken in a 1950 speech in Wheeling, West Virginia, Senator Joseph McCarthy embarked on a path that would make him the most reviled politician in America. At the time, however, McCarthy only believed the speech would make him famous and, perhaps, do some good.

Born in Wisconsin on **November 14, 1908,** McCarthy came from humble Irish Catholic stock. His father was a farmer. One brother worked in a factory; another drove a truck. McCarthy himself dropped out of school at age 14 and didn't return for six years. But after graduating from high school at age 21, his star rose fast. By 1935, McCarthy had earned a law degree. Four years later, he had a judgeship, and in 1942, he held an officer's commission in the U.S. Marine Corps.

After World War II, several well-told fibs about his military record combined with old-fashioned dirty campaigning won McCarthy a U.S. Senate seat from Wisconsin. He took office in 1947. Three unremarkable years followed. Then, in 1950, McCarthy delivered his infamous speech.

For the next four years, McCarthy helped lead a series of sensational, controversial, free-wheeling U.S. Senate subcommittee investigations focused on the presence of communists in America's government. Although the public initially cheered the investigations (and McCarthy), the senator's penchant for playing fast and loose with the facts soon got him into trouble. Moreover, McCarthy's grandstanding compromised the investigations, ultimately causing them to produce more heat than light. Fed up with his demagoguery and bullying, the Senate censured McCarthy in 1954. His approval ratings tanked.

Decades later, decoded Soviet intelligence revealed that communist infiltration of the U.S. government was no figment of McCarthy's imagination. But McCarthy didn't live to see that day. With his reputation lost, he turned to heavy drinking, dying at age 48, in 1957.

November 15: THE CATHOLIC SUFFRAGETTE

Lucy Burns had money. She also had a father committed to giving his sons and daughters an equally rigorous education. Those were two advantages few Irish Catholic women in early twentieth-century New York could claim, and Burns made the most of them, studying at Columbia, Vassar, and Yale, before leaving for Europe in 1906. There, the 27-year-old Burns studied German at the Universities of Bonn and Berlin and literature at Oxford University.

In England, Burns' studies fell by the wayside when she became involved in the women's suffrage movement. Along with her fellow American, Alice Paul, she picketed, preached on street corners, and endured hunger strikes in English prisons. Eventually, Burns and Paul decided they needed to do the same at home and returned to America in 1912, to help the National American Woman Suffrage Association (NAWSA). Two years later, strategic differences led Burns and Paul to break away from the group and form what became the National Women's Party (NWP).

For the next six years, Burns organized political protests and coordinated her organization's publicity and education campaigns. She also went to jail—repeatedly. Arrested in both June and September of 1917, Burns headed back to jail that November to serve six months in the rat-infested Occoquan Workhouse, in Washington, D.C.

Five days into her sentence, on **November 15, 1917,** Burns endured what history calls her "Night of Terror." After brutally beating Burns, prison guards handcuffed her hands above her head, stripped her naked, and left her for the night. The following morning, Burns and her fellow prisoners began a hunger strike. It lasted three days, only ending when five guards held Burns down and forcibly fed her through a tube.

Before women received the vote in 1920, Burns would spend more time in jail than any other American suffragette. As soon as the vote was won, though, an exhausted Burns walked away from the women's movement. She spent the rest of her life raising an orphaned niece and assisting the Catholic Church. She died in Brooklyn in 1966.

Goodwife "Goody" Ann Glover was the last "witch" hung in Boston. Her real crime, however, wasn't witchcraft; it was being an Irish Catholic.

During the 1650s, Glover and her husband numbered among the 50,000 Catholics that Oliver Cromwell arrested and sold into indentured servitude when he occupied Ireland. Shipped to Barbados, the couple lived a quiet life until Ann's husband refused to relinquish his Catholic faith. He was executed, and his wife and daughter came to America.

The women arrived in Boston sometime after 1680, and found work in John Goodwin's house. The trouble began in 1688, when Glover's daughter fought with her employer's children over some trivial matter. Soon afterwards, four of the five young Goodwins began experiencing seemingly uncontrollable fits. Their father called a doctor, who concluded that "nothing but a hellish witchcraft could be the origin of these maladies." Glover was subsequently arrested, imprisoned, and brought to trial.

The influential Puritan minister Reverend Cotton Mather led the prosecution. Describing Glover as "a scandalous old Irishwoman, very poor, a Roman Catholic, and obstinate in idolatry," Mather lamented that the defendant couldn't even say the Lord's Prayer. That was false. She could say it, just not in English; in Gaelic and Latin, she managed fine. But that, combined with her inability to defend herself in any language other than Gaelic only seemed further proof of "devilry" to the court.

Quickly found guilty, Glover was hung at Boston Neck on **November 16, 1688**. According to one eyewitness:

> *Before her executioners she was bold and impudent, making to forgive her accusers and those who put her off. She predicted that her death would not relieve the children, saying that it was not she that afflicted them. She did not renounce her Catholic faith, and her prediction that her death would not relieve the Goodwin children was true.*

Four years later, Cotton Mather helped lead the charge against the "witches" of Salem. Three hundred years later, Boston declared Glover's death unjust and designated November 16, as "Goody Glover Day."

November 17: THE LITTLE PIANO GIRL OF
EAST LIBERTY

In November 1976, Mary Lou Williams' calendar was packed. In one week's time, her manager had scheduled the jazz legend to play New York's The Cookery club, give a benefit concert at the Waldorf Astoria, and perform at a gala fund-raiser for the famed Town Hall. She also needed to deliver two lectures at New York University. Nevertheless, in the midst of all that, on the afternoon of **November 17, 1976,** Williams still found time to visit Our Lady of Victory Catholic School in the Bronx and put on an impromptu concert for the children.

Williams loved playing for children. She was only a child herself when she first ventured out of her East Liberty neighborhood in 1917, to play in Pittsburgh's jazz clubs. An instant sensation, locals called the seven-year-old performer "The Little Piano Girl of East Liberty."

After that, success came fast, first on the famed Orpheum Circuit at age 14, then with Duke Ellington's band at age 15. She later moved on to partnering with jazz greats such as Earl Hines, Benny Goodman, Dizzy Gillespie, and Thelonious Monk.

After her 1942 divorce from saxophonist John Williams, Williams moved to New York, where she performed in downtown clubs and hosted a radio show. In the mid-1950s, she began contemplating retirement. That changed when Dizzy Gillespie introduced her to Father John Crowley, a jazz-loving Catholic priest who advised Williams to "offer up her playing for others." Williams liked the advice. She liked Father Crowley's Church too, and in 1956, became Catholic.

For the remainder of her career, with an Irish-American priest (Father Peter F. O'Brien, S.J.) as her manager, Williams devoted her talents to the Church. She composed hymns, Masses, and other religious works; organized youth choirs; and regularly played concerts in inner-city Catholic schools. She also set up a private charity for musicians who struggled with substance abuse.

Before her death in 1981, Williams explained her love affair with music and the Church, saying, "I am praying through my fingers when I play."

For as long as Rose Philippine Duchesne could remember, she had dreamed of evangelizing Native Americans. She dreamed of it as a schoolgirl in pre-Revolutionary France. She dreamed of it after the Reign of Terror drove her out of the Visitandine convent in which she began her religious life. And she continued dreaming of it after the Napoleonic Wars, while she served as novice mistress for the Society of the Sacred Heart in Paris.

At last, in 1817, Duchesne found a way to make her dream a reality. That year, Bishop Louis William DuBourg of the Diocese of Louisiana and the Two Floridas visited Duchesne's convent. After she met with him and heard his stories of the American frontier, she begged her Superior for permission to return with DuBourg to St. Louis. She agreed, and Mother Duchesne sailed for America in 1818 with four other sisters.

It took 70 days to make the crossing. It took several weeks more to travel to St. Louis. And when Duchesne arrived, she found precious few Native Americans. Most had already moved westward. Forced to set aside her dream of serving America's Indians yet again, Duchesne focused on building a convent for her order and a school for Catholic children. Within a year, the school opened. Within 10 years, the Society of the Sacred Heart established more than a half-dozen other schools across Missouri, Louisiana, and Kansas.

Not until 1841, however, did the 72-year-old Duchesne finally receive permission to travel to Kansas and open a school for Potawatomi children. Unfortunately, by then Duchesne's advanced years made it difficult for her to learn the Potawatomi's language and impossible for her to teach them. So, while the younger sisters spent their days in the classroom, Duchesne spent her days in the chapel. The children called her *Quahkah-kanumad* or "Woman Who Prays Always."

After only one year in Kansas, Duchesne's superiors called her back to St. Louis. She died 10 years later, on **November 18, 1852**. She became Saint Rose Philippine Duchesne in 1988.

Frederick Walz owned property in New York. Walz also paid property taxes in New York. And Walz didn't understand why the churches in New York didn't pay property taxes too. As he saw it, his taxes subsidized their religious activity, thus violating the separation of Church and State mandated by the First Amendment.

To stop what he believed was unconstitutional entanglement, Walz filed suit in the late 1960s. The New York Supreme Court dismissed the case on summary judgment, but Walz appealed, and on **November 19, 1969,** *Walz v. Tax Commission of the City of New York* came before the U.S. Supreme Court.

The verdict came five months later. Eight justices agreed with the New York courts that no First Amendment violation existed. One justice agreed with Walz.

Writing for the majority, Chief Justice Warren Burger noted that in granting the exemption, the government gave no preferential treatment to any one religion or denomination: Catholics, Baptists, and Jews received the same exemption. Moreover, he explained, the government extended the exemption to churches as well as other non-profit groups, such as hospitals and schools, because: "The State has an affirmative policy that considers these groups as beneficial and stabilizing influences in community life and finds this classification useful, desirable, and in the public interest."

Burger further noted that the very tax exemptions to which Walz objected actually made possible the separation of Church and State that Walz wanted maintained. States avoiding a relationship with Churches by not taxing them could not constitute entanglement; religious organizations subsidizing the State with their taxes most definitely could.

Near the end of his opinion, Burger delivered one final shot, writing:

> *No one has ever suggested that tax exemption has converted libraries, art galleries, or hospitals into arms of the state or put employees "on the public payroll." There is no genuine nexus between tax exemption and establishment of religion. As Mr. Justice Holmes commented in a related context, "a page of history is worth a volume of logic."*

In the nineteenth century, the Catholic Church had the Kenrick brothers—Archbishops Francis and Peter. In the twentieth century, the Church had the Lawler brothers—Thomas and Ronald.

Thomas was born first, in 1920. Ronald (christened "David") came six years later. As young men, both discerned a religious vocation with the Capuchins, but only the younger Lawler continued his formation. Thomas entered the military instead.

In 1951, their paths further diverged. Ronald became a Capuchin priest, and the newly married Thomas became a spy. For the next 26 years, during the height of the Cold War, Thomas served his country in the Central Intelligence Agency (CIA), while Father Ronald served the Church. Over the course of the younger Lawler's career, he taught in more than a half-dozen universities and seminaries—including Oxford University, The Catholic University of America, and the Pontifical College Josephinum. He also mentored future archbishops such as Philadelphia's Charles Chaput and Boston's Seán Patrick Cardinal O'Malley.

While Thomas could never tell friends about his day job, he could talk about the work he did after hours: editing the Ancient Christian Writers series and co-authoring *The Teaching of Christ,* with his brother Father Ronald and then-Bishop Donald Wuerl of Pittsburgh. Published in 1976, the bestselling catechism became a touchstone for Catholics in the midst of post-Vatican II confusion.

Thomas retired from the CIA in 1977 with the Intelligence Medal of Merit. He then devoted himself to serving the Church as the first director of Religious Education for the Diocese of Arlington. In 2001, when Thomas received the *Pro Ecclesia et Pontifice* award, he became the only man in history to win both America's highest award for spying and the Church's highest award for laymen.

The same year that Thomas retired, Ronald founded the Fellowship of Catholic Scholars to preserve faithful Catholic voices in academia. He too later went to work for a diocese—Pittsburgh—and served as its longtime catechetical consultant.

In 2003, Ronald lost his life to cancer. Thomas followed two years later, dying on **November 20, 2005.**

In 1864, Father Peter Whelan spent four months in hell. And he did it by choice.

Born in Ireland in 1802, and ordained a priest for the Diocese of Charleston on **November 21, 1830,** Whelan spent years riding the missionary circuit in North Carolina, before founding Georgia's first Catholic Church in 1837. Twenty-four years later, when the American Civil War began, Whelan was in Savannah, working as vicar-general for the newly established Georgia diocese.

In late 1861, the 60-year-old Whelan went to nearby Fort Pulaski to serve as chaplain. He was there when Fort Pulaski fell the following April. Union officers offered Whelan his freedom, but he refused and went to New York City as a prisoner with his men. For months, he ministered to the imprisoned troops, saying Mass daily and securing food, medicine, and clothing from local Catholics.

In August, the soldiers went home in a prisoner exchange, and Whelan resumed his duties in Savannah. Then, in 1864, Father William Hamilton came calling.

Hamilton had just accidentally happened upon Georgia's Andersonville Prison, where he found 30,000 Union soldiers crowded into a camp built for 6,000. The men had no shelter, no bedding, and only one creek for both their drinking water and a latrine. Violence, vermin, and disease were everywhere.

When Hamilton reached Savannah, he told Bishop Augustin Verot that he'd witnessed hell on earth and begged him to send a priest to the prison. Verot asked Whelan to go, and Whelan agreed. He arrived in June, right along with the summer heat. Three times younger priests came to join him. None stayed longer than two weeks. Whelan, however, remained until the prison was almost empty, caring for the sick, praying for the dying, and going into debt to buy bread for starving men.

In 1871, Whelan died from tuberculosis contracted in the prison. It's said his funeral procession stretched for miles, with men from both the North and the South coming to mourn the man they called the "Angel of Andersonville."

As a boy, Carlos Rodríguez contemplated becoming a priest. He also contemplated marrying and having a large family. But neither came to pass.

Born in Caguas, Puerto Rico, on **November 22, 1918,** Rodríguez spent most of his childhood crowded into his grandmother's home with his parents and four siblings. From his grandmother, Rodríguez learned the habits of deep devotion. From his parents, he learned the joys of family life. Both vocations attracted him, but when he was still an adolescent, a dog attacked one of his baby cousins. Rodríguez jumped in to save the baby, only to have the dog turn on him. The encounter left Rodríguez severely wounded and possibly contributed to the intestinal problems that plagued him throughout his life.

Too sick to marry or enter religious life, Rodríguez chose to see his illness as an opportunity to serve the Church with singular devotion as a layperson. He found work as an office clerk, but dedicated nearly all his free time (and salary) to catechizing Puerto Rico's young people. Rodríguez's many and varied catechetical endeavors included self-publishing a magazine, *Liturgy and Christian Culture;* organizing campus ministry programs at the University of Puerto Rico; and teaching the catechism to Puerto Rican school children.

An ardent supporter of liturgical renewal, Rodríguez also spent countless hours researching lost traditions and encouraging their recovery. Of all those traditions, the one he most valued was the Easter Vigil, which Pope Pius XII reintroduced in 1951. Rodríguez's personal motto was *Vivimos para esa noche* ("We live for that night")—"that night" meaning the Easter Vigil.

Summing up "the why" behind his work, Rodríguez wrote, "We need Catholics who are alert to the present moment, Catholics who know how to nourish themselves in the past but whose eyes are fixed on the future."

Cancer took Rodríguez's life in 1963. Thirty-eight years later, in 2001, he became the first North American layman beatified by the Catholic Church.

November 23: THE ITALIAN PROBLEM

As the nineteenth century drew to a close, the American bishops had what they called an "Italian problem."

In 1880, only 44,000 Italian immigrants lived in the United States. By 1900, that number had risen tenfold, to more than 484,000. Within another decade, it would multiply yet again to 2.1 million. The bishops' problem, however, had less to do with numbers than it did with the fact that most Italians spoke little to no English and came to America proclaiming the anti-clerical opinions that dominated late-nineteenth-century Italy. Few attended church, their children ran wild in the streets, and crime and poverty plagued their neighborhoods.

The American clergy, largely made up of Irish-Americans, were confounded. They simply didn't know how to reach Italian Catholics.

But they knew someone who did.

As early as 1884, American bishops began pleading with Father John Bosco to send Salesian priests to the United States. Bosco's order had made tremendous progress working with disadvantaged young people in Italy, and the American bishops trusted the Salesians would make similar progress in New York, Boston, and San Francisco. Bosco believed the same. He just didn't have priests to spare, and asked the bishops to wait.

Ultimately, the bishops waited 12 years. Bosco died in 1888. Eight years later, on **November 23, 1896,** his order signed a contract with Archbishop Patrick Riordan to send four Salesians to San Francisco. The priests arrived in early 1897. They did not receive a warm welcome.

Instead, as the Salesians walked through the streets, Italian children threw rocks at them. While the Salesians slept, grown men defaced their churches and nailed obscene cartoons to the parish's doors. When they offered Mass, fewer than 10 people came.

History repeated itself two years later, when more Salesians arrived in New York. But in both cities, the order persevered and, in due course, thrived. By 1920, the Salesians had flourishing parishes and schools in most major American metropolitan centers. And the bishops no longer had an Italian problem.

November 24: THE STANDARD-BEARER OF CONSERVATISM

"In the United States at this time Liberalism is not only the dominant but even the sole intellectual tradition," wrote the literary critic Lionel Trilling in 1950. "For it is the plain fact that there are no conservative or reactionary ideas in general circulation."

One year later, William F. Buckley, Jr., stepped onto the American intellectual scene with his debut book *God and Man at Yale*. He then spent the rest of his life upending Trilling's thesis.

Born into a large, wealthy Catholic family in New York City on **November 24, 1925,** Buckley traveled the world with his parents as a boy, and served in the U.S. Army during World War II. After the war, he studied at Yale University, before embarking on a two-year tour of duty with the Central Intelligence Agency (CIA).

Buckley was still with the CIA when his critique of Yale's liberal intellectual environment went to press. Few alumni and even fewer faculty appreciated the book, but their vocal displeasure thrust Buckley into the limelight. It also did wonders for sales.

Four years later, with a growing reputation for his erudite commentary and polysyllabic vocabulary, Buckley launched the magazine *National Review*. After that, Buckley authored another 55 books (both fiction and non-fiction). He also delivered thousands of lectures, penned more than 4.5 million words for his syndicated column, and hosted the PBS show *Firing Line* for 33 years. It was an impressive body of work. But none of it had the same game-changing effect on America's political landscape as *National Review*.

Buckley's magazine ultimately turned Trilling's assessment of Liberalism on its head, bringing conservative political thought into the American mainstream and helping form a generation of thinkers, leaders, and voters. It also helped set the agenda for conservative policies and priorities, giving shape to the modern Conservative Movement.

Beyond politics, Buckley loved sailing, the Catholic Church, the Latin Mass, his son, Christopher, and his wife of 57 years, Pat. She died in 2007. He died one year later. His magazine survives him still.

November 25: THE KLAN'S SECOND COMING

In 1915, William J. Simmons went to the movies. *The Birth of a Nation*—
D. W. Griffith's American Civil War epic—was playing. It didn't disappoint. Simmons found the film entertaining. More problematical, he
found it inspiring. The Alabama native left the theater filled with resolve:
he would resurrect the Ku Klux Klan.

Forty years earlier, the original Klan had died out, but Griffith's posi-
tive portrayal of the Klan convinced Simmons that it held the key to
keeping America "American." Only this time around, Simmons believed
the Klan needed to concern itself with more than just African-Americans.
He also wanted it to impede the rising influence of Catholics, Jews, and
immigrants.

After Simmons returned home from the movies, he found an old
Klan manual and started recruiting. Months later, on **November 25,
1915,** he and 15 others climbed Georgia's Stone Mountain and torched a
cross, just as the Klan did in *The Birth of a Nation*. It was Simmons' way
of announcing the Klan's rebirth.

After that, the Klan grew quickly, with its anti-Catholic, anti-
immigrant stance attracting perhaps more Northerners than Southern-
ers. By 1924, when the Klan defeated the Catholic Al Smith's presidential
nomination at the Democratic National Convention, it claimed nearly
5 million members.

Catholics, needless to say, were less than thrilled with the Klan's
agenda. In 1924, hundreds of students at the University of Notre Dame
rioted when the Klan held their annual convention in South Bend, Indiana. Around the same time, when the Klan successfully prevented Texas
public schools from hiring Catholic teachers and ousted Catholic officials from public office in California, Catholic bishops took to the press,
denouncing the group.

In the end, scandal did what rioting students and protesting bishops
couldn't. In the wake of a leading Klansman's 1925 murder conviction,
membership plummeted, and the second incarnation of the Ku Klux
Klan faded away. Like the South, it too promised to rise again. And it
did. But not before Simmons died in 1945.

The Catholics of Galveston, Texas, wanted a church. They also wanted a priest. For years, they had neither. First, the Mexican War for Independence cost them their Spanish priests. Then, the 1836 separation of Texas from Mexico cost the territory its two remaining missionaries.

For five years, the entire Republic of Texas went without both a bishop and clergy, while its churches fell into disrepair. Finally, in 1841, Father Jean-Marie (John) Odin arrived in Galveston from New Orleans. A year later, Odin would become Texas' first bishop and Vicar Apostolic of Texas. But before then, he worked with Galveston Catholics to build the island's first church. They completed the small wooden structure days before Odin's consecration and called it St. Mary's.

Within the year, though, Bishop Odin began planning for St. Mary's replacement. After enduring two hurricane seasons in Galveston, he recognized that the original St. Mary's wouldn't withstand the destructive storms that plagued Galveston Island.

Odin's designs for a new church inched closer to reality in 1845, when he secured 500,000 bricks from Belgium. When Galveston became a diocese, in 1847, Odin broke ground, with plans to build a cathedral inspired by Oxford University's King's College Chapel. Just one year later, on **November 26, 1848,** Odin dedicated the new St. Mary's as the first cathedral in Texas.

No building codes for hurricanes existed in 1848, but the cathedral's architect, Charles G. Bryant, did his best to build Odin a sturdy church. He largely succeeded. In 1900, St. Mary's was one of the few buildings in Galveston still standing after a hurricane blew through and left 6,000 people dead. It still stood 79 hurricane seasons later, when Pope John Paul II designated it as a basilica. In 2008, Hurricane Ike almost proved too much for St. Mary's, inflicting more than $1 million in damage. But after a lengthy restoration, the Mother Church of Texas and co-cathedral of the (renamed) Archdiocese of Galveston-Houston opened its doors on Easter Sunday 2014.

Today, it stands ready to withstand many more hurricane seasons to come.

November 27: THE RUSSIAN BARONESS

Catherine de Hueck Doherty never pulled any punches. One southern woman, disgusted by Doherty's civil rights work in 1940's Harlem, learned that the hard way. "You smell of the Negro," the woman told Doherty.

"And you stink of Hell," Doherty replied.

As a nobleman's daughter, Doherty was an unlikely champion of the oppressed. Russian born and raised, she entered into an arranged (and troubled) marriage with her cousin, Baron Boris de Hueck, in 1912, at the age of 15. Several years later, when the Russian Revolution began, the couple fled to England. In London, on **November 27, 1919,** the young baroness became Catholic. She'd long been attracted to the Catholic Faith, but conversion only became possible once she left Russia.

From England, the impoverished de Huecks moved to Toronto, where Catherine gave birth to a son. Although the family's financial situation improved, the marriage did not, and as the Great Depression began, the de Huecks' marriage ended in abuse, divorce, and (eventually) annulment. For Catherine, however, the divorce became an opportunity to follow the growing desire of her heart: to sell everything she had and work with the poor.

In the 1930s, that desire brought her to Harlem, where she established a Friendship House, an interracial ministry committed to social justice. Eventually, more than a dozen Friendship Houses would operate across North America. To help fund her ministry, the single mother wrote and lectured. In the course of her work, she met and married the American newspaperman Eddie Doherty.

In both her work with Friendship House and Madonna House—the Catholic community she later established in Canada—Doherty followed what she described as her "Little Mandate"—a rule of life that demanded preaching the Gospel with simplicity and uncompromising directness. She also taught those who worked with her to abide by "the duty of the moment," meaning "what you should be doing at any given time, in whatever place God has put you."

Doherty died in 1985. Her cause for canonization opened in 2000.

In 1844, Bishop Andrew Byrne arrived in Arkansas via horseback. Waiting for him, he found one Catholic church, one Catholic school, a few Sisters of Loretto, and maybe 700 Catholics.

Most of those families were remnants of the days when France and Spain governed the Arkansas territory and Catholics dominated the region. Not until after the Louisiana Purchase, in 1803, did Protestants from the American North come to Arkansas. But by **November 28, 1843,** when Little Rock became a diocese, the number of Arkansas' Protestants dwarfed the number of Catholics.

Little Rock's first bishop wanted to change that. As Byrne saw it, Arkansas started off as Catholic country, and, with a little work, it could become Catholic once more.

After deciding that immigration offered him the best prospects for increasing his flock, Byrne purchased 640 acres near Fort Smith, Arkansas. He then persuaded 300 men and women to leave Ireland and build a Catholic colony on the newly acquired land.

Before the Irish sailed, Byrne built the diocese's first cathedral, the Cathedral of St. Andrew, completing it in 1845, and established St. Andrew's College at Fort Smith in 1849. Later that same year, the colonists arrived. Unfortunately, their numbers didn't approach 300. Some had died aboard ship and others decided to settle in St. Louis instead. Byrne recognized it as a setback, but he didn't despair. His prospects even seemed to brighten in 1851, when the Sisters of Mercy arrived to start a school.

Then, the Know-Nothings got to work. In 1854, they burned down the parish Byrne built in Helena, Arkansas. Later, they tried to invalidate his land purchases in Fort Smith. After that, Byrne couldn't convince any more Irish immigrants to join him, even though he traveled to Ireland twice to personally make the case. As the American Civil War approached and troops took over St. Andrew's College, Byrne recognized he wouldn't live to see his dream realized.

Byrne died in 1862, leaving the work of building the Church in Arkansas to future generations.

Dorothy Day defended the Faith, served the poor, campaigned for justice, and fasted for peace. For that, her admirers called her a saint.

"Don't," was her reply. "I don't want to be dismissed so easily."

Soon, she may not have a say in the matter.

Born in New York in 1897, Day grew up in California and Illinois. After spending two years at the University of Illinois at Champaign-Urbana, she dropped out and moved to New York to work as a journalist. In the pages of radical left-wing papers, the equally radical Day advocated for socialism, free love, and anarchy. When the Bolsheviks took over Russia in 1917, she celebrated. And when she found herself pregnant and single, she had an abortion.

Gradually, however, Day found herself drawn as powerfully to God as she was to progressive ideologies. While living in New York in the early 1920s, she started sneaking into a Catholic church to pray. When her work took her to New Orleans, she went regularly to Benediction services at St. Louis Cathedral. And when she gave birth to a baby girl in 1926—after believing her abortion had left her barren—she had the baby baptized Catholic.

"I did not want my child to flounder as I had often floundered," she explained. "I wanted to believe, and I wanted my child to believe, and if belonging to a Church would give her so inestimable a grace as faith in God, and the companionable love of the Saints, then the thing to do was to have her baptized a Catholic."

Day followed her daughter into the Church in December 1927. In the years that followed, she allowed the Gospel to transform both her life and politics. She believed and practiced the Faith in all its fullness, embracing the Church's teachings on faith and morals, and heeding the Gospel's call to serve the poor. She did the latter, in large part, through the Catholic Worker movement she helped found.

Dorothy Day died on **November 29, 1980**. Today, her official cause for canonization is moving forward . . . whether she likes it or not.

In 1539, New Spain buzzed with rumors. Explorers had reported that far to the north, across hundreds of miles of desert, stood seven cities built entirely of gold. Hoping the rumors might prove true, Francisco Vázquez de Coronado decided to investigate.

Before Coronado and his expedition departed, Father Juan de Padilla, the guardian of the local Franciscan monastery, approached him. The priest doubted the expedition would find cities of gold, but he knew it would find people who needed the Gospel, and he wanted to accompany the expedition.

Coronado agreed. The following February, they set out, heading north into present-day New Mexico. Coronado soon realized that the seven cities were a myth, but decided to continue exploring the region anyhow.

About a year later, the party met a Native American who they named "the Turk." The Turk told them of his home in Quivera, a land rich with gold, and offered to lead the Spaniards there. In truth, he only wanted to get home . . . or lead Coronado to his death. No one quite knows. Regardless, Coronado took the bait and went looking for Quivera. He found present-day Kansas instead. He was less than pleased.

Coronado left for home in 1542, and Padilla accompanied him as far as New Mexico. Padilla then decided he wanted to remain in the north as a missionary. With two companions, he headed back to Kansas.

Although accounts differ, it's widely believed that for almost two years, Padilla lived among the Wichita. In late 1544, however, he decided other tribes needed to hear the Gospel too and left. He didn't get far.

Just days into his journey, on **November 30, 1544,** a party of Native Americans stopped him and his companions. Some sources say the natives were Wichita, angry over his departure. Others say they were Kansa, suspicious of their enemies' "medicine man." Either way, his companions escaped; Padilla did not. Somewhere on the plains of Kansas, he became America's first Catholic martyr. His body was never found.

December

December 1: THE SPECTRE OF CAHENSLYISM

At a **December 1, 1883,** meeting in Rome, Baltimore's Archbishop James Cardinal Gibbons sang the praises of the St. Raphael Society. Those were the last kind words the cardinal ever uttered about the group.

Soon after returning to America, Gibbons entered into a decades-long battle with the St. Raphael Society and its founder, the German layman Peter Cahensly. That battle divided the American hierarchy, pitted immigrant Catholic communities against one another, and gave Rome no end of trouble.

The whole situation, however, began innocently enough. In 1871, Cahensly organized the St. Raphael Society to assist German Catholics who immigrated to America. It carried out that mission to almost universal applause until 1883, when Cahensly visited the United States and didn't like what he found.

According to Cahensly, the heavily Irish-American episcopacy neglected Germans immigrants and didn't provide them with sufficient numbers of German-speaking priests. As a result, he contended, 16 million immigrants had left the Church. To solve the problem, he proposed greater autonomy for immigrant communities and asked Rome to appoint German bishops for German-Americans. In due course, similar pleas came from Polish-Americans and Italian-Americans.

Several American bishops sided with Cahensly. Most, however, found his allegations outrageous and argued that dividing up the Church into ethnic enclaves would weaken the Faith and hurt Catholic immigrants who needed to adjust to life in America.

Rome tended to agree with those arguments, but because of delicate diplomatic relations with Germany, didn't say so as directly as they might have. That allowed the controversy to needlessly drag on in both the press and American parishes. Moreover, Cahensly would not be put off by the Vatican's gentle rebuffs; he continued asking for German bishops for German-Americans until as late as 1910. It also didn't help that bishops like Gibbons and Saint Paul, Minnesota's John Ireland found Cahenslyism a convenient distraction from the much more real problem of Americanism.

Nevertheless, as the nineteenth century ended, the spectre of Cahenslyism slowly faded away, ending for good with Cahensly's death in 1923.

December 2: FROM THE EAST

In 1880, a few hundred Greek Catholics lived in Pennsylvania. A century later, hundreds of thousands of Byzantine Catholics, Maronite Catholics, and other Eastern Rite Catholics lived across America in cities big and small.

At first, the promise of work brought those Catholics to the United States. As the twentieth century progressed, however, jobs became a secondary motivation. Far more often, civil war, revolution, and persecution at the hands of their countries' communist governments drove Eastern Rite Catholics westward.

Once in America, they found themselves enduring a different kind of persecution, as Latin Rite Catholics struggled to accept Catholics with traditions different from their own. Many also bore the cross of remembrance, unable to forget what they endured in their homelands. Other Eastern Rite Catholics suffered in spirit, as their friends and relatives living in the Soviet Union's shadow continued to endure persecution for their faith.

On **December 2, 1983,** Pope John Paul II acknowledged those struggles. He also affirmed the richness Eastern Catholics brought to the Church in America and the importance of preserving their traditions in the New World. During their bishops' *ad limina* visit to Rome, he said:

> As you come in pilgrimage to this Apostolic See, you bring with you the hopes and joys, the problems and aspirations of your beloved people. All of these aspects of life are linked to some extent with the origin of your ancestors, the conditions of their emigration and the reality of your present situation. Your history, which I honor today, is one that has been dominated by that Christian hope which finds its source in the Paschal Mystery of the death and Resurrection of our Lord Jesus Christ . . .

The pope concluded his remarks, saying, "I pray for the success of your devoted efforts to rebuild the fabric of unity with your Christian brethren who, like you, are mindful of the Lord's desire for perfect unity in faith and love."

December 3: EXPOSED TO THE LIGHT

In June 1953, Bishop Vincent Waters had strong words for Catholics in the Diocese of Raleigh. Two months earlier, the bishop had forbidden parishes in his diocese (which then encompassed the entirety of North Carolina) from discriminating against African-Americans. Neither people nor priests, he told them, could prohibit black Catholics from worshipping in their parishes; nor could they demand that blacks sit or kneel in designated areas.

The offenders ignored him. So, Waters tried again, writing a letter and ordering every pastor to read it from the pulpit on Sunday, June 21, 1953.

In the letter, Waters warned his flock that Satan uses the "spirit of division" to wage war on God's people. He then stated, in all capital letters:

> *THERE IS NO SEGREGATION OF RACES TO BE TOLERATED IN ANY CATHOLIC CHURCH IN THE DIOCESE OF RALEIGH. THE PASTORS ARE CHARGED WITH THE CARRYING OUT OF THIS TEACHING AND SHALL TOLERATE NOTHING TO THE CONTRARY.*

He continued in normal typeface:

> *I am not unmindful, as a Southerner, of the force of this virus of prejudice among some persons in the South, as well as in the North. I know, however, that there is a cure for this virus and that is, our Faith . . . I revolt against our children being infected with this virus, when men and women of goodwill everywhere can preserve them from it. The virus will not die out of itself, it has to be killed by being exposed to the light of Faith.*

Many Catholics objected to Waters' letter, and at some parishes, angry mobs showed up when the bishop came to discuss his decision. Nevertheless, they obeyed. In the fall of 1953, one year before *Brown v. Board of Education* desegregated America's classrooms, North Carolina's Catholics desegregated both their parishes and their schools.

Waters, for his part, lived long enough to see the restoration of full civil rights to African-Americans in the South. He passed away at age 70, on **December 3, 1974.**

In October 1869, the recently widowed Episcopal minister James Kent Stone wrote his mother. He had news to share: he was entering the Catholic Church.

"I am as sure that the Roman Catholic Church is the true Church of Our Lord Jesus Christ as I am that there is a God in heaven," he explained. "He has called me . . . Can I refuse to go? Nay, I have given up everything for His sake—everything."

Stone was wrong. He'd given up much to become Catholic: his position as president of Hobart College, his reputation as a top Episcopal scholar, and the good opinion of his prominent Boston family. But he hadn't given up everything. He still had two daughters.

Soon, God asked for that sacrifice as well.

After his conversion, Stone felt called to the priesthood. At the time, however, the Church didn't make exceptions for former Episcopal ministers. Stone couldn't be both priest and father. He had to choose. He agonized over the decision, but in the end, he entrusted his girls to a California family and became a priest in 1872.

Stone spent the next five decades preaching missions across the Americas, first for the Paulists and later for the Passionists. In the process, he became one of the most famous Catholic apologists of his day. Even President Chester A. Arthur came to hear the preaching of the man who, as a **December 4, 1926,** essay in *The Tablet* noted, was celebrated as America's John Henry Newman.

Stone never forgot his daughters, though, and once wept when a little girl hugged him. He had promised the adoptive parents he would never contact the children, but as an old man, he broke down and sent a letter. When it came back unopened, he begged the Virgin Mary for some sign that they forgave him. In 1921, he received that sign when his youngest daughter wrote, inviting him to visit. He left for California that fall and spent several happy weeks with his girls. While there, he fell ill. He died holding their hands.

December 5: THE MILL HILL MISSIONARIES

Archbishop Martin John Spalding had a problem.

In the immediate aftermath of the American Civil War, hundreds of thousands of former slaves had moved north. Few could read or write and the religious formation of most had been negligible. After assessing the situation, the Tenth Provincial Council of Baltimore decreed in 1869 that all Catholic bishops in the province must establish schools and missions for African-Americans in their dioceses. As Archbishop of Baltimore, Spalding led the charge for that decree. But once it passed, he didn't know how he could implement it in his own see. He lacked both money and priests.

Recognizing that the American bishops couldn't address the problem on their own, Spalding began writing to missionary societies in Europe. After two years of searching, he found a society willing to help: the Mill Hill Missionaries of London.

On **December 5, 1871,** four Mill Hill missionary priests (who called themselves "the Josephites") arrived in Baltimore with their order's founder, Father Herbert Vaughan. At Spalding's request, they took over St. Francis Xavier Church, which housed the oldest African-American Catholic congregation in the country.

Almost from the start, problems plagued their work.

At first, disputes arose over what building the missionaries were supposed to use. Then, the religious order that had formerly occupied the building demanded that the Josephites assume their debts. Before they could resolve the disagreements, Spalding died. After that, the missionaries' particular style of preaching and celebrating the liturgy—which they adopted to appeal to African-Americans' more Protestant sensibilities—caused trouble with their fellow Catholics. Finally, the priests clashed with their London house.

In 1893, the American Mill Hill missionaries resolved the latter difficulty by separating from their European brothers. That year, they formed a new order: the St. Joseph Society of the Sacred Heart. Although the decades that followed brought new troubles (most often in the form of entrenched prejudice against African-Americans), the order survived and grew. Today, the Society—still known as the Josephites—continues to serve African-American Catholics in Maryland, Virginia, and beyond.

December 6: BEAUTIFUL PATHS

Joyce Kilmer had a wife and five children. As a father, he didn't have to go to war. But he went anyway, enlisting in April 1917, just days after President Woodrow Wilson asked Congress for "a war to end all wars."

Born on **December 6, 1886,** Kilmer was only 30 when he left for the Western Front, but he already enjoyed a reputation as one of America's preeminent writers. Most knew him for his poetry, especially his 1913 poem, "Trees" (*"I think that I shall never see/ A poem lovely as a tree."*). He also, however, was a popular lecturer and essayist, who wrote regularly for the *New York Times Sunday Magazine.*

Four years before Kilmer enlisted, both he and his wife had converted to the Catholic Faith. Raised as an Episcopalian, Kilmer had long contemplated conversion; he agreed with the Church on questions of aesthetics and ethics, and, at least intellectually, was convinced of her claims. What his head knew, however, his heart just couldn't believe. That frustrated Kilmer, who wanted to believe. So, he began visiting a Catholic church every morning to ask God for the gift of faith. When his infant daughter Rose contracted polio in 1912, faith came at last. Conversion followed.

"Her lifeless hands led me," Kilmer explained. "I think her tiny feet know beautiful paths."

Kilmer left for France in October 1917. Six months later, his coolness under fire and willingness to take on dangerous missions earned him a promotion to military intelligence. That same daring led to his death. While out on a reconnaissance mission, a sniper's bullet pierced his brain, ending his life in July 1918.

Before he left on that fatal mission, Kilmer wrote another poem, "Prayer of a Soldier in France." It began with a meditation: *My shoulders ache beneath my pack/(Lie easier, Cross, upon His back).* And ended with a prayer: *Lord, Thou didst suffer more for me /Than all the hosts of land and sea./So let me render back again/This millionth of Thy gift. Amen.*

December 7: AN HONORARY AMERICAN

Gilbert du Motier, Marquis de Lafayette was determined to fight in the American Revolution. But fate seemed equally determined to stop him.

In 1775, the 18-year-old Catholic learned about America's bid for independence. The colonists' struggle captured Lafayette's young heart, and he longed to join the fight. Lafayette knew, however, that King Louis XVI would object: the Marquis was one of the wealthiest noblemen in France and husband to the king's cousin.

Nevertheless, the following winter, Lafayette met with the American Silas Deane, who'd come to Paris to enlist French support. Deane promised Lafayette that if he went to America, he could fight as a major general. On **December 7, 1776,** the two contracted an agreement, and Lafayette prepared to depart.

Right away, a problem of financing arose. Lafayette learned that the Continental Congress couldn't pay for his passage. Undeterred, Lafayette hired his own ship. Next, British spies learned of his plan, and the British ambassador seized Lafayette's ship. So the Marquis secured passage on another. Finally, the king found out about Lafayette and threatened him with prison if he sailed. Lafayette sailed anyway, sneaking aboard ship dressed as a woman. He also bought the ship's cargo, so the captain wouldn't need to stop along the way.

At last, in June 1777, Lafayette landed in America. He didn't, however, receive the welcome he expected. The Continental Congress, weary of "French glory seekers," refused him his commission. Only when Lafayette offered to fight for free (and the Congress learned of his wealth), did the commission come through.

Over the next four years, Lafayette became one of General George Washington's most trusted commanders. He led men to victory in battle and secured both troops and money from France, more than earning the honorary citizenship granted to him at the war's end. He left America a hero in 1781, and returned to France to work for liberty there.

When Lafayette died, in 1834, his son sprinkled dirt from Bunker Hill over his grave. To this day, an American flag flies above his tomb.

December 8: THE HOUSE ON HUMILITY STREET

Trouble was brewing in Italy. The country's government, as part of its ongoing war against the Vatican, had decided that the American Catholic seminary on Humility Street in Rome belonged to the State. In early 1884, they moved to repossess the building and prepare it for sale.

Immediately, the American bishops objected. They attempted to explain to the Italians that the seminary was theirs, not the Vatican's. While Pope Pius IX did buy the building for $42,000 in 1859, he didn't buy it for himself. The pope had considered it of the utmost importance that Americans have a seminary college in Rome. The seminary building—an early seventeenth-century convent known as *Casa Santa Maria*—was his contribution to the endeavor.

The bishops also explained to the Italians that they had spent far more than $42,000 repairing the damage done by the building's former tenants—French soldiers—and as of **December 8, 1859,** the day the seminary officially opened, had managed the building without any help from the Holy See.

In short, they told the Italians, the building is ours, and you can't have it.

When the Italians didn't listen, New York's Archbishop John Cardinal McCloskey wrote to President Chester A. Arthur, asking him to intervene. At the end of the letter, McCloskey noted the urgency of the case and requested that all further "communications be by cable." There was no time to waste.

Arthur agreed. He asked his Secretary of State to contact the American ambassador in Italy. The American ambassador in turn told the Italian government that the United States would not take kindly to the confiscation of its citizens' property. Within three weeks of the initial letter, McCloskey had a cable from Rome: "College exempted from Propaganda sale."

American seminarians continued to live at the house on Humility Street until 1953, when they moved to the reestablished Pontifical North American College on the Janiculum Hill. Today, the building Pope Pius IX bought and President Arthur saved houses American clergy doing graduate studies in Rome.

December 9: THE QUOTABLE CATHOLIC

Archbishop Fulton J. Sheen was, arguably, the most quotable Catholic of the twentieth century. In his 73 books, countless homilies, and hit radio and television programs—*The Catholic Hour, Life Is Worth Living,* and *The Fulton Sheen Program*—Sheen successfully distilled two thousand years of Catholic teaching into understandable nuggets of truth. Likewise, as a priest, professor, auxiliary bishop of New York, bishop of Rochester, and titular archbishop of Newport (Wales), Sheen's wit never failed him.

Accordingly, between 1930 and 1968, up to 30 million people each week tuned in to hear the Illinois native talk about faith and life. They also looked forward to him delivering lines such as:

- *Sometimes the only way the good Lord can get into some hearts is to break them.*
- *Unless there is a Good Friday in your life, there can be no Easter Sunday.*
- *If you don't behave as you believe, you will end by believing as you behave.*
- *Hearing nuns' confessions is like being stoned to death with popcorn.*
- *You must remember to love people and use things, rather than to love things and use people.*
- *Love is a mutual self-giving which ends in self-recovery.*
- *America, it is said, is suffering from intolerance. It is not. It is suffering from tolerance: Tolerance of right and wrong, truth and error, virtue and evil, Christ and chaos. Our country is not nearly so overrun with the bigoted as it is overrun with the broadminded.*
- *Fasting detaches you from this world. Prayer reattaches you to the next world.*
- *Nothing is more harmful to a man than his resistance to Grace.*

The quotable archbishop passed away at age 84 on **December 9, 1979**. Known not only for his wisdom, but also for his kindness, humility, and generosity, Sheen was declared "Venerable" by Pope Benedict XVI in 2012.

December 10, 1884, was Election Day in Boston, and fear was in the air. Before that day, not once in Boston's 254-year history had a Catholic, let alone an Irish Catholic, held the mayor's office. But in 1884, Hugh O'Brien, a popular alderman headed the Democrat ticket, and Irish immigrants constituted more than 40 percent of the city's population. For the incumbent Protestant mayor, Augustus Martin, the situation looked grim.

As far as Irish politicians went, Boston's Protestants knew they could do worse than O'Brien. Born in Ireland in 1827, the prospective mayor came to Boston with his parents at the age of five. As a young man, he worked hard, learned the printing trade, and by the end of the American Civil War ran the most successful print shop in Boston. Boston's businessmen respected O'Brien. So did Boston's politicians. In the seven years the Irishman had served as a city alderman, he'd acquitted himself well.

Nevertheless, no matter how respectable the candidate might be, Boston's Protestants did not want a Catholic mayor. And as an O'Brien victory became increasingly certain, even those Protestant politicians who liked the man began to panic. They were sure that a flood of Irishmen would follow him into office and take control of the city. Accordingly, in the weeks leading up to the election, the Massachusetts legislature passed laws to guard against that possibility. First, they changed the process for hiring and promoting public employees. Then, they removed the police department and the oversight of liquor licensing from the mayor's jurisdiction.

O'Brien, however, surprised them all. After his decisive victory on Election Day, he focused on cutting taxes, not hiring relatives. He managed the city's finances well, built a library and a park, and behaved in such a responsible, frugal way, that even the Protestants couldn't find fault. As a result, O'Brien served four consecutive terms as mayor.

The first Irish Catholic mayor of Boston died in 1895.

December 11: AMERICAN'S FIRST CATHOLIC NOVELIST

In 1823, the Nativists had a new weapon to use against the Catholic Church: the Scottish novel *Father Clement*. The book, which depicted a Catholic priest losing his faith, was nothing more than thinly disguised, badly written propaganda. But it was effective propaganda, and similar books, equally popular, soon followed.

Six years later, though, the recently ordained Father Charles Constantine Pise, S.J., took a page from the Nativists' book when he published *Father Rowland*. The first Catholic novel published in the United States, *Father Rowland* told the story of a Protestant family converted by the sound reasoning of a Catholic priest. Like *Father Clement,* the novel was pure propaganda, with next to no plot, but the public loved it just the same.

Pise—a Maryland native of Italian and Irish descent—went on to write three more novels, a history of the Catholic Church, numerous essays, and a book of poetry. His good friend Washington Irving often published Pise's writing in his magazine, *The Knickerbocker,* and Pope Gregory XVI rewarded Pise by making him a knight and Count Palatine of the Sacred Palace of Lateran.

Even the U.S. Senate took note of the priest, and on **December 11, 1832,** Senator Henry Clay nominated Pise to serve as Senate Chaplain. Once elected, Pise became the first (and to date only) Catholic to hold that position. Not surprisingly, the Nativists raised a fuss, contending that Catholicism and patriotism couldn't co-exist. Pise responded to the charges with a poem, "The American Flag." It included the lines:

> *They say that bolts of thunder,*
> *Cast in the forge of Rome,*
> *May rise and bring thee under,*
> *Flag of my native home . . .*

> *False are the words they utter,*
> *Ungenerous their brand;*
> *And rash the oaths they mutter;*
> *Flag of my native land.*

Lauded as one of the leading Catholic intellectuals of his era, Pise ended his priesthood as a pastor in New York, dying in 1866.

December 12: THE BISHOP'S SIGN

The sun had yet to rise on December 9, 1531, when Juan Diego passed by Tepeyac Hill, on his way to morning Mass in México City. A brilliant light, however, stopped the Aztec Indian peasant in his tracks. On top of the hill, stood the Blessed Virgin Mary.

"I am your merciful Mother," she told him. She then explained that she wanted México City's archbishop, Juan de Zumárraga, O.F.M., to build a church for her on the hill, so she could make her love known to mankind.

Diego did as she asked, but Zumárraga wouldn't believe him without proof. Three days later, on **December 12, 1531,** he got his proof. Mary had appeared again to Juan Diego, filled his rough cloak with roses from the archbishop's native Castile, and sent the peasant on his way. When Diego arrived at Zumárraga's house and unfurled the cloak, they found not only the roses, but also Mary's image emblazoned inside.

Within two weeks, "Our Lady of Guadalupe," as she became known, had her church on Tepeyac Hill. As the years passed and more Mexican people came to believe in the Virgin's Son, the small chapel gave way to a magnificent basilica. For centuries, Mexican Catholics honored Juan Diego's Mary there, as well as in their homes and churches. In the United States, however, devotion to Our Lady of Guadalupe didn't spread much beyond the Southwest and California.

That changed after 1945, when Pope Pius XII declared Our Lady of Guadalupe "Patroness of the Americas." In the years since, Catholics of all ethnic backgrounds and across the United States have embraced the devotion as their own. The country's grandest tributes to her include the shrine of Our Lady of Guadalupe in La Crosse, Wisconsin, built by then-Bishop Raymond Burke; the new Cathedral of Our Lady of Guadalupe in the Diocese of Dodge City, Kansas, built in 2001; and the recently constructed Fraternity of St. Peter seminary in Nebraska, Our Lady of Guadalupe Seminary.

Likewise, every December 12, the whole Church now pays tribute to Our Lady of Guadalupe during the universal feast held in her honor.

December 13: THE FAITH OF WALKER PERCY

For more than 50 years, people have searched for an explanation for Walker Percy's Catholic faith, with critics, biographers, and fans positing a dozen different reasons as to why the Southern medical doctor turned quasi-existentialist novelist entered the Church on **December 13, 1947**.

The most common explanations center on Percy's troubled family history. For generations, suicide ran in the Percy line like blue eyes do in others. One ancestor died from a morphine overdose; another from drowning. Percy's father and grandfather both shot themselves in the attics of their homes—separately, 12 years apart, but with the same shotgun. Even Percy's mother died under mysterious circumstances, driving her car off a bridge and into a creek.

According to various theories, Percy found comfort, stability, and strength in the Catholic Faith, with some hypothesizing that it gave him a courage his ancestors lacked and others speculating that it enabled him to cope with so much loss, so early in life.

Another theory, however, points to Percy's medical degree, which he earned from Columbia University in 1941, and his subsequent stay in a sanitarium, where he recovered from tuberculosis and brooded over the meaning of life. In the Catholic Faith, the theory goes, Percy reconciled those two experiences: his early belief that science held all the answers and his later conviction that the beauty and tragedy of existence defied a purely scientific explanation.

Perhaps all the explanations have some truth in them. Or perhaps the answer was as simple as the one Percy gave when people put the question to him: "I believe what the Catholic Church proposes is true."

Either way, after Percy entered the Church in 1947, he never walked away. He lived a quiet life with his wife and daughters in Louisiana, writing numerous non-fiction books and six novels, including the 1962 U.S. National Book Award winner, *The Moviegoer*.

Lauded as one of America's greatest Catholic authors, Percy died of prostrate cancer in 1990. He was 73.

December 14: THE BLAINE AMENDMENT

On the surface, nothing about the Blaine Amendment seemed patently anti-Catholic. Introduced in the U.S. House of Representatives on **December 14, 1875,** by Republican Congressman James G. Blaine, the proposed constitutional amendment prohibited public funds from going to schools affiliated with religious organizations.

The Blaine Amendment's seeming neutrality, however, was exactly that—seeming. Throughout the nineteenth century, America's public schools were bastions of Protestantism, with school prayers, Bible lessons, and even textbooks designed to inculcate Protestant teachings. When Protestants constituted the vast majority of Americans, few people minded.

But as the Catholic population grew, so did Catholic resentment over public schools indoctrinating their children. Catholics initially responded by founding parish schools. They quickly tired, however, of paying taxes to support Protestantism in public schools, and some started agitating for government funding of Catholic schools.

Blaine, who had presidential aspirations, thought he'd struck political gold. In proposing the amendment, he believed he would solidify the Republican base of Protestant voters and help his scandal-dogged party gain the moral high ground. If the amendment passed, Protestantism would remain ensconced in public schools and Catholics would be on their own.

Blaine's plan, however, failed him. A year later, he narrowly lost the Republican presidential nomination, and his amendment passed the U.S. House of Representatives but not the U.S. Senate.

Nevertheless, after the amendment's initial defeat, dozens of states succeeded in putting similarly worded amendments into their state constitutions. The U.S. Congress likewise mandated that all states admitted to the Union after 1876 needed to do the same. More than two-thirds of the states eventually passed laws implementing some version of the Blaine Amendment. Nearly all remain in force.

December 15: THE BLOOD OF THE MARTYRS

In 1915, the Ottoman government decided to take advantage of the global chaos wrought by World War I and do a little house cleaning. Systematically, it began purging Armenians from their historic homeland within the Ottoman Empire (present-day Turkey). The purge began with the ruling Turks and Kurds massacring able-bodied Armenian men. It continued as they sent women, children, the infirm, and the elderly marching to their death in the Syrian Desert. All told, nearly 1.5 million Armenians died.

Some, however, escaped to the West.

The Armenian Catholic immigration to the United States had begun in the late 1880s, with the first Armenian priest, Mardiros Megerian, arriving in New York in 1896. During Father Megerian's first years in America, congregants were few. But the Armenian genocide, which brought thousands of refugees to the city, changed that.

By 1921, Armenian Catholics had spread out across New York, New Jersey, and Pennsylvania. Only two Armenian Catholic priests, however, lived in the United States at the time—one in New York, another in New Jersey—and the demands of their parishes, combined with the needs of the ongoing flood of refugees, prevented them from traveling. As a result, Armenian Catholics in Philadelphia went without a priest for years.

Finally, on **December 15, 1923,** Father Stephen Stepanian arrived in the city. Straightaway, Philadelphia's St. Columba's Catholic Church offered the priest the use of their basement for the Armenian Divine Liturgy. Just over two years later, with the help of Philadelphia's Archbishop Dennis Joseph Cardinal Dougherty, Stepanian built St. Mark's Armenian Catholic Church, the oldest continuously operating Armenian Catholic parish in America.

In the decades that followed, Armenian Catholics founded parishes in Boston, Los Angeles, Detroit, and New York, as well as in Little Falls, New Jersey, and Glendale, California. In 1981, Pope John Paul II established the Apostolic Exarchate for Armenian Catholics in the United States and Canada. In 2005, Pope Benedict XVI elevated the exarchate to the Eparchy of United States & Canada of the Patriarchal Armenian Catholic Church.

Today, approximately 25,000 Armenian Catholics live in the United States.

December 16: LA CONQUISTADORA

In 1625, a Franciscan friar arrived in the Spanish settlement of Santa Fe. In his arms, he carried a statue of the Blessed Mother, carved a decade earlier in Europe. The statue stood one yard tall and wore a wooden garment painted over with gold leaf. The friar called the statue by the name she received in Spain: "Our Lady of the Assumption." After his arrival, though, the Franciscans of Santa Fe gave the statue a different title: "Our Lady of the Conception." They then dressed her in silks and installed her in the tiny Church of the Assumption.

For more than 50 years, Spanish settlers in Santa Fe venerated the statue. And, in 1680, when the Pueblo people threatened revolt, the whole town resolved to pray the Rosary before it, asking Mary to intercede on their behalf. Revolt still came, but when it did, most of Santa Fe's residents escaped to safety. Their statue of Mary escaped with them.

Twelve years later, in 1692, Don Diego de Vargas led the re-conquest of New Mexico with an image of Mary on his banner and a promise, should he succeed, to restore Our Lady of the Conception to the Assumption Chapel. When he achieved that re-conquest with virtually no bloodshed, he credited his victory to the Virgin's intercession. He also gave the statue a new title: *La Conquistadora* or "Our Lady of the Conquest."

After Vargas' victory, Spanish settlers and *La Conquistadora* marched back to Santa Fe. They arrived at the city's gates on **December 16, 1693**. When they entered the city, however, they found *La Conquistadora*'s former home in ruins. So, Vargas promised to build her a new one.

In 1717, the home built in *La Conquistadora*'s honor—the Church of St. Francis—finally stood complete. It continued to house the statue until 1869, when Santa Fe's first archbishop, Jean-Baptiste Lamy, replaced it with the Cathedral of St. Francis.

Today, America's oldest, continually venerated statue of the Virgin Mother dwells in the *La Conquistadora* Chapel of the Cathedral Basilica of St. Francis of Assisi.

December 17: THE WORK

José Luis Múzquiz had doubts about Opus Dei from the first. Despite what his friends told him about the lay Catholic movement, the Spanish civil engineering student didn't think it possible, as Opus Dei taught, for lay people to seriously pursue holiness while living in the world.

Then, in late 1934, Múzquiz met the movement's founder, Father Josemaría Escrivá. Múzquiz was immediately taken with the Spanish priest. Maybe, he thought, Opus Dei had potential after all.

Before Múzquiz could explore the question further, the Spanish Civil War began. Escrivá went into hiding, and Múzquiz enlisted in the Nationalist Army. When peace came, Múzquiz embraced the Opus Dei way of life, learning to see the ordinary work of each day as an occasion for extraordinary grace. He no longer doubted Escrivá's vision for the Catholic laity. But, in time, he decided God was calling him to a different path: the priesthood.

In 1944, Múzquiz became one of the first three priests ordained for Opus Dei. Five years later, with only a few dollars in his pocket, he boarded a plane bound for Chicago. There, Father Múzquiz established the first Opus Dei center in America. From Chicago, he moved on to Boston, Chicago, South Bend, Milwaukee, Madison, Saint Louis, and Washington, D.C., establishing centers, recruiting members, and encouraging vocations. Múzquiz also traveled to Asia in 1958, to help establish Opus Dei in Japan. The following year, on **December 17, 1959,** he was in Japan once more, this time to lead a retreat and meet with new members.

Despite his international travels, Múzquiz believed he would remain in America until his death, and he became a U.S. citizen. But in 1961, Escrivá called him back to Europe.

Múzquiz returned to his adopted country in 1976, to serve first as the head of Opus Dei in America and then as chaplain at the Arnold Hall Conference Center near Boston. There, in 1983, Múzquiz died.

The Archdiocese of Boston opened Múzquiz's cause for canonization in 2011.

Isaac Hecker was a born mystic. But he wasn't a born Catholic. Hecker, who entered the world on **December 18, 1819,** came from German Methodist stock. As a young boy growing up in New York City, however, he began hungering for more than what Methodism gave.

That hunger grew as Hecker passed out of adolescence and found himself regularly dreaming that he stood in the presence of heavenly beings. Looking to better understand what God wanted from him, Hecker went to live at Brook Farm, and later to Fruitlands—both utopian communes. When Utopianism failed to satisfy, Hecker turned to Catholicism. In 1844, with the help of the writer Orestes Brownson and the future cardinal Father John McCloskey, he entered the Catholic Church.

The following year, Hecker left for Belgium to begin his formation with the Redemptorists. "All my seeking," he told his family, "is now ended."

Hecker returned to America, in 1851, as a Redemptorist priest and traveled across the northeast, preaching parish missions. The more Catholics Father Hecker encountered, the more convinced he became that Protestant America could become Catholic if lay Catholics would just live their faith more fully and if the Church would more actively evangelize Protestants.

Hecker's Redemptorist Superiors didn't agree. They feared that any organized attempt to convert Protestants would lead to an anti-Catholic backlash. So, in 1858, Hecker and three fellow Redemptorists, with the backing of Pope Pius IX, founded a new order dedicated to calling both Catholics and non-Catholics to conversion: the Paulists.

For the remainder of his life, Hecker strove to evangelize America, speaking from coast to coast in churches, music halls, and town squares. Often, he addressed primarily Protestant audiences. He also founded a nineteenth-century media apostolate, which published books, magazines, and more. Leukemia slowed Hecker down during his last years, but he nevertheless remained an active apologist until his death in 1888.

Recognizing Hecker as a forerunner to the New Evangelization, the Archdiocese of New York opened his cause for canonization in 2008.

December 19: BORKED

Robert Bork was a respected lawyer, scholar, and jurist who served multiple presidential administrations with distinction. Thanks to his 1987 confirmation hearings in the U.S. Senate, however, one of the would-be Supreme Court Justice's most lasting legacies is a word: *bork*.

Defined by the Oxford English Dictionary as "To defame or vilify (a person) systematically, esp. in the mass media, usually with the aim of preventing his or her appointment to public office," *borking* has become business as usual in American politics. But in 1987, the level of vitriol unleashed by Bork's Supreme Court nomination was unprecedented. The media invaded his privacy, legislative aids combed through the most intimate details of his personal history, and politicians denounced him in apocalyptic language, with Senator Ted Kennedy thundering:

> *Robert Bork's America is a land in which women would be forced into back-alley abortions, blacks would sit at segregated lunch counters, rogue police could break down citizens' doors in midnight raids, schoolchildren could not be taught about evolution, writers and artists could be censored at the whim of the Government, and the doors of the Federal courts would be shut on the fingers of millions of citizens.*

The Reagan Administration was floored. The U.S. Senate had already confirmed the man for the U.S. Court of Appeals, D.C. Circuit, in 1982. Bork had also served as U.S. Solicitor General and taught at Yale. But by 1987, his conservative views, particularly on the right to privacy and how to interpret the Constitution, suddenly struck Senate Democrats as beyond the pale. They did everything in their power to kill the nomination, and Bork became a verb.

He also, at age 76, became a Catholic. While working at the American Enterprise Institute for Public Policy Research, teaching at Ave Maria School of Law, and authoring the bestselling book *Slouching Towards Gomorrah*, Bork slowly came to believe in the Faith that his wife, Mary Ellen, had long embraced. He entered the Church in 2003.

Nine years later, on **December 19, 2012,** the most contentious Supreme Court nominee in history passed away.

December 20: MOTHER BEASLEY

Nobody today knows exactly where Mathilda Taylor was born, although most suspect somewhere around New Orleans. Nor does anybody know when she was born; many guess 1834. As for her parents, records suggest Taylor's mother was a dark-skinned French Creole woman and her father was a Native American. Again, the exact details remain a mystery.

Regardless, sometime in the 1850s, the well-educated Catholic made her way from Louisiana to Georgia, and began teaching Savannah's free blacks how to read and write. Had the authorities discovered Taylor's illegal school, they would have punished her with "a fine and a whipping." No one did discover it, however, and Taylor continued to teach African-Americans in Savannah until 1865. She then went to work in a restaurant. In 1869, Taylor married the restaurant's owner, Abraham Beasley, a free black who, before the American Civil War, made a comfortable living from the slave trade.

Only eight years after their marriage, Abraham died, leaving Mathilda Beasley a relatively wealthy woman. Beasley didn't want the money, though. Wealth didn't interest her, and wealth gained through the slave trade interested her even less. With no children to support, Beasley decided instead to deed her husband's estate to the Catholic Church and set sail for England. There, she entered a Catholic convent in York.

Several years later, wearing the black Franciscan habit, Beasley returned to America and became the first black Catholic religious sister in Georgia. Once back in Savannah, she established the Franciscan Sisters of the Third Order Regular for African-American women and took over the administration of St. Francis Home, the orphanage her money had founded.

Mother Beasley continued running St. Francis Home until 1901. Despite persistent financial difficulties, she enjoyed the support of her bishop and most of white Savannah, Catholic and Protestant. When she died, on **December 20, 1903,** the *Savannah Morning News* eulogized her on the paper's front page, noting that, "her unequaled charities had made her almost the idol of the poor."

Joseph P. Machebeuf grew up in the mountains of France. Ordained a priest on **December 21, 1836,** he believed he would grow old in those mountains. But in 1839, Bishop John Baptist Purcell persuaded Machebeuf and his best friend, Jean-Baptiste Lamy, to come to Cincinnati.

Together, the two priests spent 11 years ministering in Ohio, before Rome tasked Lamy with shepherding the new Vicariate Apostolic of New Mexico. When Lamy set off for Santa Fe in 1850, Machebeuf followed as vicar-general. There, the ever-loyal Machebeuf ran point for his friend, reprimanding New Mexico's rebellious clergy. Machebeuf described New Mexico as "a vineyard over run with thorns and thistles," and said of himself, "I am always the one to whip the cats."

To reach the cats, Machebeuf rode on horseback across deserts and mountains, usually sleeping outside under his old buffalo robe. In time, Machebeuf came to love the Southwest as much as he'd loved the mountains of France and the hills of Ohio.

In 1860, however, the Vatican transferred Colorado to the Diocese of Santa Fe, and Lamy asked his friend to go north. Again, Machebeuf agreed. He spent most of the next 29 years on the move, traveling through Colorado's mountains in a specially outfitted wagon, which served as his altar for Mass and his bed when it rained. Even when resting in Denver, Machebeuf kept busy, growing vegetables in the summer and chopping wood in the winter for the nuns who lived next door.

Named Vicar Apostolic of Colorado and Utah in 1868, and Bishop of the Diocese of Denver in 1887, Machebeuf's boundless energy ensured the Church's future in Colorado. He bought property; built parishes, hospitals, and schools; and recruited religious orders. Unlike many other early American bishops, though, Machebeuf built no grand cathedral. He explained, "A cathedral is a question of money . . . while my work was, and should have been, a question of souls."

Denver's beloved bishop died in 1889, surrounded by mountains he called "great, strong, lonesome prayers reaching up to heaven."

December 22: THE LAST OF THE BLACK ROBES

On **December 22, 1852,** a sickly Sicilian boy named Joseph Cataldo entered the Jesuit novitiate in Palermo. The boy was only 15 and had spent much of his childhood in bed. Some questioned the Jesuits' decision to admit him. The Superior at Palermo, however, believed God had something great planned for Cataldo.

Ten years later, Cataldo was alive but still frail. Although he had two years of formation to complete, the Jesuits decided it best not to wait and ordained him that year. They then sent him off to America to finish his studies and learn English. Upon his arrival in Boston, Father Cataldo's American Superiors likewise worried about the young priest's precarious health and transferred him to their mission in sunny California.

After two years in Santa Clara, Cataldo appeared strong enough to endure harsher climes, and in 1865, he traveled north to the Jesuit's Rocky Mountain Mission in northern Idaho. There, the Sicilian priest ministered to both Native Americans and white settlers. First in Coeur d'Alene and Lewiston, Idaho; and later in Spokane, Washington; Pendleton, Oregon; and other settlements across the Pacific Northwest, Cataldo established missions, built churches, and worked to make peace between the region's natives and its new inhabitants. To that end, he mastered multiple Native American languages and translated the Gospels into Nez Percé.

In 1881, Father Cataldo handed over $936 in silver dollars to purchase a piece of land in Washington that the Native Americans called "that old piece of gravel near the falls." There, he opened Gonzaga College (now Gonzaga University) to prepare young men for the priesthood.

With the new school up and running, Cataldo continued crisscrossing Washington, Oregon, and Idaho on multiple missionary journeys. Despite his perpetually frail health, the Jesuit lived long enough to earn the title "the last of the Black Robes" from the Native Americans he served.

Cataldo died in Oregon in 1928, at age 91.

December 23: GETHSEMANI

On **December 23, 1949,** Father Thomas Merton summed up his life at Gethsemani Abbey.

"The sun shines in a very happy room this morning," he wrote in his diary, "in which a monk is where he belongs, in silence, with angels, his hand and eye moved by the loving God in deep tranquility."

The sun, however, didn't always shine quite so happily on Gethsemani.

In 1805, the first French Trappists arrived in America from Switzerland. Upon the invitation of Father Stephen Badin, they traveled to the Diocese of Bardstown and established a monastery in central Kentucky. They were monks, though, not pioneers, and after only four years, returned to Europe, preferring the comforts of their motherhouse to life on the frontier.

Thirty-nine years later, in 1848, another band of French Trappists came to Kentucky to try again. They purchased the first Trappists' land from the Sisters of Loretto and built a new monastery. They called it the Abbey of Our Lady of Gethsemani.

Before long, some of the Trappists began to doubt the wisdom of their return. American Catholics looked with suspicion on the contemplative life, and in the monastery's first 30 years, only eight men entered the order. Not one stayed. To make matters worse, the American bishops decided the Trappist monastery was just the place to send troublesome priests for a life of prayer and penance.

The monks endured the trials as best as they could, but many returned to France. Numbered among those who left were two of Gethsemani's first three abbots. The first resigned because of ill health, the third because he unknowingly put a pederast and embezzler in charge of the abbey's school.

By 1949, however, Gethsemani had found its footing. The abbey no longer welcomed wayward priests; the school had burned down, leaving the monks free to pursue their vocation of work and contemplation; and in 1948, Merton published his spiritual autobiography, *The Seven Storey Mountain*. After that, spiritual seekers and men discerning vocations arrived at Gethsemani in droves.

Today, they're arriving still.

December 24: HARRY WHO?

Harry Warren learned how to sing in his parish choir in Brooklyn, New York. He liked the singing, but he didn't much care for the hymns. So, in 1909, the 16-year-old Warren quit the choir, dropped out of school, and started performing a different kind of music in his godfather's touring carnival band.

Warren, who was born to Italian immigrants on **December 24, 1893,** spent the next eight years bouncing from one low-paying job in entertainment to the next. In 1917, however, he fell in love and married. That meant it was time to get serious about making a real living. Warren considered his options, and decided to give songwriting a try. He never tried anything else.

Between 1918 and 1981, Warren wrote more than 800 songs, most for Hollywood musicals and films. Forty-two of those songs made *Your Hit Parade's* top ten. Twenty-one made it to the number one spot. Included among those hits were enduring classics such as " Jeepers-Creepers," "I Only Have Eyes for You," "At Last," "That's Amore," "Chattanooga Choo-Choo," and "I Got a Gal in Kalamazoo." Warren also won three Academy Awards for his work on "Lullaby of Broadway," "You'll Never Know," and "On the Atchison, Topeka, and the Santa Fe."

In 1962, Warren took a break from motion picture song writing to try his hand at composing a Latin Mass. It took him more than a decade to find a choir to perform it, though, and it was never recorded.

During his lifetime, Warren jokingly referred to himself as "Harry Who." That was most people's response when they heard his name. Although Warren wrote more hit songs than Irving Berlin, he worked in relative obscurity and few Americans outside of show business ever knew of the composer. Nevertheless, through his song writing, Warren did what he set out to do: he provided for his wife of 54 years, and for their two children.

Harry Warren died in 1981, leaving his last musical, *Manhattan Melody,* unfinished.

December 25: THE HIGHBINDER RIOTS

For parishioners of Old St. Peter's Catholic Church in New York, Midnight Mass in 1806, was a Mass to remember.

That evening, the streets were quiet and cold as men, women, and children made their way to the city's lone Catholic church. Inside St. Peter's, candles lit both sanctuary and nave, and the whole church was adorned in its Christmas best. For a short while, peace reigned. Then, noises began drifting in from outside. As the Mass continued, the noises grew louder; the congregation could hear shouts and slurs mixed in with the prayers of the priest. After the dismissal, they discovered the source of those shouts and slurs.

Outside a large crowd of sailors, journeymen, and local toughs—called "the Highbinder Gang" in some reports—had gathered. As parishioners left the church, insults and threats of violence greeted them. Fortunately, the city's watchmen soon showed up and stopped the Nativists from carrying out their threats. Everyone returned home safely.

The next day, the parishioners who came to Old St. Peter's for Christmas Day Mass didn't come alone. Irish thugs from the Sixth Ward (known as "Irishtown") joined them. Not normally much for church going, the thugs had heard about the previous night's events and decided they should go to Old St. Peter's just in case the Nativists returned to make good on their threats. In part, they wanted to protect their more virtuous neighbors. They also loved a good fight.

On **December 25, 1806,** they got one.

In the late morning, the Nativists returned in force to Old St. Peter's and found the Irish waiting. The fighting commenced immediately. From the steps of Old St. Peter's to the homes and business of the Sixth Ward, the Irish and Nativists waged their miniature war all afternoon and into the night. At least one policeman died, hundreds were injured, and numerous shops in Irishtown were destroyed.

At the end of the day, however, the police only arrested the Irish thugs. The Nativists, to a man, walked free.

December 26: INTO THE WILD

On the day Charles Seghers was born—**December 26, 1839**—no Catholic priest had yet set foot in Alaska. But by the time of Seghers' death, in November 1886, Catholic missions dotted America's northernmost territory.

In the intervening 46 years, Seghers entered seminary, left his native Belgium to serve as a missionary in Canada, and, at just 33 years old, became bishop of Vancouver Island (in present-day British Columbia).

As bishop, Seghers committed himself to personally proclaiming the Gospel in the most remote parts of his diocese. In temperatures that routinely plunged 40 degrees below zero, he traveled across western Canada and Alaska by schooner, canoe, dogsled, and foot. A master linguist, Seghers always preached to the people in their native dialects, not trusting translators to get the theology right.

In 1879, Seghers reluctantly left Vancouver Island to become the coadjutor bishop (and in 1880, archbishop) of the Archdiocese of Oregon City (now Portland). Of his work in his new see, which consisted of present-day Oregon, Montana, and Idaho, Seghers wrote, "When I am preaching, I rest from riding. When I am riding, I rest from preaching."

He didn't ride for long. In late 1883, Seghers learned Vancouver Island needed a bishop and asked Pope Leo XIII's permission to return. Leo agreed, and by 1885, Seghers was riding dogsleds through the wilderness once more. During his first year back, he visited all existing missions and established two new ones. He also began building a new pro-cathedral and a bishop's residence in Victoria. In July 1886, with those projects underway, Seghers set sail for Alaska yet again. It would be his final trip.

As his party traveled through Alaska's interior, one of Seghers' companions—a laymen named Francis Fuller—began showing signs of mental illness. One morning in late November, Seghers awoke to find Fuller standing over him with a shotgun. Seconds later, the archbishop was dead.

Seghers' murder shocked the country, but as news of his work spread, young priests flocked to Alaska's missions. Today, Seghers is considered the "Father of Catholicism" in Alaska.

December 27: THE IRISH RADICAL

John Boyle O'Reilly grew up poor and hungry in mid-nineteenth-century Ireland. His schoolteacher father made sure he received an education, but the family's Catholic Faith limited O'Reilly's career opportunities. Radicalized by circumstance, the teenage O'Reilly joined the Fenians, a secret society plotting to end British rule in Ireland.

The planned rebellion never came to pass. In 1865, the British government discovered the society, arrested 21-year-old O'Reilly, and shipped him to Australia on a convict ship. There, he fell in love with his warden's daughter, got his heart broken, and, in a fit of grief, made a failed attempt at suicide on **December 27, 1868**. Once he recovered, O'Reilly became determined to escape. With the help of a priest, he broke out of the prison camp and bribed his way onto an American whaling ship.

Upon his arrival in Philadelphia, in late 1869, O'Reilly's fellow Irishmen greeted him as a hero. They expected he'd continue organizing the Irish resistance from America and stood ready to help. But soon after he began writing for *The Pilot,* a Catholic newspaper in Boston, O'Reilly decided freedom was best won by peaceful means and distanced himself from the Fenians.

From that point forward, as a poet, journalist, and (eventually) editor and co-owner of *The Pilot,* O'Reilly became one of post-Civil War America's greatest champions of human rights. In him, Jewish and Chinese immigrants found one of their few friends. So too did Native Americans and African-Americans. At O'Reilly's invitation, Frederick Douglass contributed to *The Pilot* and marched in Boston's St. Patrick's Day Parade.

In 1872, O'Reilly married a fellow Irish-American journalist, Mary Murphy. The couple had four daughters before O'Reilly's death from accidental poisoning in 1890.

Commemorated by his countrymen with a memorial on Boston's Irish Heritage Trail, O'Reilly was also honored by John F. Kennedy—who considered the Irishman his favorite poet—and by the band U2—who dedicated their song "Van Diemen's Land," on 1988's *Rattle and Hum,* to him.

Bishop Louis William DuBourg's friends understood that shepherding New Orleans was no cakewalk. For years, the city's Catholics had resisted DuBourg's authority and made his life difficult. Nevertheless, in 1817, when the bishop of Louisiana and the Two Floridas decided to move his episcopal seat from New Orleans to the remote frontier town of St. Louis, those same friends thought the decision a bit rash.

But DuBourg would not be swayed. As one historian explained, "The bishop's optimism was equaled only by his imagination, which always bypassed the difficulties involved in the arrangements he proposed."

One of the first things DuBourg imagined for his new cathedral town was a college, and before 1818 ended, St. Louis Academy opened. Operating out of a private residence, the school depended entirely on the efforts of local clergy. Because the diocese was so large, however, and priests so few, that arrangement quickly crumbled. The overworked clergy looked to DuBourg for help. The bishop, in turn, looked to the Jesuits.

DuBourg first asked the Society of Jesus to take over the school, recently renamed St. Louis College, in 1822. They declined. In 1823, DuBourg attempted to sweeten the deal by offering the Jesuits his cathedral property and the opportunity to open a school for Native Americans. They accepted that offer, but again refused to run the college. Not until 1824, after the first Jesuits arrived in Missouri, did they assure DuBourg that once they had enough men, they would operate his college too.

Three years later, in 1827, the Society of Jesus formally assumed responsibility for St. Louis College, and on **December 28, 1832,** the Missouri Legislature granted the school its charter. After that, the college became a university as it went on to establish the first schools of law, business, and medicine in the American West. In 1944, it also became the first university in Missouri to officially welcome African-Americans.

Today, DuBourg's school continues to prosper as St. Louis University. It is the oldest university west of the Mississippi.

On **December 29, 1937,** Theon and Mary Bowman welcomed their daughter Bertha into the world. Nine years later, the Bowman's little girl announced that she wanted to become Catholic.

The Bowmans were surprised—as African-American Methodists living in Mississippi, they knew little about Catholicism. But they agreed. When the teenage Bertha announced her desire to become a Franciscan sister, however, her parents put their collective foot down. Although Theon's father had been born into slavery, he was a physician and his wife was a teacher. The family wanted more for their daughter than religious life.

But Bertha wouldn't take no for an answer. She stopped eating and told her parents she would remain on a hunger strike until they consented. Which, in due course, they did. Her father didn't stop begging her to change her mind, though, and in 1953, as the 16-year-old prepared to depart for her novitiate in Wisconsin, he uttered one final warning: "They won't like you."

"I will make them like me," she replied.

And she did. At first, the mostly German-Irish Franciscan Sisters of Perpetual Adoration didn't know what to make of Bowman (who took the name "Sister Thea"); she was always singing and talking about Jesus in a way Northerners didn't. In time, however, Bowman's songs and smiles won them over, just as they won over the rest of America.

As an elementary school teacher, a doctoral student, and a professor of literature at Viterbo College in Wisconsin and Xavier University of Louisiana in New Orleans, Bowman committed herself to two things: the Catholic Faith and racial harmony. Likewise, in partnership with the Diocese of Jackson, Mississippi, Bowman spent years talking to (and singing with) Catholics across America, telling the black Catholic story and calling more African-Americans to the Church.

In 1989, Bowman delivered the keynote address at a conference hosted by the U.S. bishops. As she concluded, the bishops thanked her by joining her in singing, "We Shall Overcome."

Bowman died of cancer the following year.

December 30: CALL ME AL

On **December 30, 1873,** a baby boy was born to a poor Irish couple in New York's Fourth Ward. They named him Alfred Smith, Jr., after his father. His friends just called him "Al."

The young Smith spent his childhood doing what most boys in the Fourth Ward's overcrowded tenements did: he attended a Catholic school by day, ran wild in the Lower East Side by night, and served Mass at his parish on Sundays. To supplement the family income, he also hawked newspapers on street corners. After his father's death in 1887, however, Smith needed to do more than sell papers. At the age of 14, he quit school and found work as a fishmonger. Smith later said he learned everything he needed to know about people at the fish market.

Born with a flair for the dramatic, Smith flirted with the idea of becoming a professional actor. But he loved his childhood sweetheart, Catherine, more than the stage, and before their marriage, in 1900, opted instead for the steady income that politics could provide.

Beginning with a desk job in Tammany Hall, Smith rose quickly through the Democratic ranks. By 1911, he was Majority Leader in the New York State Assembly. By 1918, he was Governor of New York. He would win the office three more times.

As governor, Smith mostly steered clear of Tammany corruption and fought for laws to protect workers and families. He also fought prohibition and openly flouted the Volstead Act, even serving alcohol at the Executive Mansion. His disdain for the country's "drys," who were in favor of Prohibition, contributed to Smith's losing his bid for the White House in 1928 to Herbert Hoover. Although Smith handily won the Democratic nomination, he lost the general election in a landslide—done in, it was said, by "Prohibition, Prejudice, and Prosperity." In other words, his drinking and Catholic faith cost him Protestants' and prohibitionists' votes. The country's healthy economy did the rest.

After his 1928 loss, Smith retired to the private sector. He died in October 1944, five months after his beloved Catherine.

December 31: SWEETNESS

As a boy, playing baseball with his friends in Puerto Rico, Roberto Clemente used a guava tree branch for a bat, a coffee bean sack for a glove, and knotted up rags for a ball. But despite his family's poverty and the limited opportunities for Latino and African-American ballplayers in the 1950s, Clemente was determined to make it to America's big leagues.

"I am convinced that God wanted me to be a baseball player," he later explained. "I was born to play baseball."

The Catholic ballplayer got his chance in 1954, when the Brooklyn Dodgers drafted him for their farm team in Montreal. After Montreal failed to field Clemente, the Pittsburgh Pirates swooped in. Over the next 18 years, all with the Pirates, Clemente (dubbed "Sweetness" by fans) built one of baseball's most impressive records: 12 Gold Glove Awards, 4 National League batting titles, 12 All-Star Game selections, 2 World Series Championships, the National League's Most Valuable Player (MVP) Award in 1966, and the World Series MVP Award in 1971. As his crowning achievement, in September 1972, Clemente collected his 3,000th hit.

Being one of the greatest baseball players in the history of the game, however, wasn't enough for Clemente. "Any time you have an opportunity to make a difference in this world and you don't, then you are wasting your time on Earth," he said.

Clemente didn't waste time. Off the field, he could be found either with his family or doing charitable work. Over the course of his career, Clemente raised hundreds of thousands of dollars in material aid for the poor and spent hundreds of hours running baseball camps for underprivileged children. In 1972, when an earthquake devastated Nicaragua, Clemente arranged three deliveries of aid packages to the country. And when corrupt government officials stole the aid, Clemente decided to personally accompany a fourth relief flight.

Tragically, the overloaded plane carrying Clemente and the aid packages crashed immediately after takeoff, on **December 31, 1972**. Everyone on board died.

APPENDIX A: THE AMERICAN CANON

SAINTS

Frances Xavier Cabrini, *born* July 15, 1850; *died* December 22, 1917; *feast* November 13

Marianne Cope, *born* January 23, 1838; *died* August 9, 1918; *feast* January 23

Katharine Drexel, *born* November 26, 1858; *died* March 3, 1955; *feast* March 3

Rose Philippine Duchesne, *born* August 29, 1769; *died* November 18, 1852; *feast* November 18

René Goupil, *born* May 15, 1608; *died* September 29, 1642; *feast* October 19

Theodora Guérin, *born* October 2, 1798; *died* May 14, 1856; *feast* October 3

Isaac Jogues, *born* January 10, 1607; *died* October 18, 1646; *feast* October 19

Jean de Lalande, *born* (unknown); *died* October 18, 1646; *feast* October 19

John Neumann, *born* March 28, 1811; *died* January 5, 1860; *feast* January 5

Elizabeth Ann Seton, *born* August 28, 1774; *died* January 4, 1821; *feast* January 4

Kateri Tekakwitha, *born* 1856; *died* April 17, 1680; *feast* July 14

Damien de Veuster, *born* January 3, 1840; *died* April 15, 1889; *feast* May 10

BLESSEDS

Miriam Teresa Demjanovich, *born* March 26, 1901; *died* May 8, 1927

Carlos Manuel Rodríguez Santiago, *born* November 22, 1918; *died* July 13, 1963

Francis Xavier Seelos, *born* January 11, 1819; *died* October 4, 1867

Junípero Serra, *born* November 24, 1713; *died* August 28, 1784

VENERABLES

Nelson Henry Baker, *born* February 16, 1841; *died* July 29, 1936

Frederic Baraga, *born* June 29, 1797; *died* January 19, 1868

Mary Magdalena Bentivoglio, *born* 1834; *died* 1905

Celestina Bottego, *born* December 20, 1895; *died* August 20, 1980

Solanus Casey, *born* November 25, 1870; *died* July 31, 1957

Cornelia Connelly, *born* January 15, 1809; *died* April 18, 1879

Rafael Cordero, *born* October 24, 1790; *died* July 5, 1868

Henriette DeLille, *born in 1813; died* November 17, 1862

Mary Theresa Dudzik, *born* August 30, 1860; *died* September 20, 1918

Maria Kaupas, *born* January 6, 1880; *died* April 17, 1940

Antonio Margil, *born* August 18, 1657; *died* August 6, 1726

Samuel Charles Mazzuchelli, *born* November 4, 1806; *died* February 23, 1864

Mary Angeline Teresa McCrory, *born* January 21, 1893; *died* January 21, 1984

Michael J. McGivney, *born* August 12, 1852; *died* August 14, 1890

Fulton J. Sheen, *born* May 8, 1895; *died* December 9, 1979

Pierre Toussaint, *born* June 27, 1766; *died* June 30, 1853

Félix Varela y Morales, *born* November 20, 1788; *died* February 27, 1853

APPENDIX B: DIOCESES OF THE CATHOLIC CHURCH IN THE UNITED STATES DATE OF FOUNDING

Archdiocese of Anchorage:
    January 22, 1966
Diocese of Fairbanks: August 8, 1962
Diocese of Juneau: June 23, 1951

Archdiocese of Atlanta:
    February 10, 1962
Diocese of Charleston: July 11, 1820
Diocese of Charlotte:
    November 12, 1971
Diocese of Raleigh: March 3, 1868
Diocese of Savannah: July 3, 1850

Archdiocese of Baltimore:
    November 6, 1789
Diocese of Arlington: May 28, 1974
Diocese of Richmond: July 11, 1820
Diocese of Wheeling-Charleston:
    July 19, 1850
Diocese of Wilmington: March 3, 1868

Archdiocese of Boston: April 8, 1808
Diocese of Burlington: July 29, 1853
Diocese of Fall River: March 12, 1904
Diocese of Manchester: April 15, 1884
Diocese of Portland: July 29, 1853
Diocese of Springfield in Massachusetts:
    June 14, 1870
Diocese of Worcester: January 14, 1950

Archdiocese of Chicago:
    November 28, 1843
Diocese of Belleville: January 7, 1887
Diocese of Joliet: December 11, 1948
Diocese of Peoria: February 12, 1875
Diocese of Rockford:
    September 23, 1908

Diocese of Springfield in Illinois:
    October 26, 1923

Archdiocese of Cincinnati:
    June 19, 1821
Diocese of Cleveland: April 23, 1847
Diocese of Columbus: March 3, 1868
Diocese of Steubenville:
    October 21, 1944
Diocese of Toledo: April 15, 1910
Diocese of Youngstown: May 15, 1943

Archdiocese of Denver: August 16, 1887
Diocese of Cheyenne: August 2, 1887
Diocese of Colorado Springs:
    November 10, 1983
Diocese of Pueblo: November 15, 1941

Archdiocese of Detroit: March 8, 1833
Diocese of Gaylord: December 19, 1970
Diocese of Grand Rapids: May 19, 1882
Diocese of Kalamazoo:
    December 19, 1970
Diocese of Lansing: May 22, 1937
Diocese of Marquette: July 29, 1853
Diocese of Saginaw: February 26, 1938

Archdiocese of Dubuque: July 28, 1837
Diocese of Davenport: June 14, 1881
Diocese of Des Moines: August 12, 1911
Diocese of Sioux City: January 15, 1902

Archdiocese of Galveston-Houston:
    May 4, 1847
Diocese of Austin: November 15, 1947
Diocese of Beaumont: June 25, 1966
Diocese of Brownsville: July 10, 1965

Diocese of Corpus Christi:
March 23, 1912
Diocese of Tyler: February 24, 1987
Diocese of Victoria in Texas:
April 13, 1982

Archdiocese of Hartford:
November 28, 1843
Diocese of Bridgeport: August 6, 1953
Diocese of Norwich: August 6, 1953
Diocese of Providence: February 17, 1872

Archdiocese of Indianapolis:
May 6, 1834
Diocese of Evansville: October 21, 1944
Diocese of Fort Wayne-South Bend:
January 8, 1857
Diocese of Gary: December 17, 1956
Diocese of Lafayette in Indiana:
October 21, 1944

Archdiocese of Kansas City in Kansas:
May 10, 1947
Diocese of Dodge City: May 19, 1951
Diocese of Salina: December 23, 1944
Diocese of Wichita: August 2, 1887

Archdiocese of Los Angeles:
July 11, 1936
Diocese of Fresno: October 6, 1967
Diocese of Monterey in California:
October 6, 1967
Diocese of Orange: March 24, 1976
Diocese of San Bernardino: July 14, 1978
Diocese of San Diego: July 11, 1936

Archdiocese of Louisville: April 8, 1808
Diocese of Covington: July 29, 1853
Diocese of Knoxville: May 27, 1988
Diocese of Lexington: January 14, 1988
Diocese of Memphis: June 20, 1970
Diocese of Nashville: July 28, 1837
Diocese of Owensboro:
December 9, 1937

Archdiocese of Miami: October 7, 1958
Diocese of Orlando: June 18, 1968
Diocese of Palm Beach: June 16, 1984
Diocese of Pensacola-Tallahassee:
October 1, 1975
Diocese of St. Augustine:
March 11, 1870
Diocese of St. Petersburg:
March 2, 1968
Diocese of Venice in Florida:
June 16, 1984

Archdiocese of Milwaukee:
November 28, 1843
Diocese of Green Bay: March 3, 1868
Diocese of La Crosse: March 3, 1868
Diocese of Madison: January 9, 1946
Diocese of Superior: May 3, 1905

Archdiocese of Mobile: May 15, 1829
Diocese of Biloxi: March 1, 1977
Diocese of Birmingham in Alabama:
June 28, 1969
Diocese of Jackson: July 28, 1837

Archdiocese of New Orleans:
April 25, 1793
Diocese of Alexandria in Louisiana:
July 29, 1853
Diocese of Baton Rouge: July 20, 1961
Diocese of Houma-Thibodaux:
June 5, 1977
Diocese of Lafayette in Louisiana:
January 11, 1918
Diocese of Lake Charles:
January 29, 1980
Diocese of Shreveport: June 16, 1986

Archdiocese of New York: April 8, 1808
Diocese of Albany: April 23, 1847
Diocese of Brooklyn: July 29, 1853
Diocese of Buffalo: April 23, 1847
Diocese of Ogdensburg:
February 15, 1872

Diocese of Rochester: March 3, 1868
Diocese of Rockville Centre:
April 6, 1957
Diocese of Syracuse:
November 26, 1886

Archdiocese of Newark:
December 10, 1937
Diocese of Camden: December 9, 1937
Diocese of Metuchen:
November 19, 1981
Diocese of Paterson: December 9, 1937
Diocese of Trenton: August 2, 1881

Archdiocese of Oklahoma City:
December 13, 1972
Diocese of Little Rock:
November 28, 1843
Diocese of Tulsa: December 13, 1972

Archdiocese of Omaha:
January 6, 1857
Diocese of Grand Island: April 11, 1917
Diocese of Lincoln: August 2, 1887

Archdiocese of Philadelphia:
April 8, 1808
Diocese of Allentown: January 28, 1961
Diocese of Altoona-Johnstown:
October 9, 1957
Diocese of Erie: July 29, 1853
Diocese of Greensburg:
March 10, 1951
Diocese of Harrisburg: March 3, 1868
Diocese of Pittsburgh: August 11, 1843
Diocese of Scranton: March 3, 1868

Archdiocese of Portland in Oregon:
July 29, 1850
Diocese of Baker: June 19, 1903
Diocese of Boise: August 25, 1893
Diocese of Great Falls-Billings:
May 18, 1904
Diocese of Helena: March 7, 1884

Archdiocese of St. Louis: July 18, 1826
Diocese of Jefferson City: July 2, 1956
Diocese of Kansas City-St. Joseph:
September 10, 1880
Diocese of Springfield-Cape Girardeau:
August 24, 1956

Archdiocese of Saint Paul and
Minneapolis: July 19, 1850
Diocese of Bismarck: December 31, 1909
Diocese of Crookston:
December 31, 1909
Diocese of Duluth: October 3, 1889
Diocese of Fargo: November 10, 1889
Diocese of New Ulm:
November 18, 1957
Diocese of Rapid City: August 6, 1902
Diocese of St. Cloud:
September 22, 1889
Diocese of Sioux Falls:
November 12, 1889
Diocese of Winona: November 26, 1889

Archdiocese of San Antonio:
August 28, 1874
Diocese of Amarillo: August 3, 1926
Diocese of Dallas: July 15, 1890
Diocese of El Paso: March 3, 1914
Diocese of Fort Worth: August 9, 1969
Diocese of Laredo: July 3, 2000
Diocese of Lubbock: March 25, 1983
Diocese of San Angelo: October 16, 1961

Archdiocese of San Francisco:
July 29, 1853
Diocese of Honolulu: January 25, 1941
Diocese of Las Vegas: March 21, 1995
Diocese of Oakland: January 13, 1962
Diocese of Reno: March 27, 1931
Diocese of Sacramento: May 28, 1886
Diocese of Salt Lake City:
January 27, 1891
Diocese of San Jose in California:
January 27, 1981

Diocese of Santa Rosa in California:
January 13, 1962
Diocese of Stockton: January 13, 1962

Archdiocese of Santa Fe: July 23, 1850
Diocese of Gallup: December 16, 1939
Diocese of Las Cruces: August 17, 1982
Diocese of Phoenix: December 2, 1969
Diocese of Tucson: May 8, 1897

Archdiocese of Seattle: June 23, 1951
Diocese of Spokane:
December 17, 1913
Diocese of Yakima: June 23, 1951

Archdiocese of Washington:
November 15, 1947
Diocese of St. Thomas:
April 30, 1960
Archdiocese of Agaña: March 1, 1911

Diocese of Caroline Islands:
December 19, 1905
Diocese of Chalan Kanoa:
November 8, 1984
Apostolic Prefecture of the Marshall
Islands: April 23, 1993

Archdiocese of Samoa-Apia:
August 20, 1850
Diocese of Samoa-Pago Pago:
September 10, 1982

Archdiocese of San Juan de Puerto Rico:
August 8, 1511
Diocese of Arecibo: April 30, 1960
Diocese of Caguas: November 4, 1964
Diocese of Fajardo-Humacao:
March 11, 2008
Diocese of Mayagüez: March 1, 1976
Diocese of Ponce: November 21, 1924

APPENDIX C: AMERICA'S MINOR BASILICAS, DATES OF DESIGNATION BY THE HOLY SEE

January 18, 1926. Basilica of St. Mary, Minneapolis, Minnesota

July 14, 1926. Our Lady of Victory Basilica and National Shrine, Lackawanna, New York

March 10, 1929. Basilica of St. Josaphat, Milwaukee, Wisconsin

July 14, 1937. Basilica of the National Shrine of the Assumption of the Blessed Virgin Mary

Baltimore, Maryland

August 7, 1940. Basilica of the Immaculate Conception, Conception, Missouri

April 22, 1949. Basilica of the Blessed Virgin of Gethsemani, Trappist, Kentucky

February 6, 1952. Basilica of the National Shrine of St. Francis of Assisi, San Francisco, California

October 19, 1953. Cathedral Basilica of the Assumption, Covington, Kentucky

September 8, 1954. Basilica and Shrine of Our Lady of Perpetual Help, Roxbury, Massachusetts

August 22, 1955. St. Vincent Archabbey Basilica, Latrobe, Pennsylvania

May 4, 1956. Our Lady of Sorrows Basilica, Chicago, Illinois

May 11, 1956. Basilica of St. Francis Xavier, Dyersville, Iowa

February 5, 1960. Basilica of Mission San Carlos Borroméo del rio Carmelo, Carmel, California

January 27, 1961. Basilica of St. Louis, King of France (Old Cathedral), St. Louis, Missouri

March 10, 1962. Cathedral Basilica of the Immaculate Conception, Mobile, Alabama

March 26, 1962. Queen of All Saints Basilica, Chicago, Illinois

June 30, 1962. Basilica of the Sacred Heart of Jesus, Conewago Township, Pennsylvania

December 9, 1964. Cathedral-Basilica of St. Louis, King of France, New Orleans, Louisiana

September 5, 1969. Basilica of Our Lady of Perpetual Help, Brooklyn, New York

March 14, 1970. Basilica of St. Francis Xavier (The Old Cathedral), Vincennes, Indiana

October 21, 1971. Basilica and National Shrine of Our Lady of Consolation, Carey, Ohio

January 21, 1972. St. Joseph's Basilica, Alameda, California

July 14, 1975. Basilica of the National Shrine of Our Lady of Fatima, Lewiston, New York

November 17, 1975. Mission Basilica of San Diego de Alcalá, San Diego, California

September 27, 1976. Cathedral-Basilica of Sts. Peter and Paul, Philadelphia, Pennsylvania

December 4, 1976. Cathedral-Basilica of St. Augustine, St. Augustine, Florida

August 2, 1979. St. Mary Cathedral Basilica, Galveston, Texas

August 22, 1979. Basilica of St. Adalbert, Grand Rapids, Michigan

November 3, 1979. Cathedral Basilica of the Immaculate Conception, Denver, Colorado

May 6, 1982. Cathedral Basilica of St. James, Brooklyn, New York

September 2, 1985. St. Mary's Basilica, Phoenix, Arizona

October 26, 1988. Basilica of St. James, Jamestown, North Dakota

June 30, 1989. Basilica of Sts. Cyril and Methodius, Danville, Pennsylvania

August 10, 1989. Basilica of St. John the Apostle, Des Moines, Iowa

October 12, 1990. Basilica of the National Shrine of the Immaculate Conception, Washington, D.C.

February 13, 1991. Basilica of the National Shrine of St. Elizabeth Ann Seton, Emmitsburg, Maryland

June 25, 1991. Basilica of St. Stanislaus, Chicopee, Massachusetts

July 9, 1991, Basilica of St. Mary of the Immaculate Conception, Norfolk, Virginia

November 23, 1991. Basilica of the Most Sacred Heart, Notre Dame, Indiana

April 6, 1993. Basilica of St. Lawrence, Asheville, North Carolina

December 22, 1995. Cathedral Basilica of the Sacred Heart, Newark, New Jersey

December 22, 1995. Cathedral Basilica of St. Joseph, San Jose, California

August 29, 1996. Basilica of the National Shrine of St. Ann, Scranton, Pennsylvania

September 9, 1996. Basilica of St. Michael the Archangel, Loretto, Pennsylvania

April 4, 1997. Cathedral Basilica of St. Louis, St. Louis, Missouri

June 23, 1998. St. Joseph Basilica, Webster, Massachusetts

July 27, 1998. Our Lady Mary Help of Christians Basilica at the Abbey, Belmont, North Carolina

July 27, 1998. Basilica of the Sacred Heart of Jesus, Syracuse, New York

August 27, 1998. Basilica of the National Shrine of the Little Flower, San Antonio, Texas

September 8, 1998. St. Mary Basilica, Natchez, Mississippi

June 12, 1999. Basilica of the National Shrine of Our Lady of San Juan del Valle, San Juan, Texas

February 14, 2000. Mission Basilica of San Juan Capistrano, San Juan Capistrano, California

July 18, 2001. Basilica of St. Joseph Proto-Cathedral, Bardstown, Kentucky

June 21, 2003. Basilica of St. Hyacinth, Chicago, Illinois

October 4, 2004. Basilica of Sts. Peter and Paul, Lewiston, Maine

October 4, 2005. Cathedral Basilica of St. Francis of Assisi, Santa Fe, New Mexico

January 20, 2006. Basilica of St. Paul, Daytona Beach, Florida

July 11, 2006. St. Anthony Cathedral Basilica, Beaumont, Texas

July 11, 2006. Basilica of the National Shrine of Mary, Help of Christians at Holy Hill, Hubertus, Wisconsin

February 9, 2008. Basilica of the Immaculate Conception, Waterbury, Connecticut

June 21, 2008. Basilica of San Albino, Mesilla, New Mexico

February 22, 2009. Basilica of the Immaculate Conception, Natchitoches, Louisiana

June 3, 2009. Basilica of the National Shrine of Mary, Queen of the Universe, Orlando, Florida

July 16, 2009. Basilica of St. John the Evangelist, Stamford, Connecticut

November 9, 2009. Basilica of the Co-Cathedral of the Sacred Heart, Charleston, West Virginia

February 22, 2010. Basilica of the Sacred Heart of Jesus, Atlanta, Georgia

March 17, 2010. Basilica of St. Patrick's Old Cathedral, New York, New York

May 3, 2011. Basilica of Sts. Peter & Paul, Chattanooga, Tennessee

November 10, 2011. Basilica of St. Stanislaus Kostka, Winona, Minnesota

November 30, 2011. Basilica of the Sacred Hearts of Jesus and Mary, Southampton, New York

December 28, 2011. Basilica of St. Michael the Archangel, Pensacola, Florida

February 11, 2012. Basilica of St. Mary Star of the Sea, Key West, Florida

June 6, 2012. Basilica of St. John the Baptist, Canton, Ohio

October 19, 2012. Basilica of Regina Pacis, Brooklyn, New York

June 13, 2013. Basilica of St. Mary of the Assumption, Marietta, Ohio

August 15, 2013. Basilica of the Immaculate Conception, Jacksonville, Florida

August 2, 2013. Basilica Shrine of St. Mary, Wilmington, North Carolina

February 21, 2014. Basilica of St. Fidelis, Victoria, Kansas

ACKNOWLEDGMENTS

The book you're holding is the result of many long months of work undertaken by numerous hands and many minds. Chief among those minds is our research assistant, Tom Crowe. Over the past year, Crowe spent countless hours tracking down stories, searching for hard-to-find facts and dates, and finding a place in the almanac for as many American Catholic "greats" as possible. For Tom's hard work, enthusiasm, and readiness to take on any and every task sent his way, we owe him our deepest thanks.

We also owe thanks to the Catholic Vote family—Kara Mone, Josh Mercer, Patrick Gillen, and Thomas Peters—for their encouragement, support, and helpful advice. Kara was particularly instrumental in helping facilitate much of the administrative work throughout the process, as was Nicholas DiGregory, who assisted with the seemingly never-ending busywork that goes into an undertaking such as this one.

Unfortunately, over the last several decades, countless books on the men and women who built the Church in America have gone out of print and disappeared from library shelves. But because Mike Aquilina and Rob Corzine generously opened up their sizable personal libraries to us, we never lacked for the resources we needed.

The team at Image—especially Gary Jansen and Amanda O'Connor—has been equally generous with their time, enthusiasm, and ongoing support. From the first, they eagerly embraced our vision for *The American Catholic Almanac* and moved heaven and earth to meet a rigorous production schedule.

We'd also like to thank the Diocese of Peoria for permission to reprint passages from Bishop John Spalding's *North American Review* essay (see September 1), and the United States Conference of Catholic Bishops for permission to reprint parts of their June 26, 2013, press release on the U.S. Supreme Court's decision to overturn the Defense of Marriage Act (see June 26). Along similar lines, it's important to note that a handful of other entries (Saint Marianne Cope, Saint Kateri Tekakwitha, Blessed Francis Xavier Seelos, Blessed Carlos Rodriguez, and Blessed Junípero

Serra) began as part of an article written by Emily for *Our Sunday Visitor* in 2009. It was a small start to such a large project, but it helped set us on the right path nonetheless.

Most important, to our friends and families we owe a debt that no words of gratitude can repay. We could never have completed this book without the prayers, patience, and sacrifices of Christopher Chapman, Shannon Walsh, Rob Corzine, David Matthews, Sara Meredith, and the entire Burch clan—Brian's wife, Sara, and their children Martin, Bridget, Therese, Mary Hope, Samuel, Benedict, and Grace—as well as our parents, Brian and Beverly Burch and Gary and Ricki Stimpson. Writing and editing this book has, at times, claimed far more of our lives than work properly has a right to claim, and for the unfailing support of those who've had to put up with us the most, we will be forever grateful.

Last but not least, we want to thank the men and women whose stories are told in these pages. Over the last year, we've met some of the most fascinating, funny, brilliant, brave, compassionate, confounding, and breathtakingly beautiful men and women who've called America "home." No matter how challenging or stressful writing this book felt at times, learning their stories and having the chance to retell them was always a great gift. We've been blessed by that gift, just as we've been blessed by all the ways the men and women we met said yes to God. We pray that learning their stories will inspire many more men and women to say the same.